LITIGATING THE RIGHT TO HEALTH IN AFRICA

Litigating the Right to Health in Africa

Challenges and Prospects

Edited by

EBENEZER DUROJAYE
University of the Western Cape, South Africa

Routledge
Taylor & Francis Group
LONDON AND NEW YORK

First published 2015 by Ashgate Publishing

2 Park Square, Milton Park, Abingdon, Oxfordshire OX14 4RN
52 Vanderbilt Avenue, New York, NY 10017

Routledge is an imprint of the Taylor & Francis Group, an informa business

First issued in paperback 2020

British Library Cataloguing in Publication Data
A catalogue record for this book is available from the British Library.

Library of Congress Cataloging-in-Publication Data
Litigating the right to health in Africa: challenges and prospects / by Ebenezer Durojaye.
pages cm
Includes bibliographical references and index.
ISBN 978-1-4724-6867-3 (hardback) – ISBN 978-1-4724-6868-0 (ebook) – ISBN 978-1-4724-6869-7 (epub)
1. Right to health – Africa, Sub-Saharan. I. Durojaye, Ebenezer, editor.
KQC581.5.L58 2015
344.6704'1–dc23

2015011088

ISBN 13: 978-1-4724-6867-3 (hbk)
ISBN 13: 978-0-367-59782-5 (pbk)

Contents

Notes on Contributors

Emma Justine Broster (LLB, LLM UKZN; LLM, University of Michigan Law School) is an Attorney and Grant Manager at the Legal Resources Centre (LRC) in Johannesburg, South Africa. The LRC is a pro bono human rights firm that focuses on strategic impact litigation. Broster's areas of interest include access to medicine and education. Prior to working at the LRC, she clerked for Justice Yacoob at the South African Constitutional Court in 2009. In 2010 Broster worked as an intern at Intellectual Property Watch in Geneva, Switzerland, as part of the Global Health Fellows programme of Duke University. Her Master of Laws at the University of KwaZulu-Natal focused on the right to access to health care in the South African context and examined flexibilities under international intellectual property law as possible solutions for increasing access to medicine in South Africa.

Enoch MacDonnell Chilemba (LLB, Malawi; LLM Human Rights and Democratisation, Pretoria; LLD, Western Cape) is a lecturer in law at the Faculty of Law, University of Malawi, Chancellor College. During the course of his doctoral studies (2012–2014) he served as a doctoral researcher at the Community Law Centre and the Centre of Disability Law and Policy at the Faculty of Law, University of the Western Cape. He also served as post-doctoral researcher at the Community Law Centre, University of the Western Cape, during the later months of 2014 and the early months of 2015. He worked as Senior State Advocate with the Ministry of Justice & Constitutional Affairs of Malawi between February 2009 and September 2010, providing legal advice to government departments and representing government in civil and criminal matters. He has been with the Faculty of Law of the University of Malawi, Chancellor College, since October 2010. His research interests are in the fields of constitutionalism, constitutional law and human rights law, especially the rights of children and persons with disabilities in Africa. He is thus involved in research on socio-economic rights, evictions in South Africa, implementation of inclusive education for children with disabilities in Africa, obstacles to constitutionalism in Malawi and independent monitoring of domestic implementation of rights of persons with disabilities in Africa.

Ebenezer Durojaye (LLB, Lagos; LLM, LLD, Free State) is an Associate Professor of Law and Head of the Socioeconomic Rights Project at the Dullah Omar Institute, University of the Western Cape, South Africa. His research interests include human rights issues raised by access to HIV/AIDS treatment, the intersection between gender inequality and HIV/AIDS response in Africa, women's health and adolescents' sexual and reproductive rights in Africa. He has written widely on these issues in international journals. He is the co-editor of *Strengthening the Protection of Sexual and Reproductive Health through Human Rights in the African Region* (PULP, 2014). He is one of the Independent Experts of the African

Commission on Human and Peoples' Rights for the Committee on the Protection of the Rights of People Living with HIV (PLHIV) and those at Risk, Vulnerable to and Affected by HIV.

Gladys Mirugi-Mukundi (LLM in Human Rights and Democratisation in Africa from the Centre for Human Rights, University of Pretoria) is a researcher at the Dullah Omar Institute, a law and policy research centre based at the University of the Western Cape. Her research expertise and interests include human rights, socio-economic rights, social justice and social inclusion, women and access to housing, rule of law and corruption.

Satang Nabaneh (LLB (Hons) University of The Gambia; LLM University of Pretoria) is a Lecturer in Law, Faculty of Law, University of The Gambia. She has been involved in advocacy and research work on human rights in The Gambia and other parts of Africa. Satang is a seasoned human rights defender with in-depth knowledge which she has translated into capacity building, programme development, research and practical engagement with grassroots, national, regional and international organisations and platforms. She is one of Africa's greatest young women leaders as a MILEAD Fellow. In 2012, she received the award for the best article on Gender and Political Participation in Africa organised by the Association of African Women for Research and Development (AAWORD). She is also the founder of Think Young Women (TYW), a young-women led non-profit organisation in The Gambia that focuses on leadership development and advocacy for the realisation of women's rights. Currently, she is the Programme Development Consultant for Safe Hands for Girls, a US based NGO dedicated to helping women and girls that have gone through FGM or are at risk of going through the practice.

Salima Namusobya (LLB, Uganda Christian University; LLM degree in Human Rights and Democratisation in Africa from the University of Pretoria) is the Executive Director of the Initiative for Social and Economic Rights (ISER) and an expert member of the Working Group on Economic, Social and Cultural Rights of the African Commission on Human and Peoples' Rights. She is a lawyer and human rights advocate who has specialised in international human rights law and forced migration. She has been a visiting scholar at the University of Columbia in New York, participating in the Human Rights Advocates Program, and has also completed courses on litigating social and economic rights from the Harvard School of Public Health and the institute for Human Rights at the Abo Akademi in Turku, Finland. She is co-author of the textbook *Civil Procedure and Practice in Uganda* (Law Africa, 2007). Previously, she worked in various capacities with the Refugee Law Project (RLP), School of Law, Makerere University and also served as the Eastern Africa coordinator for International Law in Domestic Courts (ILDC) – an online project of the Amsterdam Center for International Law and the Centre for Human Rights at the University of Pretoria, published by Oxford University Press. She has served on the boards of several NGOs. She is a member of the Uganda Law Society, the Federation of Female Lawyers in Uganda (FIDA) and the East African Law Society.

Jacinta Nyachae (LLB, Nairobi; Post-graduate Diploma in Law and Certificate in Intellectual Property Rights and Access to Medicines) has over seven years experience working on issues of human rights relating to health. She is an Advocate of the High Court of Kenya and the Executive Director of AIDS Law Project (ALP), a local NGO that focuses on promoting and protecting rights of people living with HIV. She is also a pro bono advocate and volunteers working with girls at the informal settlements within Nairobi through mentorship programmes. She has co-authored a number of papers on access to medicines as well as presented abstracts in conferences and meetings on health and human rights. She is a member of the Law Society of Kenya, Federation of Kenya Women Lawyers (FIDA) and Young Women's Christian Association (YWCA). Nyachae is a recipient of the Mary Robinson Award for Young Women Leadership in Human Rights.

Judy A. Oder (LLM in Human Rights, Raoul Wallenberg Institute, Sweden) is an international human rights expert with experience working on right to health issues at national and regional levels. She has contributed to the African human rights system by working on various issues using litigation, capacity building, institution building and development of standards. Judy previously worked at the Institute for Human Rights and Development in Africa and the International Centre for the Legal Protection of Human Rights (INTERIGHTS).

Josephine Odikpo (LLB Edo State University now Ambrose Alli University, Ekpoma; BL Nigerian Law School) is the Executive Director of the Centre for Rights and Development. She has been a relentless advocate canvassing for the promotion and protection of the human rights of people living with or affected by HIV in Nigeria. She has also been in the forefront of those advocating for universal access to HIV treatment for people living with HIV, especially vulnerable and marginalised groups. She has been involved in the drafting of policies and legislation in relation to HIV/AIDS at state and national levels. In addition, in a number of cases she has represented people living with HIV to seek legal redress for human rights violations. In 2009, in recognition of her work as an advocate and activist for women, children and persons living with HIV or affected by AIDS, she was nominated for the 2009 distinguished Nation Builders' Merit Award and also the 2009 US Department of State International Visitor Leadership programme Alumni on 'Grassroots Democracy' in the USA.

Paul Ogendi (LLM University of Nairobi; LLM, Human Rights and Democratisation in Africa, Pretoria) is an advocate of the High Court of Kenya. He is a researcher at the Institute for International and Comparative Law in Africa and LLD candidate at the Centre for Human Rights, University of Pretoria. He is also a Researcher assisting the Working Group on Death Penalty and Extra-judicial, Summary or Arbitrary Killings at the African Commission on Human and Peoples' Rights.

Olubayo Oluduro (LLB, LLM, Lagos; PHD Ghent) is a Professor of Law and Dean at the Faculty of Law Adekunle Ajasin University Ondo Sate, Nigeria. His research interests include environmental law, health law, HIV/AIDS and human rights, constitutional law and human rights. He has published extensively in these areas in international journals across the world. He is the author of *Oil Exploitation and Human Rights Violations in Nigeria's Oil Producing Communities* (Intersentia, 2014).

Oscar Parra-Vera (Bachelor in Law (JD) and master (LLM) in legal theory from the National University of Colombia) is a Colombian lawyer working as a Senior Legal Officer at the Inter-American Court of Human Rights (Costa Rica). He coordinates one of the working groups of the Court's permanent Registry. He has been a visiting researcher to the European Court of Human Rights. Prior to joining the Inter-American Court, Parra-Vera served as 'Romulo Gallegos' Fellow and consultant for social rights at the Inter-American Commission on Human Rights (Washington, DC). He has worked as a researcher at the Ombudsman Office of Colombia, the Colombian Commission of Jurists and as a clerk for the Constitutional Court of Colombia. He has also worked as a consultant for the Inter-American Institute for Human Rights (Costa Rica), the Judicial School of Colombia, the Human Rights Center of the University of Chile and the International Institute of Humanitarian Law in Sanremo (Italy). He was a professor in FLACSO-Mexico's Master's programme in Human Rights and Democracy. He is a Member of the Editorial Board of the *Inter-American & European Human Rights Journal* and of the Advisory Group and researcher at the Leverhulme International Network on the Inter-American Human Rights System.

Amar Roopanand Mahadew (LLM degree in Human Rights and Democratisation in Africa from the University of Pretoria) is a lecturer in the Department of Law at the University of Mauritius. He lectures on human rights law, environmental law and public international law. He is currently an LLD candidate at the Community Law Centre, University of Western Cape in Cape Town. His thesis is on land grabbing issues in African countries.

Preface

The seed for this publication was sown in 2012 during a consultative session on the right to health in Africa organised by INTERIGHTS in Nairobi, Kenya. At that meeting, several scholars and activists working on the right to health in Africa assembled to discuss various issues and challenges relating to this right and how to develop possible strategies to overcome these challenges. After this meeting, it became very clear that attempts to seek legal redress for the violation of the right to health in many African countries have not been well documented. This inspired the idea for a publication to capture the experiences of researchers and activists in Africa with regard to litigating the right to health. Further research and discussions with Judy Oder of then INTERIGHTS and Alicia Yamin of the FXB Center for Health and Human Rights, Harvard School of Public Health confirmed that there is a gap in this area that needs to be filled. Africa remains troubled by various health challenges and many African governments continue to fail in their obligations to deliver decent health care services in line with their commitments under international human rights law. This has led to poor health outcomes for many Africans. Apart from being regarded as the epicentre of the HIV/AIDS pandemic, Africa remains the continent with the worst maternal mortality ratio and studies would seem to show that many Africa countries are unlikely to meet Millennium Development Goal 5 relating to reducing maternal deaths by 75 per cent from the 1990s figures. The high maternal death rate recorded in many African countries can be attributed to a high incidence of early or child marriage and poor access to family planning services.

The constitutions of many African countries have provisions that can be directly or indirectly invoked to advance the right to health. In addition, regional human rights instruments such as the African Charter on Human and Peoples' Rights, the African Charter on the Rights and Welfare of the Child and the Protocol to the African Charter on the Rights of Women all contain provisions that can be used to advance the right to health. Despite these provisions, health rights litigation is still is an emerging phenomenon in Africa. A careful review of the literature on this issue reveals that attention has tended to focus on the situation in South Africa while little has been said of experiences in other African countries. This book aims to bridge this knowledge gap by providing information about health rights litigation in other African countries. While other publications have highlighted the importance of social rights litigation in some African countries, this is one of the few publications specifically to address health rights litigation in Africa. An important lesson to be drawn from this book is that litigation can provide a powerful tool not only to hold governments accountable for failure to realise the right to health but to also to empower people to seek redress for the violation of the right to health. It will certainly be useful to researchers, students, academia and members of civil society groups.

Acknowledgments

Many people in various ways have played crucial roles in ensuring the success of this book. I am eternally grateful to colleagues, friends and family members for their moral support. First, I would like to thank the contributing authors for their commitment towards the publication of this book. Second, I would like to thank Alison Kirk and Alex Buckley of Ashgate and their colleagues for their support and understanding during the production process. I am equally grateful to the reviewers of this book for their very useful comments and suggestions to ensure its quality. In the course of my journey in life my path has crossed those of other people who have influenced my life positively. In this regard, I remain grateful to Professor Charles Ngwena of the Centre for Human Rights University of Pretoria, Professor Akin Oyebode of the University of Lagos and Adeyinka Mojisola for their moral support always. Thanks also go to Professors Jaap de Visser, the Director, Dullah Omar Institute, University of the Western Cape, South Africa, Nico Steytler SARCHL Chair in Multilevel Government, Law and Development, University of the Western Cape, Bernard Martins, Dean of the Faculty of Law, University of the Western Cape and Rebecca Cook, co-director of the International Sexual and Reproductive Health Programme, University of Toronto for their encouragement. I would also like to thank Ademola Abass, Toun Adebanjo, Samuel Ayembo, Toluwani Darasimi, Ibukunoluwa David, Stella Iheadiri, Nkatha Murungi, Nontobeko Ncinitwa, Kola Odeku, Olubayo Oluduro, Sola Omotayo, Kay Sapto, N. Tengetile and Ireoluwade Tobiloba for their good wishes and support.

I would like to thank especially Dr Enoch Chilemba for his wonderful assistance and painstaking technical support on the manuscript of this book.

Introduction

The Relevance of Health Rights Litigation in Africa

Ebenezer Durojaye

Over the years litigation on the right to health has increased across the globe. From Africa to Asia, Europe and even South America, cases relating to the violation of the right to health are constantly being brought before the courts. Most of these cases touch on issues such as denial of emergency medical treatment, denial of access to life-saving medication, denial of access to health goods and services such as contraception, and denial of health care services based on age, sex, HIV status or marital status. These cases are a reminder of the importance attached to the right to health worldwide. The increase in attempts to litigate health rights issues is buoyed by the fact that nearly 70 per cent of constitutions worldwide recognise the right to health in one form or another, while this right is explicitly enforceable in about 40 per cent of constitutions.[1] The recognition of human rights in national or international human rights documents may amount to mere paper promises if these rights are not effectively implemented by governments. This is often the case with socio-economic rights, including the right to health. More often than not, poor countries of the world, particularly those in Africa, are quick to raise the excuse of limited resources to justify their unwillingness or reluctance to realise their citizens' rights to health care services. Nowhere is this act of nonchalance more tellingly revealed than in the area of life-threatening diseases such as HIV/AIDS.

The Importance of Social Rights Litigation

Litigation generally, and public interest litigation in particular, is relevant in the sense that it provides an avenue for individuals or groups of people to redress human rights violations that they have suffered. Although litigation is by no means the only way to realise the right to health, it remains one of the most important tools for achieving change in society.[2] Litigation provides a catalyst for changes in law such that its application can reach beyond the individual case and affect a large number of people. For instance, the US case of *Brown*

---

1 C Jung et al, 'Economic and Social Rights in National Constitutions' (2014), available at papers.ssrn.com/sol3/Delivery.../SSRN_ID2456339_code1258627.pdf? (accessed 13 February 2015).

2 Center for Reproductive Rights, *Briefing Paper: Reproductive Rights in European Court of Human Rights* (Center for Reproductive Rights 2004) 3.

v Board of Education of Topeka[3] was meant to provide justice for an individual denied the right to education because of his colour, however the decision in that case has had a far-reaching effect across the whole of the USA. In short, it has remained an authoritative and historical decision affirming the equal rights of all citizens to education. Beyond the fact that the case addressed discrimination in relation to the right to education, it also sent out a strong statement of condemnation of racial discrimination. Indeed, it was the first case, so to speak, to dismantle the wall of racial discrimination or segregation in the USA. Thus, it may be argued that litigation can become a source of legal reform especially in the case of public-interest litigation.[4]

Equally, litigation can easily generate public awareness over an issue. This is true in the case of class actions where a case is brought on behalf of a large number of people on a particular issue. Bringing such matters before the court may generate publicity and bring the attention of the public to a hitherto unnoticed issue. This may lead to public support or sympathy for the issue in question. For instance, the *Brown* case drew the attention of civil rights advocates all over the world.

With regard to health rights litigation, Gloppen has argued that such litigation can be used to hold a government accountable for its failure to realise the right to health within its jurisdiction.[5] Her argument is based on the grounds that people and institutions entrusted with powers and responsibilities have the obligation to justify that those powers and responsibilities have been used appropriately. Thus, she explains:

> Governments' accountability for the right to health stems from the understanding that they hold powers in trust on behalf of the people and that their mandate includes an obligation to respect, protect, and fulfil the right to health. Failure to act in accordance with these obligations may, in a democracy, result in electorates replacing their governments.[6]

While she observes that elections remain the most vital and legitimate means of holding a government accountable in a democracy, because of their infrequent nature and the fact that they are subject to manipulation, particularly in Africa, reliance on them is uncertain. Therefore, litigation can provide an alternative means of holding governments accountable to their responsibilities with regard to the right to health. This position has been echoed by Hogerzeil et al.:

> Skilful litigation can help to ensure that governments fulfil their constitutional and international treaty obligations. Such assurances are especially valuable in countries in which social security systems are still being developed.[7]

3 347 US 483 (1954).

4 See JM Singh et al, 'Do Human Rights Matter to Health?' (2007) 370 *Lancet* 521.

5 S Gloppen, 'Litigating as a Strategy to Hold Governments Accountable for Implementing the Right to Health' (2008) 10 *Health and Human Rights* 21.

6 Ibid, 22.

7 HV Hogerzeil et al, 'Is Access to Essential Medicines as Part of the Fulfilment of the Right to Health Enforceable through the Courts?' (2006) 368 *Lancet* 305.

A good example of a case where a government has been held accountable for its obligation to realise the right to health is the South African case of *Treatment Action Campaign*.[8] In that case, the South African government argued that providing Nevirapine in public hospitals to prevent transmission of HIV from pregnant women to their children was too expensive and that there was no medical proof guaranteeing the safety and efficacy of the drug. In its judgment, the Constitutional Court rejected the government's excuse of a lack of resources and found that its refusal to make the drugs available in public health institutions contravened the right to health guaranteed under section 27 of the Constitution. The Court then ordered the government to ensure that these drugs were made available in public health institutions. This decision underlies the important role of the court in holding the executive arm of the government accountable to its responsibilities. It equally affirms the relevance of litigation as a tool for monitoring governments' obligations to realise the right to health under national and international human rights law. According to Forman, the decision in *Treatment Action Campaign* 'broke the deadlock on a social struggle where political debates had consistently failed to achieve satisfactory outcome'.[9] It should be noted, however, that the Constitution of South Africa remains unique as one of the very few to explicitly recognise socio-economic rights as enforceable rights. This may have contributed in no small way to the success recorded in the *Treatment Action Campaign* case. However, as this book will demonstrate, the mere fact that a country's constitution does not contain an explicit provision on the right to health is not necessarily a barrier to health rights litigation.

With regard to access to medicine, it has been argued that health rights litigation has the potential to redistribute wealth in society, especially among the poor.[10] This is evidenced in the litigation concerning the high price of HIV/AIDS drugs. It has been noted that litigation to bring down the price of antiretroviral drugs in South Africa during the early 2000s led to a substantially reduced cost for the drugs and prevented unnecessary expense by the government.[11] Thus the result was positive both for individuals who needed to purchase the drugs and for the government which needed to budget for the drugs. This in turn provided the opportunity for the government to use its resources for something more beneficial to society.

Furthermore, as Pieterse has contended, albeit ambitiously, litigation can become a tool for achieving social justice in society.[12] This is based on the fact that litigation can improve the lives of vulnerable and marginalised groups. Such an assumption is particularly true in a country where the courts are able to exhibit some degree of activism and dynamism in purposively interpreting the provisions of the constitution. In such a situation, litigating socio-economic rights generally, and the right to health in particular, has the potential

---

8 *Minister of Health and Others v Treatment Action Campaign (TAC)* [2002] 10 BCLR 1033 (CC).

9 L Forman, 'Ensuring Reasonable Health: Health Rights, the Judiciary, and South African HIV/AIDS Policy' (2006) *Journal of Law, Medicine and Ethics* 711, 719.

10 See M Heywood, 'South Africa's Treatment Action Campaign: Combining Law and Social Mobilisation to Realise the Right to Health' (2009) 1 *Journal of Human Rights Practice* 14, 24.

11 Ibid.

12 See M Pieterse, 'The Potential of Socio-economic Rights Litigation for the Achievement of Social Justice: Considering the Example of Access to Medical Care in South African Prisons' (2006) 50 *Journal of African Law* 118.

to tangibly alleviate the suffering of vulnerable groups and to ensure them affirmative remedies that will satisfy their immediate vital needs within society.[13] This view is echoed by Gauri and Brinks when they argue that social rights litigation has the potential to achieve redistributive justice for the poor.[14] Based on a five-country study that was carried out in developing countries, Gauri and Brinks conclude that the impact of social rights litigation varies but is positive and pro-poor in two of the five countries (India and South Africa), distributive-neutral in another two (Indonesia and Brazil) and anti-poor in Nigeria.

Despite the importance of litigation it must be admitted that it has its limitations. Sometimes success in the court may not translate to any meaningful impact in the lives of the litigants especially if it is a class action. For instance, some years after the historic decision of the South African Constitutional Court in *Grootboom*,[15] access to housing remains elusive to many citizens.[16] In fact, when Irene Grootboom (the applicant in that case) died in 2008 she was still without a house.[17] Indeed, Ferraz has argued that social rights litigation to advance the right to health in Brazil has not benefited the poor but instead has the potential to harm them.[18] Moreover, as Cook et al. correctly suggest, litigation should be a means of last resort to redress human rights violations, after all other avenues have failed.[19] In Hogerzeil's view, 'redress mechanisms through the courts should be used as a last resort. Rather, policymakers should ensure that human rights standards guide their health policies and programmes from the outset.'[20] Rosenberg warns that using the court to effect reforms in the health sector has limited impact and may not be best way to utilise scarce resources.[21] Notwithstanding these limitations, Pieterse has argued that litigation remains 'a potentially invaluable tool for the construction of an ultimately more

---

13 See S Liebenberg, 'Needs, Rights and Transformation: Adjudicating Social Rights' (2005) Center for Human Rights and Global Justice Working Paper 8 (Economic and Social Rights Series) 6–7.

14 V Gauri and D Brinks, *Courting Social Justice: Judicial Enforcement of Socioeconomic Rights in Developing World* (Cambridge University Press 2010).

15 *Government of the Republic of South Africa and Others v Grootboom and Others* 2001 (4) SA 46 (CC); 2000 (11) BCLR 1169 (CC). This was the first major socio-economic case in which the Constitutional Court clearly laid down the criteria of reasonableness as a tool for measuring effectiveness of the government's laws and policies in relation to access to housing.

16 See R Dixon, 'Creating Dialogue about Socio-economic Rights: Strong-form versus Weak-form Judicial Review Revisited' (2007) *International Journal of Constitutional Law* 391; see also Gloppen (n 5 above).

17 See G Marcus and S Budlender, *A Strategic Evaluation of Public Interest Litigation in South Africa* (Atlantic Philanthropies 2008) 7.

18 OL Ferraz, 'Harming the Poor through Social Rights Litigation: Lessons from Brazil' (2011) *Texas Law Review* 1643.

19 RJ Cook et al, *Reproductive Health and Human Rights: Integrating Medicine, Ethics and Law* (Oxford University Press 2003) 234; see also Hogerzeil et al (n 7 above) 305.

20 Hogerzeil et al (n 7 above) 305.

21 G Rosenberg, *The Hollow Hope: Can Courts Bring about Social Change?* (Chicago University Press 2008).

just society'.[22] To sum up these arguments, Yamin concludes that the impact of health rights litigation lies somewhere between the two extremes.[23]

Health Rights Litigation in Africa

In recent times, health rights litigation in Africa has seemed to be on the increase. However, the focus has always been on the developments in South Africa without any consideration of developments in other parts of the region. This may be due to the point made earlier that the South African Constitution of 1996 explicitly guarantees the right to health in section 27. Experience has shown that more and more health rights cases are originating from other African countries such as Kenya, Uganda and Nigeria. Publications focusing on socio-economic rights in Africa do exist but little attention has been given to health rights issues. For example, a publication on the role of international human rights in domestic litigation assigns just one chapter to health rights litigation in the region.[24]

More recently, a publication dealing with health rights litigation across the globe contained a chapter on Africa, but like most other publications its focus was on South Africa.[25] Also, the five-country study by Gauri and Brinks mentioned above includes only South Africa and Nigeria from within Africa. One of the most recent publications on this issue, by Flood and Gross, is a 16-country study that aims to understand the role and impact of litigating health rights issues within health care systems made up of diverse mixes.[26] This comparative study of 16 countries (made up of high- and middle-income countries) of diverse socio-economic, cultural and political backgrounds emphasises the cautious role of the court in protecting the right to health of vulnerable and disadvantaged groups.

The current book is a collection of essays dealing with the challenges and prospects for health rights litigation in Africa. It aims to show that even in jurisdictions where the right to health has not been explicitly guaranteed, attempts have been made to litigate on this right. Conversely, it demonstrates that in some countries where the right to health has been explicitly recognised in the constitution, health rights litigation remains scanty. Unlike Flood and Gross' book, which seeks to evaluate the impact of health rights litigation in a 16-country study, the focus of this book is Africa. Its concern is with understanding the legal framework for the recognition of the right to health, the challenges people encounter in litigating health rights issues, and prospects for litigating future health rights cases in the continent. Thus, the book seeks to answer the following questions: What are the health challenges that African countries often encounter? What legal frameworks are

---

22 Pieterse (n 12 above) 119.

23 A Yamin, 'Promoting Equity in Health: What Role for Courts?' (2014) *Health and Human Rights* 1, 2.

24 M Kilander, *International Law and Domestic Human Rights Litigation* (Pretoria University Law Press 2010).

25 A Yamin and S Gloppen, *Litigating Health Rights: Can Courts Bring More Justice to Health?* (Harvard University Press 2011).

26 C Flood and A Gross, *The Right to Health at the Private/Public Divide: A Global Comparative Study* (Cambridge University Press 2014).

there in African countries to realise the right to health? What challenges are encountered in litigating the right to health in Africa and what possible recommendations can be made in this regard?

Given the diverse nature of the African region it is not possible to cover all the countries in the continent and therefore the case studies in this book are carefully selected to reflect as much of this diversity as possible. They cover nearly all the sub-regions of the continent. The book, which contains contributions from activists and scholars from across Africa, is divided into three sections. The first section deals with the normative framework for the right to health, while the second section contains case studies from selected African countries. The final section reviews the comparative approach to litigating the right to health before regional human rights bodies.

The Normative Framework

In Chapter 1, Olubayo Oluduro and Ebenezer Durojaye examine the normative framework for the realisation of the right to health as set out in international human rights instruments such as the International Covenant on Economic, Social and Cultural Rights (ICESCR) and other relevant regional human rights treaties. They further discuss the main elements of the right to health and the recent developments of international, regional and national laws. The authors then review the clarifications of the right to health as provided by the UN Committee on Economic, Social and Cultural Rights, which monitors compliance with the ICESCR. In addition, they examine the roles of academics, UN Special mechanisms such as the Special Rapporteur on health, national courts and the African Commission on Human and Peoples' Rights in contributing to the understanding of the right to health.

In Chapter 2, Gladys Mirugi-Mukundi examines universal access to reproductive rights in sub-Saharan Africa from a human rights perspective. After explaining what a rights-based approach entails, Mirugi-Mukundi discusses some of the challenges facing African countries with regard to universal access to sexual and reproductive health services. She argues that addressing access to reproductive health care as a human rights issue, and not just a developmental issue, provides a holistic framework for overcoming some of the challenges, such as a lack of resources, often cited by states to avoid responsibility for meeting the needs of the people. She identifies with the former UN High Commissioner for Human Rights, Navi Pillay, who argues that maternal mortality is often a result of violations of key human rights principles including accountability, equality, non-discrimination and meaningful participation. In conclusion Mirugi-Mukundi notes that litigation may serve as one of the means of ensuring accountability and thus universal access to sexual and reproductive health care services.

Country Case Studies

Part II begins, in Chapter 3, with Enoch Chilemba's analysis of the legal enforcement of the right to health in Malawi with particular focus on litigation. Chilemba observes that

Malawi is a state party to a number of human rights treaties that recognise the right to health. It also has a legal framework, including a justiciable Bill of Rights contained in the Constitution, which could facilitate the realisation of the right. Despite this, Malawi continues to face obstacles that derail the realisation of the right to health. These challenges include lack of access to health care facilities, poor provision of services that constitute underlying determinants of health, high prevalence of major diseases and maternal health problems. Chilemba notes that despite the various health challenges facing the country, the courts in Malawi have yet to determine a case raising substantive health rights issues.

In order to establish whether it provides avenues for redress through litigation, Chilemba critically evaluates Malawi's legal implementation framework relating to the right to health. He explores the challenges and prospects for litigating the right to health in Malawi, observing that one of the main factors that derails health rights litigation in the country is the confusion that exists regarding whether or not the right to health is justiciable in terms of Malawi's domestic legal framework. In his view, Malawi should resolve this misconceived conundrum and more attempts should be made to litigate the right to health in the country. In conclusion, in the light of the persistent health challenges that the country continues to face, Chilemba sees litigation as the only trigger for the appropriate implementation of the right to health in Malawi.

In Chapter 4, Emma Broster discusses some developments in health rights litigation in South Africa. She notes that while the focus of the chapter is on litigating the right to health care, in many circumstances the translation of socio-economic rights from the text of the Bill of Rights into improvements on the grounds is best achieved by the executive and legislative branches of government. According to Broster, for reasons of resources, expertise and legitimacy the courts are, in most cases, ill-equipped to ensure implementation of socio-economic rights on the ground. She reasons that while the Constitutional Court's jurisprudence on socio-economic rights has shied away from creating a minimum core content, it has provided concrete examples of where the Court will intervene to ensure that the state complies with its constitutional obligations. After discussing some of the health challenges facing the country, she examines the legal framework on the right to health and how the courts have interpreted the government's obligations in this regard. She concludes by offering useful suggestions for a more holistic approach to realising the right to health guaranteed under the South African Constitution.

Chapter 5, by Salima Namusobya, discusses the health challenges facing Uganda and the existing legal framework to address these challenges. Namusobya argues that while Uganda has ratified international and regional human rights instruments guaranteeing the right to health, including the International Covenant on Economic, Social and Cultural Rights, the African Charter and the Protocol to the African Charter on the Rights of Women, these instruments have not been properly implemented at the national level. Moreover, she observes that no specific provision in the Ugandan Constitution explicitly guarantees the right to health. This has made it almost impossible for Ugandans to enjoy their right to health. She identifies the existing structures that are relevant to safeguarding the right to health in the country. According to Namusobya, litigating health rights cases in Uganda had a progressive but inconsistent beginning. She discusses some relevant cases and points out some of the challenges that hinder health rights litigation in the country. She concludes by providing concrete suggestions to address these challenges.

In Chapter 6, Josephine Odikpo and Ebenezer Durojaye discuss the health situation in Nigeria, highlighting some of the challenges the country faces such as HIV/AIDS and high maternal mortality. They review the legal framework for realising the right to health in Nigeria, pointing out that the Constitution does not explicitly contain such a provision. According to the authors, health rights litigation in Nigeria before 2000 was sparse due to the negative attitude of the court to social rights litigation. However, things began to change in the early 2000s when people became dissatisfied with the situation on the ground and made attempts to litigate in court. In this regard, the authors discuss two important cases relating to the rights of HIV positive persons and how the cases may impact on future litigation on the right to health in Nigeria. They further review some of the factors that hinder health rights litigation in the country and provide some important suggestions for the way forward.

An overview of the health situation and major health challenges in Mauritius is provided by Amar Roopanand Mahadew in Chapter 7. Roopanand Mahadew notes that the right to health is not explicitly recognised under the Constitution of Mauritius and he discusses some of the drawbacks of not recognising it as a constitutionally protected right. In so doing, he reviews some decisions of the Supreme Court of Mauritius, arguing that they are merely based on medical negligence and do not necessarily influence policy-making. Roopanand Mahadew then discusses the constraints that exist with regard to litigating the right to health in Mauritius and provides useful recommendations.

In Chapter 8, Jacinta Nyachae and Paul Ogendi discuss some of the health challenges in Kenya and examine the legal framework for realising the right to heath in the country. More importantly, they discuss the attempt by the Kenyan court to clarify the nature of the government's obligations in relation to the right to health. The authors examine in detail two recent cases that deal with the implications of anti-counterfeiting legislation for access to life-saving medications for people living with HIV as well as the health impact of detention of a TB patient within the prison environment in Kenya. Nyachae and Ogendi consider the strengths and weaknesses of these cases for the realisation of the right to health and provide relevant suggestions on how Kenya can better guarantee this right.

Satang Nabaneh, in Chapter 9, discusses the legal framework in Mozambique governing the right to health. She critically examines the challenges encountered with human rights litigation, which has resulted in the absence of such cases, including health-related cases, in the Mozambican legal system. She identifies barriers such as the requirement of *locus standi*, and the lack of knowledge on the part of judges and lawyers. Nabaneh argues that despite these challenges, the recognition of the right to health as a justiciable right in the Constitution and the recent establishment of the National Human Rights Commission serve as opportunities for litigating the right to health in Mozambique. She concludes by providing useful recommendations on improving litigation on the right to health in the country.

Comparative Regional Study

Chapter 10, by Judy Oder, examines some of the key right to health challenges in Africa and how litigation could be used to respond to them. After identifying some of the health challenges facing the region, Oder examines the legal and human rights framework for the realisation of the right to health under the African Human Rights System. She analyses the strengths and weaknesses of cases concerning regional mechanisms on the right to health or indirectly touching on the underlying determinants of the right to health. These include a comparative analysis of the jurisprudence of the African Commission on Human and Peoples' Rights with that of other regional bodies, eliciting lessons that can be learnt by litigants in Africa. She then discusses the challenges and opportunities for future litigation of right to health issues in Africa and concludes with concrete recommendations, which include the need to embark on targeted strategic litigation on health rights in the region and nuanced and purposive interpretation of socio-economic rights provisions in national constitutions and regional human rights instruments.

In Chapter 11, Oscar Parra-Vera discusses some of the advances made by the Inter-American Commission on Human Rights and the Inter-American Court on Human Rights in the development of standards and norms regarding the right to health in the context of individual petitions. He observes that due to the difficulty in accessing the system, some commentators have argued against the justiciability of economic, social and cultural rights in the Inter-American System. He further notes that there is a strong argument for a direct protection of the right to health under article 26 of the American Convention on Human Rights or indirect protection through civil and political rights. He considers some of the arguments and provides an overview of eight subthemes about the direct and indirect protection of the right to health, including justiciability under the American Declaration, the relevance of article 26 of the American Convention, the protection of the right to health through the right to 'life with dignity', and the duty to guarantee inspection, surveillance and control in the rendering of health care services. Thereafter, the chapter considers specific issues regarding vulnerable groups. In particular, Parra-Vera analyses the right to health and its connection with the right to personal integrity, with emphasis on health care for persons with disabilities and persons deprived of liberty.

References

Books, Chapters, Articles, etc.

Center for Reproductive Rights, *Briefing Paper: Reproductive Rights in European Court of Human Rights* (Center for Reproductive Rights 2004).

Cook, RJ, Dickens, BM and Fathalla, MF, *Reproductive Health and Human Rights: Integrating Medicine, Ethics and Law* (Oxford University Press 2003).

Dixon, R, 'Creating Dialogue about Socio-economic Rights: Strong-form versus Weak-form Judicial Review Revisited' (2007) *International Journal of Constitutional Law* 391–418.

Ferraz, OL, 'Harming the Poor through Social Rights Litigation: Lessons from Brazil' (2011) *Texas Law Review* 1643–1668.

Flood, C and Gross, A, *The Right to Health at the Private/Public Divide: A Global Comparative Study* (Cambridge University Press 2014).

Forman, L, 'Ensuring Reasonable Health: Health Rights, the Judiciary, and South African HIV/AIDS Policy' (2006) *Journal of Law, Medicine and Ethics* 711–724.

Gauri, V and Brinks, D, *Courting Social Justice: Judicial Enforcement of Social and Economic Rights in the Developing World* (Cambridge University Press 2010).

Gloppen, S, 'Litigating as a Strategy to Hold Governments Accountable for Implementing the Right to Health' (2008) 10 *Health and Human Rights* 21–36.

Heywood, M, 'South Africa's Treatment Action Campaign: Combining Law and Social Mobilisation to Realise the Right to Health' (2009) 1 *Journal of Human Rights Practice* 14–36.

Hogerzeil, HV, Samson, M, Casanovas, JV and Rahmani-Ocora, L, 'Is Access to Essential Medicines as Part of the Fulfilment of the Right to Health Enforceable through the Courts?' (2006) 368 *Lancet* 305–311.

Jung, C, Hirschl, R and Rosevear, E, 'Economic and Social Rights in National Constitutions' (2014) available at papers.ssrn.com/sol3/Delivery.../SSRN_ID2349680_code1258627.pdf? (accessed 13 February 2015).

Kilander, M, *International Law and Domestic Human Rights Litigation* (Pretoria University Law Press 2010).

Liebenberg, S, 'Needs, Rights and Transformation: Adjudicating Social Rights' (2005) Center for Human Rights and Global Justice Working Paper 8 (Economic and Social Rights Series) 6–7.

Marcus, G and Budlender, S, *A Strategic Evaluation of Public Interest Litigation in South Africa* (Atlantic Philanthropies 2008).

Pieterse, M, 'The Potential of Socio-economic Rights Litigation for the Achievement of Social Justice: Considering the Example of Access to Medical Care in South African Prisons' (2006) 50 *Journal of African Law* 118–131.

Rosenberg, G, *The Hollow Hope: Can Courts Bring about Social Change?* (Chicago University Press 2008).

Singh, JM, Govender, M and Mills, EJ, 'Do Human Rights Matter to Health?' (2007) 370 *Lancet* 521–527.

Yamin, A, 'Promoting Equity in Health: What Role for Courts?' (2014) *Health and Human Rights* 1–9.

Yamin, A and Gloppen, S, *Litigating Health Rights: Can Courts Bring More Justice to Health?* (Harvard University Press 2011).

Cases

Brown v Board of Education of Topeka 347 US 483 (1954).

Government of the Republic of South Africa and Others v Grootboom and Others 2001 (4) SA 46 (CC); 2000 (11) BCLR 1169 (CC).

Minister of Health and Others v Treatment Action Campaign (TAC) [2002] 10 BCLR 1033 (CC).

PART I
The Normative Framework on the Right to Health

Chapter 1

The Normative Framework on the Right to Health under International Human Rights Law

Olubayo Oluduro and Ebenezer Durojaye

The right to the enjoyment of the highest attainable standard of health, popularly referred to as 'the right to health', has evolved at the international level over a number of years. While at an early stage the content and nature of this right was sketchy, in recent times ample jurisprudence – at both international and regional levels – has developed the concept of the right to health. Despite the positive development of the right to health the international community still faces numerous health challenges ranging from HIV/AIDS, malaria and tuberculosis to highly infectious diseases such as bird flu and more emerging health concerns over non-communicable diseases. Almost 30 years into HIV/AIDS epidemic, its devastating impact has not been halted. Millions of people worldwide are still at risk of infection, and mortality associated with the epidemic remains high. While it is important to point out that great strides have been made with regard to creating awareness about the epidemic and providing access to life-saving medication for people in need, it remains a source of concern that more than 1 million HIV-related deaths still occur each year.[1] Most of these deaths occur in developing countries, particularly sub-Saharan Africa. It also important to note that the impact of the epidemic is felt most among women, who constitute about 50 per cent of the total number of people living with HIV worldwide and about 60 per cent of those in sub-Saharan Africa.

In the 60 plus years since the World Health Organization (WHO) declared in the preamble to its constitution that the enjoyment of the right to health is a fundamental right, various developments have shaped the meaning and content of the right to health. Notable among these is the clarification provided by UN treaty monitoring bodies such as the Committee on Economic, Social and Cultural Rights (CESCR) and the Committee on the Convention on the Elimination of All Forms of Discrimination against Women (CEDAW). For instance, in its General Comment No 14, the CESCR clarifies the essential elements of the right to health as guaranteed under article 12 of the International Covenant on Economic, Social and Cultural Rights (ICESCR). It also attempted to clarify the nature and scope of obligations of states. In its General Recommendation 24, the CEDAW Committee has explained the meaning and scope of the right to health of women guaranteed under article 12 of the Convention. More recently, the Human Rights Council

1 See, for instance, UNAIDS, *AIDS Epidemic Report* (UNAIDS 2013).

has adopted resolutions and guidelines with regard to maternal mortality as a human rights challenge. These clarifications have proved a useful guide to states, individuals and civil society groups, providing a better understanding of the right to health.

In a recent Global Status Report on Non-communicable Diseases the WHO noted that non-communicable diseases pose a great threat to millions of lives across the world.[2] According to the report, in 2008 an estimated 4 million people worldwide died as a result of non-communicable diseases. The report urges countries across the world to pay more attention to the negative consequences of non-communicable diseases by creating awareness and educating people about this fact. Given these recent developments and in view of the importance of the right to health, an understanding of its normative framework is required. A normative framework on the right to health would help to delimit the criteria used to identify and enforce the right, thus creating the preconditions for its enforceability and justiciability.

Against this backdrop, this chapter examines the normative framework for the realisation of the right to health as set out in international human rights instruments such as the ICESCR and other relevant regional human rights treaties. It provides a general overview of the sources and content of the right to health but does not engage in critical analysis of this right. It further discusses the main elements of the right to health and recent attempts at providing clarification of this right at international, regional and national levels. In this regard, the chapter examines the different interpretations provided by the CESCR, which monitors compliance with the ICESCR, and the role of academics, UN Special mechanisms such as the Special Rapporteur on health, national courts and the African Commission on Human and Peoples' Rights in contributing to the understanding of the right to health.

The Right to Health: International Normative and Legal Standards

The problem of defining and implementing a right to health is threefold: indeterminacy (how to characterise it), justiciability (how to enforce it) and progressive realisation (how to raise the standard over time).[3] In order to make the right to health an enforceable right, it must be specified and clearly defined. As pointed out by Gostin, 'a right to health that is too broadly defined lacks clear content and is less likely to have a meaningful effect'.[4] The right to health may also be viewed as 'a right to a functioning system of health protection rather than simply in terms of buildings, doctors, nurses, medicines, water and sanitation'.[5]

2 World Health Organization, *The Global Status Report on Non-communicable Diseases* (WHO 2011).

3 PK Sandhu, 'A Legal Right to Health Care: What can the United States Learn from Foreign Models of Health Rights Jurisprudence? (2007) 95 *California Law Review* 1159.

4 LO Gostin, 'The Human Right to Health: A Right to the "Highest Attainable Standard of Health"' (2001) *Hastings Center Report* 29–30, quoted in LN Kingston et al, 'Debate: Limitations on Universality: The "Right to Health" and the Necessity of Legal Nationality' (2010) 10 *BMC International Health and Human Rights* 11.

5 International Federation of Health and Human Rights Organisations (IFHRO) *Our Right to the Highest Attainable Standard of Health* (2005), available at http://www.paho.org/hr-ecourse-e/

As equal human beings, this right belongs to every human being and so governments of every nation must guarantee to every individual in society an equal opportunity to enjoy the highest attainable standard of both physical and mental health. This right has been recognised as a fundamental human right for several years. Indeed, the 1946 Constitution of the World Health Organization asserts that

> Health is a state of complete physical, mental and social well-being and not merely the absence of disease or infirmity. The enjoyment of the highest attainable standard of health is one of the fundamental rights of every human being without distinction of race, religion, political belief, economic or social condition … The extension to all peoples of the benefits of medical, psychological and related knowledge is essential to the fullest attainment of health.[6]

Health is of 'foundational importance … for human happiness, the exercise of rights and privileges, and the formation of family and social relationships'.[7]

Although the WHO definition of health 'captures the full dimensions of the state of health, it is probably too broad a definition for government policy makers charged with the responsibility for a nation's health care'.[8] Also, there is no consensus on what type and amount of health care services constitutes adequate care, nor is there an understanding of the true cost or quality of those services.[9] However, attempts have been made by scholars to delineate the important 'issue of what governments should assure or provide in terms of health care services and, specifically, what may be the content of a morally acceptable package of health care services'.[10] Suffice to say that the right to health implies more than just access to medical care and medicines; to limit the right to health to mere provision of health services appears restrictive and limiting. It goes beyond health care to include the satisfaction of basic needs that make health possible, such as access to sanitation, food, potable water, housing, clothing and so forth, as the absence of these results in most of the world's diseases.

A close look at the development of public health in the nineteenth century in Europe and the United States reveals that the most remarkable interventions for the promotion and improvement of the health of populations do not involve health services per se, but rather are dependent on the realisation of economic, social and cultural rights: food, housing,

---

assets/_pdf/Module2/Lesson1/M2_L1_4.pdf (accessed 7 January 2015).

6 The Constitution of the World Health Organization was adopted in New York in June 1945 and opened for signature on 22 July 1946. World Health Organization Constitution 14 UNTS 185.

7 L Gostin, 'Securing Health or Just Healthcare? The Effect of the Healthcare System on the Health of America' (1994) 39 *St. Louis University Law Journal* 7, 11.

8 ED Kinney and BA Clark, 'Provisions for Health and Health Care in the Constitutions of the Countries of the World' (2004) *Cornell International Law Journal* 285, 289.

9 Ibid.

10 Ibid. See also AE Buchanan, 'The Right to a Decent Minimum of Health Care' (1984) 13 *Philosophy and Public Affairs* 55.

hygiene and so on.[11] In other words, the right to health is intrinsically linked to many other rights, categorised as civil and political – rights to life, not to be subjected to torture or cruel, inhuman or degrading treatment, and to information – and economic, social and cultural – rights to food, housing, hygiene, clothing, food, work, water, education, healthy occupational and environmental conditions, and access to health-related education and information – which are contained in international treaties and domestic constitutions. For example, misuse of information about ill-health may compromise the right of an individual to enjoy his other fundamental rights and actively contribute to the democratic process or exercise the privileges or carry out his responsibilities as a citizen of his country. It may hinder the fulfilment of all rights – personal liberty, autonomy,[12] human dignity, exercise of franchise and so on – in the sense that the capacity of individuals to claim and enjoy these rights may depend on their physical, mental and social well-being. The HIV status of an individual may lead to restrictions of the right to education and to housing, arbitrary termination or denial of employment, violations of the right to marry and found a family, limitations of freedom of movement, arbitrary detention or exile, protection from abuse and neglect, and even cruel, inhuman or degrading treatment.[13] The CESCR, in its General Comment No 14, has observed that

> The right to health is closely related to and dependent upon the realisation of other human rights, as contained in the International Bill of Rights, including the rights to food, housing, work, education, human dignity, life, non-discrimination, equality, the prohibition against torture, privacy, access to information, and the freedoms of association, assembly and movement. These and other rights and freedoms address integral components of the right to health.[14]

Some decisions of domestic courts in jurisdictions such as India, South Africa and Costa Rica appear to support this assertion. For example, the Indian Supreme Court has held that a denial of right to emergency medical care constitutes a violation of the right to life guaranteed under the Indian Constitution.[15] The Supreme Court in Costa Rica has held that a denial of access to life-saving medications for people infected with HIV will undermine their right to life.[16] Thus, the right to health is indivisible from other rights and may only be fully achieved by realising these other human rights. The 'right to health' as

---

11 M Özden, *The Right to Health: A Fundamental Human Right Affirmed by the United Nations and Recognised in Regional Treaties and Numerous National Constitutions* (Human Rights Programme of the Europe-Third World Centre (CETIM) 2006).

12 See *Washington v Glucksberg* 521 US 702, 732 (1997).

13 JM Mann et al, 'Health and Human Rights' (1994) 1 *Health and Human Rights* 6, 14.

14 Committee on Economic, Social and Cultural Rights, General Comment No 14, 'The right to highest attainable standard of health' (2000) para 3.

15 *Pachim Banga Khet Majoor Samity v State of Bengal* (1996) 4 SCC 37.

16 *Alvarez v Ccaja Costarricense de Seguro Social* Exp 5778-V-97, No 5934–97, cited in E Durojaye and O Oluduro, 'Enforcement of Social and Economic Rights in Africa: Lessons from South African Case of *Government of the Republic of South Africa and Others v Grootboom and Others* 2000 (11) BCLR 1169 (CC)' (2006) 3 *Fountain Quarterly Law Journal* 15, 22.

an important free-standing right should not be seen or considered as separate from other human rights, but indispensable for the exercise of several of them.[17]

It can be asserted that the right to health has witnessed an unprecedented level of interpretation, both expanding its normative scope and identifying specific state obligations.[18] For example, the CESCR in its General Comment No 14 on the right to health stated that the content of the entitlement under this right should be further clarified for states to enable them progressively to realise these duties. The General Comment also identified a baseline of obligations below which no state can fall regardless of their resources, and which are not subject to progressive realisation.[19]

The right to health is to be understood neither as the right to be healthy nor as the right to the provision of health care,[20] since the state cannot afford protection against every possible cause of illness. Importantly, there are several factors outside the direct control of states that combine to influence good health, such as an individual's biological make-up and socio-economic conditions. The right to health refers to the right to the enjoyment of a variety of goods, facilities, services and conditions necessary for its realisation.[21] Thus, it implies an obligation on the part of the government to create the conditions necessary for individuals to achieve their optimal health status.[22]

Individual right-holders are conferred with certain normative advantages by the right to health. As stated by the CESCR General Comment, the right to health contains both freedoms and entitlements. The *freedoms* include the right to control one's health and body, including sexual and reproductive freedom, and the right to be free from interference, such as the right to be free from torture, non-consensual medical treatment and experimentation. By contrast, the *entitlements* include the right to a system of health protection that provides equality of opportunity for people to enjoy the highest level of health.[23] It is necessary for states to meet these underlying determinants of health for the right to be adequately protected. The right takes into account the relationship between states and individuals, particularly in matters relating to health. Thus, the notion of the highest attainable standard of health takes into account both the individual's biological and socio-economic preconditions and the state's available resources.[24]

---

17 World Health Organization, *25 Questions and Answers on Health & Human Rights* (WHO 2002) 10.

18 S Nixon and L Forman, 'Exploring Synergies between Human Rights and Public Health Ethics: A Whole Greater than the Sum of its Parts' (2008) 8 *BMC International Health and Human Rights* 2.

19 Committee on Economic, Social and Cultural Rights, General Comment No 14, para 30.

20 E Minelli, *World Health Organization: The Mandate of a Specialized Agency of the United Nations* (Geneva Foundation for Medical Education and Research 2003).

21 World Health Organization and Office of the United Nations High Commissioner for Human Rights, 'The Right to Health', Fact sheet No 31 (2000) 5.

22 D Tarantola et al, *Human Rights, Health and Development: Initiative for Health and Human Rights* (University of New South Wales Initiative for Health and Human Rights 2008).

23 Committee on Economic, Social and Cultural Rights, General Comment No 14, para 8.

24 Minelli (n 20 above).

No one should be unfairly deprived of the chance to enjoy good health by reason of sex, religion, race, age, language, colour, disability, health status (e.g. HIV/AIDS), national or social origin, sexual orientation, political or other opinion, property, birth or civil, political, social or other status as this is incompatible with the right to health. Also, health services must be provided in a manner that respects cultural differences.[25] As noted by Thoraya Obaid, the former Executive Director of the United Nations Population Fund (UNFPA), 'cultural sensitivity ... leads to higher levels of programme acceptance and ownership by the community, and programme sustainability'.[26] Where a state fails to take appropriate steps to address discriminatory practices in a health system, it can be called to account and be required to take remedial measures. The Limburg Principles provide that the grounds of discrimination mentioned in article 2(2) (ICESCR) are not exhaustive and therefore call for 'special measures to be taken for the sole purpose of advancing the interest of certain groups in order to ensure that these groups enjoy the benefit of economic, social and cultural rights'.[27] Special attention must be given to vulnerable members of society, which includes women, children, adolescents, elderly persons, the disabled and indigenous communities. Hence the need to address issues that directly or indirectly affect the health of marginalised and vulnerable groups in society. These issues may include violence against women, violence and abuse at home and at work, harmful traditional practices, including female genital mutilation, lack of voice in household and community decision-making, lack of access to education, inadequate or non-existent social protection, and lack of birth registration or identity papers.[28] However, the insistence on the principle of non-discrimination and on the indivisibility of the right to health from other human rights has been a major source of concern for many policy-makers who have to contend with the reality of scarce resources.[29] In such a situation, tough choices have to be made to give priority to some rights over others and to the claims of some rights-holders over others, such as between young and old, those living in urban areas and those in remote rural areas, and those with chronic diseases that are expensive to treat and those with minor diseases that can be catered for under basic primary health care.[30]

---

25 See World Health Organization, *Basic Documents*, 45th edn, Supplement (WHO 2006), available at http://www.who.int/governance/eb/who_constitution_en.pdf (accessed 23 January 2015).

26 United Nations Population Fund, *Culture Matters: Working with Communities and Faith-based Organizations* (UNFPA 2005) v.

27 Limburg Principles on the Implementation of the International Covenant on Economic, Social and Cultural Rights (1986) paras 36 and 39.

28 World Health Organization, *Human Rights, Health and Poverty Reduction Strategies* (WHO 2008) 23.

29 L Munro, '"The Human Rights-based Approach to Programming": A Contradiction in Terms?' in S Hickey and D Mitlin (eds) *Rights-based Approaches to Development: Exploring the Potential and Pitfalls* (Kumarian Press 2009) 187, 197–201, quoted in J Tobin, 'Introduction' in J Tobin, *The Right to Health in International Law* (Oxford University Press 2011), University of Melbourne Legal Studies Research Paper 562, 8.

30 Ibid.

Sources of the Right to Health in International Law

The international human right to health is recognised by various declarations and treaties of the UN and other international and regional bodies, and states parties are required to respect, protect and fulfil these. In 1948 the UN formally mentioned the international human right to health in connection with other economic, social and cultural rights in the Universal Declaration of Human Rights (UDHR), which is the basis of all human rights.[31] It indirectly refers to the right to health. Article 25 of the Declaration provides that 'Everyone has the right to a standard of living adequate for the health and wellbeing of himself and of his family, including food, clothing, housing and medical care and necessary social services, and the right to security in the event of unemployment, sickness, disability, widowhood, old age or other lack of livelihood in circumstances beyond his control.'[32] At the time the UDHR was adopted by the UN General Assembly, it was a non-binding instrument but it has since assumed the status of customary international law for most of its provisions.[33]

The most important and comprehensive provision on the right to health is article 12 of the ICESCR, which provides the most authoritative expression of the right in international law.[34] It provides that state parties to the Covenant shall recognise the right of everyone to the enjoyment of the highest attainable standard of physical and mental health. It further lists measures that the states parties should take to guarantee the full realisation of such a right:

> (a) the provision of the reduction of the stillbirth-rate and of infant mortality for the healthy development of the child;
>
> (b) the improvement of all aspects of environmental and industrial hygiene;
>
> (c) the prevention, treatment and control of epidemic, endemic, occupational and other diseases;
>
> (d) the creation of conditions which would assure to all medical service and medical attention in the event of sickness.

Saddled with the responsibility for promoting, implementing and enforcing this covenant is the UN Committee on Economic, Social and Cultural Rights.

While not providing directly for the right to health, the International Covenant on Civil and Political Rights (ICCPR) provides in article 6 that states parties are under an obligation

---

31 Universal Declaration of Human Rights, GA Res 217A (III), UN Doc A/810 at 76 (1948).

32 Ibid.

33 E Riedel, 'The Human Right to Health: Conceptual Foundations' in A. Clapham and M Robinson (eds) *Realizing the Right to Health* (Rüffer & Rub 2009) 21, 22.

34 International Covenant on Economic, Social and Cultural Rights, GA Res 2200 (XXI) A (UN Doc A/6316) at 49 (Dec. 16, 1966).

to protect every human being's inherent right to life. Some states parties with no specific provision for the right to health in their constitutional or other legislative documents have used this provision in relation to the right to health.[35] In addition, the Committee on Human Rights in its General Comment No 6 on the right to life has explained that the right to life should not be interpreted narrowly but must be seen to intercept with maternal health, food and housing.[36] Further, article I of the Declaration of Alma Ata states that

> health, which is a state of complete physical, mental and social well-being, and not merely the absence of disease or infirmity, is a fundamental human right and that the attainment of the highest level of health is a most important world-wide social goal whose realisation requires the action of many other social and economic sectors in addition to the health sector.[37]

The International Convention on the Elimination of all Forms of Racial Discrimination (ICERD) in its article 5(e) iv states that: 'States Parties undertake ... to guarantee the right of everyone ... to public health, medical care, social security and social services'.[38] Moreover, article 11(1)(f) of the Convention on the Elimination of all Forms of Discrimination against Women provides that 'States Parties shall take all appropriate measures ... to ensure on a basis of equality of men and women ... the right to protection of health'.[39] Articles 12(1) and 12(2) of the same Convention provide that: 'States parties shall take all appropriate measures to eliminate discrimination against women in the field of health care' and that 'States Parties shall ensure to women appropriate services in connection with pregnancy, confinement and the post-natal period, granting free services where necessary, as well as adequate nutrition during pregnancy and lactation'. Article 14(2)(b) states that 'States Parties shall take all appropriate measures to eliminate discrimination against women in rural areas ... and, in particular, shall ensure to such women the right: To have access to adequate health care facilities, including information, counselling and services in family planning.' The CEDAW Committee in its General Recommendation No 24 has further provided clarification on the nature of states' obligations regarding the right to health guaranteed in the Convention.[40] According to the Committee, states are under an obligation to ensure that policies and laws facilitate equal access to health care for women

---

35 Riedel (n 33 above) 25.

36 Report of the Human Rights Committee, 'The Right to Life', UN GAOR 37th session Supp No 40.

37 International Conference on Primary Health Care, held in Alma-Ata, URSS, September 1978, Declaration of Alma-Ata (1978), available at www.who.int/hpr/archive/docs/almaata.html (accessed 3 January 2015).

38 International Convention on the Elimination of All Forms of Racial Discrimination, 21 December 1965, United Nations Treaty Series vol. 660, 195, available at http://www.unhcr.org/refworld/docid/3ae6b3940.html (accessed 12 February 2015).

39 Convention on the Elimination of All Forms of Discrimination against Women (1979), available at http://www.un.org/womenwatch/daw/cedaw/ (accessed 3 January 2015).

40 Committee on the Elimination of Discrimination against Women, General Recommendation No 24, 'Women and Health', UN Doc A/54/38 Rev 1 (1999).

in a non-discriminatory manner. The Committee further notes that health care services must be gender sensitive, taking into account the particular needs of women.[41]

The Convention on the Rights of the Child states in article 24(1) that 'States parties recognise the right of the child to the enjoyment of the highest attainable standard of health and to facilities for the treatment of illness and rehabilitation of health. States Parties shall strive to ensure that no child is deprived of his or her access to such health care services.'[42] Article 24(2)(c) requires states parties, among other things, to take appropriate measures 'To combat disease and malnutrition, including within the framework of primary health care, through, inter alia, the application of readily available technology and through the provision of adequately nutritious foods and clean drinking-water, taking into consideration the dangers and risks of environmental pollution.' Recently, the Committee on the Rights of the Child (CRC) in its General Comment No 15 has elaborated on the nature of states' obligation regarding the right to health of children as guaranteed under article 24 of the Convention. According to the Committee, the right to health guaranteed in article 24 should be interpreted as an inclusive right:

> extending not only to timely and appropriate prevention, health promotion, curative, rehabilitative and palliative services, but also a right to grow and develop to their full potential, and live in conditions that enable them to attain the highest standard of health by implementing programmes that address the underlying determinants of health.[43]

The Committee urges states parties to adopt a holistic approach to advancing children's right to health. In this regard, the Committee notes that not 'only is children's right important in and of itself, but also the realisation of the right to health is indispensable for the enjoyment of all the other rights in the Convention'.[44] The Committee reasons further that the notion of 'highest attainable standard of health' must take into cognisance a child's biological, social, cultural and economic preconditions. It notes that states' available resources should include supplementary resources from other sources, including non-governmental organisations, the international community and the private sector.

The UN Millennium Declaration adopted by the UN General Assembly also emphasises the importance of health care and prevention of disease.[45] It stressed the need for states to improve their maternal and child health, and combat HIV/AIDS, malaria and other major diseases. Of the eight UN Millennium Development Goals (MDGs), three – MDG 4, reducing child mortality, MDG 5 improving maternal health and MDG 6 combating HIV/AIDS, malaria and other diseases – have a direct implication for the enjoyment of the right

41 Ibid.

42 Convention on the Rights of the Child 1989 A/RES/44/25. See also arts 28, 43(e) and 45 of the International Convention on the Protection of the Rights of all Migrant Workers and Members of their Families (1990) and art 25 of the Convention on the Rights of Persons with Disabilities (2006).

43 Committee on the Rights of the Child, General Comment No 15, 'The right of the child to the enjoyment of highest attainable standard of health' (17 April 2013) CRC/C/GC/15.

44 Ibid, para 7.

45 UN General Assembly Millennium Declaration (December 2000).

to health. In addition, MDG 8 calls for cooperation with pharmaceutical companies, in order to provide access to affordable essential drugs in developing countries.[46]

The right to health, particularly in the areas of reproductive health and women's health, also features in several UN world summits such as the Vienna Declaration and Programme of Action, which alluded to the right to health in several of its paragraphs, stressing the importance of health care and protection,[47] the Programme of Action of the United Nations International Conference on Population and Development[48] and the Declaration and Programme of Action of the Fourth World Conference on Women.[49] In Chapter 2, Gladys Mirugi-Mukundi discusses in detail the obligations of African governments to realise universal access to sexual and reproductive health services.

In addition to the various developments mentioned above, in April 2002, the Commission on Human Rights appointed a Special Rapporteur on the right to health to focus among other things on clarifying the scope of the right to health and state obligations.[50] The Special Rapporteur has declared that 'the legal content of the right is not yet well established', thereby serving as an impediment to the realisation of the right to health.[51] With respect, this may not be the reason as there is plethora of legislation on the right to health as discussed above, in particular the definition of the WHO as well as the above mentioned article 12 of the ICESCR, which constitute a sufficient framework within which to conceive policies for realising the right to health at both the national and international level.[52] Recent developments at the UN level have further raised the profile of the right to health under international law. For instance, in 2009, the Human Rights Council adopted a resolution on maternal mortality, where it noted that pregnancy-related deaths and morbidities amount to gross violations of women's fundamental rights as enshrined in various human rights instruments.[53] The Council thus called on governments across the world to take appropriate steps and measures, including law reforms and abrogation of cultural practices that discriminate against women, in order to stem the rates of maternal death in the world.

46 Riedel (n 33 above) 24.

47 Adopted by the World Conference on Human Rights (Vienna), 14–25 June 1993, particularly paras 11, 18, 24, 31 and 41.

48 International Conference on Population and Development (ICPD) UN A/CONF.171 (13) (18 October 1994).

49 Fourth World Conference on Women, Beijing, 15 September 1995, A/CONF.177/20.

50 Special Rapporteurs are independent experts appointed by the UN to monitor and report back on a country situation or a specific human rights theme through the presentation of annual reports.

51 Report of the Special Rapporteur on the right of everyone to the enjoyment of the highest attainable standard of physical and mental health, Paul Hunt, submitted in accordance with Commission resolution 2002/31 (February 2003) E/CN.4/2003/58, para 39.

52 Özden (n 11 above) 7–8.

53 Human Rights Council, 'Preventable Maternal Mortality and Morbidity and Human Rights' (16 June 2009) A/HRC/11/L.16/Rev 1.

At the regional level, the African Charter on Human and Peoples' Rights (hereafter African Charter) in its article 16 guarantees the right to health.[54] It provides that everyone has the right to enjoy the best attainable state of physical and mental health, and enjoins states party to the Charter to take the necessary measures to protect the health of their people and ensure that they receive medical attention when they are sick. In *Social and Economic Rights Action Center (SERAC) and Another v Nigeria*,[55] which deals with various allegations of human rights violations, including environmental pollution and threats to a healthy environment against the Nigerian government, the African Commission on Human and Peoples' Rights (hereafter African Commission) found that the Nigerian government violated articles 4 (right to life), 16 (right to health) and 24 (right of peoples to a satisfactory environment), among others. The Commission further held that the right to enjoy the best attainable state of physical and mental health enunciated in Article 16(1) of the African Charter and the right to a general satisfactory environment favourable to development obligate governments to desist from directly threatening the health and environment of their citizens. Also, the Commission found that the right to health under the Charter is not limited to health care and that the right is justiciable as against the previous prevailing view.[56]

In *Purohit v The Gambia*,[57] the complainants were mental health advocates, who submitted communication on behalf of patients detained at a psychiatric unit in The Gambia, under the Mental Health Acts of the Republic of The Gambia. They alleged that there were no review or appeal procedures against determination or certification of one's mental state for both involuntary and voluntary mental patients under the Lunatics Detention Act (LDA) and no remedy for wrong certification/diagnosis. Also, that the LDA fails to lay out fixed periods of detention for those persons found to be of unsound mind, which may lead to an indefinite detention of a mental patient. The complainants also stated that there was no independent examination of administration, management and living conditions within the unit itself. The complainants thus alleged, inter alia, a violation of article 16 (right to health) of the African Charter. The African Commission held that the right to health is vital to all aspects of a person's life and well-being, and is crucial to the realisation of all the other fundamental human rights. It declared that this right includes 'the right to health facilities, access to goods and services to be guaranteed to all without discrimination of any kind'.[58] In other words, the right to the highest attainable standard of health should be concerned not only with outcomes but also with processes. It should be concerned 'in not only what a health system does (for example, providing access to essential medicines and safe drinking water), but also how it does it (for example, transparently, in a participatory manner, and

---

54 African Charter on Human and Peoples' Rights, OAU Doc CAB/LEG/67/3/Rev 5, adopted on 27 June 1981, entered into force 21 October 1986. See also the African Charter on the Rights and Welfare of the Child, art 14.

55 (2001) AHRLR 60 (ACHPR 2001).

56 S Kiapi, 'Interpreting the Right to Health under the African Charter' (2005) 11 *East African Journal of Peace & Human Rights* 1.

57 (2003) AHRLR 96.

58 Ibid, para 80.

without discrimination)'.[59] The Commission, however, considered the financial and other challenges facing African countries in realising the right to health:

> [M]illions of people in Africa are not enjoying the right to health maximally because African countries are generally faced with the problem of poverty which renders them incapable to provide the necessary amenities, infrastructure and resources that facilitate the full enjoyment of this right. Therefore, having due regard to this depressing but real state of affairs, the African Commission would like to read into article 16 the obligation on part of states party to the African Charter to take concrete and targeted steps, while taking full advantage of its available resources, to ensure that the right to health is fully realised in all its aspects without discrimination of any kind.[60]

This suggests that the Commission is leaning towards adopting standards developed by the CESCR in its General Comments, especially No 3[61] on socio-economic obligations.[62] It acknowledges the constraints a state may encounter, due to the limits of available resources in Africa, and provides for progressive realisation of the socio-economic rights 'to the maximum of its available resources'. However, the Commission cautions that this should not be misinterpreted to mean that states could take deliberate retrogressive measures to render the enjoyment of socio-economic rights meaningless. This coincides with the reasoning of the CESCR, which noted that a state party seeking to be exempted from liability for failing to meet its socio-economic rights due to lack of available resources must demonstrate that every effort has been made to use all resources that are at its disposition in an effort to satisfy, as a matter of priority, those minimum essential levels of socio-economic rights.[63]

More recently, the Commission has made attempts to explain the content of the right to health under the African Charter through issuance of resolutions and General Comments. For instance, the Commission has issued a resolution calling on African governments to adopt a human rights-based approach to addressing the impact of HIV/AIDS in the region. According to the Commission, it is imperative that all efforts adopted by African governments towards curbing the spread of HIV must be respectful of individuals' human rights.[64] Also, the Commission has issued resolutions relating to topical issues affecting the sexual and reproductive lives of Africans. For instance, in 2008 the Commission issued

---

59 P Hunt and G Backman, 'Health Systems and the Right to the Highest Attainable Standard of Health (2008) 10 *Health and Human Rights* 81, 83.

60 *Purohit v The Gambia* (n 57 above) para 84.

61 Committee on Economic, Social and Cultural Rights, General Comment No 3, 'The nature of state parties' obligations' (5th session, 1990) UN Doc E/1991/23, annex III 86 (1991).

62 C Mbazira, 'Enforcing the Economic, Social and Cultural Rights in the African Charter on Human and Peoples' Rights: Twenty Years of Redundancy, Progression and Significant Strides' (2006) 6 *African Human Rights Law Journal* 333, 353.

63 Committee on Economic, Social and Cultural Rights, General Comment No 3, paras 9 and 10.

64 African Commission on Human and Peoples' Rights, 'Resolution on the HIV/AIDS Pandemic – Threat against Human Rights and Humanity' (2001) ACHPR/Res 53/(XXIX)01.

two important resolutions dealing with access to medicines[65] and maternal mortality.[66] The need to promote and protect the sexual and reproductive health and rights of Africans, particularly women, continues to be a great challenge. Women remain highly marginalised and vulnerable and therefore are helpless and hopeless in matters relating to their sexual and reproductive well-being. For the first time in the history of the African Commission, a General Comment on article 14(1)(d) and (e) of the Protocol to the African Charter on the Rights of Women was issued in December 2012. The General Comment explains that women and young girls are disproportionately affected by HIV due to a number of factors including multiple forms of discrimination based on various grounds such as race, sex, sexuality, sexual orientation, age, pregnancy, marital status, HIV status and social and economic status. The Commission recognises that 'women in Africa have the right to the highest attainable standard of health, which includes sexual and reproductive health and rights'.[67] It further notes that due to the high prevalence and significant risk of HIV exposure and transmission, women are unable to fully enjoy these rights. In Chapter 10 Judy Oder discusses in detail the right to health under the African Human Rights system.

Despite all these positive developments, however, scepticism remains with regard to the content and justiciability of the right to health. For instance, as Riedel has noted:

> While all these instruments with relevance to health matters have either been adopted or approved by the UN General Assembly or the ECOSOC, strictly speaking they have no legally binding effect on states and governments. Still, the mere fact that these instruments have been followed by states, as if they were binding, has illustrated that they form an important component within the international movement to promote and protect the physical and mental health of all persons worldwide.[68]

In other words, 'these international declarations of rights to health either include mere suggestions for enforcement or have no schemes for domestic enforcement at all, and thus have no "bite"'.[69] They might, at best, offer moral direction for policy-making to international organisations like the WHO, without affording protection for individuals seeking access to health care.[70] In the words of Friesen, 'a human right, even one supported by international law, is not a legal right – it is not justiciable, and thus cannot be used as a tool by … citizens who wanted to be proactive in improving and maintaining the quality of their public health care'.[71] Given the recent developments regarding the right to health discussed above, it would seem that these criticisms are unfounded and misplaced.

---

65 African Commission on Human and Peoples' Rights, 'Resolution on Access to Health and needed Medicines in Africa' (2008) ACHPR/Res 141 (XXXXIIII)08.

66 African Commission on Human and Peoples' Rights, 'Resolution on Maternal Mortality in Africa' (2008) ACHPR/Res 135 (XXXXIIII)08.

67 General Comment on Art 14 (1)(d) and (e) of the Protocol to the African Charter on the Rights of Women, para 5.

68 Riedel (n 33 above) 24.

69 Sandhu (n 3 above) 1159.

70 Ibid.

71 T Friesen, 'The Right to Health Care' (2001) 9 *Health Law Journal* 205.

Understanding the Nature and Content of the Right to Health

As noted above, in 2000 the UN Committee on Economic, Social and Cultural Rights published General Comment No 14 to the ICESCR[72] which articulates the normative substance of the right to health, the obligations associated with it and its implementation and enforcement by delineating how universal expectations are to be met in economically, socially and culturally diverse states.[73] While General Comment No 14 is not a complete, perfect or a binding document, it nonetheless affirms that the right to the highest attainable standard of health cannot be dismissed as a rhetorical device.[74] As provided by the General Comment, the right to health has a core content, referring to the minimum essential level of the right[75] and provides direction to countries on what is required of them for the delivery of health services. General Comment No 14 provides that the right to health extends not only to timely and suitable health care but also to the underlying determinants of health, such as adequate sanitation and access to safe and potable water, an adequate supply of safe food, nutrition and housing, healthy occupational and environmental conditions and access to health-related education. These underlying determinants and facilities must be available, accessible, acceptable and of good quality. These four interrelated criteria set out by General Comment No 14 on how to assess the right to health – availability, accessibility, acceptability and quality (AAAQs) – are discussed below.

Availability

This implies that the following must be available in sufficient quantity: safe and potable drinking water and adequate sanitation facilities; trained medical and professional personnel receiving domestically competitive salaries; hospitals, clinics, essential drugs, as defined by the WHO; nutritious food; and adequate housing and shelter.[76]

Accessibility

This has four overlapping components: non-discrimination, physical accessibility, economic accessibility and information accessibility. A state has a legal obligation to ensure that there is access to health facilities, goods and services on a non-discriminatory basis in law and in fact (non-discrimination); that the health facilities are in safe reach of all sections of the population including rural populations, persons with disabilities, persons with HIV, children, ethnic minorities, indigenous peoples, women, adolescents and older

---

72 Committee on Economic, Social and Cultural Rights, 'Substantive Issues Arising in the Implementation of the International Covenant on Economic, Social and Cultural Rights', UN Doc E/C.12/2000/4.

73 Kinney and Clark (n 8 above) 289.

74 G Backman et al, 'Health Systems and the Right to Health: An Assessment of 194 Countries' (2008) 372 *Lancet* 2048.

75 ED Kinney, 'Realizing the International Human Right to Health: The Challenge of For-profit Health Care (2010) 113 *West Virginia Law Review* 49, 51.

76 World Health Organization, *Human Rights, Health and Poverty Reduction Strategies* (n 28 above) 22.

persons (physical accessibility); that the health services are affordable to all, including economically disadvantaged groups, and that the poor should not be disproportionately burdened with health expenses when compared to the rich members of society (economic accessibility); and that information about different health services, medicines or preventive measures are freely available to all groups, such as adolescents, within the community (information accessibility).[77]

Acceptability

All health facilities, goods and services must be respectful of medical ethics and culturally appropriate – that is, respectful of the culture of individuals, minorities and communities, and sensitive to gender and life cycle requirements[78] – as well as respecting the confidentiality and improving the health status of those concerned.

Quality

This requires that all health services and facilities must be of good quality and that available drugs are scientifically approved and unexpired; that health personnel are trained and skilled; that hospital equipment is adequate and safe; and that places of employment are safe and healthy.[79] For example, in Nigeria, the National Agency for Food and Drug Administration and Control was set up to curb, among other things, the importation and consumption of fake and counterfeit drugs through public enlightenment campaigns, and this has helped to improve the safety and quality of drugs and medicines in the country.

Indicators are presently being designed by the WHO to determine the level of compliance of states with these criteria. Any law, policies or regulations that unreasonably restrict health services according to these criteria would not comply with the right to health.[80] For example, a law or policy requiring unnecessary qualifications for health care providers has the tendency to limit the availability of a service that contributes to safe motherhood and jeopardises health services, notwithstanding the fact that such policies may have been proposed in good faith so as to ensure excellence in women's health care delivery.[81] All these elements are necessary to achieving the right to health in any nation.

Progressive Realisation of the Right to Health

States parties by their ratification of human rights treaties are required to give effect to the rights contained in the covenants within their states. Importantly, in recognition of the

77 Ibid.

78 Ibid.

79 Ibid, 22–23.

80 RJ Cook et al, *Reproductive Health and Human Rights: Integrating Medicine, Ethics, and Law* (Oxford University Press 2003) 189.

81 Ibid.

fact that the right to the highest attainable standard of health cannot be realised overnight, article 2(1) of the ICESCR stresses that states have the obligation to progressively achieve the full realisation of the rights under the Covenant – that is, an implicit recognition that states have resource constraints on their ability to immediately fully implement rights.[82] Some governments have taken the flexibility offered by the progressive realisation standard to mean that socio-economic rights 'merely represented programmatic goals or promotional obligations, non-self-executing norms, whereby it would be up to the States Parties concerned to decide, by way of discretion, if, and how, the right promised at the international level would be operationalised at the national level'.[83] This approach clearly contravenes the intent and purpose of the Covenant. The resource availability mentioned in article 2(1) of the Covenant should not be an excuse for states to avoid their obligations under the Covenant. States, including developing countries, must take reasonable, deliberate and new steps towards addressing major impediments to health and ensuring the realisation of the right to health. The fundamental nature of the right to health, as a basis for the right to life, can be seen in the words of the Supreme Court of Costa Rica:

> In a state of law, the right to life, and in consequence the right to health, receives particular protection. Any economic criterion that pretends to annul the exercise of such rights must cede in importance … because without the right to life all of the other rights are useless … Of what use are all other rights and guarantees, the institutions and programs, the advantages and benefits of our system of liberties, if even one person cannot count on having the rights to health and life guaranteed?[84]

The South African Constitutional Court in *Soobramoney v. Minister of Health KwaZulu Natal*[85] examined the right to health claims within the context of limited resources. The case concerned a renal patient who was refused regular kidney dialysis at a government health clinic because of a government-instituted system of priorities owing to severe shortage of dialysis machines and trained nursing staff. Dismissing his application, the Court found that the state has a constitutional obligation within its available resources to provide health care, as well as sufficient food, water and social security. The Court was very clear concerning the large margin of discretion it would grant the state to set budgetary priorities, declaring that the Court 'will be slow to interfere with rational decisions taken in good faith by the political organs and medical authorities'.[86] Sachs J stated that: 'In open and democratic societies based upon dignity, freedom and equality, the rationing of access to life-prolonging resources is regarded as integral to, rather than incompatible with, a human rights approach to health care.'[87] Notwithstanding that the Court granted

82 WHO and Office of the United Nations High Commissioner for Human Rights (n 21 above) 23.

83 Riedel (n 33 above) 29.

84 *Alvarez v Caja Costarricense de Seguro Social* Exp. 5778-V-97, No 5934–97.

85 1997 (12) BCLR 1696.

86 Ibid, para 29.

87 Ibid, para 52.

the Minister of Health discretion in the allocation of resources, it required a standardised priority system and reaffirmed the principle of progressive realisation.[88]

In *Government of the Republic of South Africa v Grootboom*,[89] the plaintiff, Irene Grootboom, and her family who occupied privately held land meant for a low-income housing development were evicted and thus became homeless. Since they could not return to their previous shelter, in a shanty settlement, because others now occupied their space, the plaintiff's family erected plastic sheeting on a sports field, which proved to be inadequate shelter from the rain. Even though the Court found that the state's ongoing programme on low-income housing development met its obligation under section 26(2), it declared, however, that the fact that the constitution allows for the progressive realisation of social rights was not a reason for the legislature to claim poverty for not realising the right to housing, health care and other social rights. It can be seen from the above that even though the courts arrived at different outcomes for the individuals in *Soobramoney*, *Grootboom* and *Treatment Action Campaign*, the plaintiffs were able to compel the government to justify its policy decisions.[90] The court's attention in *Soobramoney*, for example, 'forced the government to describe the policy, explain its decision-making process, and reevaluate whether the policy accorded with its constitutional obligations'; in *Grootboom*, 'its careful scrutiny of the government's housing policy signaled to the political branches that they must actively pursue the progressive realisation of social rights – that they are "binding obligation[s]"'; while in *Treatment Action Campaign*, its 'ruling gave teeth to the Section 27 health care right by holding that while the government has a wide range of discretion, it does not have the discretion not to act in certain cases'.[91]

Thus, while recognising 'the formidable structural and other obstacles resulting from international and other factors beyond the control of States that impede the full realisation of article 12 in many States parties',[92] the CESCR stated in paragraph 47 of General Comment No 14 that 'it is important to distinguish the inability from the unwillingness of a State party to comply with its obligations'. Accordingly, the Committee notes that

> A State which is unwilling to use the maximum of its available resources for the realisation of the right to health is in violation of its obligations … If resource constraints render it impossible for a State to comply fully with its Covenant obligations, it has the burden of justifying that every effort has nevertheless been made to use all available resources at its disposal in order to satisfy, as a matter of priority, the obligations outlined above.[93]

---

88 P Roger, 'South Africa's Right to Health Care: International and Constitutional Duties in Relation to HIV/AIDS Epidemic' (2004) *Human Rights Brief* 11.

89 2000 (11) BCLR 1169 (CC). See also *Minister of Health v Treatment Action Campaign* 2002 (10) BCLR 1033 (CC). In *Moore v Gambia* (241/2001), the African Commission on Human and Peoples' Rights stated that the state has an obligation to realise the right to health of mental health patients to the maximum of available resources.

90 Sandhu (n 3 above) 1180.

91 Ibid, 1180–1181.

92 Committee on Economic, Social and Cultural Rights, General Comment No 14, para 5.

93 Ibid. See also *Minister of Health v Treatment Action Campaign* (n 89 above).

The Committee, in paragraphs 50–52 of General Comment No 14, lists various elements that constitute the failure by a state to fulfil its duty, including:

> the denial of access to health facilities, goods and services to particular individuals or groups as a result of *de jure* or *de facto* discrimination; ... the suspension of legislation or the adoption of laws or policies that interfere with the enjoyment of any of the components of the right to health; and the failure of the State to take into account its legal obligations regarding the right to health when entering into bilateral or multilateral agreements with other States, international organisations and other entities, such as multinational corporations.[94]

> the failure to regulate the activities of individuals, groups or corporations so as to prevent them from violating the right to health of others; the failure to protect consumers and workers from practices detrimental to health ... the failure to protect women against violence or to prosecute perpetrators; the failure to discourage the continued observance of harmful traditional medical or cultural practices.[95]

> the failure to adopt or implement a national health policy designed to ensure the right to health for everyone; insufficient expenditure or misallocation of public resources which results in the non-enjoyment of the right to health by individuals or groups, particularly the vulnerable or marginalized.[96]

As part of the obligation to realise the right to health, the Committee reasons that developing countries are under an obligation to seek international cooperation and assistance where they are not able to meet even the minimal requirements. In this regard, developed countries have an international obligation under Article 2(1) ICESCR to provide cooperation and assistance, notwithstanding that obligation is not specified in any detail by way of concrete amounts.[97] They should assist low-income countries in fulfilling their core obligations in particular.

Levels of Protection Accorded the Right to Health

The health care system has obligations to people's right to health, and these include the obligations to respect, to protect and to fulfil the right to health. It has to respect and protect the 'freedoms' and to fulfil the 'entitlements' embodied in the right to health, failing which it can be held in violation of the right to health.[98] The right to health just like

94 Committee on Economic, Social and Cultural Rights, General Comment No 14, para 50.

95 Ibid, para 51.

96 Ibid, para 52.

97 Riedel (n 33 above) 30.

98 Cook et al (n 80 above) 37.

any other rights imposes three basic obligations on states parties, namely respect, protect and fulfil.[99]

The obligation to respect requires the system to refrain from interfering directly or indirectly with the enjoyment of the right to health in that no health policy, practice or programme should directly violate the right to health of the individual. Explaining further in General Comment No 14, the CESCR notes as follows:

> States should refrain from limiting access to contraceptives and other means of maintaining sexual and reproductive health, from censoring, withholding or intentionally misrepresenting health-related information, including sexual education and information, as well as from preventing people's participation in health-related matters. States should also refrain from unlawfully polluting air, water and soil.[100]

Also, the UN Commission on Human Rights in one of its resolutions in 2002 noted that 'access to medication in the context of pandemics such as HIV/AIDS is one fundamental element for achieving progressively the full realization of the right of everyone to the enjoyment of the highest attainable standard of physical and mental health'.[101] The resolution enjoined states at the national level, on the basis of non-discrimination, 'to refrain from taking measures which would deny or limit equal access for all persons to preventive, curative or palliative pharmaceuticals or medical technologies used to treat pandemics such as HIV/AIDS or the most common opportunistic infections that accompany them'.[102]

The obligation to protect requires the system to prevent third parties from interfering with the freedom of people to enjoy their right to health. It entails

> [the] duties of States to adopt legislation or to take other measures ensuring equal access to health care and health-related services provided by third parties; to ensure that privatisation of the health sector does not constitute a threat to the availability, accessibility, acceptability and quality of health facilities, goods and services; to ensure that harmful social or traditional practices do not interfere with access to pre- and post-natal care and family planning; to prevent third parties from coercing women to undergo traditional practices, e.g. female genital mutilation.[103]

It implies that states must appropriately regulate such important non-state actors as the health care industry, including private health care, pharmaceutical and health insurance companies, and, more importantly, national and multinational enterprises, as each of the

99 Committee on Economic, Social and Cultural Rights, General Comment No 14, paras 33–37.

100 Committee on Economic, Social and Cultural Rights, General Comment No 14.

101 Office of the High Commissioner for Human Rights, Access to Medication in the Context of Pandemics such as HIV/AIDS, Commission on Human Rights Res. 2002/32, UN Doc E/2002/23-E/CN.4/2002/200.

102 Ibid.

103 Committee on Economic, Social and Cultural Rights, General Comment No 14.

activities of these actors has the capacity to promote and protect, or to neglect and violate, the right to health.[104]

The obligation to fulfil requires states to ensure that people have access to a system of health care that provides equal opportunity for everyone.[105] It requires 'States parties, inter alia, to give sufficient recognition to the right to health in the national political and legal systems, preferably by way of legislative implementation, and to adopt a national health policy with a detailed plan for realizing the right to health.'[106] States are also required to ensure the provision of health care services, including immunisation programmes against the major infectious diseases, and to ensure equal access for all to the underlying determinants of health, such as nutritiously safe food and potable drinking water, basic sanitation and adequate housing and living conditions.[107]

The prospect of improving the health situation of citizens in developing countries diminishes in the face of government reduction in expenditure on health. Analysis of health sector expenditure in most African countries shows that the budgetary allocation to the health sector has continued to decrease over the years, thus militating against the achievement of the UN's health MDGs.[108] In April 2001, heads of state of African Union (AU) countries met in Abuja and pledged to commit at least 15 per cent of their annual budget to improve the health sector.[109] They also urged donor countries to 'fulfil the yet to be met target of 0.7% of their Gross National Product (GNP) as official Development Assistance (ODA) to developing countries'.[110] According to the WHO, since 2010, only Rwanda and South Africa had achieved the Abuja Declaration target of 'at least 15 per cent and only eight countries in Africa were on track to meet the MDGs – Algeria, Cape Verde, Egypt, Eritrea, Madagascar, Rwanda, Seychelles and Tunisia. Indeed, most African countries are achieving less than 50 per cent of the gains required to reach the goals by 2015.[111] In contrast, the African Union Commission reports that six AU member states have met the 15 per cent benchmark – Rwanda (18.8 per cent), Botswana (17.8 per cent), Niger (17.8 per cent), Malawi (17.1 per cent), Zambia (16.4 per cent) and Burkina Faso (15.8 per cent).[112]

---

104 Tarantola et al (no 22 above) 6.

105 Cook et al (n 80 above) 37.

106 Committee on Economic, Social and Cultural Rights, General Comment No 14, para 36.

107 Ibid.

108 See, for example, Partners in Population and Development Africa Regional Office (PPD ARO), 'Meeting the Abuja Promise by African Governments to Commit 15% of Total National Budgets to Health', available at http://www.ppdafrica.org/docs/policy/abuja-e.pdf (accessed 4 February 2015).

109 Organisation of African Unity, Abuja Declaration on HIV/AIDS, Tuberculosis and other Related Infectious Diseases (2001) OAU Doc OAU/SPS/ABUJA/3.

110 World Health Organization, 'The Abuja Declaration: Ten Years On' (2010), available at www.who.int/healthsystems/publications/Abuja10.pdf (accessed 3 February 2015).

111 Ibid.

112 Partners in Population and Development Africa Regional Office (PPD ARO) (n 108 above).

Furthermore, the AU states that in sub-Saharan Africa, government spending on health currently averages US$25–27 per capita, yet 32 of the 54 AU member states invest less than US$20 (including four of the six countries who have met the 15 per cent benchmark). Nigeria, Burkina Faso, Burundi, Cameroun, Chad, Comoros, Congo, Cote d'Ivoire, Djibouti, Ghana, Guinea Bissau, Liberia, Mali, Mozambique, Senegal, Uganda and Zambia are the 17 African countries that spend less than US$33 per capita on health in their national budgets, implying that most African countries are not yet on track to achieve the health-related MDGs.[113] African governments must show a genuine commitment to health by devoting an increasing share of their own resources to the health sector compared to areas such as defence and infrastructure. At the same time, donor countries should be committed to fulfilling the yet to be met target of 0.7 per cent of their GNP as official Development Assistance to developing countries.

What Constitutes the Minimum Core of the Right to Health?

The minimum core obligation serves as the marking scheme to determine whether a state has failed in its obligation under the ICESCR. In its General Comment No 3, the CESCR explained:

> On the basis of the extensive experience gained by the Committee, as well as by the body that preceded it, over a period of more than a decade of examining States parties' reports the Committee is of the view that a minimum core obligation to ensure the satisfaction of, at the very least, minimum essential levels of each of the rights is incumbent upon every State party. Thus, for example, a State party in which any significant number of individuals is deprived of essential foodstuffs, of essential primary health care, of basic shelter and housing, or of the most basic forms of education is, *prima facie*, failing to discharge its obligations under the Covenant.[114]

What constitutes the minimum core would seem unclear from the above quotation. In support of this position, Russell has argued that the concept of minimum state obligation under international law is one of the most difficult and controversial concepts in economic, social and cultural rights, bridging the gap as it does between fundamental entitlements and scarce resources.[115]

Expatiating on what constitutes a minimum core obligation, in its General Comment No 15 on the right to water, the CESCR maintained among other things that violation of the right occurs through the failure of the state parties' 'insufficient expenditure or misallocation of public resources which results in the non-enjoyment of the right to

---

113 Ibid.

114 Committee on Economic, Social and Cultural Rights, General Comment No 3, para 10.

115 S Russell, 'Introduction – Minimum State Obligations: International Dimensions' in D Brand and S Russell (eds) *Exploring the Core Content of Socio-economic Rights: South African and International Perspectives* (Protea Book House 2005) 11, 12.

water by individuals or groups, particularly the vulnerable or marginalized' and its failure 'to ensure that the minimum essential level of the right is enjoyed by everyone'.[116] The CESCR in General Comment No 14 lists the following core obligations of the right to health, which all states (whether rich or poor) must meet:

1. To ensure the right of access to health facilities, goods and services on a non-discriminatory basis, especially for vulnerable or marginalized groups;

2. To ensure access to the minimum essential food that is nutritionally adequate and safe, to ensure freedom from hunger to everyone;

3. To ensure access to basic shelter, housing and sanitation, and an adequate supply of

4. safe and potable water;

5. To provide essential drugs, as defined according to the WHO Action Programme on Essential Drugs;

6. To ensure equitable distribution of all health facilities, goods and services; and

7. To adopt and implement a national public health strategy and plan of action that is based on epidemiological evidence, addressing the health concerns of the whole population; the strategy and plan of action shall be devised, and periodically reviewed, on the basis of a participatory and transparent process.[117]

These core obligations that are 'non-derogable and in many respects do not depend on a state's development level'[118] affect the 'existential minimum', which every individual requires to survive. The CESCR has thus continued to address specifically the failure of states in providing essential drugs to curb epidemic diseases such as HIV/AIDS.[119] While these essential levels are, to some extent, resource-dependent, states are required to give core obligations priority in their efforts to realise the rights under the Covenant.[120] States are under obligation not to adopt retrogressive measures that undermine the realisation of the right to health. For instance, a state administering a programme to provide antiretroviral drugs is not permitted to

---

116 Committee on Economic, Social and Cultural Rights, General Comment No 15, 'The right to water' (2002) UN Doc E/C.12/2002/11, para 44.

117 M Mulumba et al, 'Constitutional Provisions for the Right to Health in East and Southern Africa', EQUINET Discussion Paper 18 (2010) 5.

118 AE Yamin, 'Not Just a Tragedy: Access to Medications as a Right under International Law' (2003) 21 *Boston University International Law Journal* 325, 337.

119 See Committee on Economic, Social and Cultural Rights, Concluding Observations, Honduras (UN Doc E/C.12/1/Add 57 (2001); Yamin (n 118 above), 337.

120 World Health Organization and Office of the United Nations High Commissioner for Human Rights (n 21 above) 26.

backslide because of budgetary difficulties.[121] However, differences in the resources available in different countries serve as a serious challenge to the establishment of uniform economic, social and cultural rights standards that can be internationally recognised.[122] The reality is that most low-income countries are too poor to fulfil the core obligations or even provide a basic package of health services for all, which the WHO estimates would cost US$40 per person per year.[123] And in assessing the ability of low-income countries to fulfil their core obligations, one should consider both the state's domestic resources and the resources it receives through international assistance and cooperation.[124]

The CESCR in its General Comment No 14 (para 44) has noted that other obligations that must be accorded comparable priority include:

> (a) To ensure reproductive, maternal (pre-natal as well as post-natal) and child health care; (b) To provide immunisation against the major infectious diseases occurring in the community; (c) To take measures to prevent, treat and control epidemic and endemic diseases; (d) To provide education and access to information concerning the main health problems in the community, including methods of preventing and controlling them; (e) To provide appropriate training for health personnel, including education on health and human rights.

Notwithstanding the above, suffice it to say that the right to health does not have a universal legal force. Rather,

> it holds little or no enforceability in non-democratic or autocratic jurisdictions such as China and Myanmar. Similarly, the domestic legal force of ratified human rights treaties may vary considerably, and may depend on domestic implementation of treaties at the national level. Nonetheless, it is increasingly evident that in spite of these lacunae and variations, the right to health is enjoying greater enforceability in domestic courts due to increased ratifications of international human rights treaties, increased entrenchment in domestic bills of rights and increased judicial willingness to enforce health rights. The right to health is, therefore, not merely a 'manifesto' right nor simply a rhetorical tool for advocacy, but an increasingly well-developed and enforceable legal right.[125]

Conclusions

This chapter has discussed the normative framework for the right to health under international law. Promoting and securing the right to enjoyment of the highest attainable

---

121 AE Yamin, 'The Right to Health Under International Law and its Relevance to the United States' Critical Concepts for Reaching Populations at Risk' (2005) 95 *American Journal of Public Health* 1157.

122 Kiapi (n 56 above) 6.

123 R Hammonds et al, 'Under the (Legal) Radar Screen: Global Health Initiatives and International Human Rights Obligations' (2012) *BMC International Health and Human Rights* 1, 3.

124 Ibid.

125 Nixon and Forman (n 18 above).

standard of health is ethical; it is a legal obligation and a move towards bringing an end to poverty, discrimination and exclusion.[126] The majority of states now accept that the right to health is a fundamental right and have commenced the adoption of a rights-based approach in the realisation of this right at the domestic level. However, much work still needs to be done, particularly in developing countries, to ensure the full realisation of this right, particularly within disadvantaged and marginalised groups. Governments must ensure that their policies and programmes on health issues are well targeted towards and meaningful to the vast majority of the global poor, the vulnerable and the worst off so that, as suggested by Pogge, the poor and disadvantaged will no longer be seen merely as 'shrunken wretches begging for our help', but rather will be addressed as 'persons with dignity who are claiming what is theirs by right'.[127]

Efforts must be made by states to advance a normative framework more attentive to the health needs and well-being of the vulnerable. States must also take steps to include in their constitutions explicit provisions regarding health and health care. While it may be true that not all countries that entrench a constitutional right to health care have lived up to their mandates,[128]

> a statement on health or health care in a national constitution is important in and of itself as it represents explicit commitment regarding health and health care for the country's population. These commitments can be useful as they may be implemented in the future, and their existence is helpful to those advocating for better health and health care as well as for implementation of the international human right to health.[129]

Entrenchment of the right to health in the constitution will serve as a constructive and important tool for citizens as well as those in the health sector to develop equitable policies and programmes to strengthen the health care system, and to hold the government and the international community accountable. The recognition of the right to health has not only helped to generate judicial decisions that have improved the delivery of health-related services, but has also resulted in non-judicial mechanisms of accountability, such as the Right to Health Unit established by the Uganda Human Rights Commission, thus leading to enhanced health policy and practice.[130]

---

126 N Pillay, 'Right to Health and the Universal Declaration of Human Rights (2008) 372 *Lancet* 2005, 2006.

127 T Pogge (ed), *Freedom from Poverty as a Human Right: Who Owes What to the Very Poor* (Oxford University Press 2007) 4.

128 A Littell, 'Can a Constitutional Right to Health Guarantee Universal Health Care Coverage or Improved Health Outcomes? A Survey of Selected States' (2002) 35 *Connecticut Law Review* 289, 308–309. Littell finds no correlation between infant mortality or the presence of universal health coverage and a constitutional right to health in a survey of eleven countries (quoted in Sandhu (n 3 above) 1168).

129 Kinney and Clark (n 8 above) 298.

130 Backman et al (n 74 above) 2078.

References

Books, Chapters, Articles, etc.

Backman, G et al, 'Health Systems and the Right to Health: An Assessment of 194 Countries' (2008) 372 *Lancet* 2047–2085.

Buchanan, AE, 'The Right to a Decent Minimum of Health Care' (1984) 13 *Philosophy and Public Affairs* 55–78.

Cook, RJ, Dickens, BM and Fathalla, MF, *Reproductive Health and Human Rights: Integrating Medicine, Ethics, and Law* (Oxford University Press 2003).

Durojaye, E and Oluduro, O, 'Enforcement of Social and Economic Rights in Africa: Lessons from South African Case of *Government of the Republic of South Africa and Others v Grootboom and Others* 2000 (11) BCLR 1169 (CC)' (2006) 3 *Fountain Quarterly Law Journal* 15–30.

Friesen, T, 'The Right to Health Care' (2001) 9 *Health Law Journal* 205–222.

Gostin, L, 'Securing Health or Just Healthcare? The Effect of the Healthcare System on the Health of America' (1994) 39 *St. Louis University Law Journal* 7–43.

Gostin, LO, 'The Human Right to Health: A Right to the "Highest Attainable Standard of Health"' (2001) *Hastings Center Report* 29–30.

Hammonds, R, Ooms, G and Vandenhole, W, 'Under the (Legal) Radar Screen: Global Health Initiatives and International Human Rights Obligations' (2012) 12 *BMC International Health and Human Rights* 1–19.

Hunt, P and Backman, G, 'Health Systems and the Right to the Highest Attainable Standard of Health' (2008) 10 *Health and Human Rights* 81–92.

International Federation of Health and Human Rights Organisations (IFHRO), *Our Right to the Highest Attainable Standard of Health* (2005), available at http://www.paho.org/hr-ecourse-e/assets/_pdf/Module2/Lesson1/M2_L1_4.pdf (accessed 7 January 2014).

Kiapi, S, 'Interpreting the Right to Health under the African Charter' (2005) 11 *East African Journal of Peace & Human Rights* 1–20.

Kingston, LN, Cohen, EF and Morley, CP, 'Debate: Limitations on Universality: The "Right to Health" and the Necessity of Legal Nationality' (2010) 10 *BMC International Health and Human Rights* 11.

Kinney, ED, 'Realising the International Human Right to Health: The Challenge of For-profit Health Care' (2010) 113 *West Virginia Law Review* 49–66.

Kinney, ED and Clark, BA, 'Provisions for Health and Health Care in the Constitutions of the Countries of the World' (2004) *Cornell International Law Journal* 285–355.

Littell, A, 'Can a Constitutional Right to Health Guarantee Universal Health Care Coverage or Improved Health Outcomes? A Survey of Selected States' (2002) 35 *Connecticut Law Review* 289–318.

Mann, JM et al, 'Health and Human Rights' (1994) 1 *Health and Human Rights* 6–23.

Mbazira, C, 'Enforcing the Economic, Social and Cultural Rights in the African Charter on Human and Peoples' Rights: Twenty Years of Redundancy, Progression and Significant Strides' (2006) 6 *African Human Rights Law Journal* 333–357.

Minelli, E, *World Health Organization: The Mandate of a Specialized Agency of the United Nations* (Geneva Foundation for Medical Education and Research 2003).

Mulumba, M, Kabanda, D and Nassura, V, 'Constitutional Provisions for the Right to Health in East and Southern Africa', EQUINET Discussion Paper 18 (2010).

Munro, L, '"The Human Rights-Based Approach to Programming": A Contradiction in Terms?' in S Hickey and D Mitlin (eds) *Rights-based Approaches to Development: Exploring the Potential and Pitfalls* (Kumarian Press 2009) 187–206.

Nixon, S and Forman, L, 'Exploring Synergies between Human Rights and Public Health Ethics: A Whole Greater than the Sum of its Parts' (2008) 8 *BMC International Health and Human Rights* 2.

Özden, M, *The Right to Health: A Fundamental Human Right Affirmed by the United Nations and Recognised in Regional Treaties and Numerous National Constitutions* (Human Rights Programme of the Europe-Third World Centre (CETIM) 2006).

Partners in Population and Development Africa Regional Office (PPD ARO), 'Meeting the Abuja Promise by African Governments to Commit 15% of Total National Budgets to Health', available at http://www.ppdafrica.org/docs/policy/abuja-e.pdf.

Pogge, T (ed), *Freedom from Poverty as a Human Right: Who Owes What to the Very Poor* (Oxford University Press 2007).

Pillay, N, 'Right to Health and the Universal Declaration of Human Rights' (2008) 372 *Lancet* 2005–2006.

Riedel, E, 'The Human Right to Health: Conceptual Foundations' in A. Clapham and M Robinson (eds) *Realizing the Right to Health* (Rüffer & Rub 2009) 21–39.

Roger, P, 'South Africa's Right to Health Care: International and Constitutional Duties in Relation to HIV/AIDS Epidemic' (2004) *Human Rights Brief* 11–13.

Russell, S, 'Introduction – Minimum State Obligations: International Dimensions' in D Brand and S Russell (eds) *Exploring the Core Content of Socio-economic Rights: South Africa and International Perspectives* (Protea Book House 2002) 11–21.

Sandhu, PK, 'A Legal Right to Health Care: What can the United States Learn from Foreign Models of Health Rights Jurisprudence? (2007) 95 *California Law Review* 1159–1192.

Tarantola, D et al, *Human Rights, Health and Development: Initiative for Health and Human Rights*, Technical Series Paper # 08.1 (University of New South Wales Initiative for Health and Human Rights 2008).

Tobin, J, 'Introduction', in J Tobin, *The Right to Health in International Law* (Oxford University Press 2011), University of Melbourne Legal Studies Research Paper 562.

UNAIDS, *AIDS Epidemic Report* (UNAIDS 2013).

United Nations Population Fund, *Culture Matters: Working with Communities and Faith-based Organizations* (UNFPA 2005).

World Health Organization, *25 Questions and Answers on Health & Human Rights* (WHO 2002).

World Health Organization, *Basic Documents* (45th edn, Supplement, WHO 2006), available at http://www.who.int/governance/eb/who_constitution_en.pdf.

World Health Organization, *Human Rights, Health and Poverty Reduction Strategies* (WHO 2008).

World Health Organization 'The Abuja Declaration: Ten Years On' (2010), available at *www.who.int/healthsystems/publications/Abuja10.pdf*.

World Health Organization, *The Global Status Report on Non-communicable Diseases* (WHO 2011).

World Health Organization and Office of the United Nations High Commissioner for Human Rights, 'The Right to Health', Fact sheet No 31 (2000).

Yamin, AE, 'Not Just a Tragedy: Access to Medications as a Right under International Law' (2003) 21 *Boston University International Law Journal* 325–371.

Yamin, AE, 'The Right to Health Under International Law and its Relevance to the United States' Critical Concepts for Reaching Populations at Risk' (2005) 95 *American Journal of Public Health* 1156–1161.

International and Regional Instruments

Abuja Declaration on HIV/AIDS, Tuberculosis and other Related Infectious Diseases (2001) OAU Doc OAU/SPS/ABUJA/3.

African Charter on Human and Peoples' Rights, OAU Doc CAB/LEG/67/3/Rev 5, adopted 27 June 1981, entered into force 21 October 1986.

African Charter on the Rights and Welfare of the Child, OAU Doc CAB/LEG/24.9/49, adopted 1990, entered into force 29 November 1999.

African Commission on Human and Peoples' Rights, 'Resolution on the HIV/AIDS Pandemic – Threat against Human Rights and Humanity' (2001) ACHPR/Res 53/(XXIX)01.

African Commission on Human and Peoples' Rights, 'Resolution on Access to Health and Needed Medicines in Africa' (2008) ACHPR/Res 141 (XXXXIIII)08.

African Commission on Human and Peoples' Rights, 'Resolution on Maternal Mortality in Africa' (2008) ACHPR/Res 135 (XXXXIIII)08.

Committee on Economic, Social and Cultural Rights, General Comment No 3, 'The nature of state parties' obligations' (5th session, 1990) UN Doc E/1991/23, annex III 86 (1991).

Committee on Economic, Social and Cultural Rights, General Comment No 14, 'The right to highest attainable standard of health', UN Doc E/C.12/2000/4 (2000).

Committee on Economic, Social and Cultural Rights, Concluding Observations, Honduras, UN Doc E/C.12/1/Add.57 (2001).

Committee on Economic, Social and Cultural Rights, General Comment No 15, 'The right to water', UN Doc E/C.12/2002/11 (2002).

Committee on Economic, Social and Cultural Rights, 'Substantive Issues Arising in the Implementation of the International Covenant on Economic, Social and Cultural Rights', UN Doc E/C.12/2000/4 (Aug. 11, 2004).

Committee on the Elimination of Discrimination against Women, General Recommendation No 24, 'Women and Health' (Twentieth session, 1999) UN Doc A/54/38 Rev 1 (1999).

Committee on the Rights of the Child, General Comment No 15, 'The right of the child to the enjoyment of highest attainable standard of health' (17 April 2013) CRC/C/GC/15.

Convention on the Elimination of All Forms of Discrimination against Women (CEDAW), GA Res 54/180, UN GAOR 34th session Supp No 46, UN Doc A/34/46 (1980), adopted 18 December 1979, entered into force 3 September 1981.
Convention on the Rights of the Child, A/RES/44/25, adopted 20 November 1989, entered into force 2 September 1990.
Convention on the Rights of Persons with Disabilities, A/RES/61/106, adopted 13 December 2006, entered into force 3 May 2008.
Declaration of Alma-Ata, adopted at the International Conference on Primary Health Care, held in Alma-Ata, USSR, September 1978, available at www.who.int/hpr/archive/docs/almaata.html.
Fourth World Conference on Women, Beijing, 15 September 1995, A/CONF.177/20.
General Comment on Art 14(1)(d) of the Protocol to the African Charter on the Rights of Women.
Human Rights Council, 'Preventable Maternal Mortality and Morbidity and Human Rights' A/HRC/11/L.16/Rev 1 (16 June 2009).
International Conference on Population and Development (ICPD), UN A/CONF.171 (13) (18 October 1994).
International Covenant on Economic, Social and Cultural Rights, A/Res/21/2200, adopted 16 December 1966, entered into force 3 January 1976.
International Convention on the Elimination of All Forms of Racial Discrimination, adopted 21 December 1965, entered into force 4 January 1969.
International Convention on the Protection of the Rights of all Migrant Workers and Members of their Families, A/RES/45/158, adopted 18 December 1990, entered into force 1 July 2003.Limburg Principles on the Implementation of the International Covenant on Economic, Social and Cultural Rights, UN Doc E/CN.4/1987/17, Annex (1987).
Office of the High Commissioner for Human Rights, 'Access to Medication in the Context of Pandemics such as HIV/AIDS', Commission on Human Rights Res 2002/32, UN Doc E/2002/23-E/CN/4/2002/200.
Report of the Human Rights Committee, 'The Right to Life', UN GAOR 37th session Supp No 40.
Report of the Special Rapporteur on the right of everyone to the enjoyment of the highest attainable standard of physical and mental health, Paul Hunt, submitted in accordance with Commission resolution 2002/31, 13 Feb. 2003, E/CN.4/2003/58.
Universal Declaration of Human Rights, GA Res 217A (III), UN Doc A/810 (1948).
UN Millennium Declaration, A/RES/55/2, adopted September 2000, entered into force September 2005.
Vienna Declaration and Programme of Action, A/CONF.157/23, adopted by the World Conference on Human Rights (Vienna), 14–25 June 1993.

Cases

Alvarez v Ccaja Costarricense de Seguro Social Exp 5778-V-97. No. 5934–97.
Government of RSA v Grootboom 2000 (11) BCLR 1169 (CC).

Minister of Health v Treatment Action Campaign 2002 (10) BCLR 1033 (CC).
Pachim Banga Khet Majoor Samity v State of Bengal (1996) 4 SCC 37.
Purohit and Another v The Gambia (2003) AHRLR 96 (ACHPR 2003).
Social and Economic Rights Action Center (SERAC) and Another v Nigeria (2001) AHRLR 60 (ACHPR 2001).
Soobramoney v. Minister of Health KwaZulu Natal 1997 (12) BCLR 1696.
Washington v Glucksberg 521 US 702, 732 (1997).

Chapter 2

A Human Rights-based Approach to Realising Access to Sexual and Reproductive Health Rights in sub-Saharan Africa

Gladys Mirugi-Mukundi[1]

Sexual and reproductive health and rights (SRHR) remain one of the weakest areas in the context of human rights protection in Africa.[2] Given that sub-Saharan Africa accounts for more than half of all maternal deaths in the world, African states have not treated the problem with a corresponding level of urgency. Deaths arising from pregnancy or childbirth-related complications leave millions of children without mothers in Africa. Studies reveal that children who have lost their mothers are 10 times more likely to die prematurely than those who have not.[3]

The United Nations Population Fund (UNFPA) estimates that illnesses and deaths from poor reproductive health account for one-fifth of the global burden of disease.[4] The World Bank estimates that 74 per cent of maternal deaths are preventable if all women had access to necessary interventions for addressing complications of pregnancy and childbirth such as access to reproductive health services.[5] Provision of sexual and reproductive health services is thus a significant contribution to women's health in line with the UN Millennium Development Goals (MDGs). However, lack of access to universal reproductive health care services is the norm in most African states. While numerous reasons are cited for this state of affairs, factors such as socio-economic status, cultural

---

1 The author would like to express her sincere appreciation to the anonymous reviewers for their valuable and insightful comments. The author takes responsibility for all errors and omissions in the chapter.

2 Progress towards universal access to sexual and reproductive health (SRH) as envisioned in Millennium Development Goal (MDG) 5 in the African region has been below expectation. See World Health Organization, *Accelerating Universal Access to Sexual and Reproductive Health: Agenda for the African Region of the World Health Organization* (WHO 2013) foreword.

3 Campaign on Accelerated Reduction of Maternal Mortality in Africa, at http://esaro.unfpa.org/public/public/lang/en/pid/7130 (accessed 15 January 2015).

4 UNFPA, *Reducing Poverty and Achieving the Millennium Development Goals: Arguments for Investing in Reproductive Health and Rights* (UNFPA 2005).

5 A Wagstaff and M Claeson, *The Millennium Development Goals for Health: Rising to the Challenges* (World Bank 2004).

norms, the health care system, infrastructure and ignorance are largely to blame.[6] Greater commitment and investment is required to ensure universal access to reproductive health care in Africa.[7]

This chapter examines universal access to reproductive rights in sub-Saharan Africa from a human rights perspective. The chapter is divided into four main sections. The first surveys the scope and definition of universal access to reproductive health from a human rights perspective. The second identifies key human rights principles, standards and obligations at the international and regional levels, as well as policy responses and trends in Africa. The following section assesses the challenges encountered towards achieving universal access to reproductive health in sub-Saharan Africa. The final section concludes the chapter and argues that African governments need to do more if they are to achieve MDG 5b on universal access to reproductive health. This chapter advocates that a human rights-based approach is necessary if sub-Sahara Africa is to achieve universal access to reproductive rights.

Access to Sexual and Reproductive Health Services: Scope and Definition from a Human Rights Perspective

While issues relating to sexual and reproductive health (SRH) constitute fundamental rights, they remain controversial, particularly in a region like Africa.[8] According to Yamin and Boulanger the initial MDG 5 target – to reduce the maternal mortality ratio by three-quarters – focused on narrow select interventions even within the health sector, leaving out broader SRHR.[9] Indeed it was not until the World Summit at the United Nations in September 2005 that the goal of achieving universal access to reproductive health by 2015 was integrated into internationally agreed strategies and development goals within the MDG framework.[10]

---

6 C Abouzahr, 'Maternal Mortality: Helping Mothers Live', *OECD Observer*, at http://www.oecdobserver.org/news/archivestory.php/aid/374/Maternal_mortality:_helping_mothers_live.html#sthash.y8tPekBg.dpuf (accessed 24 December 2014).

7 See various research reports such as Centre for Reproductive Rights and Women Advocates Research and Documentation Centre, *Broken Promises: Human Rights, Accountability and Maternal Death in Nigeria* (CRR and WARDC 2008); Amnesty International, *Giving Life, Risking Death: Maternal Mortality in Burkina Faso* (Amnesty International 2009); Amnesty International, *Out of Reach: The Cost of Maternal Health in Sierra Leone* (Amnesty International 2009); Human Rights Watch, *'Stop Making Excuses': Accountability for Maternal Healthcare in South Africa* (Human Rights Watch 2011).

8 W Nowicka, 'Sexual and Reproductive Rights and the Human Rights Agenda: Controversial and Contested' (2011) 19 *Reproductive Health Matters* 119.

9 AE Yamin and V Boulanger, 'Taking Measure of the Elephant in the Room: Sexual and Reproductive Health and Rights, MDG 5, and Where We Want to Go from Here', Working Paper Series, FXB Center (2013).

10 In 2006, the UN Secretary-General introduced a set of new targets to follow up on the Millennium Declaration. See Report of the Secretary-General on the work of the Organization, Sixty-first Session Supplement No 1 (A/61/1).

The reproductive health agenda was first clearly articulated at the International Conference on Population and Development (ICPD) in 1994.[11] The ICPD Programme of Action contains principles that provide a human rights framework and inform governments and community initiatives that guide laws, policies and programmes on SRH.[12] According to the ICPD, reproductive health can be defined as a

> state of complete physical, mental and social well-being … in all matters relating to the reproductive system and to its functions and processes. Reproductive health therefore implies that people are able to have a satisfying and safe sex life and that they have the *capability to reproduce* and the freedom *to decide if, when and how often to do so … to be informed and to have access to safe, effective, affordable and acceptable methods of family planning of their choice …* and the right of access to appropriate health-care services that will enable women to go safely through pregnancy and childbirth and provide couples with the best chance of having a healthy infant.[13]

In adopting a rights-based approach to reproductive health, the ICPD acknowledges that 'reproductive rights embrace certain human rights that are already recognised in national laws, international human rights documents'. It advocates for the highest standard of sexual and reproductive health that would include 'their right to make decisions concerning reproduction free of discrimination, coercion and violence, as expressed in human rights documents'.[14] The ICPD establishes that SRHR are linked to women's rights and the ability of women to survive pregnancy and childbirth and to exercise autonomy over decisions relating to their reproductive lives.[15]

The Committee on Economic, Social and Cultural Rights (CESCR) in its General Comment No 14 expounds on sexual and reproductive health services to include 'access to family planning, pre- and post-natal care, emergency obstetric services and access to information, as well as to resources necessary to act on that information' as important measures towards the achievement of the right to maternal, child and reproductive health.[16] This indicates that the right to SRH is a fundamental part of the right to health.[17] The Committee on the Convention on the Elimination of All Forms of Discrimination against Women (hereafter CEDAW committee) equally affirms that 'access to health care,

11 United Nations Population Fund, Report of the International Conference on Population and Development (ICPD) Programme of Action (1994) A/CONF.171/13/Rev 1.

12 Ibid, chap II.

13 Ibid, para 7.2.

14 Ibid, para 7.3.

15 Human Rights Council, 'Study by the World Health Organization on mortality among children under five years of age as a human rights concern' (2013) UN Doc A/HRC/24/60, para 36.

16 Committee on Economic, Social and Cultural Rights, General Comment No 14, para 14; International Covenant on Economic, Social and Cultural Rights, art 12.2(a) the right to maternal, child and reproductive health.

17 See Reports of the UN Special Rapporteur on the right of everyone to the enjoyment of the highest attainable standard of physical and mental health, Paul Hunt.

including reproductive health is a basic right under the Convention on the Elimination of All Forms of Discrimination against Women'.[18]

Furthermore, MDG 5b on universal access to reproductive health sets out the indicators to include contraceptive prevalence rate, adolescent birth rate, antenatal care coverage (at least one visit and at least four visits), and unmet need for family planning.[19] According to the World Health Organization (WHO), the indicators can be used to 'monitor progress on removing barriers, improving health systems, and positively addressing sexual and reproductive health needs and risks'.[20] This indicates that sexual and reproductive health laws, policies and programmes have to be evaluated within the existing and evolving standards and obligations on the right to health. In essence, women's reproductive rights include 'the right of access to appropriate health-care services that will enable women to safely go through pregnancy and childbirth'.[21]

From the foregoing, access to sexual and reproductive health from a human rights perspective entails two recurring themes, namely equitable access to sexual and reproductive health services and non-discriminatory access to health facilities, goods and services.

What is a Human Rights-based Approach to Access to Sexual and Reproductive Health?

A human rights-based approach provides specifically that human rights norms and principles should guide relationships between rights-holders (individuals and groups with rights) and the duty-bearers (actors with an obligation to fulfil those rights, such as states).[22] With regard to access to SRH services, a human rights-based approach is intended to strengthen the capacities of rights-holders to claim their entitlements and to enable duty-bearers to meet their obligations through the design, implementation and monitoring of programmes and policies.[23]

---

18 Committee on the Elimination of Discrimination against Women, General Recommendation 24, para 1.

19 Millennium Development Goals Indicators, Official list of MDG indicators, 15 January 2008, available at http://mdgs.un.org/unsd/mdg/Resources/Attach/Indicators/OfficialList2008.pdf (accessed 15 January 2015). See also World Health Organization, *National-level Monitoring of the Achievement of Universal Access to Reproductive Health: Conceptual and Practical Considerations and Related Indicators* (WHO 2008).

20 World Health Organization, *National-level Monitoring* (n 18 above).

21 United Nations Population Fund, Report of the ICPD (n 10 above) para 7.2.

22 UN Development Group, 'The Human Rights Based Approach to Development Cooperation towards a Common Understanding among UN Agencies' (May 2003), available at www.undg.org/archive_docs/6959-The_Human_Rights_Based_Approach_to_Development_Cooperation_Towards_a_Common_Understanding_among_UN.pdf (accessed 15 January).

23 FXB Center for Health and Human Rights and Open Society Foundations, *Health and Human Rights Resource Guide* (5th edn, FXB Center for Health and Human Rights and Open Society Foundations 2013).

A human rights-based approach encompasses principles of human dignity, equality and non-discrimination; participation (increases and strengthens the participation of the local community) and accountability (improves transparency and accountability,[24] among others. As London rightfully puts it, 'a human rights approach to health is critical to address growing global health inequalities'.[25] In essence, a human rights-based approach to access to SRH is important because it is 'effective in reinforcing both human rights and public health objectives, particularly with respect to highly stigmatising health issues'.[26] The most common conception of a rights-based approach is the utilisation of the human rights framework in public interest litigation with the aim of holding governments accountable.

International and Regional Standards and Obligations on Access to Sexual and Reproductive Health Services

Several international and regional human rights instruments oblige governments to fulfil their mandate as duty-bearers to provide and enable access to sexual and reproductive health rights.[27] In Chapter 1 of this book, Olubayo Oluduro and Ebenezer Durojaye provide a more detailed discussion on the scope of states' obligations to realise the right to health, including sexual and reproductive health. It is instructive to note that the state has a general obligation to 'respect, protect, and fulfil' fundamental human rights.[28] The state as a duty-bearer is obliged to 'respect, protect, and fulfil' the rights of all and to ensure that others do so, and take measures to enable and assist especially the most vulnerable to claim their rights and entitlements.[29] The duty to protect and promote SRH is comparable to minimum core obligations which a state cannot justify its non-compliance with.[30]

This section surveys how some of these instruments address access to SRH as a human rights issue. To illustrate the significance of addressing SRH as a human right, the

---

24 Ibid.

25 L London, 'What is a Human Rights-Based Approach to Health and Does It Matter? (2008) 10 *Health and Human Rights* 65, 65.

26 V Gauri and S Gloppen, *Human Rights Based Approaches to Development: Concepts, Evidence, and Policy*, World Bank Policy Research Working Paper 5938 (2012), available at http://elibrary.worldbank.org/content/workingpaper/10.1596/1813-9450-5938 (accessed 15 January 2015).

27 International Covenant on Economic, Social, and Cultural Rights (ICESCR) (16 December 1966, entered into force 3 January 1976); Convention on the Elimination of all Forms of Discrimination against Women (CEDAW) (1981); Convention on the Rights of the Child (CRC) (1989); Protocol to the African Charter on Human and Peoples' Rights on the Rights of Women in Africa (2003).

28 Committee on Economic, Social and Cultural Rights, General Comment No 14, para 33.

29 Ibid, paras 33, 34, 35, 36, 37.

30 Minimum core obligations are obligations considered to be of immediate effect to meet the minimum essential levels of a human right. If a state fails to meet these because it does not have the resources, it must demonstrate that it has made every effort to use all available resources to satisfy, as a matter of priority, these core obligations. See Committee on Economic, Social and Cultural Rights, General Comment No 3 (1990) para 10.

issues are examined within the purview of three core human rights principles: universality, accessibility and participation.

Sexual and Reproductive Rights are Universal, Indivisible, Interdependent and Interrelated

SRHR is linked to women's rights and the ability of women to survive pregnancy and childbirth and to exercise autonomy over decisions relating to their reproductive lives.[31] These rights are indivisible, interdependent, interrelated and all of equal importance for human dignity.

Article 12 of the International Covenant on Economic, Social and Cultural Rights (ICESCR) provides that state parties shall 'recognise the right of everyone to the enjoyment of the highest attainable standard of physical and mental health'. The CESCR in its General Comment No 14 elucidates on the content of the right to health and notes that the right to health intersects with other rights such as 'the rights to food, housing, work, education, human dignity, life, non-discrimination, equality, the prohibition against torture, privacy, access to information, and the freedoms of association, assembly and movement'.[32] Even though it is a non-binding document, General Comment No 14 affirms that the right to health encompasses access not only to health care, but also to the 'underlying determinants of health, such as safe water, adequate sanitation, a healthy environment, health-related information, and freedom from discrimination'.[33] This demonstrates that all human rights are 'universal, indivisible, interdependent, interrelated, and of equal importance for human dignity'.[34]

In addition, the inclusion of SRH in the MDGs was an acknowledgement that it is a prerequisite for achieving MDG 5 on improving maternal health, MDG 3 on promoting gender equality and empowerment and MDG 6 on combating HIV and other diseases. The lack of universal access for women to reproductive health services thus undermines the possibility of achieving MDGs 5 and 6.[35] The United Nations Development Fund for Women (UNIFEM) encourages states to promote working 'with men and communities to promote their recognition of and respect for women's sexual and reproductive rights,

---

31 Human Rights Council, 'Study by the World Health Organization on mortality among children under five' (n 14 above) para 36.

32 Committee on Economic, Social and Cultural Rights, General Comment No 14, para 3. The CESCR is a UN body authorised to monitor compliance with the ICESCR and has issued general comments/recommendations and concluding observations.

33 P Hunt, 'Right to the Highest Attainable Standard of Health' (2007) 320 *Lancet* 369-371.

34 Maastricht Guidelines on Violations of Economic, Social and Cultural Rights (1997) para 4. See further Vienna Declaration and Programme of Action (1993) part 1, chap III.

35 AIDS Rights Alliance for Southern Africa (ARASA), 'The Women's Rights Protocol' (June 2010) *HEARD Issue Brief* (June 2010), available at http://www.google.com/url?sa=t&rct=j&q=&esrc=s&source=web&cd=1&ved=0CB4QFjAA&url=http%3A%2F%2Fwww.heard.org.za%2Fdownloads%2Fsadc-donors-brief-on-international-legal-obligations.pdf&ei=MWoyVdm1OIXhaJHsgaAF&usg=AFQjCNFa7DNk0YLurjSu_-xKzILSXl1ICA&sig2=9C4R-E524I4iQ9L_27vtDQ&bvm=bv.91071109,d.d2s (accessed 15 January 2015).

and encourage men to take responsibility for their own sexual health and fertility and to help them exercise those responsibilities'.[36] As Mann et al rightfully put it 'intersection of health and human rights may provide practical benefits to those engaged in health or human rights work, may help reorient thinking about major global health challenges, and may contribute to broadening human rights thinking and practice'.[37]

Sexual and Reproductive Rights should be Available, Accessible and Acceptable

CESCR General Comment No 14 further affirms that although the right to health is subject to progressive realisation due to the limits of available resources, governments have a 'continuing obligation to move as expeditiously and effectively as possible towards the full realization'.[38] In other words the government must take 'deliberate, concrete and targeted steps towards the full realization of the right to health'.[39] In addition governments are obliged to fulfil this duty by adopting 'appropriate legislative, administrative, budgetary, judicial, promotional and other measures towards the full realization of the right to health'.[40] The state is the duty-bearer that should be held to account for failure to respect, protect and fulfil that right.[41] CESCR General Comment No 14 articulates that 'the realization of women's right to health requires the removal of all barriers interfering with access to health services, education and information, including in the area of sexual and reproductive health'.[42]

According to CESCR General Comment No 14, the right to health in all its forms including reproductive rights contains these interrelated and essential elements, namely availability, accessibility, acceptability and good quality.[43] By making health facilities and services 'available', it implies that governments have to ensure that they are 'available in sufficient quantity'. 'Accessibility' implies that governments have a responsibility to ensure equal access to quality health care services for all, without discrimination.[44] The CESCR

---

36 UNIFEM, *Making the MDGs Work for All Gender-responsive Rights-based Approaches to the MDGs* (UNIFEM 2008) 68.

37 J Mann et al, 'Health and Human Rights' (1997) *Health and Human Rights* 1, available at http://www.hhrjournal.org/wp-content/uploads/sites/13/2014/03/2-Mann3.pdf (accessed 15 April 2015).

38 Committee on Economic, Social and Cultural Rights, General Comment No 14, para 9.

39 Committee on Economic, Social and Cultural Rights, General Comment No 3, paras 2 and 43.

40 Committee on Economic, Social and Cultural Rights, General Comment No 14, para 33.

41 Ibid, paras 33 and 37. See also Report of the UN Special Rapporteur on extreme poverty and human rights, Magdalena Sepúlveda Carmona (March 2013) UN Doc A/HRC/23/26, para 65.

42 Committee on Economic, Social and Cultural Rights, General Comment No 14, para 14. Also see Committee on the Elimination of Discrimination against Women, General Recommendation No 24, para 24.

43 Committee on Economic, Social and Cultural Rights, General Comment No 14, para 35.

44 UNFPA and Danish Institute for Human Rights, *Reproductive Rights are Human Rights: A Handbook for National Human Rights Institutions* (UNFPA and DIHR 2014).

further elaborates that 'accessibility' encompasses four main aspects.[45] These include non-discrimination and equal treatment to health care services;[46] physical accessibility for 'all sections of the population, especially vulnerable or marginalized groups, such as ethnic minorities and indigenous populations, women, children, adolescents, older persons, persons with disabilities and persons with HIV/AIDS';[47] economic accessibility, which is financial affordability of health facilities, goods and services; and information accessibility, including the right to seek and receive information on health issues.

The CEDAW Committee emphasises that 'measures to eliminate discrimination against women are considered to be inappropriate if a health care system lacks services to prevent, detect and treat illnesses specific to women'.[48] It recommends that state parties 'prioritize the prevention of unwanted pregnancy through family planning and sex education and reduce maternal mortality rates through safe motherhood services and prenatal assistance. When possible, legislation criminalizing abortion should be amended to remove punitive provisions imposed on women who undergo abortion.'[49]

In light of societal, cultural, traditional and economic pressures, the CEDAW Committee further emphases that governments should take all appropriate steps to combat traditional practices that are harmful and prejudicial to the health and well-being of women and children, such as female circumcision, which is predominant in Africa.[50] In recognition that female genital mutilation continues to violate the human rights of women, in 2014 the UN General Assembly adopted a resolution on the elimination of female genital mutilation.[51]

At the regional level, the African human rights system provides an appropriate framework and mechanism to address sexual and reproductive health and rights.[52] The Protocol to the African Charter on Human and Peoples' Rights on the Rights of Women [53] requires states parties to enact and implement laws to prohibit discrimination and harmful practices that endanger women's health (art 2), respect women's right to health (art 14(1)), provide adequate, affordable and accessible health services to women (art 14(2)), and establish and strengthen pre-natal, delivery and post-natal health and nutrition services for pregnant and breast- feeding women (art 14(2)).

---

45 Committee on Economic, Social and Cultural Rights, General Comment No 14, para 12(b).

46 Committee on Economic, Social and Cultural Rights, General Comment No 14, paras 18-19.

47 Committee on Economic, Social and Cultural Rights, General Comment No 14, para 12(b).

48 CEDAW, General Recommendation No 24, para 11.

49 CEDAW, General Recommendation No 24, para 31(c).

50 CEDAW, General Recommendation No 14 (1990).

51 UN General Assembly, 'Resolution on intensifying global efforts for the elimination of female genital mutilations' (2014) UN Doc A/RES/69/150.

52 K Toure et al, 'Positioning Women's and Children's Health in African Union Policy-making: A Policy Analysis' (2012) 8 *Globalization and Health*, available at http://www.ncbi.nlm.nih.gov/pmc/articles/PMC3298467/#__ffn_sectitle (accessed 15 January 2015).

53 The Protocol to the African Charter on Human and Peoples' Rights on the Rights of Women (adopted in 2003, entered into force 25 November 2005).

Accountable and Meaningful Participation in Access to Sexual Reproductive Health Services

Participation in the context of health systems includes 'identifying overall strategy, policy-making, implementation and accountability'.[54] The UN Special Rapporteur on Health highlights in several reports that an integral feature of the right to health is the active and informed participation of individuals and communities in health decision-making that affects them.[55] To strengthen community participation in health decision-making and accountability of health facilities, the Special Rapporteur on Health advises that 'States have a human rights responsibility to establish institutional arrangements for the active and informed participation of all relevant stakeholders, including disadvantaged communities.'[56] Therefore participation in the process of decision-making by all those who are potentially affected, particularly women, is critically important.

Reproductive health has a greater impact on women and girls than on men and boys. As Leeuwen points out, unlike men, women have specific human rights that need to be promoted and protected.[57] The WHO acknowledges that 'Women's comprehensive understanding of their sexual and reproductive health is imperative to ensuring their ability to protect their health and make informed decisions about sexuality and reproduction.'[58]

In 2009, the Human Rights Council adopted a resolution on maternal mortality.[59] The resolution emphasises and recognises participation to enhance accountability as an operational principle of a rights-based approach.[60]

Accountability is a critical feature of a human rights approach to participation[61] –accountability that enables rights-holders – females and males – to claim their rights and ensures that the state fulfils its obligations as duty-bearer. In the health

54 Report of the Special Rapporteur on the right of everyone to the enjoyment of the highest attainable standard of physical and mental health, Paul Hunt (31 January 2008) UN Doc A/HRC/7/11, para 41.

55 Report of the Special Rapporteur on the right of everyone to the enjoyment of the highest attainable standard of physical and mental health, Paul Hunt (19 January 2006) UN Doc E/CN.A/2006/48/Add 2, para 36; Report of the Special Rapporteur on the right of everyone to the enjoyment of the highest attainable standard of physical and mental health, Paul Hunt (11 February 2005) UN Doc E/CN.4/2005/51, paras 59-61.

56 Report of the Special Rapporteur, Paul Hunt (n 53 above) para 41. See also H Potts, 'Human Rights in Public Health: Rhetoric, Reality and Reconciliation' (PhD thesis, Monash University, 2006).

57 F Leeuwen, *Women's Rights are Human Rights: The Practice of the United Nations Human Rights Committee and the Committee on Economic, Social and Cultural Rights* (Intersentia 2010) 36.

58 Human Rights Council, 'Study by the World Health Organization on mortality among children under five years of age' (n 14 above) para 29.

59 Human Rights Council, 'Preventable maternal mortality and morbidity and human rights' (2009) UN Doc A/HRC/11/L.16/Rev 1.

60 E Durojaye, 'The Human Rights Council's Resolution on Maternal Mortality: Better Late than Never' (2010) 10 *African Human Rights Law Journal* 293.

61 Report of the Special Rapporteur, Magdalena Sepúlveda Carmona (n 40 above) para 65.

system, especially where reproductive health is concerned, accountability between health workers and the users they serve is linked to internal accountability between health workers and the health systems in which they work.[62]

There are various approaches to dealing with the accountability of governments for failure to meet their obligations in fulfilling the right to SRH. Strategic litigation is the most common of these approaches.[63] Litigation can compel governments to act to fulfil their obligations under national and international law. As the UN Special Rapporteur on Health has emphasised, 'accountability can be used to expose problems and identify reforms that will enhance health systems for all'.[64]

Factors Limiting Access to Sexual and Reproductive Health Services in Africa

The 2010 MDG Review Summit noted that

> the challenges facing member countries in their quest to attain MDGs are slow growth prospects; resource constraints; lack of institutional reforms; inadequate capacity development; uneven income distribution; global economic situation; lack of political will and commitment to the MDGs; lack of an enabling environment to attract investment and encourage private sector development; and the lack of inclusive growth.[65]

A study by Amnesty International equally notes that these barriers include, but are not limited to,

> lack of information on sexual and reproductive health and rights; women's low socio-economic status (in the household and in society at large), which undermines their right to decide whether, when and how many children to have; economic barriers, notably the cost of medical treatment; geographic barriers obstructing access to health facilities; and poor quality of treatment due to shortage of medical supplies and qualified personnel.[66]

Other notable human rights issues that contribute to the lack of universal access to reproductive services in Africa include denial of women's sexual and reproductive rights, gender discrimination and early marriage and pregnancy.

Various studies indicate that women face many barriers in obtaining necessary health care services, including long distances to health care facilities, ineffective referral services

---

62 UNFPA and Danish Institute for Human Rights (n 43 above) 82.

63 S Gloppen, 'Litigation as a Strategy to hold Governments Accountable for Implementing the Right to Health' (2008)10 *Health Human Rights* 21.

64 Report of the Special Rapporteur, Paul Hunt (n 53 above) para 122.

65 Islamic Development Bank, 'The Challenge of Achieving the Millennium Development Goals in IDB Member Countries in the Post-crisis World', IDB Occasional Paper No 16 (June 2011).

66 Amnesty International, *Giving Life, Risking Death* (n 6 above) 1.

and financial barriers.[67] This is compounded by conflict. Several African countries still endure persistent conflicts or severe governance problems that frustrate or slow attainment of the MDGs.

Among developing countries, sub-Saharan Africa faces the greatest challenge in achieving the MDG on universal access to sexual and reproductive health.[68] Some exogenous factors have contributed to the difficulties it faces: the HIV/AIDS pandemic, political instability, reduced aid flow, limited health budgets and inadequate data on maternal mortality. Although Africa presents a bag of mixed blessings, the status of Africa's achievements towards 2015 should be viewed within its social, economic and cultural context.

This section focuses on five main challenges: societal norms, customary and traditional practices in Africa; the HIV/AIDS epidemic in sub-Saharan Africa; limited budgets; weak public health system and shortage of health care personnel.

Challenges in Relation to Right-Holders

Societal norms, customary and traditional practices

Societal norms, customary and traditional views and practices about sexuality, such as gender orientation and abortion, and harmful traditional practices like child marriages and female genital mutilation/cutting (FGM) compromise women's and girls' endeavours to access reproductive health services. Although many African countries have laws and policies that prohibit FGM and circumcision of girls, the practice is still prevalent.[69] FGM, which is strongly anchored in cultural belief and norms,[70] exposes women and girls to health hazards such as obstructed labour, haemorrhage and even death. A 2006 study by the WHO found that women and girls who have undergone FGM suffer serious complications during childbirth.[71] FGM is thus tantamount to the violation of human

67 Amnesty International, *From Promises to Deliveries: Putting Human Rights at the Heart of the Millennium Goals* (Amnesty International 2010); R Kagbe, 'Wasted Lives: Why do Chadian Women Still Die in Child Birth?' *50.50 inclusive democracy*, 30 August 2012, available at https://www.opendemocracy.net/5050/kagbe-rachel/wasted-lives-why-do-chadian-women-still-die-in-childbirth (accessed 15 April 2015); Centre for Reproductive Rights and Asian-Pacific Resource & Research Centre for Women (Arrow), *Women of the World: Laws and Policies Affecting their Reproductive Lives. East and Southeast Asia* (CRR and Arrow 2005).

68 World Health Organization, *Accelerating Universal Access to Sexual and Reproductive Health* (n 1 above).

69 United Nations Children's Fund, *Female Genital Mutilation/Cutting: A Statistical Overview and Exploration of the Dynamics of Change* (UNICEF 2013).

70 K Odeku et al, 'Female Genital Mutilation: A Human Rights Perspective' (2009) 19 *Journal of Psychology in Africa* 55.

71 World Health Organization (Study Group on Female Genital Mutilation and Obstetric Outcome), 'Female Genital Mutilation and Obstetric Outcome: WHO Collaborative Prospective Study in Six African Countries' (2006) 367 *Lancet* 1835.

rights of girls and women.[72] Beyond sexual and reproductive health, other rights that could be violated in this regard include the right to life and dignity.

According to data from the WHO, in much of 'sub-Saharan Africa and south Asia motherhood is often simply seen as "what girls are for" – their social value is firmly rooted in their capacity for reproduction'.[73] And as such early child marriage is common.[74] In addition, this complex practice of child marriage is often driven by poverty. However, early child marriage risks locking adolescent girls into relationships in which they have limited voice to shape their reproductive health choices.

Adolescent pregnancy is common in most developing countries particularly in sub-Saharan Africa.[75] Pregnant adolescents require special care because they are at higher risk of maternal and newborn death (up to five times for maternal mortality than for women older than 19 years) as well as associated complications such as pre-term delivery and low birth weight.[76] In acknowledging that adolescents are particularly vulnerable in most countries because of their lack of information and access to relevant services, the ICPD has called on countries to develop integrated approaches to the special nutritional, general and reproductive health, education and social needs of girls and young women.[77] According to the WHO, family planning is a key concern of 'Countdown to 2015' because of its contribution to reducing unintended pregnancies and unsafe abortions, as well as to enabling women to control their reproductive lives.[78] Abortion is illegal in most African countries except when the pregnancy endangers the mother's life.[79] However, the existence of legal abortion does not mean that the abortion is safe.[80] Granted, unsafe abortions account for 13 per cent of maternal deaths in Africa and constitute one of the five leading direct causes of maternal deaths, and can result in permanent injuries and death due to

---

72 United Nations, 'A world fit for children' (10 May 2002) UN Doc A/RES/S-27/2. Also see O Nnamuchi, 'Circumcision or Mutilation – Voluntary or Forced Excision – Extricating the Ethical and Legal Issues in Female Genital Ritual' (2012) 25 *Journal of Law and Health* 85, 85.

73 World Health Organization, 'Adolescent Pregnancy' (2008) 1 *MPS Notes*, available at www.who.int/maternal_child_adolescent/documents/mpsnnotes_2_lr.pdf (15 January 2015).

74 International Center for Research on Women, *New Insights on Preventing Child Marriage: A Global Analysis of Factors and Programs* (ICRW 2007).

75 The adolescent birth rate remained high in the African region at 117 per 1,000 women aged 15-19 years as compared to 50 per 1,000 for the global estimate in 2010. See World Health Organization, *World Health Statistics Report* (WHO 2012).

76 United Nations, *Millennium Development Goals Report* (UN 2009) 28.

77 United Nations Population Fund, Report of the ICPD (n 10 above) para 4.20.

78 World Health Organization and UNICEF, *Countdown to 2015: Accountability for Maternal, New Born & Child Survival: The 2013 Update* (Countdown 2013).

79 Abortion is not permitted for any reason in 14 African countries. Four countries in Africa have relatively liberal abortion laws: Zambia permits abortion on socio-economic grounds, and Cape Verde, South Africa and Tunisia allow pregnancy termination without restriction as to reason, but with gestational limits. For more details, see Guttmacher Institute, 'Facts on Abortion in Africa' (2012), available at http://www.guttmacher.org/pubs/IB_AWW-Africa.pdf (accessed 15 January 2015).

80 G Sedgh et al, 'Induced Abortion: Rates and Trends Worldwide' (2007) 370 *Lancet* 1338.

complications.[81] Unsafe abortions account for 13 per cent of maternal deaths, and 20 per cent of the total mortality and disability burden due to pregnancy and childbirth.[82] This could be eliminated if women had universal access to family planning.[83] Further, most African countries have laws that criminalise abortion.[84] The Kenyan case of *Republic v Nyamu and Others*[85] demonstrates 'the difficulties that can arise for health-care practitioners charged with providing abortion services'.[86] In that case Dr. Nyamu and two of his staff members were arrested for providing illegal abortion services. This came after 15 foetuses were discovered along a rive in Nairobi. It was alleged that the documents accompanying the foetuses pointed to tow health clinics that Dr. Nyamu worked as a gynaecologist. Although this case was dismissed for a lack of evidence, it led to a successful campaign for the new provisions on reproductive health in the Kenyan Constitution of 2010. Anti-abortion legislation forces women to seek backstreet abortions from illegal providers who are at times unqualified to handle even minor obstetric procedures.

According to International Pregnancy Advisory Services (IPAS), 'this denies women control over their own reproductive decision-making ... by unduly limiting their self-determination and impeding equal participation in their nations' social, political and economic life'.[87] The former UN Special Rapporteur on Health has advised that 'women with unwanted pregnancies should be offered reliable information and compassionate counseling, including information on where and when a pregnancy may be terminated legally'.[88] Various studies by the IPAS and the Centre for Reproductive Health reveal that where abortions are legal, they must be safe.[89] Programmes to increase access to pregnancy prevention services and protect young women from unsafe abortions are greatly needed.[90]

---

81 World Health Organization, *Unsafe Abortion: Global and Regional Estimates of the Incidence of Unsafe Abortion and Associated Mortality in 2003* (5th edn, WHO 2007) 5.

82 Ibid.

83 UNFPA Executive Director (Dr Babatunde Osotimehin) at the High-level forum. See 'UN Secretary-General, UNFPA Call for Accelerated Action to Prevent Women and Girls from Dying Unnecessarily' *UNFPA News*, 23 September 2013, at http://www.unfpa.org/public/home/news/pid/15056#sthash.2PK4EceV.dpuf (accessed 15 January 2015). Also see S Singh et al, *Adding It Up: The Costs and Benefits of Investing in Sexual and Reproductive Health* (Guttmacher Institute 2014).

84 Guttmacher Institute 'Facts on Abortion in Africa' (n 78 above).

85 Case No 81 of 2004 Kenya High Court.

86 Center for Reproductive Rights, the International Programme on Reproductive and Sexual Health Law at the University of Toronto, and the University of the Free State, *Legal Grounds: Reproductive and Sexual Rights in African Commonwealth Courts*, Vol II (CRR et al 2010) 96.

87 IPAS, 'Ensuring Women's Access to Safe Abortion: A Key Strategy for Achieving Millennium Development Goals' (2011). For further analysis of abortion-related cases, see *KL v Peru*, Human Rights Committee, Communication No 1153/2003, CCPR/C/85/D1153/ 2003, views adopted on 24 October 2005; *RR v Poland* (Appl. No. 27617/04, 26 May 2011).

88 Report of the United Nations Special Rapporteur on the right of everyone to the enjoyment of the highest attainable standard of physical and mental health, Paul Hunt (February 2004) UN Doc E/CN.4/2004/49, para 30.

89 IPAS (n 86 above).

90 BA Levandowski et al, 'Reproductive Health Characteristics of Young Malawian Women Seeking Post-abortion Care' (2012) 16 *African Journal of Reproductive Health* 253.

It is instructive to note that the African Women's Protocol is the first regional instrument to expressly provide for the right to abortion.[91] It is also worth noting that despite regressive penal laws against abortion in most African countries, there is a growing trend towards liberalisation of national laws decriminalising safe abortions in Africa.[92] The African Women's Protocol requires member states to 'protect women's reproductive rights by authorising medical abortion in cases of sexual assault, rape and incest'.[93] Further, article 24(3) of the Convention on the Rights of the Child obliges states parties to take all effective and appropriate measures with a view to abolishing traditional practices prejudicial to the health of children, including such harmful practices as child marriage, which impair women's and girls' ability to make decisions about their sexual and reproductive lives and have negative effects on child survival.

According to the former UN Special Rapporteur on Health, 'Rape and other forms of sexual violence, including forced pregnancy, non-consensual contraceptive methods (such as forced sterilization and forced abortion), female genital mutilation/cutting, and forced marriage, all represent serious breaches of sexual and reproductive freedoms, and are fundamentally and inherently inconsistent with the right to health.'[94] In essence, many legal provisions and legal frameworks on reproductive rights and abortion ought to be reviewed. Various international and regional bodies and organisations have called on state parties to address harmful practices, such as child marriage, and ensure access to the information and services needed by women and girls to make informed decisions about their sexual and reproductive lives.[95] An understanding of local customs, traditional beliefs and women's social status is therefore essential to inform policies and programmes on SRH.

HIV/AIDS pandemic

According to UNAIDS, sub-Saharan Africa has the highest number of people living with HIV in the world.[96] By 2010 sub-Saharan Africa had the largest proportion of maternal deaths attributed to HIV at 10 per cent, while the Caribbean had the second largest at 6 per

---

91 Protocol to the African Charter on Human and People's Rights on the Rights of Women in Africa (2003) art 14(2); Guttmacher Institute (n 78 above); IPAS, 'The Impact on Young Women when Abortion is a Crime' (2014), available at http://www.ipas.org/~/media/Files/Ipas%20Publications/FSCRYTHE14.ashx?utm_source=resource&utm_medium=meta&utm_campaign=FSCRYTHE14 (accessed 15 January 2015).

92 World Health Organization, *Unsafe Abortion: Global and Regional Estimates of the Incidence of Unsafe Abortion and Associated Mortality in 2008* (6th edn, WHO 2011).

93 Protocol to the African Charter on Human and People's Rights on the Rights of Women in Africa (2003) art 14(2).

94 Report of the United Nations Special Rapporteur, Paul Hunt (n 87 above) para 25.

95 See United Nations Population Fund, Report of ICPD (n 10 above) para 7.3.

96 In 2010, approximately 68 per cent of all people living with HIV resided in sub-Saharan Africa, a region with only 12 per cent of the global population. See UNAIDS, 'World AIDS Day Report' (2011) 7, available at http://www.unaids.org/en/media/unaids/contentassets/documents/unaidspublication/2011/jc2216_worldaidsday_report_2011_en.pdf.

cent.[97] HIV-positive women have a higher risk of maternal death. In fact, HIV has been noted as a leading cause of death during pregnancy in African countries with high HIV prevalence.[98] The effect of HIV/AIDS in sub-Saharan Africa is likely to have contributed to the slow pace of decline in maternal mortality.[99]

As well as high death rates, the HIV/AIDS pandemic has presented challenges to women's right to choice[100] that have resulted in ills such as coerced abortions and sterilisation for HIV-positive women.[101] Such was the situation in the case of *LM and Others v Government of the Republic of Namibia*[102] where three HIV-positive women were forcibly sterilised in public hospitals in Namibia. The court reiterated that the principle of acceptability implies that the health facility, goods and services should be culturally sensitive and that personnel should respect patients' confidentiality.[103] In terms of quality, health facilities should be 'culturally acceptable … scientifically and medically appropriate and of good quality'. This encompasses the requirement of skilled personnel.[104] The Government of Namibia was found in breach of its human rights obligation to respect patient's right of choice.

For example, according to the report by the South African Department of Health, HIV prevalence among antenatal patients has increased rapidly since the first case was reported in 1990. In 2004, HIV prevalence among women attending antenatal care within the public health sector in South Africa was reported to be 29.5 per cent.[105] This situation prompted the Treatment Action Campaign to challenge the Minister of Health to roll out a comprehensive national programme (by providing Nevirapine and other medications) to prevent mother-to-child transmission of HIV in *Treatment Action Campaign v Minister of Health*.[106] The South African Constitutional Court found the government's policy to limit Nevirapine to 18 sites to be unreasonable and in breach of the government's obligation to realise the right to health guaranteed in section 27 of the Constitution.

---

97 World Health Organization et al, *Trends in Maternal Mortality 1990-2010* (Who et al 2012) 23.

98 Ibid.

99 J Wilmoth et al, 'Maternal Deaths Drop by One-third from 1990 to 2008: A United Nations Analysis' (2010) *Bulletin of the World Health Organization* 718.

100 M Mushariwa, 'The Right to Reproductive Health and Access to Health Care Services within the Prevention of Mother-to-Child Transmission Programme: The Reality on the Ground in the Face of HIV/AIDS' in B Goldblatt and K McLean (eds) *Women's Social and Economic Rights: Developments in South Africa* (Juta 2011) 183, 202.

101 See P Nair, 'Litigating against the Forced Sterilization of HIV-positive Women: Recent Developments in Chile and Namibia' (2010) 23 *Harvard Human Rights Journal* 223.

102 [2012] NAHC 211.

103 Committee on Economic, Social and Cultural Rights, General Comment No 14, para 12(c).

104 Committee on Economic, Social and Cultural Rights, General Comment No 14, para 12(d).

105 Republic of South Africa Department of Health, 'National HIV and Syphilis Antenatal Sero-prevalence Survey in South Africa 2004' (2005).

106 2002 (4) BCLR 356.

Challenges in Relation to the Duty-bearers

Limited budgets allocations

One of the major challenges to health sector development in Africa is limited resource allocation. This has been compounded by the integration of SRH into the national health-related budgets. In the Abuja Declaration on HIV and AIDS, Tuberculosis and other Infectious Diseases (2001), African states pledged to commit 15 per cent of their total annual budget to improving the health care system. However, most African countries spend on average a meagre 8.7 per cent of their total budget on health.[107] For instance in 2011, Africa's economic giant, South Africa, spent 8.5 per cent of GDP on health care, while Nigeria, an equally powerful economic powerhouse, spent 5.3 per cent of its GDP on health care.[108] In contrast, Liberia, a post-conflict fragile state, spends on average 19.5 per cent of its GDP on health care.[109] In fact, 24 per cent of Liberia's '2009/2010 budget is allocated towards social and community services, with 7.3% for health, 11.6% for education and 10.7% to infrastructure'.[110]

People's access to sexual and reproductive services is determined by how budgets are formulated and how those resources are distributed. CESCR General Comment No 14 describes the obligation to eliminate discrimination against women as requiring significant positive measures involving allocations of resources and strategies pursued over time.[111] It argues that the 'availability' of reproductive health services depends on resource allocation.

The health budgets are further limited by the HIV/AIDS pandemic, which, as the leading cause of death in sub-Saharan Africa, has been given high priority thereby relegating other health priorities such as universal access to reproductive services to the margins. This further undermines women's right to reproductive and sexual health. The underfunding and under-prioritising of sexual and reproductive services and goods that mostly women and girls require amounts to discrimination against women and is contrary to two of the most fundamental elements of international human rights, namely non-discrimination and equality.

Limited health budgets are a poor reflection of the standards of health in a country. Budgeting for reproductive health should be more than a line item on a budget table. Limited health budgets exemplify the lack of attention paid to women's health. If the

---

107 World Bank, 'Health Expenditure, Total (% of GDP)', at http://data.worldbank.org/indicator/SH.XPD.TOTL.ZS. According to the World Bank 'Total health expenditure is the sum of public and private health expenditure. It covers the provision of health services (preventive and curative), family planning activities, nutrition activities, and emergency aid designated for health but does not include provision of water and sanitation.'

108 Ibid.

109 Ibid.

110 Liberia Ministry of Planning and Economic Affairs, 'Liberia 2010 MDG Report – Achieving 2015: Progress, Prospects, Constraints: Liberia's Progress towards the Millennium Development Goals' (September 2010).

111 B Porter, 'The Crisis of Economic, Social and Cultural Rights and Strategies for Addressing it' in J Squires et al (eds) *The Road to a Remedy: Current Issues in the Litigation of Economic, Social and Cultural Rights* (University of New South Wales Press 2005) 43.

risks of maternal mortality are to be reduced, and women's right to the highest attainable standard of health protected, governments must allocate and effectively spend more to strengthen their health system.[112] Improving sexual and reproductive rights for women requires improvements and greater investment in the health system.

A weak public health care system

Many low-income African countries have weak health systems partly because adequate resources – both financial and human – are not invested in the health sector. Apart from resources, a strong health system also depends on a structure of policies and regulations that ensures that health services are distributed fairly, such as referral programmes and the integration of related services; non-discrimination policies and complaint/recourse mechanisms; training programmes for health providers, including informed consent and confidentiality; mechanisms for health services to marginalised groups; and the research and monitoring of health outcomes.[113]

An 'effective, integrated, responsive health system accessible to all' is an essential element of a healthy and equitable society.[114] The UN emphasises that 'an effective health system is a core social institution, no less than a court system or political system'.[115] According to a report by the former UN Special Rapporteur on Health, factors contributing to Africa's inadequate achievement of MDG 5b on universal access to reproductive health services include weak health systems (physical and financial barriers to essential health services, shortage of medicine, poor human resources) and poor conditions as determinants of health (household education, income, insufficient and inappropriate nutritional practices, poor sanitation facilities).[116]

The WHO has noted that the poor uptake of family planning services that include contraceptives and obstetrics care can also be attributed to a multitude of interrelated factors such as too few health services and providers, and poor infrastructure and transport.[117] Access to quality and adequate reproductive health services such as family planning services and obstetric care could significantly reduce maternal deaths and injuries.

A number of African countries are increasingly adopting strategies and policies such as free obstetric care or risk-pooling mechanisms with the goal of increasing the coverage of effective health services. However, illiteracy and lack of information reduce

---

112 International Budget Partnership and the International Initiative on Maternal Mortality and Human Rights, *The Missing Link: Applied Budget Work as a Tool to Hold Governments Accountable for Maternal Mortality Reduction Commitments* (IBP and IIMMHR 2009).

113 Engender Health et al, *Advancing the Sexual and Reproductive Health and Human Rights of People Living with HIV: A Guidance Package* (Engender Health et al 2009) 16.

114 Report of the Special Rapporteur, Paul Hunt (n 53 above) para 122.

115 Report of the Special Rapporteur, Magdalena Sepúlveda Carmona (n 40 above) para 20. See also LP Freedman, 'Achieving the MDGs: Health Systems as Core Social Institutions' (2005) 48 *Development* 19.

116 African Development Bank (AfDB), *Assessing Progress in Africa toward the Millennium Development Goals. MDG Report 2013. Food Security in Africa: Issues, Challenges and Lessons* (AfDB 2013).

117 Harmonisation for Health in Africa, *Investing in Health for Africa: The Case for Strengthening Systems for Better Health Outcomes* (Harmonisation for Health in Africa 2011).

the number of people who are able and even willing to access the services. In Kenya, for instance, despite the maternity fee waiver, it was reported that many women prefer to stay clear of government health facilities for fear that the fee waiver will worsen the quality of health care.[118] In Nigeria, although an innovative Midwives Service Scheme has been implemented,[119] the proportion of births attended by a skilled health worker has remained low and heightens the risks of maternal death.[120] A Rapid Maternal Needs Assessment conducted in Liberia for the draft Operational Plan to Reduce Maternal and Neonatal Mortality revealed that maternal mortality is affected by inadequate facilities, equipment and drug supplies; health workers' inability to perform essential procedures; lack of an adequate transport system; and lack of alignment between traditional practices and standard of care.[121] A 2009 report notes that 'the overall weakness of health systems is responsible for many of the gaps that impede the full enjoyment by people living with HIV of their sexual and reproductive health and rights'.[122]

Issues of quality of service delivery, particularly in the health sector, and inequality in access to services, especially among vulnerable and marginalised groups such as young people, remain high on the agenda. The availability of SRH services such as contraceptives and efficient birth attendances by qualified medical obstetrics personnel have been emphasised as contributing factors towards achieving MDG 5 on reducing maternal mortality and promoting universal access to reproductive health services.

Through public interest litigation, civil society organisations in Africa have been successful in compelling governments to take account. In *Minister for Health v. Treatment Action Campaign*, the Constitutional Court of South Africa ordered the government, 'to devise and implement a comprehensive and coordinated programme to progressively realize the right of pregnant women and their newborn children to have access to health services to combat mother-to-child transmission of HIV'.[123] The Court rejected the government's excuse of a lack of resources and found its policy to limit access to antiretroviral therapy

118 M Gathigah, 'Kenya's Mothers Shun Free Maternity Healthcare', Interpress News Agency (July 2013), at http://www.ipsnews.net/2013/07/kenyas-mothers-shun-free-maternity-health-care/ (accessed 15 January 2015).

119 Under the scheme, the federal government, as a stop-gap measure, has embarked on the massive engagement of midwives on a cost-sharing basis among the three tiers of government. This initiative is aimed at rapidly improving the MDG indicator on the proportion of births attended by skilled health personnel.

120 Government of the Federal Republic of Nigeria, *Nigeria Millennium Development Goals Report* (2010), available at www.mdgs.gov.ng (accessed 15 January 2015).

121 Liberia Ministry of Planning and Economic Affairs (n 109 above).

122 Engender Health et al (n 112 above), 9. Support for the sexual and reproductive health of people living with HIV requires a specific set of services, including the diagnosis, management and treatment of HIV and other STIs; sex education and information; psychosocial support to cope with living with HIV; family planning; safe abortion and/or post-abortion care; services to assist conception; antenatal, delivery; services to address gender- and sexuality-based violence; commodities and social support for HIV prevention.

123 Constitutional Court of South Africa, Case CCT 8/02, para 135 (2)(a).

to prevent mother-to-child transmission of HIV to be unreasonable and a failure of its constitutional obligation to realise the right to health.

Harris cautions that for fragile and post-conflict states priority is usually given to rebuilding 'state security forces due to their role in past violence', while little attention is given to the health system as a 'potential facilitator of social reconstruction and peace building', 'to the detriment of the whole peace building enterprise'.[124] Where the court is moved to evaluate what entails basic health services, Nnamuchi emphasises the utilisation of the interpretative formula of the minimum core obligations, which refer to a threshold that must be met by countries.[125]

Dearth of health care personnel

One of the greatest challenges facing health systems in many African countries has to do with lack of skilled or trained health care personnel to provide SRH services to the people, particularly women. This sometimes leads to a situation where women and girls seeking SRH services experience abuse and mistreatment at the hands of health care personnel.[126] Slattery notes that 'reproductive rights violations in healthcare settings include: verbal, physical and sexual abuse; coercive practices, such as forced sterilization; and denial of abortion and post-abortion care services'.[127]

It is essential to ensure that health care workers comply with relevant national and international standards on reproductive health care. This has been the subject of a court case in Uganda which seeks a declaration that non-provision of essential maternal health commodities in government health facilities leading to the death of expectant mothers is an infringement of their rights to life and health.[128] However, the Court refused to find against the government based on the principle of political question.

Patients may be dissuaded from seeking reproductive health services because of the poor attitudes of health care providers. In a study in South Africa by Human Rights Watch, women and girls gave accounts of inconsiderate or humiliating treatment by

---

124 B Harris et al, 'Bringing Justice to Unacceptable Healthcare Services? Street-level Reflections from Urban South Africa' (2014) 8 *International Journal of Transitional Justice* 141, 143; PN Pham et al, 'Human Rights, Transitional Justice, Public Health and Social Reconstruction' (2010) 70 *Social Science and Medicine* 98. See also J Negin, 'The Central Role of Health in Building Peaceful Post-conflict Societies' (2007) 10 *Journal of Peace Conflict and Development* 1, 3.

125 O Nnamuchi, 'Millennium Development Goal 5, Human Rights, and Maternal Health in Africa: Possibilities, Constraints, and Future Prospects' (2014) 23 *Annals of Health Law* 92, 116; Committee on Economic, Social and Cultural Rights, General Comment No 3.

126 E Slattery, 'Out of the Silo: Using Reproductive Rights Jurisprudence to Litigate Abuses in Healthcare Settings' (2011) 16 *INTERIGHTS Bulletin* 185.

127 Ibid. See Center for Reproductive Rights, 'Reproductive Rights Violations as Torture and Cruel, Inhuman, or Degrading Treatment or Punishment: A Critical Human Rights Analysis' (2011), available at http://reproductiverights.org/sites/ - crr.civicactions.net/files/documents/TCIDT.pdf (accessed 15 January 2015).

128 Constitutional Petition No 16 of 2011 (now Constitutional Appeal No 1 of 2013). Also see Center for Health, Human Rights and Development, 'Constitutional Court Begins Hearing Maternal Deaths Case' (2011), available at http://www.cehurd.org/2011/09/constitutional-court-.

providers at health facilities.[129] The study further revealed that the 'systemic problems such as understaffing, poor pay, heavy workloads, and lack of equipment and medical supplies contribute to negative attitudes, abuses and poor quality of care'.[130] The negative attitudes of health workers, especially those assigned to attend adolescent mothers, deter adolescents from accessing contraceptive and family planning services.[131]

Conclusions

This chapter discusses a human rights-based approach to access to sexual and reproductive health rights and services in Africa. The chapter argues that governments can be held accountable for failure to fulfil their obligations as set out by the international and regional instruments on access to sexual and reproductive health services and rights. However, despite progressive provisions at the international and regional levels most sub-Saharan African states lag far behind in ensuring compliance with and implementing those provisions. This is largely due to sexual and reproductive health issues being viewed as peripheral matters relative to access to health care and their association with controversial family planning methods such as abortion. Criminalisation of abortion and limited support of the use of contraceptives in some countries compound the problem.

As Nnamuchi correctly points out, one of the major challenges to health sector development in Africa is 'government's ability to elicit support of the general public for its programs'.[132] It is commendable that non-state actors such as civil society organisations have continued to actively participate in 'translating official government objectives into tangible benefits for the people'[133] through advocacy strategies, lobbying for policy change, public interest litigation and human rights education on access to reproductive health. As the world focuses on the post-2015 sustainable development agenda, concerns have been raised on access to sexual and reproductive health rights of many women and girls in sub-Saharan Africa; reproductive health services remain elusive, resulting in the perpetuation of lack of human dignity, lack of equality and discrimination.

If African countries are to make substantive progress in realisation of reproductive and sexual health, it is important that states engage with the matter as a human rights issue rather than as mere development. Treated as a human rights issue, SRH would receive adequate allocation of resources and investment in the public health system. Significant efforts to achieve 'equitable access to reproductive health care' have been made since the International Conference on Population and Development in 1994. Many African countries, through their laws and policies, have designed programmes to facilitate access to sexual and reproductive health services. Such policies and programmes aim to 'protect

---

129 Human Rights Watch, *'Stop Making Excuses'* (n 6 above).

130 Ibid, 39.

131 LS Zabin and K Kiragu, 'The Health Consequences of Adolescent Sexual and Fertility Behavior in sub-Saharan Africa' (1998) 29 *Studies in Family Planning* 210.

132 Nnamuchi (n 124 above) 117.

133 Ibid.

individuals and to guide programmes to improve access to maternal and child health, to make family planning more widely accessible, to prevent and treat HIV and to provide support to those living with the virus'.[134] These policies and programmes have gone a long way to improving the lives of citizens in various ways.[135] However, many challenges still remain. As Navi Pillay (then UN High Commissioner for Human Rights) emphasised, the rights and obligations embedded in human rights treaties, including regional frameworks, must be translated into services on the ground.[136] With only limited time remaining to achieve the MDGs, urgent action is required by African countries to improve women and children's health needs.

References

Books, Chapters, Articles, etc.

Abouzahr, C, 'Maternal Mortality: Helping Mothers Live', *OECD Observer*, at http://www.oecdobserver.org/news/archivestory.php/aid/374/Maternal_mortality:_helping_mothers_live.html#sthash.y8tPekBg.dpuf (accessed 24 December 2014).

Center for Health, Human Rights and Development, 'Constitutional Court Begins Hearing Maternal Deaths Case' (2011), available at http://www.cehurd.org/2011/09/constitutional-court-.

Durojaye, E, 'The Human Rights Council's Resolution on Maternal Mortality: Better Late than Never' (2010) 10 *African Human Rights Law Journal* 293-322.

Freedman, LP, 'Achieving the MDGs: Health Systems as Core Social Institutions' (2005) 48 *Development* 19-24.

FXB Center for Health and Human Rights and Open Society Foundations, *Health and Human Rights Resource Guide* (5th edn, FXB Center for Health and Human Rights and Open Society Foundations 2013).

Gathigah, M, 'Kenya's Mothers Shun Free Maternity Healthcare', Interpress News Agency (July 2013), at http://www.ipsnews.net/2013/07/kenyas-mothers-shun-free-maternity-health-care/ (accessed 15 January 2015).

Gauri, V and Gloppen, S, *Human Rights Based Approaches to Development: Concepts, Evidence, and Policy*, World Bank Policy Research Working Paper 5938 (2012), available at http://elibrary.worldbank.org/content/workingpaper/10.1596/1813-9450-5938 (accessed 15 January 2015).

134 UNFPA, *How Universal is Access to Reproductive Health? A Review of the Evidence* (UNFPA 2010).

135 The WHO Global Reproductive Health Strategy has articulated the five priority aspects of sexual and reproductive health as improving antenatal, delivery, postpartum and new-born care; providing high-quality services for family planning, including infertility services; eliminating unsafe abortion; combating sexually transmitted infections, including HIV, reproductive tract infections, cervical cancer and other gynaecological morbidities; and promoting sexual health.

136 United Nations High Commissioner for Human Rights, 'Strengthening the United Nations Human Rights Treaty Body System' (June 2012) UN Doc A/66/860.

Gloppen, S, 'Litigation as a Strategy to hold Governments Accountable for Implementing the Right to Health' (2008) 10 *Health Human Rights* 21-36.

Guttmacher Institute, 'Facts on Abortion in Africa' (2012), at http://www.guttmacher.org/pubs/IB_AWW-Africa.pdf (accessed 15 January 2015).

Harmonisation for Health in Africa, *Investing in Health for Africa: The Case for Strengthening Systems for Better Health Outcomes* (Harmonisation for Health in Africa 2011).

Harris, B, Eyles, J, Penn-Kekana, L, Fried, J et al, 'Bringing Justice to Unacceptable Health Care Services? Street-Level Reflections from Urban South Africa' (2014) 8 *International Journal of Transitional Justice*, 141-161.

Hunt, P, 'Right to the Highest Attainable Standard of Health' (2007) 320 *Lancet* 369-371.

Kagbe, R, 'Wasted Lives: Why do Chadian Women Still Die in Child Birth? *50.50 inclusive democracy*, 30 August 2012, at https://www.opendemocracy.net/5050/kagbe-rachel/wasted-lives-why-do-chadian-women-still-die-in-childbirth (accessed 15 April 2015).

Leeuwen, F, *Women's Rights are Human Rights: The Practice of the United Nations Human Rights Committee and the Committee on Economic, Social and Cultural Rights* (Intersentia 2010).

Levandowski, BA, Pearson, E, Lunguzi, J and Katengeza, HR, 'Reproductive Health Characteristics of Young Malawian Women Seeking Post-abortion Care' (2012) 16 *African Journal of Reproductive Health* 253-261.

London, L, 'What is a Human Rights-Based Approach to Health and Does It Matter? (2008) 10 *Health and Human Rights* 65-80.

Mann, J et al, 'Health and Human Rights' (1997) *Health and Human Rights* 1, available at http://www.hhrjournal.org/wp-content/uploads/sites/13/2014/03/2-Mann3.pdf (accessed 15 April 2015).

Mushariwa, M, 'The Right to Reproductive Health and Access to Health Care Services within the Prevention of Mother-to Child Transmission Programme: The Reality on the Ground in the Face of HIV/AIDS' in B Goldblatt and K McLean (eds) *Women's Social and Economic Rights: Developments in South Africa* (Juta 2011) 183.

Nair, P, 'Litigating against the Forced Sterilisation of HIV-Positive Women: Recent Developments in Chile and Namibia' (2010) 23 *Harvard Human Rights Journal* 223-231.

Negin, J, 'The Central Role of Health in Building Peaceful Post-conflict Societies' (2007) 10 *Journal of Peace Conflict and Development* 1-22.

Nnamuchi, O, 'Circumcision or Mutilation – Voluntary or Forced Excision – Extricating the Ethical and Legal Issues in Female Genital Ritual' (2012) 25 *Journal of Law and Health* 85-122.

Nnamuchi, O, 'Millennium Development Goal 5, Human Rights, and Maternal Health in Africa: Possibilities, Constraints, and Future Prospects' (2014) 23 *Annals of Health Law* 92-140.

Nowicka, W, 'Sexual and Reproductive Rights and the Human Rights Agenda: Controversial and Contested' (2011) 19 *Reproductive Health Matters* 119-128.

Odeku, K, Rembe, S and Anwo, J, 'Female Genital Mutilation: A Human Rights Perspective' (2009) 19 *Journal of Psychology in Africa* 55-62.

Pham, PN, Vinck, P and Weinstein, HM, 'Human Rights, Transitional Justice, Public Health and Social Reconstruction' (2010) 70 *Social Science and Medicine* 98-105.

Porter, B, 'The Crisis of Economic, Social and Cultural Rights and Strategies for Addressing it' in J Squires, M Langford and B Thiele (eds) *The Road to a Remedy: Current Issues in the Litigation of Economic, Social and Cultural Rights* (University of New South Wales Press 2005) 43-69.

Potts, H, 'Human Rights in Public Health: Rhetoric, Reality and Reconciliation' (PhD thesis, Monash University, 2006).

Sedgh, G et al, 'Induced Abortion: Rates and Trends Worldwide' (2007) 370 *Lancet* 1338-1345.

Singh, S et al, *Adding It Up: The Costs and Benefits of Investing in Sexual and Reproductive Health* (Guttmacher Institute 2014).

Slattery, E, 'Out of the Silo: Using Reproductive Rights Jurisprudence to Litigate Abuses in Healthcare Settings' (2011) 16 *INTERIGHTS Bulletin* 185-187.

Toure, K, Sankore, R, Kuruvilla, S, Scolaro, E, Bustreo, F and Osotimehin, B, 'Positioning Women's and Children's Health in African Union Policy-making: A Policy Analysis' (2012) 8 *Globalization and Health* 3, available at http://www.ncbi.nlm.nih.gov/pmc/articles/PMC3298467/#__ffn_sectitle (accessed 15 January 2015).

Wagstaff, A and Claeson, M, *The Millennium Development Goals for Health: Rising to the Challenges* (World Bank 2004).

Wilmoth, J, Mathers, C, Say, L and Mills, S, 'Maternal Deaths Drop by One-third from 1990 to 2008: A United Nations Analysis' (2010) *Bulletin of the World Health Organization* 718-718A.

World Health Organization (Study Group on Female Genital Mutilation and Obstetric Outcome), 'Female Genital Mutilation and Obstetric Outcome: WHO Collaborative Prospective Study in Six African Countries' (2006) 367 *Lancet* 1835-1841.

World Health Organization, 'Adolescent Pregnancy' (2008) 1 *MPS Notes*, at www.who.int/maternal_child_adolescent/documents/mpsnnotes_2_lr.pdf (accessed 15 January 2015).

Yamin, AE and Boulanger, V, 'Taking Measure of the Elephant in the Room: Sexual and Reproductive Health and Rights, MDG5, and Where We Want to Go from Here', Working Paper Series, FXB Center for Health and Human Rights, Harvard School of Public Health (2013).

Zabin, LS and Kiragu, K, 'The Health Consequences of Adolescent Sexual and Fertility Behavior in sub-Saharan Africa (1998) 29 *Studies in Family Planning* 210–232.

International and Regional Instruments

Abuja Declaration on HIV and AIDS, Tuberculosis and other Infectious Diseases (2001) OAU/SPS/ABUJA/3.

African Charter on Human and Peoples' Rights, adopted 17 June 1981, entered into force 21 October 1986.

Committee on Economic, Social and Cultural Rights, General Comment No 3, 'The nature of state parties' obligations' (Fifth session, 1990), UN Doc E/1991/23, annex III at 86 (1991), reprinted in Compilation of General Comments and General Recommendations Adopted by Human Rights Treaty Bodies, UN Doc HRI/GEN/1/Rev 6 at 14 (2003).

Committee on Economic, Social and Cultural Rights, General Comment No 14, 'The right to the highest attainable standard of health' (Twenty-second session, 2000), UN Doc E/C.12/2000/4 (2000), reprinted in Compilation of General Comments and General Recommendations Adopted by Human Rights Treaty Bodies, UN Doc HRI/GEN/1/Rev 6 at 85 (2003).

Committee on the Elimination of Discrimination against Women, General Recommendation No 14, 'Female Cicrcumcision' (Ninth session, 1990), UN Doc A/45/38 (1990).

Committee on the Elimination of Discrimination against Women, General Recommendation No 24, 'Women and Health' (Twentieth session, 1999), UN Doc A/54/38 (1999).

Convention on the Elimination of All Forms of Discrimination against Women (CEDAW), adopted 18 December 1979, entered into force 3 September 1981.

Convention on the Rights of the Child, A/RES/44/25, adopted 20 November 1989, entered into force 2 September 1990.

International Covenant on Economic, Social and Cultural Rights, A/Res/21/2200, adopted 16 December 1966, entered into force 3 January 1976.

Maastricht Guidelines on Violations of Economic, Social and Cultural Rights (1997), UN Doc E/C.12/2000/13.

Protocol to the African Charter on Human and People's Rights on the Rights of Women in Africa, CAB/LEG/66.6, adopted 11 July 2003, entered into force 25 November 2005.

United Nations Population Fund (UNFPA), Report of the International Conference on Population and Development, Cairo, 5-13 September 1994, 1995, A/CONF.171/13/Rev.1.

UN General Assembly, 'Resolution on intensifying global efforts for the elimination of female genital mutilations' (2014) UN Doc A/RES/69/150.

Vienna Declaration and Programme of Action, UN Doc A/CONF.157/23, adopted 25 June 1993.

Reports

African Development Bank (AfDB), *Assessing Progress in Africa toward the Millennium Development Goals. MDG Report 2013. Food Security in Africa: Issues, Challenges and Lessons* (AfDB 2013).

AIDS Rights Alliance for Southern Africa (ARASA), 'The Women's Rights Protocol' (June 2010) *HEARD Issue Brief* (June 2010), available at http://www.google.com/url?sa=t&rct=j&q=&esrc=s&source=web&cd=1&ved=0CB4QFjAA&url=http%3A%2F%2Fwww.heard.org.za%2Fdownloads%2Fsadc-donors-brief-on-international-legal-obligations.pdf&ei=MWoyVdm1OIXhaJHsgaAF&usg=AFQjCNFa7DNk0YLurjSu_-xKzILSXl1ICA&sig2=9C4R-E524I4iQ9L_27vtDQ&bvm=bv.91071109,d.d2s (accessed 15 January 2015).

Amnesty International, *Giving Life, Risking Death: Maternal Mortality in Burkina Faso* (Amnesty International 2009).

Amnesty International, *Out of Reach: The Cost of Maternal Health in Sierra Leone* (Amnesty International 2009).

Amnesty International, *From Promises to Deliveries: Putting Human Rights at the Heart of the Millennium Goals* (Amnesty International 2010).

Centre for Reproductive Rights, 'Reproductive Rights Violations as Torture and Cruel, Inhuman, or Degrading Treatment or Punishment: A Critical Human Rights Analysis' (2011), available at http://reproductiverights.org/sites/-crr.civicactions.net/files/documents/TCIDT.pdf (accessed 15 January 2015).

Centre for Reproductive Rights and Asian-Pacific Resource & Research Centre for Women, *Women of the World: Laws and Policies Affecting their Reproductive Lives. East and Southeast Asia* (CRR and Arrow 2005).

Center for Reproductive Rights, the International Programme on Reproductive and Sexual Health Law at the University of Toronto, and the University of the Free State, *Legal Grounds: Reproductive and Sexual Rights in African Commonwealth Courts*, Vol II (CRR et al 2010).

Centre for Reproductive Rights and Women Advocates Research and Documentation Centre, *Broken Promises: Human Rights, Accountability and Maternal Death in Nigeria* (CRR and WARDC 2008).

Engender Health et al, *Advancing the Sexual and Reproductive Health and Human Rights of People Living with HIV: A Guidance Package* (Engender Health et al 2009).

Government of the Federal Republic of Nigeria, *Nigeria Millennium Development Goals Report* (2010), available at www.mdgs.gov.ng (accessed 15 January 2015).

Human Rights Council, 'Preventable maternal mortality and morbidity and human rights' (2009) UN Doc A/HRC/11/L.16/Rev 1.

Human Rights Council, 'Study by the World Health Organization on mortality among children under five years of age as a human rights concern' (2013) UN Doc A/HRC/24/60.

Human Rights Watch, *'Stop Making Excuses': Accountability for Maternal Health Care in South Africa* (Human Rights Watch 2011).

International Budget Partnership and the International Initiative on Maternal Mortality and Human Rights, *The Missing Link: Applied Budget Work as a Tool to Hold Governments Accountable for Maternal Mortality Reduction Commitments* (IBP and IIMMHR 2009).

International Center for Research on Women, *New Insights on Preventing Child Marriage: A Global Analysis of Factors and Programs* (ICRW 2007).

IPAS, 'Ensuring Women's Access to Safe Abortion: A Key Strategy for Achieving Millennium Development Goals' (IPAS 2011).

Islamic Development Bank, 'The Challenge of Achieving the Millennium Development Goals in IDB Member Countries in the Post-crisis World', IDB Occasional Paper No 16 (June 2011).

Liberia Ministry of Planning and Economic Affairs, 'Liberia 2010 MDG Report – Achieving 2015: Progress, Prospects, Constraints: Liberia's Progress towards the Millennium Development Goals' (September 2010).

Report of the Office of the United Nations High Commissioner for Human Rights on preventable maternal mortality and morbidity and human rights (UN Human Rights Council 2010) A/HRC/14/39.

Report of the UN Special Rapporteur on extreme poverty and human rights, Magdalena Sepúlveda Carmona (March 2013), UN Doc A/HRC/23/36.

Report of the UN Special Rapporteur on the right of everyone to the enjoyment of the highest attainable standard of physical and mental health, Paul Hunt (February 2004), UN Doc E/CN.4/2004/49.

Report of the UN Special Rapporteur on the right of everyone to the enjoyment of the highest attainable standard of physical and mental health, Paul Hunt (11 February 2005), UN Doc E/CN.4/2005/51.

Report of the UN Special Rapporteur on the right of everyone to the enjoyment of the highest attainable standard of physical and mental health, Paul Hunt (31 January 2008), UN Doc A/HRC/7/11.

Republic of South Africa Department of Health, 'National HIV and Syphilis Antenatal Sero-prevalence Survey in South Africa 2004' (Department of Health 2005).

UNAIDS, 'World AIDS Day Report' (UNAIDS 2011), available at http://www.unaids.org/en/media/unaids/contentassets/documents/unaidspublication/2011/jc2216_worldaidsday_report_2011_en.pdf (accessed 15 January 2015).

UNFPA, *Reducing Poverty and Achieving the Millennium Development Goals: Arguments for Investing in Reproductive Health and Rights* (UNFPA 2005).

UNFPA, *How Universal is Access to Reproductive Health? A Review of the Evidence* (UNFPA 2010).

UNFPA and Danish Institute for Human Rights, *Reproductive Rights are Human Rights: A Handbook for National Human Rights Institutions* (UNFPA and DIHR 2014).

UNIFEM, *Making the MDGs Work for All Gender-Responsive Rights-Based Approaches to the MDGs* (UNIFEM 2008).

United Nations, 'A world fit for children' (10 May 2002) UN Doc A/RES/S-27/2.

United Nations, *Millennium Development Goals Report* (UN 2009).

United Nations Children's Fund, *Female Genital Mutilation/Cutting: A Statistical Overview and Exploration of the Dynamics of Change* (UNICEF 2013).

United Nations High Commissioner for Human Rights, 'Strengthening the United Nations Human Rights Treaty Body System' (June 2012) UN Doc A/66/860.

World Health Organization, *Unsafe Abortion: Global and Regional Estimates of the Incidence of Unsafe Abortion and Associated Mortality in 2003* (5th edn, WHO 2007).

World Health Organization, *National-level Monitoring of the Achievement of Universal Access to Reproductive Health: Conceptual and Practical Considerations and Related Indicators* (WHO 2008).

World Health Organization, *Unsafe Abortion: Global and Regional Estimates of the Incidence of Unsafe Abortion and Associated Mortality in 2008* (6th edn, WHO 2011).

World Health Organization, *World Health Statistics Report* (WHO 2012).

World Health Organization, *Accelerating Universal Access to Sexual and Reproductive Health: Agenda for the African Region of the World Health Organization* (WHO 2013).

World Health Organization and UNICEF, *Countdown to 2015: Accountability for Maternal, New Born & Child Survival: The 2013 Update* (Countdown 2013).

World Health Organization, UNICEF, UNFPA and the World Bank, *Trends in Maternal Mortality 1990-2010* (WHO et al 2012).

Cases

KL v Peru, Human Rights Committee, Communication No. 1153/2003, CCPR/C/85/D1153/ 2003, views adopted on 24 October 2005.

LM and Others v Government of the Republic of Namibia [2012] NAHC 211.

Minister for Health v. Treatment Action Campaign Constitutional Court of South Africa, Case CCT 8/02.

Republic of Kenya v. Nyamu and Others Case No. 81 of 2004 Kenya High Court.

RR v Poland (Appl. No. 27617/04, 26 May 2011).

Treatment Action Campaign v Minister of Health 2012 (4) BCLR 356.

PART II
Country Case Studies

Chapter 3
The Domestic Legal Enforcement of the Right to Health in Malawi: Appraising the Litigation Potential

Enoch MacDonnell Chilemba

The right to health is fundamental in that it is considered 'indispensable for the exercise of other human rights'.[1] A number of human rights treaties recognise this right at both international and regional levels. These include the International Covenant on Economic, Social and Cultural Rights (ICESCR),[2] the Convention on the Rights of the Child (CRC)[3] and the Convention on the Rights of Persons with Disabilities (CRPD) at the international level[4] and the African Charter on Human and Peoples' Rights (ACHPR) at the African regional level.[5] Malawi is one of the states parties to these treaties.[6] States parties are expected to take measures that ensure the implementation/enforcement of human rights, including the right to health, at the national level.[7] The measures should include constitutional, legislative and judicial mechanisms, which make up the legal framework for the domestic implementation. Judicial measures entail the enforceability of the right through domestic litigation.

This chapter analyses the legal enforcement of the right to health in Malawi with particular focus on litigation.[8] After providing a general background and introduction, the chapter investigates the major health challenges facing Malawi.[9] Thereafter, it examines the extent to which the legal framework in Malawi guarantees the justiciable right to health

---

1 See Committee on Economic, Social and Cultural Rights, General Comment No 14 'The right to the highest attainable standard of health' (2000).

2 Adopted 16 December 1966, entered into force 3 January 1976. See art 12.

3 Adopted 20 November 1989, entered into force 2 September 1990. See art 24.

4 Adopted 13 December 2006, entered into force 3 May 2008. See art 25.

5 Adopted 26 June 1981, entered into force 21 October 1986. See art 16.

6 Malawi ratified the ACHPR on 17 November 1989, ratified the CRC on 2 January 1991, acceded to the CESCR on 22 December 1993 and ratified the CRPD on 27 August 2009.

7 Committee on Economic, Social and Cultural Rights, General Comment No 14, paras 53-56.

8 Accordingly, it focuses on laws (legislation) and judicial cases as opposed to policies and other measures.

9 It is noteworthy that there are successes as well as challenges in Malawi's health sector. See, for example, Malawi Government Ministry of Health (MoH), *Malawi Health Sector Strategic Plan 2011-2016: Moving towards Equity and Quality* (MoH 2011) 37. However, in accordance with its scope and purpose, this chapter only considers the challenges as it is they which necessitate litigation.

and analyses applicable domestic judicial decisions that have dealt with health matters in order to assess the potential of litigating the right in Malawi. Finally, the challenges and opportunities for Malawi's future implementation of the right to health through litigation are explored.

Major Health Challenges Facing Malawi

The ICESCR guarantees the right to health and obliges states parties to ensure 'the enjoyment of the highest attainable standard of physical and mental health'.[10] Inter alia, the ICESCR requires states to take measures necessary for the 'creation of conditions which would assure to all medical service and medical attention in the event of sickness'.[11] The Committee on Economic, Social and Cultural Rights (CESCR), which monitors the implementation of the Covenant,[12] has interpreted the right to health in General Comment No 14. According to the CESCR, the right entails that quality health care facilities must be available, accessible, affordable and acceptable to all.[13] These can be referred to as the '4As international standards' relating to the right to health that states parties such as Malawi should realise.

However, it has generally been established that the provision of health services in Malawi is beset by impediments that make compliance with the '4As standards' a pipedream. The obstacles include lack of access to health care facilities, shortage of trained medical personnel, poor provision of services that constitute 'determinants to health' and specific challenges relating to maternal mortality, disability and high prevalence of major diseases.

Lack of Access to Health Care

Malawi's health sector has always comprised both private and public facilities, with the government providing 60 per cent of all health services as early as 1995.[14] However, due to a number of factors there is a general lack of access to health care amenities such as hospitals and essential medicines. First, there are few hospitals or clinics, and these are not evenly distributed as they are often clustered in urban areas.[15] For example, there is no government health facility in Likoma Island district, while in Chitipa district, 51 per

10 Art 12(1).

11 Art 12(2)(d).

12 The Committee was established pursuant to United Nations Economic and Social Council (ECOSOC) resolution 1985/17 of 28 May 1985 to carry out the monitoring functions assigned to ECOSOC under Part IV of the ICESCR.

13 General Comment No 14, para 12.

14 See generally E Ngalande-Banda and G Walt, 'The Private Health Sector in Malawi: Opening Pandora's Box?' (1995) 7 *Journal of International Development*, 403, 405. See also E Ngalande-Banda and HP Simukonda, 'The Public/Private Mix in the Health Care System in Malawi' (1994) 9 *Health Policy and Planning* 63.

15 B Lunan et al, 'Maternal Health in Malawi: Challenges and Successes', Scotland Malawi Partnership (2010), 12-13.

cent of the population lives more than 8 km from a health facility.[16] In addition, many rural places have dysfunctional health infrastructure or none at all.[17] Furthermore, most government hospitals do not provide certain essential and important services mainly due to lack of equipment.[18]

Second, Malawi faces persistent, severe drug shortage problems especially in public health care facilities.[19] It was reported that the drug shortage had reached 95 per cent in 2013, and had reached (been reduced to) 65 per cent by January 2015.[20] This implies that Malawi had in stock only 5 per cent in 2013 and 35 per cent in 2015 of essential drugs. The problem is exacerbated by factors that include lengthy procurement processes, weak logistical information systems and inadequate and unpredictable funding.[21] Furthermore, donors contribute almost 80 per cent of Malawi's annual budget for medical supplies – a position that has been acknowledged to be unsustainable.[22] The government has also observed that the budget for medicines and medical supplies is not commensurate with the number of patients that hospitals receive.[23]

Third, Malawi's health sector suffers from a shortage of trained medical personnel.[24] This is reportedly compounded by the 'brain drain' which continues to hit the sector.[25] The shortage is acute in rural areas where, for example, only 32 per cent of rural women have a trained attendant at birth.[26] The government concedes that Malawi is not anywhere near to reaching the staff numbers needed to provide minimum standards of health service delivery.[27] In addition, Malawi has limited specialised training for professional health workers such as doctors and nurses.[28] The shortage of trained medical personnel

16 MoH, *Malawi Health Sector Strategic Plan 2011-2016* (n 9 above) 33-35.

17 Ibid.

18 Malawi Government, *Report on Health Services Reform: Improving Public Health Services Delivery in Malawi* (Public Sector Reforms Management Unit 2012) 13-14.

19 See generally 'Malawi CSO's Lament Bad Governance: Stick to Jan 13 Demo' *Nyasa Times*, 3 January 2015, at http://www.nyasatimes.com/2015/01/03/malawi-csos-lament-bad-governance-stick-to-jan-13-demo/ (accessed 26 February 2015); Oxfam, *Missing Medicines in Malawi: Campaigning against 'Stock Outs' of Essential Drugs* (Oxfam 2012); Ngalande-Banda and Walt (n 14 above) 409; World Health Organization, *Malawi: Essential Drugs Programme: Midterm Report* (WHO 1994); Refworld, 'Malawi's Never-ending Drug Shortage Problem', 29 May 2013, at http://www.refworld.org/category,COI,IRIN,MWI,51276c762,0.html (accessed 26 February 2015).

20 See 'Drug Shortage Now at 65%' *The Nation*, 8 January 2014, at http://mwnation.com/drug-shortage-now-65/ (accessed 26 February 2015).

21 MoH, *Malawi Health Sector Strategic Plan 2011-2016* (n 9 above) 30.

22 Malawi Government, *Report on Health Services Reform* (n 18 above) 13-14.

23 Ibid, iv-x.

24 See, for example, World Health Organization et al, 'Malawi: Rapid Assessment of Sexual and Reproductive Health and HIV Linkages' (2011) 6. See also UNICEF, 'Malawi', at http://www.unicef.org/malawi/health_nutrition_3951.html (accessed 25 February 2015).

25 See Help Malawi, 'Challenges in Healthcare', at http://helpchildren.org/about/why-malawi/culture/ (accessed 26 February 2015).

26 Lunan et al (n 15 above) 15.

27 MoH, *Malawi Health Sector Strategic Plan 2011-2016* (n 9 above) 31.

28 Malawi Government *Report on Health Services Reform* (n 18 above) iv-x.

compounds the lack of access to health care and derails the implementation of the right to health.

Poor Service Provision of 'Determinants of Health'

Malawi experiences obstacles to the provision of most of the 'social determinants' of health – a position which impacts negatively on the right to health.[29] For example, there is limited access to safe and potable water and sanitation, which contributes to poor health.[30] Similarly, although there were significant efforts taken in 2011 to improve drinking water sources in urban and rural areas, these efforts merely denoted about 38 per cent of piped water into premises in urban areas and only 2 per cent in rural areas.[31] Furthermore, the government's relevant strategies for implementing core obligations of socio-economic rights (SERs), including most of the social determinants of health, are not well funded or supported by the required infrastructure, skills and personnel.[32] Indeed, there is widespread malnutrition among children, which has not improved since 1992, with 46 per cent of children under the age of 5 stunted, 21 per cent underweight and 48 per cent chronically malnourished.[33]

High Prevalence of Major Diseases

Malawi registers high prevalent rates of major diseases such as malaria, tuberculosis and HIV/AIDS.[34] The HIV/AIDS prevalence rate is 12 per cent, with women accounting for

---

29 'Determinants of health' are those conditions that make it possible for persons to live and enjoy good health, and include access to safe water, adequate food and nutrition, and housing. See Committee on Economic, Social and Cultural Rights, General Comment No 14, paras 4 and 11. See also African Commission on Human and Peoples' Rights, 'Principles and Guidelines on the Implementation of Economic, Social and Cultural Rights in the African Charter on Human and Peoples' Rights' (2010) para 63.

30 See African Women's Development and Communication Network (FEMNET), *Assessment of the Implementation by Malawi Government of the International Conference on Population and Development (ICPD) and Other Relevant International and Regional Instruments* (FEMNET 2007) 28; *US Agency for International Development (USAID) 'Malawi: Water and Sanitation Profile', at http://www.wsscc.org/resources/resource-publications/malawi-water-and-sanitation-profile* (accessed 26 February 2015).

31 World Health Organization, 'Malawi: Country Profiles', at http://www.who.int/gho/countries/mwi/country_profiles/en/index.html (accessed 26 February 2015).

32 FEMNET, *Assessment of the Implementation by Malawi Government of ICPD* (n 30 above) 37.

33 Help Malawi, 'Challenges in Healthcare' (n 25 above); MoH, *Malawi Health Sector Strategic Plan 2011-2016* (n 9 above) 20. See also Committee on the Rights of the Child, 'Concluding Observations: Malawi' (2009) para 51.

34 M Lawson et al, 'Malawi Essential Health Services Campaign: For All Campaign: Country Case Study', Oxfam Research Report (2008), 10; MoH, *Malawi Health Sector Strategic Plan 2011-2016* (n 9 above) 24.

60 per cent of those living positively.[35] In addition, there are obstacles to the implementation of the national response to the HIV/AIDS problem.[36] For example, the response does not adequately reach the marginalised and vulnerable populations because programmes do not specifically target them.[37] In addition, the prevalence rate is higher for women and girls, and yet viable gender specific programmes are limited.[38] Furthermore, there is limited access to opportunistic infections (OIs) treatment and antiretrovirals (ARVs). For example, in 2011, only 32 per cent of eligible children were on ARVs and the coverage of OIs treatment was only about 20 per cent of need.[39]

Malaria remains the leading cause of death in Malawi, especially among children and pregnant women, and about six million cases occur every year.[40] The situation is attributable, among other things, to the low coverage of insecticide residual spraying and poor adherence to treatment guidelines and policies, which affect the implementation of malaria interventions.[41] Furthermore, Malawi is burdened with the problem of communicable and non-communicable diseases.[42]

Maternal and Mental Health Challenges

Malawi has one of the highest maternal mortality ratios in the world, capable of reaching 807 per 100,000 live births when it rises but occasionally dropping to 406 per 100,000.[43] This is mainly attributable to poor access to health services, including drugs.[44] For example, the relevant statistics show that only 54 per cent of women deliver in health facilities,[45]

35 World Health Organization, 'Malawi Health Profile' (2011), at http://www.who.int/gho/countries/mwi.pdf (accessed 26 February 2015); J Fleischman, *The Global Health Initiative in Malawi: New Approaches and Challenges to Reaching Women and Girls* (Centre for Strategic and International Studies 2011) 5.

36 Malawi Government, *2012 Global AIDS Response Report: Malawi Country Report for 2010 and 2011* (2012).

37 Ibid, 50.

38 Ibid, 49.

39 MoH, *Malawi Health Sector Strategic Plan 2011-2016* (n 9 above) 26 and 27.

40 Ibid, 19; UNICEF, 'Malawi' (n 24 above).

41 MoH, *Malawi Health Sector Strategic Plan 2011-2016* (n 9 above) 20.

42 See, for example, MoH, *Malawi Health Sector Strategic Plan 2011-2016* (n 9 above), 20 and 28; KP Msyamboza et al, 'The Burden of Selected Chronic Non-communicable Diseases and their Risk Factors in Malawi: Nationwide STEPS Survey' (2011) 6(5) *PLoS ONE* e20316.

43 UNICEF, 'Malawi' (n 24 above); Centre for Human Rights and Rehabilitation, 'Malawi: Submission to the UN Universal Periodic Review. Ninth Session of the UPR Working Group of the Human Rights Council' (2010) 6. Newspaper reports suggest that the rate had reduced to 460 deaths per 100,000 in 2013. See 'Malawi Continues to Reduce Maternal Deaths' *Daily Times*, 23 May 2013, at http://bnltimes.com/index.php/daily-times/headlines/national/15152-malawi-continues-to-reduce-maternal-deaths (accessed 24 May 2013).

44 Fleischman (n 35 above) 5. See also Lunan et al (n 15 above) 12 and 14; UK Kafulafula et al, 'The Challenges Facing Nurse-Midwives in Working towards Safe Motherhood in Malawi' (2005) 17(4) *Malawi Medical Journal* 125-127.

45 Help Malawi, 'Challenges in Healthcare' (n 25 above).

while about 74 per cent of maternal deaths that are attributable to poor accessibility could be prevented if all women had access to proper sexual and reproductive health care services.[46] However, a comparison of the country statistics within the Southern African Development Community region shows that it is not only Malawi that is experiencing such high maternal mortality ratios. For example, the figures compiled by the World Health Organization (WHO) and other international bodies show that in 2010 the maternal mortality ratio was 460 per 100,000 live births in Malawi, 570 in Zimbabwe, 300 in South Africa, 440 in Zambia, 490 in Mozambique and 460 in Tanzania.[47] Nevertheless, the high ratio, which includes deaths that could have been prevented, shows that maternal mortality is a challenge Malawi needs to address.

Malawi also faces health challenges pertaining to disability, especially in the field of mental health.[48] It has been observed that mental treatment is often not successful and that medication and medical professional expertise are not usually available principally because of their acute shortage.[49] Indeed, Malawi has minimal availability of skilled mental health workers with the effect that it has a 100 per cent vacancy rate for clinical psychologist positions.[50] Furthermore, persons with disabilities continue to face disability-related/based barriers to accessing health services.[51]

In view of these challenges, it can be observed that Malawi is not implementing the right to health as envisaged by international law. Hence, it would be relevant to evaluate Malawi's legal implementation framework in order to establish whether it provides avenues for redress, including through litigation.

The Legal Framework on the Right to Health in Malawi

Malawi has a dualist legal system, which requires ratified treaties to be incorporated by an Act of Parliament to become domestically enforceable.[52] However, the Constitution provides that the treaties Malawi ratified before the commencement of the 1995 Constitution automatically attain domestic applicability.[53] The Constitution and a number of laws also have provisions that have implications for the realisation of the right to health.[54]

---

46 Lunan et al (n 15 above) 15.

47 See generally World Health Organization et al, *Trends in Maternal Mortality: 1990-2010* (WHO 2012) 37-45.

48 See, for example, MoH, *Malawi Health Sector Strategic Plan 2011-2016* (n 9 above) 28.

49 Malawi Human Rights Commission, *Report on Monitoring of Mental Health Hospitals And Selected Outreach Facilities in Malawi* (Malawi Human Rights Commission 2012) 33.

50 MoH, *Malawi Health Sector Strategic Plan 2011-2016* (n 9 above) 28.

51 Ibid, 27. See also SINTEF et al, *Living Conditions of Persons with Activity Limitations in Malawi* (SINTEF 2004).

52 See Constitution of Malawi, 1995, sec 211(1); *Chakufwa Tom Chihana v The Republic* [1992] 15 MLR 86 (Supreme Court).

53 See sec 211(2). See also DM Chirwa, *Human Rights under the Malawian Constitution* (Juta 2011) 29-30.

54 See below for further discussion of the implications of the dualist/monist position.

The Constitutional Framework

The Malawi Constitution does not expressly regard health as a justiciable right. This is because the 'right' is contained in section 13, which sets out principles of national policy that are merely directory, although courts are expected to take them into account when enforcing the Constitution.[55] The principles expect the state to achieve goals that promote the people's welfare and development by 'progressively adopting and implementing policies and legislation'. Section 13 contains four principles on health, environment, nutrition and children that expressly mention (and relate to) health.[56] Regarding health, the state is expected to 'provide adequate health care, commensurate with the health needs of Malawian society and international standards of health care'. In respect of children, the state must 'encourage and promote conditions conducive to the full development of healthy, productive and responsible members of society'. Regarding the environment, it should provide a healthy living and working environment for the people through responsible environmental management. Lastly, in respect of nutrition, the state is expected to 'achieve adequate nutrition for all in order to promote good health and self-sufficiency'.

Furthermore, the Constitution's justiciable Bill of Rights contains a number of provisions that are related to health. First, section 23(2)(c) recognises the justiciable right of children to be protected from any treatment that is likely to be harmful to their health. Section 30(2) recognises the justiciable rights to access health services, food, shelter and basic resources as elements/components of the right to development. The Constitution also explicitly guarantees prisoners and other detained persons the justiciable right(s) to adequate nutrition and medical treatment at the expense of the state.[57] In addition, the Constitution contains other justiciable rights that have implications for health. For example, it protects the right to dignity and freedom from torture under section 19, which includes the right not to be subjected to medical or scientific experimentation without consent or to corporal punishment.[58] It further recognises the right to life under section 16 and the right to freedom from discrimination under section 20 with the effect that it prohibits discrimination in accessing health care services.

Therefore, although the Constitution could be regarded as not expressly recognising the justiciable right to health, it contains provisions and other justiciable rights that constitute elements of the right.[59] Indeed, in a number of cases Malawian courts have applied and 'interpreted' certain constitutional provisions relating to health.[60]

---

55 See sec 14.

56 See sec 13, paras (b), (c), (d) and (h).

57 Sec 42(1)(b).

58 Sec 19(1), (3), (4) and (5).

59 For further discussion relating to Malawi's constitutional protection of SERs, see DM Chirwa, 'A Full Loaf is Better than Half: The Constitutional Protection of Economic, Social and Cultural Rights in Malawi' (2005) 49(2) *Journal of African Law* 207.

60 See below for further discussion on how the Malawian courts have applied the constitutional and other applicable legal provisions in interpreting and enforcing health rights.

The Legislative Framework

Public Health Act, 1948

The Public Health Act (PHA) is Malawi's principal health legislation that provides for matters relating to public health.[61] It requires, inter alia, the Local Authority to take 'reasonable and practicable measures for preventing the occurrence or dealing with any outbreak or prevalence of any infectious communicable or preventable disease' and to safeguard and promote the public health.[62] Part III of the Act makes provision on how 'notifiable' diseases should be contained, which includes by cleansing and disinfecting any affected/infected premises.[63] Part V provides for measures that must be taken to contain 'formidable epidemic or endemic diseases', which include smallpox, cholera, yellow fever, cerebro-spinal meningitis, typhus, and sleeping sickness.[64] The measures include destruction or disinfection of buildings or goods and restricting the immigration to or emigration from affected areas/premises. The PHA further provides for the prevention of the introduction of infectious diseases into Malawi and also makes provision for matters relating to sanitation.[65] Furthermore, it sets out the obligation of the Local Authority to construct, provide and maintain public sewers, drainage and latrines.[66] In addition, the Act requires the prevention of water pollution, the prohibition/prevention of selling or transacting in unwholesome food or animal products such as milk[67] and the implementation of obligations relating to cemeteries, crematoria and exhumation of dead bodies.[68]

It appears that the Act was not drafted with a view to impose a duty on the state to realise the substantive right to health but to ensure public health in general through the prevention of epidemics, among other things.[69]

Pharmacies, Medicines and Poisons Act, 1988

The Act provides for the training, registration and disciplining of pharmacists, pharmacy technologists and pharmacy assistants; the licensing of traders in medicines and poisons; the general control and regulation of the profession of pharmacy in Malawi and other related matters.[70] For example, Part II of the Act establishes the Pharmacy, Medicines and

61 Chapter 34:01 of the Laws of Malawi.

62 Sec 7.

63 See also secs 13 and 16. Sec 11 provides that 'notifiable' diseases include anthrax, cerebro-spinal meningitis, cholera, diphtheria, dysentery and typhoid fever.

64 See generally Part V and secs 30 and 31(a)-(t).

65 See generally Part VI, secs 38-41 and Part IX.

66 Part X.

67 Part XIII.

68 Part XIV.

69 The Act does not contain any human rights provision. See also MG Kachedwa, 'An Investigation of the Adequacy of the Health Research Governance System in Malawi' (unpublished Mph thesis, University of Malawi, College of Medicine 2009) 57, for the views of authors such as Kachedwa on the Act.

70 Chapter 35:01 of the Laws of Malawi.

Poisons Board,[71] whose functions include regulating the training of pharmacy professionals and advising on matters relating to medicinal products and poisons.[72] Part III establishes, inter alia, a Pharmacy Committee to regulate any pharmacy business,[73] while Parts IV and V deal with matters such as licensing of any dealings in medicinal products.[74]

Occupational Health, Safety and Welfare Act, 1997

This Act regulates the safety, health and welfare of employed persons in the workplace.[75] It requires every workplace to ensure the provision or maintenance of cleanliness, first aid, medical examination, sanitary conveniences, drinking water, washing facilities, ventilation and appropriate temperature, lighting, prevention of overcrowding and drainage of floor.[76] For example, it requires the provision of an accessible and adequate supply of clean and potable drinking water,[77] a first aid box or cupboard of the prescribed standard which is readily accessible, arrangements for ensuring the removal for medical attention of employees who have suffered an accident or sudden illness,[78] and medical examination before engagement of work if it is necessary in the interest of the health or safety of the person to employed.[79]

Disability Act, 2012

This Act, which provides for rights and matters pertaining to persons with disabilities in Malawi,[80] recognises the right to health care services in section 6 and in section 7 further prohibits discrimination against persons with disabilities in accessing health services.[81] In addition, section 6(2) imposes a number of obligations on the state in realising the right. These include the duty to provide 'the same range, quality and standard of free or affordable healthcare services as provided to other persons, including sexual and reproductive health services and population based public health programmes'.[82] The Act can be regarded as Malawi's first legislation expressly to recognise the justiciable right to health care, although it applies to persons with disabilities.

---

71 See sec 3.

72 Secs 10 and 11.

73 See secs 17 and 18-33.

74 See secs 34-38 and 46-49. There is also subsidiary legislation to the Act composed of a number of regulations.

75 Chapter 55:07 of the Laws of Malawi. See Part IV.

76 See generally secs 22-34.

77 Sec 29(1) and (2).

78 Sec 33(1)-(4).

79 Sec 34.

80 Act 8 of 2012.

81 See sec 6(1), which provides in part that 'The Government shall provide appropriate health care services to persons with disabilities.' See also EM Chilemba, 'Malawi' (2014) *African Disability Rights Yearbook* 207, 225.

82 See sec 6(2)(c).

Gender Equality Act, 2012

This Act recognises the right to sexual and reproductive health (SRH) in section 19.[83] It also imposes duties on health officers pertaining to SRH in section 20, which mainly require them to respect the SRH rights of every person without discrimination and the dignity and integrity of every person accessing SRH services.[84]

Other laws

There are also other laws, such as the Mental Treatment Act,[85] which apply to the health sector.[86] For example, the Nurses and Midwives Act mainly establishes the Nurses and Midwives Council to regulate the certification, licensing and disciplining of nurses and midwives.[87] For its part, the Medical Practitioners and Dentists Act makes provision for the regulation, registration, licensing, disciplining and training of medical practitioners, dentists and allopathic physicians, and of medical personnel generally.[88] It also establishes the Medical Council of Malawi to regulate all medical practice, including private practice.[89]

Furthermore, the Second Schedule to the Local Government Act provides for a Local Assembly's health functions.[90] These include to provide, manage and maintain health facilities such as clinics and to employ medical professional and ancillary staff; to ensure sanitation and control nuisances; and to establish, maintain and manage emergency services such as ambulance and fire fighting services.[91] The Anatomy Act makes provision for the donation, examination and use of bodies, or parts of bodies, of deceased persons for educational, scientific, research, therapeutic or diagnostic purposes, including inquests and post-mortems, and for the law dealing with human tissue.[92] Lastly, the Workers' Compensation Act provides for compensation for injuries suffered or diseases contracted by workers in the course of their employment or for death resulting from such injuries or diseases.[93]

83 Act 3 of 2013.

84 See, for example, sec 20(1)(a) and (b).

85 Chapter 34:02 of the Laws of Malawi. The Mental Health Bill, 2005 has been drafted to replace the Act. Sec 55 of the Bill contains rights such as the right to 'the best available mental healthcare, which shall be part of the health and social care system'.

86 It is not within the scope of this chapter to provide a detailed discussion of such laws.

87 Act 16 of 1995.

88 Act 17 of 1986.

89 It is noteworthy that the Act recognises 'traditional medical practice'. See sec 61.

90 Act 32 of 1998.

91 See generally sec 1.

92 Chapter 34:03 of the Laws of Malawi. See generally Part II and secs 3 and 4.

93 Chapter 55:03 of the Laws of Malawi. Further discussion of the implication of the legislative framework on litigation can be found below.

The Health Rights Litigation Burden before Malawian Courts

Courts in Malawi have not yet dealt with the substantive right to health, probably because the right is not regarded as justiciable. Nevertheless, the courts have adjudicated upon a number of cases that raise health issues. It is relevant to analyse some of the cases to establish whether they point to a potential for litigation.

Health Care Services and Rights of Prisoners

Prison conditions and health care

In the *Masangano* case,[94] the applicants, who invoked the Constitution and the Prisons Act,[95] challenged the constitutionality of the deplorable conditions in prisons. They claimed that the conditions amounted to violations of their rights, particularly the right not to be subjected to torture and cruel, inhuman and degrading treatment or punishment. The High Court (sitting as the Constitutional Court) described one complaint as alleging:

> That prisoners are denied access to medical attention and the right dose for a person to fully recover and are even asked the offence they committed before receiving any medical attention and are even sometimes given wrong dosage.[96]

This complaint raises health issues relating to access to medical treatment. The other complaints, which alleged poor and insufficient food and diet, also impacted on the determinants of health. The applicants did not claim a violation of their right to health. In its judgment, the Court found the state's argument that SERs are generally not justiciable in Malawi to be 'out of touch' with modern legal and judicial thinking. The state had also argued that the claims relating to health, food and clothing are not justiciable in terms of section 13 of the Constitution. The Court found that although the principles in section 13 are only directory, courts could still invoke them in terms of section 14 of the Constitution when applying or interpreting constitutional provisions or reviewing executive decisions.

In observing that overcrowding in prisons leads to outbreak of diseases, the Court stated:

> In the case at hand, we would like to observe that the Applicants complain of overcrowding. It is the same overcrowding which the Prison Inspectorate noted was aggravated by poor ventilation and which contributed to the death of 259 inmates in a space of about 18 months … That overcrowding has been noted as one factors [sic] creating the spread of diseases in prison such as tuberculosis which has been said to be a major cause of sickness and death in prison, along with HIV (see Malawi Policy on Tuberculosis Control in Prisons, June 2007) … Put simply, the overcrowding and poor ventilation in our prisons amounts to

94 *Gable Masangano (Suing on his own behalf and on behalf of all prisoners in Malawi) v the Attorney General & Others* Constitutional Cause No 15 of 2007.

95 Chapter 9:02 of the Laws of Malawi.

96 *Masangano* case (Constitutional Cause No 15 of 2007) 5.

> inhuman and degrading treatment of the inmates and therefore contrary to Section 19 of the Republic of Malawi Constitution.[97]

It is surprising that despite finding that overcrowding causes outbreaks of disease, the Court did not mention that this could lead to a violation of the right to health. Instead, it only found a violation of the right to human dignity. Perhaps the justiciability mystery influenced its reasoning. Nevertheless, it ruled in favour of the prisoners on a number of grounds and stated:

> We would like to reaffirm that prisoners' rights include right to food, clothing, accessories and cell equipment to the minimum standards as set out in the Prisons Act and Prison Regulations ... We also affirm that prisoners have a right to appropriate prison accommodation which is not congested and which has appropriate ventilation. They have the right to access to medical attention and treatment like any other human being.[98]

The judgment is commendable as the Court acknowledged that prisoners have the right to access medical attention and treatment 'like any other human being', which is an element of the substantive right to health. However, the main drawback is that the Court did not refer to the right to health despite finding violations of its elements. Although the applicants did not invoke the right, the Court had sufficient basis to acknowledge that the deplorable conditions could threaten the right to health. Nevertheless, this case demonstrates that the courts are willing to welcome litigation that invokes the elements/determinants of the right to health.

Right to health in bail applications

In the *Mphembedzu* case,[99] the applicant requested the Court to release him from custody on bail on the ground of his ill-health, among other things. The Court ruled in his favour.[100] The case raised health issues as the medical report that was submitted showed that the applicant's health would continue to deteriorate if he remained in detention. In recognising the right to health, the Court stated:

> This Court however, concurs with Counsel for the Applicant in his submission that the authorities have a legal and moral obligation to protect the right to health of prison inmates. This Court would however, add that this obligation extends to all other citizens. This is clear from Section 13 (c) of the Constitution of the Republic of Malawi.[101]

Thus, the Court expressly stated that the Constitution protects the right to health of all citizens. It further indicated that there are sufficient domestic legal provisions that protect

---

97 *Masangano* case (Constitutional Cause No 15 of 2007) 55 and 56.

98 *Masangano* case (Constitutional Cause No 15 of 2007) 59 and 60.

99 *Chimwemwe Mphembedzu v The Republic* Bail Case No 70 of 2011; [2011] MWHC 12.

100 It is noteworthy that the state did not object to the bail application.

101 *Mphembedzu* case (Bail Case No 70 of 2011; [2011] MWHC 12) 3 and 4.

the right. This finding suggests that despite the 'right' being classified under the directory principles, the state retains the obligation to protect it. These findings are commendable and strengthen the potential for litigation.

Furthermore, although the Court did not adjudicate on the substantive right to health care, it hinted at the possibility of determining substantive health issues when it observed:

> This Court is also mindful of the fact that the present application is not concerned with the determination of the issue whether or not the authorities have provided adequate health care to the Applicant as an inmate or a prisoner. Had this been the case then this Court would have probably found the said provisions relevant.[102]

Therefore, the Court hinted that it could have adjudicated on the prisoners' substantive right to health care if it had been raised. This development is commendable and shows that there is great potential for litigating the substantive right to health in Malawi.

In the *Lambat* case,[103] the applicant applied to be released from detention on bail on the basis of ill-health. The state opposed the application. The Court conceded that 'illness of an applicant *per se* is not a ground for consideration by the court in granting bail unless the same is shown to have arisen consequent upon incarceration'.[104] The express acknowledgement of this principle alone shows that the courts (are willing to) respect the health of an individual. However, there was no evidence that the applicant's ill-health was caused by the detention. Nevertheless, the Court ruled in favour of the applicant. This further demonstrates the courts' resolve to respect the right to health.

The Individual Right to Health Care in Judicial Reviews

The right to health care as a statutory benefit

In *Ex Parte Muluzi*,[105] the applicant challenged the government's decision to refuse to fund his trip to South Africa for medical attention unless a panel of local independent doctors had examined him. The applicant argued that as a former head of state, he was entitled to medical attention and treatment at the expense of the state under the Presidents' (Salaries and Benefits) Act.[106] The Court found in his favour. The state had argued that the Constitution does not guarantee the right to free health services and that instead section 13(c) expects the state to develop health care policies and legislation. The Court took a position on the issue and observed as follows:

---

102 *Mphembedzu* case (Bail Case No 70 of 2011; [2011] MWHC 12) 4 and 5.

103 *Numtaz Maluk Lambat v The Republic* judgment of 22 September 2008; [2008] MWHC 175; Miscellaneous Criminal Application No 202 of 2008.

104 *Lambat* case (Miscellaneous Criminal Application No 202 of 2008) 7.

105 *The State and Secretary to the President and Cabinet, Ex Parte Dr Bakili Muluzi* Miscellaneous Civil Application No 3 of 2011.

106 Chapter 2:02 of the Laws of Malawi.

> It is equally true however that the legislature in its wisdom and while aware of the provision of section 13(c) above-mentioned decided to make special provision for our Presidents' and their Vices past and present salaries and benefits. Such benefits included the free medical services mentioned above ... this right is without geographical, fiscal or other limitation. He can have the medical services practically anywhere and for whatever ailment and at whatever cost. Government or the insurer will pay.[107]

Although the case raises health issues, it was not decided from the stand point of the right to health but from constitutional and administrative law perspectives. The Court found that since the law granted the applicant the benefit to access 'free' medical services once a clinical decision was made that he needed medical attention, the state could not refuse to cover the related costs. Perhaps the Court missed the opportunity to make reference to the fact that the states' delay in releasing the funds could threaten the applicant's right to health.

Furthermore, the Court made other observations that have implications on the right to health. It acknowledged, inter alia, that the right to free medical health services is not recognised in Malawi:

> It must be appreciated that medical services are not by right free in this country. The Presidents and their Vices past and present are a special class. Patients may at government hospices get treatment for free if they are lucky. They may also be called upon to even at government hospices pay a little something from time to time.[108]

Accordingly, it follows that if any person (other than prisoners) cannot afford to pay for medical services/treatment (since the state is moving away from providing free medical services[109]), the courts would be reluctant to provide an effective remedy. Since the right to health entails that medical/health services must be affordable, it would be interesting to see how the courts approach the issue of economic accessibility of health services. Hence, it can be observed that the *Ex Parte Muluzi* case does not provide many insights into the substantive right to health due to the uniqueness of the case. Apparently, the case leaves an unsolved 'justiciability conundrum' that could impact on the potential of litigating the right to health in Malawi.

The right to health as ground for compensation

In the *Nowa* case,[110] the applicant sought a review of the National Compensations Tribunal's order declining to compensate him for his ill-health which was attributable to

---

107 *Ex Parte Muluzi* case (Miscellaneous Civil Application No 3 of 2011) 16 and 17.

108 *Ex Parte Muluzi* case (Miscellaneous Civil Application No 3 of 2011) 18.

109 See generally 'Malawi to Introduce Paying Fees in Hospitals – Minister', *Nyasa Times*, 24 February 2015, at http://www.nyasatimes.com/2015/02/24/malawi-to-introduce-paying-fees-in-hospitals-minister/ (accessed 26 February 2015); 'No "Freebies": Malawi Introduces Paying Services in Public Hospitals' *Nyasa Times*, 13 May 2013, at http://www.nyasatimes.com/2013/05/13/no-freebies-malawi-reintroduces-paying-services-in-public-hospitals/ (accessed 26 February 2015).

110 *Nowa v The State and National Compensation Tribunal* [2002–2003] MLR 192 (HC).

his imprisonment. The applicant had developed severe gouty tophi due to the authorities' neglect to have him treated when he was in custody. The Court ruled that it was erroneous for the Tribunal to decline to compensate the applicant when medical reports had demonstrated the clear link between his condition and imprisonment. Accordingly, the Court awarded the applicant a sum of money in compensation.

The case is linked to the right to health since the Court acknowledged that the state's failure to provide medical treatment amounted to an 'atrocity'.[111] Therefore, although the Court did not expressly find a violation of the right to health, it protected the right by ordering the state to compensate him for perpetrating the ill-health suffered. Perhaps under the circumstances the Court should have made explicit reference to the fact that the applicant's right to health was violated. Nonetheless, this case shows the courts' willingness to entertain claims that relate to violations of the right to health or its aspects.

The Right to Health in Other Instances

The courts have further respected and protected the right to health in a number of cases. For example, in the case in which Malawi's former diplomat to Mozambique was convicted of abuse of office, the court suspended his 16 month prison sentence after he pleaded ill-health.[112] In another case in which Malawi's former president was facing criminal prosecution for the offences of abuse of office and corruption, the court postponed the commencement of the trial on numerous occasions (in 2006 and later in 2009) to allow him to seek medical attention in South Africa.[113] Consequently, it took over four years before trial finally resumed in April 2013. This demonstrates the courts' resolve to protect the right to health whenever called upon to do so.[114] Lastly, in *The Republic v Abdul Rahman*, the Magistrates Court observed:

> food, education and shelter are basic rights and are reflected in the Bill of Right Chapter of the Malawian Constitution and as a nation that ratified the Human Right Charter, we have to uphold and preserve such rights especially if the parties seeking those are asylum seekers.[115]

Although the decision might not bind the High Court as it was handed out by a subordinate court, the finding is commendable for recognising that Malawi is under obligation to 'realise' food and shelter, which are determinants of health and are explicitly mentioned in section 30(2) of the Constitution. It suggests that the courts expect these determinants to be protected.

---

111 The Constitution established the Tribunal to compensate victims of 'atrocities' committed by the one-party government, which was in power between 1964 and 1994. See sec 137.

112 *Republic v Chibambo* Criminal Case No 122 of 2007.

113 *The State v Dr Bakili Muluzi* & *Another* Criminal Case No 1 of 2009.

114 See also *Mendulo v Malawi Revenue Authority* IRC Matter No 161 of 2003, where the court's finding that the applicant's lie that his health was not suited to work in hot areas amounted to insubordination and dishonesty (impliedly) shows that the right should not be abused.

115 *The Republic v Abdul Rahman & Others (Somalians)* Criminal Cause No 26 of 2006, 4.

In light of the foregoing discussion, it can be observed that the general perception that Malawi's domestic legal framework does not recognise the substantive justiciable right to health is the major factor that militates against litigating the right to health in Malawi. As will be discussed below, this perception derails the efforts to ensure state accountability in health service provision.

Prospects for Health Rights Litigation in Malawi

Challenges to Future Litigation

It is noteworthy that domestic courts are expected to enforce legal provisions that have domestic applicability. However, Malawi's applicable legal framework does not indicate how or whether Malawi is bound to implement the 4As international standards relating to the right to health. The Constitution does not explicitly guarantee the justiciable right to health but only recognises other elements of the right that are justiciable. However, most of these are guaranteed to specific categories, including children or prisoners, or they could qualify as elements of other rights such as development.[116] Furthermore, the Constitution does not expressly recognise other determinants of health, for example food, nutrition, water and shelter, as substantive justiciable rights. Instead, they are regarded as elements of other substantive rights such as development.[117] The explicit health provisions in section 13 of the Constitution merely require the state to adopt policies and legislation to achieve the goals relating to health. Since the provisions are not justiciable, it is uncertain whether the state could be successfully sued if it fails to adopt or implement the appropriate policies and laws. This 'ambiguous' position taken by the Constitution has a negative impact on the potential of litigating the substantive right to health.

In addition, it appears that most of the applicable legislative provisions were not drafted with a view to 'recognising' the broad right to health. On the one hand, the legislation picks out certain or specific elements of the right that can be enforced before the courts. For example, the Gender Equality Act picks the right to SRH, while the Disability Act recognises the right to 'healthcare' for persons with disabilities. And again, laws such as the Occupational Health, Safety and Welfare Act recognise health rights that are guaranteed to employees within the workplace context. This position suggests that the applicable legislation merely regards some aspects of the right to health, as opposed to the substantive right itself, to be justiciable. On the other hand, most of the legislative provisions in the health generic laws that can be enforced before the court mainly relate to criminal liability and specific performance of duties that promote 'public health'. They do not expressly seek to vindicate the right to health of the individual. Indeed, a report by the WHO has observed that the legislative framework has a number of gaps such as the failure/ delay to revise the 1968 Public Health Act to 'take into account legal, socio-economic and

116 See, for example, secs 23(2)(c), 30(2) and 42(2)(d).

117 See, for example, sec 30(2).

political changes that have significant impact on health service delivery'.[118] This derails the implementation of the right.

Ultimately, this apparent justiciability ambiguity poses challenges to health rights litigation. The uncertainty is further complicated by Malawi's dualist approach to the treaties it ratified after the adoption of the 1995 Constitution since Malawi has not incorporated any of the post-1995 treaties (such as the CRPD). Indeed, this (non-)justiciability conundrum is regrettable as it could give the government a perpetual excuse not to implement the right and could also obstruct people from its litigation. It is not surprising that despite the fact that Malawi is facing many health challenges, including chronic shortages of essential medicines, the courts have not dealt with any case that has raised substantive health matters. Therefore, the omission by Malawi's legal framework to expressly recognise health as a justiciable right constitutes one of the major obstacles to domestic health rights litigation. Consequently, the continued perceived conception/misconception that health is a non-justiciable right could be the main impediment to future litigation.

Opportunities for Future Litigation

Although the perceived justiciability conundrum regarding the right to health in Malawi remains, there are signs that point to the actual and future potential of health rights litigation. First, Malawi generally follows the dualist approach with regard to ratified treaties and so far the CRC has been incorporated.[119] Second, Malawi follows the monist approach to treaties ratified before the commencement of the 1995 Constitution unless an Act of Parliament provides to the contrary. Malawi ratified the ICESCR and the ACHPR before 1995 with the effect that these treaties should form part of domestic law.[120] Hence, it is expected that the ICESCR, CRC and ACHPR provisions on health should be enforceable before the domestic courts. Indeed, the Malawi courts have held that the treaties ratified before the 1995 Constitution are domestically applicable.[121] For example, in *Malawi Telecommunications v Makande and Another*,[122] the Malawi Supreme Court of Appeal held that ILO Convention No 158 (Termination of Employment Convention (1983)) should be applicable to Malawi in terms of section 211(2) of the 1995 Constitution since there is no Act of Parliament which provides to the contrary.[123] Accordingly, the right to health should be justiciable in Malawi by virtue of the 'domestication' of the ICESCR, CRC and ACHPR.

Third, the Constitution requires the courts to have regard to the norms of international law when interpreting constitutional provisions.[124] Hence, the courts are expected to give an interpretation that is consistent with international law. Therefore, health rights issues

---

118 World Health Organization et al, 'Malawi: Rapid Assessment of Sexual and Reproductive Health' (n 24 above) 5.

119 See sec 4(c) of Third Schedule to the Child Care, Protection and Justice Act, 22 of 2010.

120 There is no legislation that outs their application in Malawi.

121 See, for example, *Kalinda v Limbe Leaf Tobacco Ltd* Civil Cause No 542 of 1995; *Banda v Dimon (Mw) Ltd* [2008] MLLR 92.

122 [2008] MLLR 35.

123 Malawi ratified ILO Convention 158 on 1 October 1986.

124 Sec 11(2)(c).

under the Constitution must be interpreted in accordance with the ICESCR and other applicable treaties. Since the Constitution contains health rights provisions, litigation would result in the courts advising government to discharge its health obligations (as envisaged) under international law. This could strengthen the potential of litigation in the enforcement of the right.

In addition, the Constitution contains certain justiciable rights that constitute elements of other substantive rights such as development in addition to the right to health. Litigating such provisions would result in the litigation of the relevant aspects of the right to health. Moreover, the courts have demonstrated their willingness to invoke any provisions of the Constitution. Indeed, in the *Masangano* case, the Constitutional Court stated:

> No part of our Constitution is a no-go area for the courts in so far as Section 9 of the same Constitution places the responsibility of interpreting, protecting and enforcing the Constitution on the Judiciary.[125]

Therefore, if the constitutional provisions on health are raised, the courts will not be intimidated by the apparent justiciability conundrum regarding the right. Indeed, in the *Mphembedzu* case, the Court hinted that it could have adjudicated on the substantive right to health care if the issue had arisen. This shows the litigation potential.

Above all, legislation that Malawi has enacted recently expressly recognises some significant justiciable aspects of the right to health. For example, the Disability Act recognises the right to health care, while the Gender Equality Act guarantees the right to SRH. In addition, the Constitution recognises the right of prisoners and other detained persons to medical treatment at the expense of the state. Accordingly, the right to health can no longer be considered as non-justiciable since its various aspects are justiciable. Therefore, despite the apparent justiciability conundrum, there are tangible opportunities for future litigation of the right to health in Malawi.

Conclusions

It can be appreciated that the main obstacle to health rights litigation in Malawi is the uncertainty engulfing the justiciability of the right to health under the Constitution. International human rights law requires states to put in place judicial mechanisms to enable redress, including provision of remedies, in cases of threats or violations of the enjoyment of human rights.[126] The CESCR has also made similar recommendations.[127] Accordingly,

125 *Masangano* case (Constitutional Cause No 15 of 2007) 35.

126 Hence, the laws should make all human rights, including SERs justiciable. See Committee on the Rights of the Child, General Comment No 5, 'General measures of implementation of the Convention on the Rights of the Child' (2003) paras 24 and 25; UNICEF, *Implementation Handbook for the Convention on the Rights of the Child* (UNICEF 2007) 55; Committee on Economic, Social and Cultural Rights, General Comment No 3, 'The nature of states parties obligations' (1990) para 4.

127 Committee on Economic, Social and Cultural Rights, General Comment No 3, para 5. See also Committee on Economic, Social and Cultural Rights, 'Guidelines on treaty-specific

as a state party to a number of applicable treaties, Malawi is obliged to recognise the justiciable right to health. In any case, as the CESCR's operative provision states in part:

> Each State Party to the present Covenant undertakes to take steps ... with a view to achieving progressively the full realization of the rights recognized in the present Covenant by *all appropriate means*, including particularly the adoption of legislative measures.[128]

It can be observed that the failure to recognise the justiciable right to health is not consistent with the obligation to take 'all appropriate means'. In addition, laws that frustrate litigation cannot be considered 'appropriate means' for implementing the right. Above all, states parties such as Malawi can only comply with their obligations to respect, protect and fulfil the right to health by taking legal measures that recognise health as a justiciable right.[129]

Furthermore, the African Commission on Human and Peoples' Rights, which monitors the implementation of ACHPR, has observed that SERs under the ACHPR should be realised progressively through the taking of particular measures.[130] For example, in *Purohit and Moore v The Gambia*,[131] the Commission reiterated the obligation to take concrete and targeted steps to ensure that the right to health is fully realised in all its aspects without discrimination of any kind.[132] The Commission has further adopted the Principles and Guidelines on SERs in which it has pointed out that certain obligations such as the duty to ensure provision of effective domestic judicial/administrative remedies must be realised immediately.[133] In Chapter 10 of this book, Judy Oder deals in great detail with the role of the African Commission in realising the right to health in Africa. Accordingly, it is

---

documents to be submitted by states parties under articles 16 and 17 of the International Covenant on Economic, Social and Cultural Rights' (2009), Annex VIII, para 3, sub-para (e).

128 Committee on Economic, Social and Cultural Rights, art 2(1), emphasis added. See also MCR Craven, *The International Covenant on Economic, Social and Cultural Rights: A Perspective on its Development* (Oxford University Press 1995) 144-150.

129 Committee on Economic, Social and Cultural Rights, General Comment No 14, paras 34-37, 59, 60 and 61.

130 See MA Baderin, 'The African Commission on Human and Peoples' Rights and the Implementation of Economic, Social and Cultural Rights in Africa' in MA Baderin and R Mccorquodale (eds) *Economic, Social and Cultural Rights in Action* (Oxford University Press 2007) 156; EA Ankumah, *The African Commission on Human and Peoples' Rights: Practice and Procedure* (Martinus Nijhoff 1996)139, 144.

131 (2003) AHRLR 96 (ACHPR 2003).

132 *Purohit* case, para 84. For further discussion on the SERs under the African Charter and the African Commission's approach to SERs, see Baderin (n 131 above); CA Odinkalu, 'Analysis of Paralysis or Paralysis by Analysis: Implementing Economic, Social and Cultural Rights under the African Charter on Human and Peoples' Rights' (2001) 23 *Human Rights Quarterly* 327.

133 See African Commission on Human and Peoples' Rights, 'Principles and Guidelines' (n 29 above) 16-30. The Commission has also adopted a resolution/declaration on SERs in Africa. See African Commission on Human and Peoples' Rights, 'Pretoria Declaration on Economic, Social and Cultural Rights in Africa' (2004).

expected that Malawi, as a state party to the ACHPR, has to ensure that SERs, including the right to health, are made justiciable.[134]

Indeed, the South African Constitution and constitutional cases such as the case of *Minister of Health & others v Treatment Action Campaign & Others* (hereafter *TAC* case)[135] demonstrate that governments have to be held accountable before national courts for their failure to provide health care in certain circumstances. In the *TAC* case, the Constitutional Court of South Africa directed the South African government to adopt reasonable measures to ensure access of the country's majority poor households to Nevirapine, an antiretroviral drug.[136] It is noteworthy that unlike in Malawi, the South African Constitution expressly contains the justiciable right to health care as a right guaranteed to everyone and a 'special protection right' accorded to children.[137] Hence, the constitutional protection of the right to health is one of the concrete ways of holding governments accountable. For example, in *Soobramoney v Minister of Health (Kwazulu-Natal)*,[138] the Constitutional Court of South Africa dealt with a matter in which the applicant claimed a right to receive renal dialysis treatment from hospital as a matter of emergency under the Constitution.[139] The Court dismissed the claim after finding that it had not been established that that the failure by the state to provide renal dialysis facilities for all persons falling within the applicant's category (of chronically ill patients) constituted a breach of its constitutional obligations. The Court observed that the right not to be refused emergency medical treatment meant

134 The Commission has also adopted a resolution on access to health and needed medicines where it recognises that the right to health 'embraces all underlying aspects of health' and emphasises states parties' obligation to ensure provision of medicines or access to them. See African Commission on Human and Peoples' Rights, 'Resolution on Access to Health and Deeded Medicines in Africa' (44th ordinary session, 2008). The Commission has further adopted a general comment relating to the right to SRH under the Protocol to the African Charter on Human and Peoples' Rights on the Rights of Women in Africa. (The Protocol was adopted on 11 July 2003 and entered into force on 25 November 2005.) See African Commission on Human and Peoples' Rights, 'General Comments on Article 14 (1) (d) and (e) of the Protocol to the African Charter on Human and Peoples' Rights on the Rights of Women in Africa' (52nd session, 2012). Since Malawi is state party to the Protocol (ratified on 20 May 2005) and Malawi's Gender Equality Act recognises the right to SRH, the General Comment and the incorporation of the Protocol would strengthen the litigation of the rights and assist in addressing the challenges being faced by women such as maternal mortality.

135 2002 5 SA 703 (CC).

136 Nevirapine is a reliable ARV drug that is used in the treatment of HIV/AIDS.

137 See Constitution of the Republic of South Africa, Act 108 of 1996, sec 27(1)(a), which provides that 'Everyone has the right to have access to – (a) health care services, including reproductive health care'; and sec 28(1)(c), which provides that 'Every child has the right – … (c) to basic nutrition, shelter, basic health care services and social services'. See also *Government of the Republic of South Africa & Others v Grootboom & Others* 2001 (1) SA 46; 2000 (CC) 11; BCLR 1169 (CC), where the Constitutional Court has indicated that the state's constitutional obligation relating to SERS in general is discharged by taking 'reasonable' legal and policy measures for the realisation of such rights.

138 1998 1 SA 765 (CC); 1997 12 BCLR 1696.

139 See sec 27(3), which provides that 'No one may be refused emergency medical treatment'.

that persons who suffer sudden catastrophes that need urgent medical attention should not be denied emergency services which are available. Emma Broster's comprehensive analysis of these cases and others is found in Chapter 4 of this book.

In view of this, it is incumbent upon Malawi to review its domestic legal framework to remove any misconceptions that suggest that the right to health is non-justiciable. This can be achieved, inter alia, by incorporating provisions in the applicable health legislation such as the PHA that expressly indicate that individuals have the right to health which should be protected by the state. In addition, Malawi could consider revising the Constitution's Bill of Rights to make provision for justiciable SERs, which should include health. Furthermore or alternatively, the courts should be expected to expressly affirm that the substantive right to health is justiciable in Malawi through the domestic applicability of the CESCR, CRC, ACHPR and other applicable treaties. Hence, the courts should hold the state accountable to fulfil its health rights obligations under international law.

Above all, considering the serious health challenges that Malawi is facing, such as habitual drug shortages, individuals or organisations could consider taking the state before the Constitutional Court to protect the right to health that is being threatened by these challenges. Such litigation could invoke the express provisions on health in the Disability Act and Gender Equality Act, which could be complemented by the constitutional provisions on health and the 'domesticated' health provisions in the ICESR, CRC and ACHPR. Indeed, the prospect of litigating the right to health in Malawi might become certain if only one such case is determined by the Court.

Therefore, it can be concluded that the (non-)justiciability conundrum surrounding the right to health in Malawi is grounded in perceived misconceptions since, as elucidated above, the right should be justiciable. Hence, there is actual and future potential for its litigation. Above all, in the light of Malawi's health challenges, it is only litigation that can trigger the appropriate implementation of the right to health in Malawi.

References

Books, Chapters, Articles, etc.

Ankumah, EA, *The African Commission on Human and Peoples' Rights: Practice and Procedure* (Martinus Nijhoff 1996).

Baderin, MA, 'The African Commission on Human and Peoples' Rights and the Implementation of Economic, Social and Cultural Rights in Africa' in MA Baderin and R Mccorquodale (eds) *Economic, Social and Cultural Rights in Action* (Oxford University Press 2007) 139-166.

Chirwa, DM, 'A Full Loaf is Better than Half: The Constitutional Protection of Economic, Social and Cultural Rights in Malawi' (2005) 49(2) *Journal of African Law* 207-241.

Chirwa, DM, *Human Rights under the Malawian Constitution* (Juta 2011).

Craven, MCR, *The International Covenant on Economic, Social and Cultural Rights: A Perspective on its Development* (Oxford University Press 1995).

'Drug Shortage now at 65%' *The Nation*, 8 January 2015, at http://mwnation.com/drug-shortage-now-65/ (accessed 26 February 2015).

Help Malawi, 'Challenges in Healthcare', at http://helpchildren.org/about/why-malawi/culture/ (accessed 21 May 2013).

Kachedwa, MG, 'An Investigation of the Adequacy of the Health Research Governance System in Malawi' (unpublished Mph thesis, University of Malawi, College of Medicine, 2009).

Kafulafula, UK, Hami, M and Chodzaza, E, 'The Challenges Facing Nurse-Midwives in Working towards Safe Motherhood in Malawi' (2005) 17(4) *Malawi Medical Journal* 125-127.

'Malawi Continues to Reduce Maternal Deaths' *Daily Times*, 23 May 2013, at http://bnltimes.com/index.php/daily-times/headlines/national/15152-malawi-continues-to-reduce-maternal-deaths (accessed 24 May 2013).

'Malawi CSO's Lament Bad Governance: Stick to Jan 13 Demo' *Nyasa Times*, 3 January 2015, at http://www.nyasatimes.com/2015/01/03/malawi-csos-lament-bad-governance-stick-to-jan-13-demo/ (accessed 26 February 2015).

'Malawi to Introduce Paying Fees in Hospitals – Minister', *Nyasa Times*, 24 February 2015, at http://www.nyasatimes.com/2015/02/24/malawi-to-introduce-paying-fees-in-hospitals-minister/ (accessed 26 February 2015).

Msyamboza, KP, Ngwira, B, Dzowela, T, Mvula, C, Kathyola, D, Harries, AD and Bowie, C, 'The Burden of Selected Chronic Non-Communicable Diseases and Their Risk Factors in Malawi: Nationwide STEPS Survey' (2011) 6(5) *PLoS ONE* e20316.

Ngalande-Banda, E and Simukonda, HP, 'The Public/Private Mix in the Health Care System in Malawi' (1994) 9 *Health Policy and Planning* 63-71.

Ngalande-Banda, E and Walt, G, 'The Private Health Sector in Malawi: Opening Pandora's Box?' (1995) 7 *Journal of International Development* 403-421.

'No "Freebies": Malawi Introduces Paying Services in Public Hospitals' *Nyasa Times*, 13 May 2013, at http://www.nyasatimes.com/2013/05/13/no-freebies-malawi-reintroduces-paying-services-in-public-hospitals/ (accessed 26 February 2015).

Odinkalu, CA, 'Analysis of Paralysis or Paralysis by Analysis: Implementing Economic, Social and Cultural Rights under the African Charter on Human and Peoples' Rights' (2001) 23 *Human Rights Quarterly* 327-369.

UNICEF, *Implementation Handbook for the Convention on the Rights of the Child* (UNICEF 2007).

International and Regional Instruments

African Charter on Human and Peoples' Rights, OAU Doc CAB/LEG/67/3 Rev 5, adopted 26 June 1981, entered into force 21 October 1986.

African Commission on Human and Peoples' Rights, 'Pretoria Declaration on Economic, Social and Cultural Rights in Africa' (2004) in C Heyns and M Killander (eds) *Compendium of Key Human Rights Documents of the African Union* (PULP 2010).

African Commission on Human and Peoples' Rights, 'Resolution on Access to Health and Deeded Medicines in Africa' (ACHPR/Res.141 (XXXXIIII) 08), 44th ordinary session held in Abuja, Federal Republic of Nigeria, 10-24 November 2008.

African Commission on Human and Peoples' Rights, 'Principles and Guidelines on the Implementation of Economic, Social and Cultural Rights in the African Charter on Human and peoples' Rights' (November 2010), available at http://www.escr-net.org/docs/i/1599552 (accessed 26 February 2015).

African Commission on Human and Peoples' Rights, General Comments on Article 14 (1) (d) and (e) of the Protocol to the African Charter on Human and Peoples' Rights on the Rights of Women in Africa, adopted during its 52nd session in Yamoussoukro, Ivory Coast, 9-22 October 2012, available at http://www.achpr.org/news/2012/11/d65/ (accessed 26 February 2015).

Committee on Economic, Social and Cultural Rights, General Comment No 3, 'The nature of states parties obligations' (Fifth session 1990) UN Doc E/1991/23, Annex III at 86 (1991).

Committee on Economic, Social and Cultural Rights, General Comment No 5, 'Persons with disabilities' (Eleventh session 1994) UN Doc E/1995/22 (1995).

Committee on Economic, Social and Cultural Rights, General Comment No 14, 'The right to the highest attainable standard of health' (Twenty-second session 2000) UN Doc E/C.12/2000/4 (2000).

Committee on Economic, Social and Cultural Rights, 'Guidelines on treaty-specific documents to be submitted by states parties under articles 16 and 17 of the International Covenant on Economic, Social and Cultural Rights' (Fortieth and Forty-first sessions 2008) UN Doc E/2009/22, E/C.12/2008/3, Annex VIII (2009).

Committee on the Rights of the Child, 'Concluding Observations: Malawi' (2002) UN Doc CRC/C/15/Add 174.

Committee on the Rights of the Child, General Comment No 3, 'Rights of children with HIV/AIDS' (2003) UN Doc CRC/GC/2003/1.

Committee on the Rights of the Child, General Comment No 5, 'General measures of implementation of the Convention on the Rights of the Child' (2003) UN Doc CRC/GC/20003/5.

Committee on the Rights of the Child, 'Concluding Observations: Malawi' (2009) UN Doc CRC/C/MWI/CO/2.

Convention on the Elimination of All Forms of Discrimination against Women, adopted 18 December 1979, entered into force 3 September 1981 (UN, *Treaty Series*, vol 1249, 13).

Convention on the Rights of the Child, adopted 20 November 1989, entered into force 2 September 1990 (UN *Treaty Series*, vol 1577).

Convention on the Rights of Persons with Disabilities, UN Doc A/61/611, adopted 13 December 2006, entered into force 3 May 2008.

International Covenant on Economic Social and Cultural Rights, adopted 16 December 1966, entered into force 3 January 1976 (UN *Treaty Series*, vol 993, 3).

Protocol to African Charter on Human and Peoples' Rights on the Rights of Women in Africa, OAU Doc CAB/LEG/66 6/Rev 1, adopted 11 July 2003, entered into force 25 November 2005.

Reports

African Women's Development and Communication Network (FEMNET), *Assessment of the Implementation by Malawi Government of the International Conference on Population and Development (ICPD) and Other Relevant International and Regional Instruments* (FEMNET 2007).

Centre for Human Rights and Rehabilitation, 'Malawi: Submission to the UN Universal Periodic Review. Ninth Session of the UPR Working Group of the Human Rights Council' (2010).

Chilemba, EM, 'Malawi' (2014) *African Disability Rights Yearbook* 207-226.

Fleischman, J, *The Global Health Initiative in Malawi: New Approaches and Challenges to Reaching Women and Girls* (Washington DC: Centre for Strategic and International Studies 2011).

Lawson, M, Mazengera, S, Nkhoma-Mbawa, F and Noel, T, 'Malawi Essential Health Services Campaign, For All Campaign: Country Case Study', Oxfam Research Report (2008).

Lunan, B, Clements, Z, Mahony, S and Hope-Jones, D, 'Maternal Health in Malawi: Challenges and Successes', Scotland Malawi Partnership (2010).

Malawi Government, *Report on Health Services Reform: Improving Public Health Services Delivery in Malawi* (Public Sector Reforms Management Unit, Office of the President and Cabinet 2012).

Malawi Government, 2012 *Global AIDS Response Report: Malawi Country Report for 2010 and 2011* (2012), available at http://www.unaids.org/en/dataanalysis/knowyourresponse/countryprogressreports/2012countries/ce_MW_Narrative_Report%5B1%5D.pdf (accessed 26 February 2015).

Malawi Government Ministry of Health (MoH), *Malawi Health Sector Strategic Plan 2011-2016: Moving towards Equity and Quality* (MoH 2011).

Malawi Human Rights Commission, *Report on Monitoring of Mental Health Hospitals and Selected Outreach Facilities in Malawi* (2012), available at http://www.panusp.org/wp-content/uploads/2013/02/FINAL-MENTAL-HEALTH-REPORT.pdf (accessed 26 February 2015).

Oxfam, *Missing Medicines in Malawi: Campaigning against 'Stock Outs' of Essential Drugs* (Oxford: Oxfam 2012), available at http://policy-practice.oxfam.org.uk/publications/missing-medicines-in-malawi-campaigning-against-stock-outs-of-essential-drugs-226732 (accessed 26 February 2015).

Refworld, 'Malawi's Never-ending Drug Shortage Problem', available at http://www.refworld.org/category,COI,IRIN,MWI,51276c762,0.html (accessed 26 February 2015).

SINTEF, CSR and FEDOMA, *Living Conditions of Persons with Activity Limitations in Malawi* (SINTEF 2004).

UNICEF, 'Malawi', at http://www.unicef.org/malawi/health_nutrition_3951.html (accessed 26 February 2015).

US Agency for International Development (USAID), 'Malawi: Water and Sanitation Profile' (2011), at http://www.wsscc.org/resources/resource-publications/malawi-water-and-sanitation-profile; http://www.wsscc.org/sites/default/files/publications/usaid_malawi_water_and_sanitation_profile.pdf (accessed 26 February 2015).

World Health Organization, 'Malawi: Country Profiles', at http://www.who.int/gho/countries/mwi/country_profiles/en/index.html (accessed 26 February 2015).

World Health Organization, *Malawi: Essential Drugs Programme: Midterm Report* (WHO 1994).

World Health Organization, 'Malawi Health Profile' (2011), at http://www.who.int/gho/countries/mwi.pdf (accessed 26 February 2015).

World Health Organization, IPPF, UNFPA, UNAIDS, 'Malawi: Rapid Assessment of Sexual and Reproductive Health and HIV Linkages' (2011), available at http://www.plosone.org/article/info:doi/10.1371/journal.pone.0020316.

World Health Organization, UNICEF, UNFPA and World Bank, *Trends in Maternal Mortality: 1990-2010* (WHO 2012).

Cases

African Commission on Human and Peoples' Rights

Purohit and Moore v The Gambia (2003) AHLR 96 (ACHPR 2003).

Malawi

Banda v Dimon (Mw) Ltd [2008] MLLR 92.

Chakufwa Tom Chihana v The Republic [1992] 15 MLR 86 (Supreme Court).

Chimwemwe Mphembedzu v The Republic [2011] MWHC 12; Bail Case No 70 of 2011.

Gable Masangano (Suing on his own behalf and on behalf of all prisoners in Malawi) v the Attorney General & Others Constitutional Cause No 15 of 2007.

Kalinda v Limbe Leaf Tobacco Ltd Civil Cause No 542 of 1995.

Malawi Telecommunications v Makande and Another [2008] MLLR 35.

Mendulo v Malawi Revenue Authority IRC Matter No 161 of 2003.

Nowa v The State and National Compensation Tribunal [2002–2003] MLR 192 (HC).

Numtaz Maluk Lambat v The Republic judgment of 22 September 2008; [2008] MWHC 175; Miscellaneous Criminal Application No 202 of 2008.

Republic v Chibambo Criminal Case No 122 of 2007.

The Republic v Abdul Rahman & Others (Somalians) Criminal Cause No 26 of 2006.

The State and Secretary to the President and Cabinet, Ex Parte Dr Bakili Muluzi Miscellaneous Civil Application No 3 of 2011.

The State v Dr Bakili Muluzi & Another Criminal Case Number 1 of 2009.

South Africa

EN & Others v Government of the Republic of South Africa & Others 2006 6 SA 575 (D); (2006) AHRLR 326 (SAHC 2006).

Government of the Republic of South Africa & Others v Grootboom & Others 2001 1 SA 46.

Minister of Health & others v Treatment Action Campaign & Others 2002 5 SA 703 (CC).

Soobramoney v Minister of Health (Kwazulu-Natal) 1998 1 SA 765 (CC); 1997 12 BCLR 1696.

Treatment Action Campaign & Others v Minister of Health & Others 2002 (10) BCLR 1033 (CC).

Van Biljon v Minister of Correctional Services & Others 1997 4 SA 441 (C).

Chapter 4

Litigating the Right to Health Care in South Africa

Emma Justine Broster

South Africa is facing great challenges as a result of its past and the growing economic disparities within the country. Despite it having one of the most progressive constitutions, the realisation of the Bill of Rights is hampered by the significant fiscal constraints of the state as it endeavours to fulfil its socio-economic rights obligations. The difficulty of realising the right of access to health care is compounded by the scale of HIV/AIDS infection in South Africa. More than ten years ago, the Constitutional Court summarised the impact of the pandemic, in *Minister of Health and Others v Treatment Action Campaign and Others* (*TAC*), as follows:

> The HIV/AIDS pandemic in South Africa has been described as 'an incomprehensible calamity' and 'the most important challenge facing South Africa since the birth of our new democracy' and government's fight against 'this scourge' as 'a top priority'. It 'has claimed millions of lives, inflicting pain and grief, causing fear and uncertainty, and threatening the economy'. These are not the words of alarmists but are taken from a Department of Health publication in 2000 and a ministerial foreword to an earlier departmental publication.[1]

South Africa has made great progress in expanding access to treatment since 2002, as it has one of the largest antiretroviral programmes in the world. However, given the scale of the pandemic and its impact in rural areas in particular, the reality is that this is still an accurate summary of the situation.

Although there are many practical obstacles facing South Africa in the provision of health care and other socio-economic rights, the inclusion of positive obligations on the state to provide access to these rights results in significant scope for litigation to ensure that the state creates and implements policies that progressively realise these rights. This chapter discusses some developments with regard to health rights litigation in South Africa. While the focus of this chapter is on litigating the right to health care, one must bear in mind that in many circumstances the translation of socio-economic rights from the text of the Bill of Rights into improvements on the ground is best achieved by the executive and the legislative branches of government. For reasons of resources, expertise and legitimacy the courts are, in most cases, ill-equipped to ensure implementation of

1 *Minister of Health v Treatment Action Campaign* (2) 2002 5 SA 721 (CC) para 1.

socio-economic rights on the ground.[2] While the Constitutional Court's jurisprudence on socio-economic rights has shied away from creating a minimum core content, it has provided concrete examples of where the Court will intervene to ensure that the state complies with its constitutional obligations. This chapter seeks to highlight these examples and to discuss avenues for future litigation. After discussing some of the health challenges facing the country, the chapter examines the legal framework on the right to health and how the courts have interpreted the government's obligations in this regard. It concludes by offering suggestions for a more holistic approach to realising the right to health guaranteed under the Constitution.

Major Health Challenges Facing South Africa

The underlying health of South Africans has degenerated as a result of historic and systemic issues, including colonialism, apartheid, growing economic disparities, incompetence and corruption.[3] When South Africa attained democratic rule in 1994, it inherited a highly dysfunctional and segregated health care sector.[4] In order to address this situation, the state must take steps to narrow disparities and to provide opportunities for people to survive childhood and have healthy, productive lives free from HIV/AIDS and other life-threatening diseases.

Apart from systemic issues, the greatest challenge facing South Africa in respect of health care is the impact of HIV/AIDS. South Africa has the highest number of HIV-positive people in the world, with more than 17 per cent of the world's population living with HIV in South Africa.[5] Its impact stretches to all aspects of life, and beyond those who become infected to include their families and how the state sets its priorities in terms of providing health care. While nearly two million people were receiving antiretroviral drugs (ARVs) in 2012, less than half of those in need of treatment were receiving it.[6] Reasons

2 M Pieterse, 'Legislative and Executive Translation of the Right to Have Access to Health Care Services' 14 (2010) *Law Democracy & Development* 1, explores further the reasons why courts are not the preferred vehicle for such translation:

For reasons of institutional legitimacy, resources, expertise, capacity and clout, the legislative and executive branches of government are typically regarded as being best place to articulate specific socio-economic entitlements and to establish the administrative and other processes through which these may effectively be claimed. Indeed, they are constitutionally mandated to do this, as reflected by the State's obligation under sections 26(2) and 27(2) of the Constitution to progressively realise socio-economic rights within its available resources by taking reasonable legislative and other measures.

3 HCJ van Rensburg, 'The History of Health Care in South Africa' in HCJ van Rensburg (ed) *Health and Health Care in South Africa* (University of Free State 2012) 61.

4 Ibid.

5 UNAIDS, 'South Africa Country Situation 2009' (10 December 2011), at http://www.unaids.org/ctrysa/AFRZAF_en.pdf (accessed 27 February 2015).

6 A Gray et al, 'Health Policy and Legislation' in A Padarath and R English (eds) *South African Health Review 2012/13* (Health Systems Trust 2013).

for this shortfall include the cost of ARV medication and the necessary personnel to administer it. To compound the problem, an additional 300,000 people are infected every year and will require treatment[7]

In addition to expanding access to medication, it is vital, at a base level, that the state ensures uninterrupted access to ARVs and other chronic medication. Systemic failures relating to a lack of planning and proper financial management have catastrophic consequences for those in need of uninterrupted medication. An example of the impact of these failures occurred in 2008 in the Free State where the hospitals stopped initiating new patients onto ARVs.[8] Despite urgent action by the National Department of Health, the Southern Africa HIV Clinicians Society estimated that an additional 30 people a day died from AIDS-related complications because they could not access ARVs.[9]

Issues surrounding expanding access to an uninterrupted supply of medication are compounded by the high prices of medicine, and in particular ARVs.[10] For this reason, ensuring access to low-cost treatments, such as generic medicines, where possible is fundamental to addressing this problem.

While mitigating the impact of HIV/AIDS is a primary focus area for the state, there are many other areas in health care that require attention. These include a shortage of doctors, in particular in the more rural parts of South Africa, and the high rate of maternal mortality, which increased from 150/100,000 pregnancies in 1998 to 650/100,000 pregnancies in 2007.[11] Addressing these problems requires very different strategies on the part of the state, as well as different legal obligations under the right to health care contained in the Constitution.

The right to health care included in the Constitution is broadly framed and has yet to be judicially interpreted in many circumstances. In discussing the legal framework of the right to health care, this chapter focuses on whether access to medicines can be said to fall within the ambit of the right to health care.

Legal Framework Relating to the Right to Health Care

South African Constitution of 1996

The South African Constitution is one of the few that contains a genuinely justiciable right to health. Like the other socio-economic rights, the right of access to health care does not necessarily include an entitlement by the individual to the immediate provision of services in every situation. However, it does require the state to develop a systematic,

7 Ibid.

8 O Adams, 'SelloMokhalipi and the Stories from the Free State Stock-Outs' *Equal Treatment Magazine for the Treatment Action Campaign* (September 2009), at http://www.tac.org.za/community/files/file/etmag/ET29/ET29English.pdf (accessed 27 February 2015).

9 Ibid.

10 UNAIDS (n 5 above).

11 Human Rights Watch, *'Stop Making Excuses': Accountability for Maternal Health Care in South Africa* (Human Rights Watch 2011).

comprehensive programme to realise these rights on a progressive basis and within its available resources. In determining whether the state has complied with this obligation the court will decide the reasonableness of the state's programme.

In view of South Africa's high prevalence of HIV/AIDS, the significant costs of ARV treatment and the high number of HIV-positive people seeking treatment in the public sector, this chapter focuses on whether the access to medicines and in particular ARVs is encapsulated within the ambit of the right to health care.

The Ambit of the Right to Health Care

The Constitution provides little guidance as to what is included within the term 'health care', except to expressly include reproductive health care. However, the right of access to health care is situated within the right of access to food, water and social security, which demonstrates an intention for the right to be broader than just health care services. In order to establish the ambit of a socio-economic right, the Constitutional Court has stated that it is determined with reference to the context of the right. This is divided into two parts: the textual setting of the right and its historical context.

Textual setting

Under Section 39(1) of the Constitution a court is obliged to consider international law as a tool to interpret the Bill of Rights.[12] This was reiterated by Chaskalson P in *S v Makwanyane and Others*:

> Public international law would include non-binding and binding law. They may both be used under the section as tools of interpretation. International agreements and customary international law accordingly provide a framework within which [the Bill of Rights] can be evaluated and understood, and for that purpose, decisions of tribunals dealing with comparable instruments ... may provide guidance as to the correct interpretation of particular provisions of the Bill of Rights.[13]

The provisions of the International Covenant on Economic, Social and Cultural Rights (ICESCR) influenced the socio-economic rights obligations contained in the Bill of Rights and therefore provide interpretive guidance.[14] Article 12 of the ICESCR states:

> 1. The States Parties to the present Covenant recognize the right of everyone to the enjoyment of the highest attainable standard of physical and mental health.

---

12 Section 39(1) states: 'When interpreting the Bill of Rights, a court, tribunal or forum (a) must promote the values that underlie an open and democratic society based on human dignity, equality and freedom; (b) must consider international law; (c) may consider foreign law.'

13 1995 3 SA 391 (CC) para 35.

14 International Covenant on Economic, Social and Cultural Rights, 19 Dec 1966, 993 UNTS 3, Can TS 1976 No 46, 6 ILM 360. Adopted by General Assembly Resolution 2200A (XXI) of 16 December 1966 and entered into force on 3 January 1976. South Africa signed the Covenant on 3 October 1994 but has yet to ratify it.

> 2. The steps to be taken by the States Parties to the present Covenant to achieve the full realization of this right shall include those necessary for:
>
> ...
>
> (c) The prevention, treatment and control of epidemic, endemic, occupational and other diseases.

The right was further clarified when the Committee on Economic, Social and Cultural Rights (CESCR) issued General Comment No 14, concluding that Article 12 extends access not only to timely and appropriate health care but also to underlying determinants of health, including adequate food, housing, water and sanitation, safe working conditions and environments, and access to health-related education and information.[15] General Comment No 14 states:

> Violations of the obligation to fulfil occur through the failure of States Parties to take all necessary steps to ensure the realization of the right to health. Examples include the failure to adopt or implement a national health policy designed to ensure the right to health for everyone; insufficient expenditure or misallocation of public resources which results in the non-enjoyment of the right to heath by individuals or groups, particularly the vulnerable or marginalised ... and the failure to take measures to reduce the inequitable distribution of health facilities, goods or services.[16]

With regard to the nature of States Parties' obligations, the CESCR stated:

> A State Party in which any significant number of individuals are deprived of essential foodstuffs, of essential primary healthcare, of basic shelter and housing, or of the most basic forms of education is, prima facie, failing to discharge its obligations under the Covenant. If the Covenant were to be read in such a way as not to establish such a minimum core obligation, it would be largely deprived of its raison d'être. By the same token, it must be noted that any assessment as to whether a State has discharged its minimum core obligations must also take account of resource constraints applying within the country concerned. Article 2(1) obligates each State Party to take the necessary steps to the maximum of its available resources. In order for a State Party to be able to attribute its failure to meet at least its minimum core obligations to a lack of available resources it must demonstrate that every effort has been made to use all resources that are at its disposition in an effort to satisfy, as a matter of priority, those minimum obligations.[17]

---

15 Committee on Economic, Social and Cultural Rights, General Comment No 14, 'The right to the highest attainable standard of health' (2000) para 4.

16 Ibid.

17 Committee on Economic, Social and Cultural Rights, General Comment No 3, 'The nature of states parties' obligations (Art. 2, par. 1)' (1991) para 10.

South Africa signed the ICESCR on 3 October 1994 but has yet to ratify it.[18] However, it seems that this ratification is likely to be back on the agenda of the government for 2014.[19] In the interim, the provisions of the ICESCR and the Committee's General Comments form part of international law and, in accordance with section 39(1) of the Constitution, must be considered in the interpretation of the Bill of Rights.

The need for universal HIV/AIDS treatment has been recognised internationally as a fundamental human right. This can be seen in relation to the Convention on the Rights of the Child, the Millennium Development Goals and the Guidelines issued by UNAIDS.

The Committee on the Convention on the Rights of the Child (CRC)[20] issued General Comment No 3 on HIV/AIDS and the Rights of the Child which states:

> [T]he obligations of States Parties under the Convention extend to ensuring that children have sustained and equal access to comprehensive treatment and care, including necessary HIV-related drugs ... It is now widely recognised that comprehensive treatment and care includes antiretrovirals and other drugs, diagnostics and related technologies for the care of HIV/AIDS, related opportunistic infections and other conditions.[21]

The Millennium Development Goals (MDGs) have become 'a universal framework for development and a means for developing countries and their development partners to work together in pursuit of a shared future for all'.[22] They relate both directly and indirectly to access to medicine and are as follows:

1. Eradicating extreme poverty and hunger
2. Achieving universal primary education
3. Promoting gender equality and the empowerment of women
4. Reducing infant mortality
5. Improving maternal health
6. Combating HIV/AIDS, malaria and other diseases, specifically with regard to HIV/AIDS: to halt and begin to reverse the spread of HIV/AIDS by 2015; and the achievement, by 2010, of universal access to treatment of HIV/AIDS for all those who need it

18 South Africa finally ratified the Covenant on 12 January 2015 but it will only take effect in April 2015.

19 Following Cabinet's announcement of its intention to ratify the Covenant in October 2012 the Department of Justice made a presentation to the Parliamentary Portfolio Committee on Justice, which subsequently approved the government's intention to ratify, together with the declaration entered to the right to education. This instrument of approval was then tabled before Parliament for final approval.

20 Convention on the Rights of the Child, 20 November 1989, 1577 UNTS 3, 28 ILM 1456 (came into force 2 September 1990). South Africa signed the Convention on 16 July 1995 but has yet to ratify it.

21 Committee on the Rights of the Child, General Comment No 3, 'HIV/AIDS and the Rights of the Child' (2003) para 25.

22 Ban Ki Moon, *Millennium Development Goals Report* (United Nations 2007), available at http://www.un.org/milleniumgoals/pdf/mdg2007.pdf (accessed 27 February 2015).

7. Ensuring environmental sustainability
8. Developing global partnerships for development.

South Africa's commitment to these goals indicates that the government considers HIV/AIDS to be a significant problem and that the provision of treatment is vital to achieving MDG 6.

In 2003 the Joint United Nations Programme on HIV/AIDS (UNAIDS) and the UN High Commissioner for Human Rights held a consultation on HIV/AIDS and Human Rights and issued a revised Guideline 6 'Access to Prevention, Treatment, Care and Support', stating

> States should enact legislation to provide for … safe and effective medication at an affordable price. States should also take measures necessary to ensure for all persons, on a sustained and equal basis, the availability and accessibility of quality goods, services and information for HIV/AIDS … treatment … including antiretroviral and other safe and effective medicines, diagnostics and related technologies for preventive, curative and palliative care of HIV/AIDS and related opportunistic infections and conditions.[23]

It is demonstrated above that international law recognises that medicines are vital to providing access to health care. Therefore from a textual perspective it can be seen that the right to access to health care in section 27(1) of the Constitution includes the right of access to ARVs. However, there is an internal limitation of section 27(2) which allows the state to demonstrate that it is doing all it can within its available resources. The importance of this provision is discussed below.

The social and historical context

As demonstrated below, the social and historical context also indicates that the right to access to health care includes access to medicines, in particular ARVs. Chaskalson P in *Soobramoney v Minister of Health (KwaZulu-Natal)* (*Soobramoney*) describes the context in which Chapter 2 should be interpreted.

> We live in a society in which there are great disparities in wealth. Millions of people live in deplorable conditions and in great poverty. There is a high level of unemployment, inadequate social security, and many do not have access to clean water or to adequate health services. These conditions already existed when the Constitution was adopted and a commitment to address them and to transform our society into one in which there will be human dignity, freedom and equality lies at the heart of our new Constitutional order. For as long as these conditions continue to exist that aspiration will have a hollow ring.[24]

---

23 Office of the UN High Commissioner for Human Rights & the Joint United Nations Programme on HIV/AIDS, 'HIV/AIDS and Human Right International Guidelines Revised Guideline 6: Access to Prevention, Treatment, Care and Support' (2006), available at http://whqlibdoc.who.int/publications/2002/9291730254.pdf (accessed 27 February 2015).

24 1998 1 SA 765 (CC) para 8.

The Constitutional Court has heard two cases specifically involving HIV/AIDS. The first was *Hoffmann v South African Airways*.[25] In this case, the Court found that the denial of employment to an HIV-positive person as a flight attendant amounted to unfair discrimination. The Court in reaching its decision held:

> People who are living with HIV constitute a minority. Society has responded to their plight with intense prejudice. They have been stigmatised and marginalized … People who are living with HIV/AIDS are one of the most vulnerable groups in our society … In view of the prevailing prejudice against HIV-positive people, any discrimination against them can, to my mind, be interpreted as a fresh instance of stigmatisation and I consider this to be an assault on their dignity.[26]

In the second case, namely *TAC*,[27] the Court dealt with the government's failure to provide Nevirapine at all public hospitals. This case is dealt with in more detail under the discussion of the internal limitation of access to health care within available resources.

These cases demonstrate the Constitutional Court's view that HIV/AIDS requires urgent action, that those who are infected with the disease deserve special protection from discrimination and that the government must 'fight this scourge as a top priority'. However, Yacoob J in *Grootboom and Others v Government of the Republic of South Africa and Others* (*Grootboom*) discussed the difficulties confronting the state in the light of South Africa's history of addressing issues concerned with the basic needs of people.[28] He stated:

> This case shows the desperation of hundreds of thousands of people living in deplorable conditions throughout the country. The Constitution obliges the State to act positively to ameliorate these conditions. The obligation is to provide access to housing, healthcare, sufficient food and water, and social security to those unable to support themselves and their dependants. The State must also foster conditions to enable citizens to gain access to land on an equitable basis. Those in need have a corresponding right to demand that this be done.[29]

It is clear that those in need of medicines have the right to demand from the state that it provide access to health care. However, this right is tempered by what Yacoob J goes on to say in his judgment:

> I am conscious that it is an extremely difficult task for the State to meet these obligations in the conditions that prevail in our country. This is recognised by the Constitution which expressly provides that the State is not obliged to go beyond available resources or to realise these rights immediately. *I stress however, that despite all these qualifications, these are rights, and the*

25 2001 1 SA 1 (CC).

26 Ibid, para 28.

27 *TAC* case (n 1 above).

28 [2000] ZACC 14, para 24.

29 Ibid, para 93.

> *Constitution obliges the State to give effect to them. This is an obligation that Courts can, and in appropriate circumstances, must enforce.*[30]

Therefore, in light of both domestic and international law it is clear that the right to access to health care includes the provision of ARVs, irrespective of the qualification in section 27(2).

Establishing the Extent of the State's Positive Obligations under Section 27(1), in Light of Section 27(2)

Section 27(2) requires that 'the state must take reasonable legislative and other measures, within its available resources, to achieve the progressive realisation of each of these rights'. The Constitutional Court in *TAC* held that rights contained in section 27(1) are not self-standing rights.

> Section 27(1) of the Constitution does not give rise to a self-standing and independent positive right enforceable irrespective of the considerations mentioned in section 27(2). Section 27(1) and 27(2) must be read together as defining the scope of the positive rights that everyone has and the corresponding obligations on the state to 'respect, protect and fulfil these rights'. The rights conferred by section 26(1) and section 27(1) are to have 'access' to the services that the state is obliged to provide in terms of section 26(2) and 27(2).[31]

O'Regan J in *Mazibuko and Others v City of Johannesburg and Others*[32] explained that the Constitutional Court in *Grootboom* had not held that section 26 entitles citizens to approach a court to claim a house from the state; instead the Court held that the scope of the positive obligation imposed on the state by section 26 is carefully delineated by section 26(2). O'Regan J applied this approach to section 27(1)(b) and held:

> It is clear that the right does not require the state upon demand to provide every person with sufficient water without more; rather it requires the state to take reasonable legislative and other measures progressively to realise the achievement of the right to access to sufficient water, within available resources.[33]

In creating this mechanism for determining the ambit of the obligations contained in section 27(1), the Court expressly avoided an objective standard for rights, or a minimum core. This has proved highly controversial as many commentators and practitioners

30 Ibid, para 94.
31 *TAC* case (n 1 above) para 39.
32 2010 4 SA 1 (CC).
33 Ibid, para 50.

consider that such an objective standard would facilitate a greater capacity for review of the state's compliance with its constitutional obligations.[34]

Minimum Core

The minimum core content was developed by the Committee on Economic, Social and Cultural Rights. It requires every state to fulfil the minimum core obligations by ensuring the satisfaction of a minimum essential level of socio-economic rights.[35] Had the Constitutional Court decided to use the minimum core obligations it would have created a far more objective standard with which to measure the level of the state's compliance.

The Constitutional Court first addressed the minimum core argument in *Grootboom* where it played down the normative strength of the ICESCR and the General Comments of the CESCR, relating to the minimum core of the right of access to housing. Yacoob J stated that it was not possible to determine the minimum threshold for the progressive realisation of the right to access to adequate housing without first identifying the needs and opportunity for enjoyment of such a right. The latter will vary according to factors such as income, unemployment, availability of land and poverty. The difference between city and rural communities will also determine the needs and opportunity for enjoyment of this right. In addition, the Constitutional Court in *TAC*, referring to the judgment in *Grootboom*, said:

> Although Yacoob J indicated that evidence in a particular case may show that there is a minimum core of a particular service that should not be taken into account in determining whether measures adopted by the state are reasonable, the socio-economic rights of the Constitution should not be construed as entitling everyone to demand that the minimum core be provided to them. Minimum core was thus treated as possibly being relevant to reasonableness under section 26(2) and not as a self-standing right conferred on everyone under section 26(1).[36]

The most recent rejection of attempts to create a minimum core occurred in *Mazibuko*. In this case, the applicants asked the Court to determine the content of the right to access to water sufficient for dignified life. The applicants attempted to persuade the Court to find that 50 litres per person per day ought to be the content of the right and that the Court should then 'decide whether the state acted reasonably in seeking to achieve the

34 See, for instance, S Liebenberg, *Socio-economic Rights: Adjudication under a Transformative Constitution* (Juta 2010); see also P Bond and J Dugard, 'Water, Human Rights and Social Conflict: South African Experiences' (2007) 1 *Law, Social Justice and Global Development*, available at http://go.warwick.ac.uk/elj/lgd/2007_1/author (accessed 23 January 2015).

35 Committee on Economic, Social and Cultural Rights, General Comment No 3, para 10, states that 'a State party in which any significant number of individuals is deprived of essential foodstuffs, of essential primary healthcare, of basic shelter and housing, or of the most basic forms of education, is prima facie failing to discharge its obligations under the Covenant'.

36 *TAC* case (n 1 above) para 34.

progressive realisation of this right'.[37] However, the Court held that the applicants had sought a decision that went further than determining a minimum, but rather sought that the Court should 'adopt a quantified standard determining the content of the right not merely its minimum core'.

The Court rejected this due to the text of the Constitution and the need for judicial deference towards decisions government makes in realisation of socio-economic rights. The Court held that in accordance with *Grootboom* and *TAC*, section 27(1) and section 27(2) must be read

> to delineate the scope of the positive obligation to provide access to sufficient water imposed on the state. That obligation requires the state to take reasonable legislative and other measures progressively to achieve the right of access to sufficient water within available resources. It does not confer a right to claim 'sufficient water' from the state immediately.[38]

O'Regan J continued by stating that the Constitution recognised that the right of access to sufficient water cannot be realised immediately in all circumstances.[39] The Court highlighted South Africa's history and socio-economic situation at the time of the drafting of the Constitution and held:

> At the time the Constitution was adopted, millions of South Africans did not have access to the basic necessities of life, including water. The purpose of the constitutional entrenchment of social and economic rights was thus to ensure that the state continue to take reasonable legislative and other measures progressively to achieve the realisation of the rights to the basic necessities of life. It was not expected, nor could it have been, that the state would be able to furnish citizens immediately with all the basic necessities of life. Social and economic rights empower citizens to demand of the state that it acts reasonably and progressively to ensure that all enjoy the basic necessities of life. In so doing, the social and economic rights enable citizens to hold government to account for the manner in which it seeks to pursue the achievement of social and economic rights.[40]

The Court also highlighted the benefit of a flexible standard which allowed for the courts to evaluate the context rather than simply employing a rigid standard.[41] This builds on the Court's judgment in *Grootboom* which emphasised the diverse circumstances in which the Court will be asked to assess the state's policies.[42]

---

37 *Mazibuko* case (n 32 above) para 51.

38 Ibid, para 56.

39 Ibid, para 58.

40 Ibid, para 59.

41 The Court stated: 'Moreover, what the right requires will vary over time and context. Fixing a quantified content might, in a rigid and counter-productive manner, prevent an analysis of context. The concept of reasonableness places context at the centre of the enquiry and permits an assessment of context to determine whether a government programme is indeed reasonable.' *Mazibuko* case (n 32 above) para 60.

42 *Grootboom* case (n 28 above) paras 32-33.

The second reason the Court in *Mazibuko* rejected a rigid minimum core approach is the principle of separation of powers[43] and the need to ensure the legitimacy of the Court. This is discussed in more detail below.

The Constitutional Court's Socio-economic Rights Jurisprudence

Given the flexible nature of the reasonableness enquiry, the only guidance as to how the court will deal with challenges to the government's compliance with its socio-economic rights obligations can be obtained from a discussion of how the court has used this enquiry in other cases.

As Pieterse argues, the focus of the Constitutional Court has been on determining the effectiveness of the legislature and executive's attempts to translate socio-economic rights into reality, as opposed to developing the content of constitutional guarantees.[44] For this reason it can be argued that the Constitutional Court's jurisprudence on socio-economic rights has been one of limitation. This can be seen in the following areas: in the extent to which it will interfere with the state's policies, in the scope of its order and in monitoring the implementation of its order. As discussed above, the Court has avoided an objective standard, such as the minimum core, to measure the state's compliance with the Constitution, preferring to adopt the reasonableness measure.[45] The reasonableness standard has been used by the Court to avoid involving itself in the creation of the

43 The Court at para 61 deals with the issue of separation of powers, it states: 'Secondly, ordinarily it is institutionally inappropriate for a court to determine precisely what the achievement of any particular social and economic right entails and what steps government should take to ensure the progressive realisation of the right. This is a matter, in the first place, for the legislature and executive, the institutions of government best placed to investigate social conditions in the light of available budgets and to determine what targets are achievable in relation to social and economic rights. Indeed, it is desirable as a matter of democratic accountability that they should do so for it is their programmes and promises that are subjected to democratic popular choice.'

44 Pieterse (n 2 above) 2.

45 The issue of the use of a minimum core as a standard in determining the state's compliance with the provision of the Bill of Rights was discussed in *Soobramoney*, *Grootboom* and *TAC*. The Court in *TAC* outlined the content of a minimum core: 'This minimum core might not be easy to define but includes at least the minimum decencies of life consistent with human dignity. No one should be condemned to a life below the basic level of dignified human existence. The very notion of individual rights presupposes that anyone in that position should be able to obtain relief from a Court' (para 28). After analysing the decisions of *Soobramoney* and *Grootboom*, the Court in *TAC* held that 'the socio-economic rights of the Constitution should not be construed as entitling everyone to demand that the minimum core be provided to them. Minimum core was thus treated as possibly being relevant to reasonableness under section 26(2), and not as a self-standing right conferred on everyone under section 26(1) … A purposive reading of section 26 and 27 does not lead to any other conclusion. It is impossible to give everyone access even to a "core" service immediately. All that is possible, and all that can be expected of the State, is that it act reasonably to provide access to the socio-economic rights identified in sections 26 and 27 on a progressive basis' (para 34).

state's policy especially regarding socio-economic rights in order to respect the separation of powers.[46]

Reasonableness

As discussed above, the reasonableness standard was first outlined by Yacoob J in *Grootboom* when deciding the ambit of the internal limitation in section 26(2).[47] He held that reasonableness is a flexible standard and is not capable of being measured objectively. It is decided on the circumstances of the case,[48] in a similar manner to the reasonableness review ground in section 6 of the Promotion of Access to Justice Act No 3 of 2000 (PAJA). The reasonableness enquiry must be viewed in the context of the Bill of Rights as a whole while remembering that 'society must seek to ensure that the basic necessities of life are provided to all if it is to be a society based on human dignity, freedom and equality'.[49]

When evaluating the reasonableness of the state's policy the Court does not investigate whether there are other more desirable measures or whether the money could have been spent better. This is because the Court must show a level of deference to the decision-maker who reviewed a wide range of possible options that could have been adopted.[50]

---

46 The Court in *TAC* stated: 'It should be borne in mind that in dealing with such matters the courts are not institutionally equipped to make the wide-ranging factual and political enquiries necessary for determining what the minimum-core standards called for by the first and second amici should be, nor for deciding how public revenues should most effectively be spent. There are many pressing demands on the public purse. As was said in *Soobramoney*: "The State has to manage its limited resources in order to address all these claims. There will be times when this requires it to adopt a holistic approach to the larger needs of society rather than to focus on the specific needs of particular individuals within society." Courts are ill-suited to adjudicate upon issues where court orders could have multiple social and economic consequences for the community. The Constitution contemplates rather a restrained and focused role for the courts, namely, to require the state to take measures to meet its constitutional obligations and to subject the reasonableness of these measures to evaluation. Such determinations of reasonableness may in fact have budgetary implications, but are not in themselves directed at rearranging budgets. In this way the judicial, legislative and executive functions achieve appropriate constitutional balance' (para 38).

47 Yacoob J said: '[t]he State is required to take reasonable legislative and other measures. Legislative measures by themselves are not likely to constitute constitutional compliance. Mere legislation is not enough. The State is obliged to act to achieve the intended result, and the legislative measures will invariably have to be supported by appropriate, well-directed policies and programmes implemented by the Executive. These policies and programmes must be reasonable both in their conception and their implementation. The formulation of a programme is only the first stage in meeting the State's obligations. The programme must also be reasonably implemented. An otherwise reasonable programme that is not implemented reasonably will not constitute compliance with the State's obligations' (para 42).

48 *Bato Star Fishing (Pty) Ltd v Minister of Environmental Affairs and Tourism* 2004 (4) SA 490 (CC) para 45.

49 *Grootboom* case (n 28 above) para 44.

50 Ibid.

However, this does not mean that the state's policies cannot be evaluated by courts in order to establish their reasonableness.[51]

In *Grootboom* the Court was faced with a challenge to the state's housing policy in that it had failed to provide basic shelter to people who had been rendered homeless as a result of being evicted from state-owned land. The Court found that while the policy dealt reasonably in addressing the medium- and long-term housing needs of its people, it had failed to develop a policy to assist those in immediate, crisis situation who need short-term assistance. The court held:

> [63] Section 26 requires that the legislative and other measures adopted by the state are reasonable. To determine whether the nationwide housing programme as applied in the Cape Metro is reasonable within the meaning of the section, one must consider whether the absence of a component catering for those in desperate need is reasonable in the circumstances. It is common cause that, except for the Cape Metro land programme, there is no provision in the nationwide housing programme as applied within the Cape Metro for people in desperate need ...
>
> [65] The national government bears the overall responsibility for ensuring that the state complies with the obligations imposed upon it by section 26. The nationwide housing programme falls short of obligations imposed upon national government to the extent that it fails to recognise that the state must provide for relief for those in desperate need. They are not to be ignored in the interests of an overall programme focussed on medium and long-term objectives. It is essential that a reasonable part of the national housing budget be devoted to this, but the precise allocation is for national government to decide in the first instance.

In *TAC*, the Court had to evaluate the reasonableness of the state's restriction of access to life-saving medication to prevent mother-to-child transmission of HIV/AIDS. The Department of Health's justification for the restriction of Nevirapine to 18 test sites was twofold: the first related to the toxicity of the medicine,[52] the second to the need to study the feasibility and cost-effectiveness of providing the necessary therapy at all public health facilities.[53] In finding that the policy of the department was unconstitutional the Court found that Nevirapine had been endorsed by the World Health Organization and the United States' Food and Drug Administration, and therefore that fears around toxicity were unfounded,[54] and that the costs of providing this medicine now fell within the

---

51 As O'Regan said in *Bato Star*: 'a Court should pay due respect to the route selected by the decision-maker. This does not mean, however, that where the decision is one which will not reasonably result in the achievement of the goal, or which is not reasonably supported on the fact or not reasonable in the light of the reasons given for it, a Court may not review that decision. A Court should not rubber-stamp an unreasonable decision simply because of the complexity of the decision or the identity of the decision-maker' (para 48).

52 *TAC* case (n 1 above) para 10.

53 Ibid, para 16.

54 Ibid, paras 57-58.

augmented budget.[55] In addition to these reasons it is clear that the Court took cognisance of the high prevalence of HIV/AIDS in South Africa, that women and children are most adversely affected by this restriction[56] and that economically women and children are disproportionately poor.[57]Also, the provision of this medicine would significantly reduce the chances of infecting the baby with HIV. These measures reduce the future burden on the public health system by decreasing the number of HIV-positive people in need of expensive and lifelong ARV treatment from the state. It can be argued that, in the light of the above, the Court was in a more comfortable position to encroach into the sphere of the executive when it ordered the state to ensure universal roll-out of Nevirapine.

Reasonableness appears to be a pragmatic mechanism for measuring the state's progress, especially as South Africa is still developing its economy and trying to uplift the circumstances of a significant proportion of the population; it allows the government to develop the policies it needs in order to bring about this upliftment over time. In addition, on a practical level this standard has been used by the Constitutional Court to make decisions which do not diminish its legitimacy with the other branches of government.[58] Roux argues that by avoiding dictating to the executive and legislature what its policy ought to be on a specific right, it ensures that its decisions are still respected by the other branches of government. He notes that 'it is … the proper function of the CCSA [Constitutional Court of South Africa] to devise review standards that allow it to remain sensitive to the political nature of its role'.[59]

The use of the reasonableness standard has created fundamental difficulty in socio-economic rights litigation, namely that the Court in making its decisions has avoided providing objective content to the rights contained in the Bill of Rights. The Court's focus rather has been on identifying and correcting flaws in the content of laws and policies aimed at translating socio-economic rights. There is a concern, as Pieterse explains, that there is a lack of clarity as to whether reasonableness will be able to perceive and correct

55 Ibid, para 71.

56 The Court held: '[78] The provision of a single dose of nevirapine to mother and child for the purpose of protecting the child against the transmission of HIV is, as far as the children are concerned, essential. Their needs are "most urgent" and their inability to have access to nevirapine profoundly affects their ability to enjoy all rights to which they are entitled. Their rights are "most in peril" as a result of the policy that has been adopted and are most affected by a rigid and inflexible policy that excludes them from having access to nevirapine.'

57 C Ngwena, 'Scope and Limits of Judicialisation of the Constitutional Right to Health in South Africa: An Appraisal of Key Cases with Particular Reference to Justiciability' (2013) R. *Dir. Sanit., Sao Paulo* 43.

58 T Roux, 'Principle and Pragmatism on the Constitutional Court of South Africa' (2008) 7 *International Journal of Constitutional Law* 106, 136. Roux argues: 'Many South African legal academics were quite indignant at the time about the CCSA's [Constitutional Court of South Africa] rejection of the minimum core content approach, which they argued amounted to an abdication of its responsibility to enforce socio-economic rights. As soon as one accepts, however, that the CCSA's concern in these cases may have been to *devise a review standard that allowed it greater flexibility to manage its relationship with the political branches*, much of the force of the criticism falls away' (emphasis added).

59 Ibid, 136.

failures by government to pass legislation or policies to ensure that socio-economic rights are realised.[60]

Perhaps in response to criticism around the lack of objective content of rights and ambiguity as to when the Court will intervene, O'Regan J in *Mazibuko* provided the clearest guidance yet on when the Court would intervene to find a policy unreasonable:

> If government takes no steps to realise the rights, the courts will require government to take steps. If government's adopted measures are unreasonable, the courts will similarly require that they be reviewed so as to meet the constitutional standard of reasonableness. From *Grootboom*, it is clear that a measure will be unreasonable if it makes no provision for those most desperately in need. If government adopts a policy with unreasonable limitations or exclusions, as in *Treatment Action Campaign No* 2, the Court may order that those are removed. Finally, the obligation of progressive realisation imposes a duty upon government continually to review its policies to ensure that the achievement of the right is progressively realised.[61]

Available Resources

In a country like South Africa the state must address many problems simultaneously, creating significant constraints on the state's resources. In the context of health care the issue of available resources is particularly pertinent. The lack of resources argument has been used in a number of cases. In *Soobramoney*, the applicant asked the Court to compel the state to provide him with renal dialysis for his chronic renal failure. This case is an extreme example of the resource debate as the applicant was ineligible for a transplant that would remedy his condition and was asking for this highly expensive treatment for the rest of his life.

The court's decision was based on a lack of resources. In finding that the state lacked the resources to provide the applicant with treatment for his chronic renal failure the court stated that this was because

> the cost of doing so would make substantial inroads into the health budget. And if this principle were to be applied to all patients claiming access to expensive medical treatment or expensive drugs, the health budget would have to be dramatically increased to the prejudice of other needs which the State has to meet.[62]

A lack of resources was also raised by the state in the health care setting in *TAC*. This was demonstrated by Dr Ntsaluba in an affidavit lodged by the applicant in which he raised the issue of resources as justification for the very limited roll-out of Nevirapine. He said that the provision of Nevirapine required the creation of infrastructure involving counselling,

60 Pieterse (n 2 above).

61 *Mazibuko* case (n 32 above) para 67.

62 *Soobramoney* case (n 24 above) para 28.

provision of formula as a substitute for breastfeeding and vitamin supplements and antibiotics. He then states:

> There are significant problems in making this package available. There are problems of resources insofar as counselling and testing are concerned and budgetary constraints affecting the expansion of facilities at public hospitals and clinics outside the research and training sites.[63]

The Court, however, did not deal with this argument in great detail. It stated: 'The cost of Nevirapine for preventing mother-to-child transmission is not an issue in the present proceedings. It is admittedly within the State's resources.'[64]

Progressive Realisation

The final element of section 27(2) is the requirement of progressive realisation. Yacoob J in *Grootboom* examined its meaning:

> The term 'progressive realisation' shows that it was contemplated that the right could not be realised immediately. But the goal of the Constitution is that the basic needs of all in our society be effectively met and the requirement of progressive realisation means that the state must take steps to achieve this goal. It means that accessibility should be progressively facilitated: legal, administrative, operational and financial hurdles should be examined and, where possible, lowered over time.[65]

The requirement of progressive realisation has room for interpretation and exploration through litigation, as it remains to be seen how the Court will deal with a challenge on the basis of slow implementation of an otherwise constitutional policy.

Possible Future Litigation

While South Africa has a constitution that contains positive obligations to ensure proper protection of the right to health care, the significant economic disparities present in the country and the many social issues that the state is constitutionally mandated to address mean that any challenge to enforce a socio-economic right will involve arguments around resources. Litigation to challenge the policy of a state for failing to cater for a class of people or to provide access to an item needed to ensure the protection of a right will have to pass the test of reasonableness.

The Court's decision to utilise the test of reasonableness rather than an objective standard has been criticised by both scholars and practitioners. However, in order to be

63 *TAC* case (n 1 above) paras 48-51.

64 Ibid, para 71.

65 *Grootboom* case (n 28 above) para 45.

successful in the litigation of these issues it is important to be mindful of the statement of O'Regan J in *Mazibuko* and to select issues which demonstrate a gap in a state's policy or a lack of implementation of such a policy. Within the field of health care, and in the light of the problems surrounding access to medicines, there are a number of issues which could be litigated. These issues include deficiencies within the supply chain of medications which results in stock-outs, particularly in relation to chronic medication or ARVs. Furthermore, given the requirement of progressive realisation, it is vital that the state continues to expand its ARV roll-out and the quality of the ARVs. In rural areas there may be communities which lack any form of access to primary health care and have to travel long distances to obtain any form of treatment or medication.

Such issues are ripe for litigation. However, due to the issues discussed in this chapter around the reasonableness standard it is vital that cases that are brought demonstrate clearly a failure of government to comply with its constitutional obligation in order to allow the court to respect the doctrine of separation of powers and its legitimacy with the executive.

Conclusions

This chapter has discussed the approaches of the court to health rights litigation in South Africa. Its focus has been on the jurisprudence of the Constitutional Court in socio-economic rights cases, particularly relating to the right to health. The chapter has shown that despite the explicit recognition in the Constitution of socio-economic rights, including the right to health, challenges remain in the full enjoyment of these rights. The chapter has discussed the approaches of the Constitutional Court to holding the government accountable for its obligations to realise socio-economic rights in general and the right to health in particular. It has been shown that the Constitutional Court has preferred the reasonableness test to the 'minimum core obligation' developed by the CESCR at the international level.

References

Books, Chapters, Articles, etc.

Adams, O, 'SelloMokhalipi and the stories from the Free State Stock-outs' *Equal Treatment Magazine for the Treatment Action Campaign* (2009), at http://www.tac.org.za/community/files/file/etmag/ET29/ET29English.pdf (accessed 27 February 2015).

Bond, P and Dugard, J, 'Water, Human Rights and Social Conflict: South African Experiences' (2007) 1 *Law, Social Justice and Global Development*, available at http://go.warwick.ac.uk/elj/lgd/2007_1/author (accessed 23 January 2015).

Gray, A, Vawda, Y and Jack, C, 'Health Policy and Legislation' in A Padarath and R English (eds) *South African Health Review* (Health Systems Trust 2012/13).

Liebenberg, S, *Socio-economic Rights: Adjudication under a Transformative Constitution* (Juta 2010).

Ngwena, C, 'Scope and Limits of Judicialisation of the Constitutional Right to Health in South Africa: An Appraisal of Key Cases with Particular Reference to Justiciability' (2013) 14 *R. Dir. Sanit., Sao Paulo* 43-87.
Pieterse, M, 'Legislative and Executive Translation of the Right to Have Access to Health Care Services' (2010) 14 *Law, Democracy & Development* 1-25.
Roux, T, 'Principle and Pragmatism on the Constitutional Court of South Africa' (2008) 7 *International Journal of Constitutional Law* 106-138.
Van Rensburg, HCJ, 'The History of Health Care in South Africa' in HCJ van Rensburg (ed) *Health and Health Care in South Africa* (2nd edn, Schaik 2012).

International and Regional Instruments

Committee on Economic, Social and Cultural Rights, General Comment No 3, 'The nature of states parties' obligations' (Fifth session 1990) UN Doc E/1991/23.
Committee on Economic, Social and Cultural Rights, General Comment No 14, 'The right to the highest attainable standard of health' (Twenty-second session 2000) UN Doc E/C.12/2000/4.
Committee on the Rights of the Child, General Comment No 3, 'HIV/AIDS and the Rights of the Child' (Thirty-second session 2003) UN Doc CRC/GC/2003/1.
Convention on the Rights of the Child, adopted 20 November 1989, entered into force 2 September 1990 (UN *Treaty Series*, vol. 1577).
International Covenant on Economic Social and Cultural Rights, adopted by General Assembly Resolution 2200A (XXI) of 16 December 1966, entered into force 3 January 1976 (UN *Treaty Series*, vol. 993, 3).

Reports

Human Rights Watch, *'Stop Making Excuses': Accountability for Maternal Health Care in South Africa* (Human Rights Watch 2011).
Moon, Ban Ki, *Millennium Development Goals Report* (United Nations 2007).
Office of the United Nations High Commissioner for Human Rights & the Joint United Nations Programme on HIV/AIDS, 'HIV/AIDS and Human Right International Guidelines Revised Guideline 6: Access to prevention, treatment, care and support' (2006), available at http://whqlibdoc.who.int/publications/2002/9291730254.pdf (accessed 27 February 2015).
UNAIDS, 'South Africa Country Situation 2009' (2011), at http://www.unaids.org/ctrysa/AFRZAF_en.pdf (accessed 27 February 2015).

Cases

Bato Star Fishing (Pty) Ltd v Minister of Environmental Affairs and Tourism 2004 4 SA 490 (CC).
Grootboom and Others v Government of the Republic of South Africa and Others [2000] ZACC 14.
Hoffmann v South African Airways 2001 1 SA 1 (CC).
Mazibuko and Others v City of Johannesburg and Others 2010 4 SA 1 (CC).

Minister of Health v Treatment Action Campaign (2) 2002 5 SA 721 (CC).
S v Makwanyane and Others 1995 3 SA 391 (CC).
Soobramoney v Minister of Health (KwaZulu-Natal) 1998 1 SA 765 (CC).

Chapter 5

Litigating the Right to Health in Uganda: The Necessity for Innovation and Activism

Salima Namusobya

Although there have been recent developments in this area, litigation as a strategy for promoting the realisation of the right to the highest attainable standard of physical and mental health remains underutilised in Uganda. While the state has the primary obligation to use its maximum available resources to establish an effective health system,[1] the country still grapples with major challenges in the effective, universal and equitable delivery of health services. According to the 2012 Poverty Status Report, 7.5 million Ugandans are still living in poverty and 13 million Ugandans, representing over 43 per cent of the population, though not in absolute poverty are still insecure.[2] This means that public goods and services including health care are a critical component of people's well-being. According to the United Nations Development Assistance Framework (UNDAF) for Uganda 2010-2014, social services, especially health and education, continue to be functionally weak, and stakeholders have noted the importance of explicitly confirming Uganda's commitment to the right to health in the National Health Policy II (NHP II) and the Health Sector Strategic Plan III (HSSP III).[3]

UN Special Rapporteur Paul Hunt identified the main features of a right to health approach in the Ugandan context as including information and education, community participation, the role of health professionals, tackling stigmatisation and discrimination, an integrated health system, enhanced research and development, the role of donors and the international community, and monitoring and accountability.[4] However, the question whether there is a justiciable right to health under Uganda's national laws remains contentious even among relevant practitioners. There is a very narrow construction of the right, and the underlying determinants of health such as a clean and healthy environment,

1 See art 2 of the International Covenant on Economic, Social and Cultural Rights (ICESCR).

2 Uganda Ministry of Finance, Planning and Economic Development, Poverty Status Reports, *Poverty Reduction and the National Development Process: Reducing Vulnerability, Equalizing Opportunities and Transforming Lives* (MFPED 2012).

3 World Health Organization and Uganda Ministry of Health, 'Health and Human Rights in Uganda: Fact Sheet' (2009).

4 Report of the UN Special Rapporteur on the right of everyone to the enjoyment of the highest attainable standard of physical and mental health, Paul Hunt (Mission to Uganda March 2005) UN Doc E/CN.4/2006/48/Add 2 (2006).

adequate housing and access to safe water and adequate sanitation have often been left out in the discussions around the right. Economic, social and cultural rights (ESCRs) are generally perceived to be development objectives rather than enforceable rights in the Ugandan context. This is also reflected in the inadequate legal protection afforded to these rights at the domestic level, as well as the attitude of government officials who continue to view the limited positive steps taken to implement ESRs as political gifts intended to secure the electoral loyalty of benefitting communities.[5] Accordingly, civil society actors have also been slow to utilise litigation as a strategy for promoting the right to health, and recent attempts have been met with a judiciary that is reluctant to adjudicate social and economic issues, as will be elaborated in this chapter. Against this backdrop, this chapter examines the legal framework for the realisation of the right to health in Uganda. More importantly, it discusses attempts to litigate the right to health in the country and identifies some challenges in this regard. It then proffers some recommendations for the way forward.

Health Challenges Facing Uganda

The 2013 Human Development Report categorised Uganda as one of the countries with low human development in the area of health, with only 48 per cent of the population satisfied with the quality of health care.[6] The country's health system has also consistently been described as ailing, and not responsive to the majority of Ugandans.[7] The government has acknowledged persistent policy and implementation challenges to be addressed, including gaps in access to health care between urban and rural areas, high and stagnant infant and maternal mortality rates, and the continued prevalence of communicable and non-communicable diseases.[8] Currently, the essential package of health services is underfunded, leading to stock-outs of essential medicines and low quality of health care. Health workers are not yet working in the required numbers in rural districts, and households risk further impoverishment due to informal fees in the public sector or formal fees in the private

5 S Namusobya, 'Why ISER' (2013) 1 *Economic and Social Rights Advocacy Brief*, available at www.iser-uganda.org (accessed 27 February 2015).

6 United Nations Development Programme, *Human Development Report 2013: The Rise of the South: Human Progress in a Diverse World* (UNDP 2013) 168, available at http://www.undp.org/content/dam/undp/library/corporate/HDR/2013GlobalHDR/English/HDR2013%20Report%20English.pdf (accessed 27 February 2015).

7 The Ugandan media has been awash with reports of failures in Uganda's health system, ranging from poor infrastructure, neglect of vulnerable groups, particularly pregnant mothers, poor access to skilled health personnel and so on.

8 Uganda Ministry of Finance, Planning and Economic Development, National Budget Framework Paper, FY 2013/2014 (MFPED 2013).

sector.[9] Mothers remain at high risk of untimely death due to complications of childbirth[10] and lack of skilled care, infant mortality is at 54/1,000,[11] while the under 5 mortality rate stands at 90/1,000 live births and HIV prevalence is 4,030/100,000 people.[12] According to the Annual Health Sector Performance Report 2011/2012, the sector did not meet most of its targets for the year, and there was a decline in some of them. For example, the maternal mortality ratio increased from 435/100,000 live births to 438/100,000, and the contraceptive prevalence rate was at 30 per cent against a target of 40 per cent for the year.[13]

Furthermore, the functionality of health facilities has been noted to be sub-optimal with lower levels of care affected more than higher levels. For example, according to a recent World Bank study, the percentage of Level II Health Centres (HC II) experiencing stock-outs of essential medicines was close to 80 per cent, and only a third of public health workers could correctly diagnose at least four out of five very common conditions such as diarrhoea with dehydration or malaria with anaemia.[14] Uganda has one of the youngest and most rapidly growing populations in the world with a total fertility rate estimated at 6.7 children per woman according to the government's data and 6.4 according to UN data.[15] If the current fertility rate and annual growth rate are maintained, Uganda's population is expected to increase to 44 million by 2020, hence placing more demands on the health sector.[16]

According to the Health Sector Strategic Plan (HSSP) 2010/11-2014/15, the government of Uganda has committed itself to deliver a basic package of services – the National Minimum Health Care Package (NMHCP) – as efficiently and equitably as possible. In particular, there is a strong commitment to target poor and disadvantaged people. The NMHCP consists of programmes which deliver both curative and preventive services under four categories: (i) Health Promotion, Disease Prevention and Community Health Initiatives, including epidemic and disaster preparedness and response; (ii) Maternal

9 Uganda Ministry of Health, Health Systems 20/20 and Makerere University School of Public Health, *Uganda Health System Assessment 2011* (Health Systems 20/20 Project, Abt Associates 2012).

10 Save the Children, *Surviving the First Day: State of the World's Mothers 2013* (Save the Children 2013) – the 14th annual State of the World's Mothers report – placed Uganda in 132nd position out of the 176 countries that were graded.

11 Uganda Bureau of Statistics and ICF International Inc., *Uganda Demographic and Health Survey 2011* (UBOS and ICF International 2012).

12 World Health Organization, 'Uganda Health Profile', last updated May 2013. Also, according to the Uganda Bureau of Statistics, *2012 Statistical Abstract* (UBOS 2012), malaria remains the highest cause of both morbidity and mortality among children below 5 years of age.

13 Uganda Ministry of Health, *Annual Health Sector Performance Report, 2011/2012*.

14 World Bank, 'Quality of Uganda's Education and Health Sectors Poses Risk to Long-term Economic Progress', World Bank press release, 19 November 2013, available at http://www.worldbank.org/en/news/press-release (accessed 27 February 2015).

15 World Bank, *Uganda – Demography and Economic Growth in Uganda* (World Bank 2011) 1, available at www-wds.worldbank.org (accessed 27 February 2015).

16 Uganda Ministry of Health, *The Second National Health Policy: Promoting Peoples' Health to Enhance Socio-economic Development* (MOH 2010) 2.

and Child Health; (iii) Prevention, Management and Control of Communicable Diseases; and (iv) Prevention, Management and Control of Non-communicable Diseases.

Notably, the Uganda Human Rights Commission (UHRC) 2012 report highlighted a number of challenges facing the health care system.[17] These included frequent drug stock-outs, and noticeable challenges in access to health services, for example in places of detention, especially in access to HIV/AIDS drugs and treatment.[18] The UHRC also found that 321 of the inspected health facilities had inadequate personnel, and noted that the proportion of the national budget for health had decreased from 8.9 per cent in 2010/11 to 8.3 per cent in 2011/12, which is below the Abuja requirement target of 15 per cent.[19]

It is against this background that subsequent sections of this chapter will discuss the legal framework relating to the right to health and the use of litigation as a strategy for realising the right to health in Uganda.

Legal Framework Relating to the Right to Health in Uganda

Uganda has ratified several international and regional human rights instruments related to the right to health. These include the International Covenant on Economic, Social and Cultural Rights (ICESCR),[20] the Convention on the Elimination of All forms of Discrimination against Women (CEDAW),[21] the Convention on the Rights of the Child (CRC),[22] the African Charter on Human and Peoples' Rights (ACHPR)[23] and the Protocol to the African Charter on Human and Peoples' Rights on the Rights of Women in Africa (Maputo Protocol).[24] However, these international commitments have not been fully incorporated into domestic law. The Constitution has a mixed system where some ESCRs are under the Bill of Rights in chapter 4, while the majority are relegated under the National Objectives and Directive Principles of State Policy (NODPSP) in the preamble to the Constitution. As noted by Oloka-Onyango, the most deafening omission from the 1995 Constitution is the broad range of ESCRs enshrined in the ICESCR, to which Uganda has been party since 1987 and which instrument has given states around the world great inspiration for their domestic constitutional and legal regimes.[25]

17 Uganda Human Rights Commission, *15th Annual Report, 2012, Popular Version* (UHRC 2012).

18 Ibid, 6.

19 Ibid, 34-35.

20 Ratified on 21 April 1987.

21 Ratified on 22 July 1985.

22 Ratified on 17 August 1990.

23 Ratified on 10 May 1986.

24 Ratified on 22 July 2010.

25 J Oloka-Onyango, 'Reviewing Chapter Four of the 1995 Constitution: Towards the Progressive Reform of Human Rights and Democratic Freedoms in Uganda', study presented to the Human Rights Network-Uganda, February 2013, 53.

Accordingly, there is no substantive provision on the right to health under the Bill of Rights, although there are rights to other determinants of health, and health care provisions for specific groups, as will be discussed below. Provisions directly related to health are instead found under the NODPSP. Objective XIV(b) enjoins the state to endeavour to fulfil the fundamental rights of all Ugandans to social justice and economic development and in particular to ensure that all Ugandans enjoy rights and opportunities and access to education, health services, clean and safe water, work, decent shelter, adequate clothing, food security and pension and retirement benefits. Objective XX further provides that the state shall take all practical measures to ensure the provision of basic medical services to the population, while objectives XXI and XXII provide for clean and safe water, and food security and nutrition respectively, both of which are determinants of the right to health.

In 2005, there was an amendment to the Constitution that among other provisions introduced article 8A, which states that:

> (1) Uganda shall be governed based on principles of national interest and common good enshrined in the national objectives and directives of state policy.
>
> (2) Parliament shall make relevant laws for purposes of giving full effect to clause (1) of this article.

It has been argued that article 8A's location in the body of Constitution is a clear indication that the country is bound by the Objectives[26] and opens up space for judicial activism for purposes of developing an integrated reading of the Constitution.[27]

Furthermore, article 45 of the Constitution is of importance to the justiciability of the right to health. It provides that rights, duties, declarations and guarantees relating to the fundamental and other human rights and freedoms specifically mentioned under Chapter IV shall not be regarded as excluding others not specifically mentioned. Article 287 of the Constitution also saves all international instruments that Uganda had signed before the coming into force of the 1995 Constitution, hence opening doors for reliance on international instruments that Uganda has ratified before the courts of law.

As noted above, the Constitution incorporates substantive rights relating to other underlying determinants of health under the Bill of Rights. Article 39, for example, provides for the right of every Ugandan to a clean and healthy environment. This provision has been restated under section 3(1) of the National Environment Act[28] and has been the basis

---

26 C Mbazira, *Public Interest Litigation and Judicial Activism in Uganda: Improving the Enforcement of Economic, Social and Cultural Rights*, Human Rights and Peace Centre Working Paper 24 (HURIPEC 2009).

27 C Mbazira, 'Uganda and the UN Treaty Bodies: Reflections on the Past and Thoughts for the Future in the Implementation of Economic, Social and Cultural Rights' in Office of the High Commissioner for Human Rights, *Uganda and the United Nations Human Rights Mechanisms: A Compilation on the Occasion of the 60th Anniversary of the Universal Declaration of Human Right*s (OHCHR 2009).

28 Sec 3(1) of the National Environment Act 1995 states that every person has a right to a healthy environment.

for litigating some cases related to health. The Constitution also has provisions relating to equality and non-discrimination[29] and provisions relating to specific groups, such as women and children.

Article 33(3) enjoins the state to protect women and their rights, taking into account their unique status and natural maternal functions. Regarding rights at work, article 40(1) requires parliament to make laws that provide for the right of persons to work under satisfactory, safe and healthy conditions, while article 40(3) states that the employer of every female worker shall accord her protection during pregnancy and after birth. Article 40 is a crucial constitutional guarantee for all workers, and it is also important because it accords female workers special treatment during pregnancy and after birth, reinforcing the principles in Article 33(3).[30]

The Constitution guarantees the health rights of children by stating under article 34(3) that no child should be deprived of medical treatment, while article 34(4) provides that children should not be employed in or required to do work that is likely to be harmful to their health. The Children Act also has various sections related to health and medical arrangements for children, although much of the responsibility is placed on non-state actors.[31]

Regarding persons with disabilities (PWDs), the Constitution provides that PWDs have a right to respect and human dignity, and that the state and society shall take appropriate measures to ensure that they realise their full mental and physical potential.[32] Other constitutional provisions related to the right to health include article 26(2), which provides that a person can be deprived of property in the interest of public health, and article 23(1)(d), which provides that a person can be deprived of their personal liberty to prevent spread of an infectious or contagious disease.

Of relevance to health litigation are the provisions on the right to life, and freedom from torture, inhuman and degrading treatment or punishment. Article 22(1) is to the effect that no person shall be deprived of life intentionally except in execution of a sentence passed in a fair trial by a court of competent jurisdiction. Article 22(2) is also relevant to the extent that it allows for abortions under circumstances authorised by law.[33] Article 24 provides for freedom from torture, while article 44 makes it a non-derogable right.

Existing Mechanisms for the Enforcement of the Right to Health in Uganda

The Ugandan legal system has a number of mechanisms that can be used to enforce the right to health. These include courts of law as well as quasi-judicial tribunals and administrative bodies.

---

29 See art 21 of the Constitution of the Republic of Uganda 1995.

30 Oloka-Onyango (n 25 above) 43.

31 See, for example, secs 5, 7, 8, 11, 37 and 66 of The Children Act 1997.

32 See art 35(1) of the Constitution of the Republic of Uganda 1995.

33 Art 22(2) states that 'No person has the right to terminate the life of an unborn child except as may be authorised by law.'

Courts of judicature

The Judiciary is established under article 126 of the Constitution. The courts are the central mechanisms for dispute resolution, and they include the Supreme Court, which is the highest court, the Court of Appeal, which also serves as the Constitutional Court, the High Court and Magistrates Courts.

Article 137(1) sets up the Constitutional Court with the powers to determine any question as to the interpretation of the Constitution. The judges of the Court of Appeal also constitute the Constitutional Court, but with a bench of five members whenever they sit as the latter.[34] The Court has jurisdiction to hear any matter where anyone alleges that an act or omission is inconsistent with, or in contravention of, a constitutional provision. The petitioner may seek a declaration or an order for redress where appropriate.[35] In cases where an order for redress is sought, the Court may grant the order or refer the matter to the High Court to investigate and determine the appropriate redress. Notably, where any question as to the interpretation of the Constitution arises in any proceedings in another court, that court shall stay its proceedings and refer the matter to the Constitutional Court if the parties request to do so.[36]

The High Court has unlimited original jurisdiction in all matters and such appellate and other jurisdiction as may be conferred on it by the Constitution or another law.[37] Accordingly, the High Court has served as the initial court for most of the cases related to enforcement of rights or seeking compensation for a violation.

Under article 50(1) of the Constitution, any person who claims that a fundamental or other right or freedom guaranteed under the Constitution has been infringed or threatened is entitled to apply to a competent court for redress, which may include compensation. The Constitution also has very flexible provision on standing, and allows for any person or organisation to bring an action against the violation of another person's or group's human rights.[38]

Quasi-judicial bodies

Ombudsman-type institutions have proved a useful complement to the courts because legal proceedings are routinely lengthy and undertaken only by trained lawyers.[39] In its first annual report in 1997, the Uganda Human Rights Commission stated that most of the people who brought complaints to the Commission were vulnerable people, who said that court procedures were too complicated for them and that they did not have the money to engage private lawyers to pursue their cases.[40]

---

34 Art 137(2) of the Constitution.

35 Art 137(3) of the Constitution.

36 See art 137(5), (6) and (7).

37 Art 139(1) of the Constitution.

38 Art 50(2) of the Constitution.

39 K Tomasevski, 'Strengthening Pro-poor Law: Legal Enforcement of Economic and Social Rights' in T O'Neil (ed) *Human Rights and Poverty Reduction: Realities, Controversies and Strategies* (Overseas Development Institute 2006) 28, available at http://www.odi.org.uk/sites/odi.org.uk/files/odi-assets/publications-opinion-files/2398.pdf (accessed 27 February 2015).

40 Uganda Human Rights Commission, *1st Annual Report* (UHRC 1997) 13.

The Uganda Human Rights Commission (UHRC) is an independent constitutional body established to promote and protect human rights. It was established under article 51(1) of the Constitution, and operationalised by the UHRC Act.[41] The UHRC has powers of court to summon witnesses and receive human rights complaints. Where a violation is proven, the UHRC can make an order for appropriate redress, such as compensation. The UHRC also has the mandate to ensure government compliance with international treaties. The Commission reported that it did not record any health rights related complaints in 2012.[42] The Centre for Health, Human Rights and Development (CEHURD) has since lodged a complaint over the continued human rights violations that occurred when electricity distributor UMEME embarked on load-shedding of public health facilities. Notably, part of the United Nations Development Programme support to the UHRC is meant to strengthen the capacity of UHRC staff in the handling and resolving of complaints related to the right to health, with specific emphasis on neglected diseases.[43] The biggest challenge facing the UHRC tribunal is the enforcement of its decisions.[44]

The Equal Opportunities Commission (EOC) was established by The Equal Opportunities Act 2007, in fulfilment of article 32(3) of the Constitution for the purpose of eliminating discrimination and inequalities against any individual or group of persons on various grounds, and to take affirmative action in favour of marginalised groups. The Commission has powers of court to discharge its functions. It is empowered to investigate or inquire into, on its own initiative or on a complaint made by any person or group of persons, any act, circumstance, conduct, omission, programme, activity or practice which seems to amount to or constitute discrimination, marginalisation or to otherwise undermine equal opportunities. In discharging this function the EOC Act empowers the Commission to proceed judiciously. The Commission may also refer any matter to another institution and recommend or order any entity to adopt or take particular steps or action which in its opinion will promote equal opportunities. Although its tribunal is not yet operational, the EOC can be used to promote the right to health.

The Uganda Medical and Dental Practitioners Council (UMDPC) regulates the medical officers and dental professionals in the country under the auspices of the Uganda Medical and Dental Practitioners Act 11 of 1996. The Council is mandated to foster good medical practices, to keep registers of qualified medical officers and dental surgeons in the country and to promote a high standard of medical education. Furthermore, the Council is mandated to protect the public from malpractice of the professionals. One of the objectives of the Council is to investigate all reported cases of alleged professional misconduct and take appropriate action.

---

41 Uganda Human Rights Commission Act 4 of 1997.

42 Uganda Human Rights Commission (n 17 above).

43 UNDP, Uganda 'Support to the Uganda Human Rights Commission' country page, available at http://www.undp.or.ug/index.php/support-to-the-uganda-human-rights-commission (accessed 27 February 2015).

44 All UHRC annual reports have pointed out the challenge of enforcement of their decisions and implementation of their recommendations to government.

Litigating the Right to Health in Uganda

The net impact of the relegation of ESCRs to the National Objectives is that it has been difficult to sustain actions such as those contending a violation of the right to health. Human rights activists are reluctant to bring these kinds of suits to the courts because one has to undertake a 'careful scrutiny' of a variety of human rights provisions, and also to read them into rights such as the right to life, in addition to seeking recourse in regional and international human rights instruments.[45] This section seeks to review current case law related to the right to health in Uganda.

A Progressive Beginning Beset by Inconsistency

One of the earliest court pronouncements related to the right to health in Uganda was in the case of *Salvatori Abuki and Another v Attorney General*.[46] In holding that the exclusion order threatened the right to life under article 29 of the Constitution, Justice Egonda-Ntende stated that:

> [T]he right to life is inviolable. I take this view guided by the National Objectives and Directive Principles of State Policy which we are enjoined to apply in interpreting this Constitution in part thereof. I take comfort in part (xiv) General Social and Economic objectives ... An exclusion order under section 7 of the witchcraft Act seems to me to be set in the opposite direction from assuring access of the person banished to any shelter, food, security, clean and safe water, and health services.[47]

The judge also noted that section 7 of the Witchcraft Act was not acceptable and demonstrably justifiable in a free and democratic society, and was therefore inconsistent with article 29(2)(a) of the Constitution of Uganda and therefore void for inconsistency.

The above judgment is commendable because the Court moved itself to refer to the national objectives relating to ESCRs, including health, and linking them to the right to life. This approach has also been taken by Indian courts, for example in the case of *Paschim Banga Khet Mazdoor Samity v State of West Bengal*,[48] where the Supreme Court established a link between the lack of adequate emergency medical treatment and the protection of the right to life.

In 2000 there were two attempts at horizontal claims by tobacco smokers to bring personal injury claims against the tobacco industry in Uganda for product liability, having suffered health problems as a result of smoking. The cases, however, stopped at the preliminary stages and there was a missed opportunity to obtain the courts' arguments on the merits. In the case of *Vincent Oribi v British American Tobacco (BAT)*,[49] the plaintiff, who

45 Oloka-Onyango (n 25 above) 54.
46 Constitutional Case No 2 of 1997.
47 Ibid.
48 (1996) 4 SCC 37.
49 Miscellaneous Application No 0569 of 2000, arising out of Civil Suit No 207 of 2000.

smoked from 1985 to 1999 and subsequently suffered detrimental health effects, brought a suit against the respondent claiming misrepresentation based on their health warnings on cigarette packs. Also, in *Thomas Okumu v BAT & Mastermind Tobacco Limited*,[50] the plaintiff contended that the defective nature of the respondents' cigarettes caused him to develop lung cancer and also sought relief for all other cigarette smokers. At the preliminary stage, the Court sought to determine whether the case was a representative/class action suit, or a public interest litigation case. The Court ruled that it was a class action, and discontinued the case on the basis that the plaintiff did not notify and seek the consent of the people he sought to represent; hence, the suit was barred in law. The judgment, however, helps practitioners to make the proper distinction between class actions and public interest litigation cases, and prepare accordingly before approaching the courts.

Notably, the majority of health-related cases in Uganda thus far have been based on the right to a clean and healthy environment. This is partly due to the fact that the right is substantively provided for under article 39 of the Constitution. Analysts have stated that although the right to a clean and healthy environment initially floundered on the rough seas of judicial intransigence and conservatism, over time the courts have become more comfortable with the idea and several cases have been decided positively on the issue.[51]

In *Uganda Electricity Transmission Company Ltd v De Samaline Incorporation Ltd*, the court elaborated the right to a clean and healthy environment as follows:

> [T]he right to a clean and healthy environment must not only be regarded as a purely medical matter. It should be regarded as a holistic socio-cultural phenomenon because it is concerned with physical and mental well-being of human beings. A clean and healthy environment is measured in both ethical and medical context. It is about linkages in human well-being. These may include social injustice, poverty, diminishing self-esteem, and poor access to health services. That right is not restricted to a clinical model.[52]

Working with the above definition, the Court concluded that the discharge of 'unpleasant, noxious, and choking dust' constituted a violation of employees' right to a clean and healthy environment under article 39 of the Uganda Constitution.

However, in the later case of *The Environmental Action Network Limited (TEAN) v British American Tobacco (BAT) Ltd*,[53] the court held that a petition concerning unregulated smoking in public places disclosed no cause of action. This judgment has been criticised for disregarding the flexible *locus standi* allowed under article 50 of the Constitution that permits anybody to bring a case in public interest regardless of whether they are affected by the violation.[54] There was a turn-around in the subsequent case of *BAT Ltd. v TEAN*

---

50 Miscellaneous Application No 0678 of 2000, arising out of Civil Suit No 465 of 2000.

51 Oloka-Onyango (n 25 above) 42.

52 High Court Miscellaneous Cause (No 181 of 2000).

53 Miscellaneous Application No 70 of 2002.

54 See E Kasimbazi and A Kibandama, *Environmental Law in Uganda* (Kluwer Law International 2011) 228.

Ltd,[55] where the court held that spirited persons or groups of persons who may feel obliged to represent those persons or groups of persons may, acting in the public interest, do so under article 50(2) of the Constitution.

Subsequently, the right to a clean and healthy environment has been upheld in several cases including *ACODE v Attorney General and National Environment Management Authority*,[56] where the court held that the right to a healthy environment entitles Ugandans to a right to an environment adequate for their health and well-being.

CEHURD & Others: A Threat to Justiciability

In 2011, CEHURD & Others petitioned the Constitutional Court seeking declarations to the effect that the non-provision of basic indispensable maternal health commodities in government health facilities and the imprudent and unethical behaviour of health workers towards expectant mothers are inconsistent with the Constitution and a violation of the right to health.[57] They argued that the high maternal mortality is caused by the government's non-provision of the basic minimum maternal health care packages, and inadequate human resources for maternal health – specifically midwives and doctors – frequent stock-outs of essential drugs and lack of Emergency Obstetric Care (EmOC) services at health centres and hospitals.

The Attorney General raised a preliminary objection based on the 'political question' doctrine and argued that the petition required a decision affecting political questions and that by adjudicating it, the Court would be interfering with the political discretion preserved for the executive and the legislature.

The Court held that although government had not allocated enough resources to the health sector and, in particular, maternal health care services, it was reluctant to determine the questions raised in the petition because the executive has the political and legal responsibility to determine, formulate and implement government policies for the good governance of Uganda. The Court further held that it had no power to determine or enforce its jurisdiction on matters that require analysis of health sector government policies and make a review or findings on them; and that by determining the issues raised in the petition, it would be substituting its discretion for that of the executive granted to it by law.

The Court relied on American jurisprudence in the cases of *Marbury v Madison*[58] and *Baker v Carr*,[59] alongside some domestic decisions, including *Attorney General v Major David Tinyefunza*,[60] to uphold the political question doctrine. It has been argued that by avoiding adjudicating the merits of a petition on health care in Uganda as a result of the political

55 High Court (Civil Application No 27/2003), arising from Miscellaneous Application No 70 of 2002.

56 High Court Miscellaneous Application (No 0100 of 2004).

57 See *CEHURD & Others v Attorney General*, Constitutional Petition No 16 of 2011 for background.

58 5 US 137 (1803).

59 369 US 186 (1962).

60 Supreme Court Constitutional Appeal No 1 of 1997.

question doctrine, the ruling of the Constitutional Court in the maternal health case is a threat to the justiciability of ESCRs in the country.[61]

The Committee on Economic, Social and Cultural Rights discussed the political question doctrine and stated that:

> It is sometimes suggested that matters involving the allocation of resources should be left to the political authorities rather than the courts. While the respective competences of the various branches of government must be respected, it is appropriate to acknowledge that courts are generally already involved in a considerable range of matters which have important resource implications. The adoption of a rigid classification of economic, social and cultural rights which puts them, by definition, beyond the reach of the courts would thus be arbitrary and incompatible with the principle that the two sets of human rights are indivisible and interdependent. It would also drastically curtail the capacity of the courts to protect the rights of the most vulnerable and disadvantaged groups in society.[62]

The above view about the political question doctrine in relation to ESCRs has been reflected in the judgments of many domestic courts. In South Africa, the main question that initially faced the Constitutional Court in all cases relating to ESCRs was how the courts could enforce the positive obligations to fulfil rights incorporated in sections 26 and 27 of the Constitution and at the same time respect the constitutional separation of powers.[63] The first challenge on adjudication of ESCRs was seen in the *Constitution Certification* case,[64] where the state argued that the inclusion of ESCRs in the Constitution would constitute a breach of the principle of separation of powers. The South African Constitutional Court however held that:

> Even when a court enforces civil and political rights such as equality, freedom of speech and the right to a fair trial, the order it makes will often have such implications. A court may require the provision of legal aid, or the extension of state benefits to a class of people who formerly were not beneficiaries of such benefits. In our view it cannot be said that by including socio-economic rights within a bill of rights, a task is conferred upon the courts so different from that ordinarily conferred upon them by a bill of rights that it results in a breach of the separation of powers.[65]

---

61 Initiative for Social and Economic Rights, 'A Political Question? Reflecting on the Constitutional Court's Ruling in the Maternal Mortality Case (*CEHURD & Others v Attorney General of Uganda*)' ISER Position Paper (2012), available at http://www.iser-uganda.org (accessed 27 February 2015).

62 Committee on Economic, Social and Cultural Rights, General Comment No 9, para 10.

63 F Coomans, 'Reviewing Implementation of Social and Economic Rights: An Assessment of the "Reasonableness" Test as Developed by the South African Constitutional Court' (2005) 65 *Heidelberg Journal of International Law* 167.

64 *Certification of the Constitution of the Republic of South Africa*, Constitutional Court of South Africa, Case CCT 23/96, September 6, 1996.

65 Ibid, para 77.

Accordingly, rather than deny claimants access to the courts, the South African Constitutional Court progressively articulated the Court's role in adjudicating ESCR issues and developed the 'reasonableness'[66] and 'proportionality' tests which they use in adjudication.[67] In the case of *Minister of Health and Others v Treatment Action Campaign and others*,[68] the Constitutional Court of South Africa rejected the separation of powers argument, and stated that the concept did not mean that courts could not or should not make orders that have implications for policies. In Chapter 4, Emma Broster discusses in detail some of the important socio-economic rights cases in South Africa.

In other countries such as India where there are no explicit provisions on the right to health, the courts have creatively found a way of rejecting the excuse of a lack of resources and have held the government accountable for health rights violations. In *Paschim Banga Khet Mazdoor Samity v State of West Bengal*, the Indian Supreme Court held that:
It is no doubt true that financial resources are needed for providing these facilities. But at the same time it cannot be ignored that it is the constitutional obligation of the State to provide adequate medical services to the people. Whatever is necessary for this purpose has to be done … In the matter of allocation of funds for medical services, the said constitutional obligation of the State has to be kept in view.[69]Furthermore, in the Colombia *Vaccination* case involving the general failure of the state to provide for the vaccination of children, the Colombian Constitutional Court concluded that:

> The negligent abstention by the State, its passivity regarding the marginalized and discriminated groups of society, does not meet its duty to put in place an equitable social order –which constitutes the basis for the legitimacy of the Welfare State under the rule of law. It also fails to comply with the constitutional provision proscribing marginalization and discrimination. In these circumstances, the role of the judiciary is not to replace public authorities which are liable for this abstention. It is rather to order the State to fulfill its duties, where it is clear that failure to act violates a fundamental constitutional right.[70]

In *Patricia Asero Ochieng*,[71] the High Court of Kenya held that any legislative measure that would have the effect of limiting accessibility and availability of antiretroviral medicines would *ipso facto* threaten the lives and health of people infected with HIV and AIDS. The Court held further, that the 'socio-economic factors that promote conditions in which people can lead a healthy life' imply a situation in which people have access to the

66 The reasonableness test was developed in the cases of *Grootboom v Oostenberg Municipality and Others* 2000 (3) BCLR 277 (C), *Minister of Health and Others v Treatment Action Campaign and Others* 2002 (5) SA 721 (CC) and *Khosa and Others v the Minister of Social Development and Others* (case CCT 12/03).

67 Initiative for Social and Economic Rights (n 61 above).

68 2002 (5) SA 721 (CC).

69 *Paschim Banga* case (n 48 above) para 16.

70 Constitutional Court of Colombia, Decision (Sentencia) SU-225/98, May 20, 1998, paragraph 29 (unofficial translation provided by International Commissions of Jurists).

71 *Patricia Asero Ochieng & Others v Attorney General*, Petition No 409 of 2009, paras 52, 63 and 88.

medication they require to remain healthy and that if the state fails to put in place such conditions, then it has violated or is likely to violate the right to health of its citizens. A detailed analysis of this case and other cases in Kenya can be found in Chapter 8 by Jacinta Nyachei and Paul Ogendi.

Having upheld the political question doctrine, the constitutional court in *CEHURD and Others* advised that 'In matters which require any court to draw an inference like in the instant petition, an application for redress can best be entertained by the High Court under article 50 of the Constitution'.

It is submitted that the above advice is flawed given that article 137(3) of the Constitution gives the Constitutional Court the discretion to make an order for redress where appropriate. Following *CEHURD & Others*, CEHURD has filed a couple of cases before the High Court under article 50 of the Constitution, including the case of *CEHURD and Others v Nakaseke District Local Administration*,[72] seeking court declarations on the rights to health, life, family and children's rights, among others, and *CEHURD and Others v Executive Director of Mulago National Referral Hospital and AG*,[73] which sought declarations on the right to health and related rights. It is, however, difficult to determine whether the choice to go to the High Court had anything to do with the advice of the court in *CEHURD & Others*. In Constitutional Petition No. 64 of 2011, CEHURD is challenging the constitutionality of some provisions of the Trial on Indictments Act and the Penal Code Act that refer to persons with mental disabilities as lunatics, idiots and imbeciles, but this case does not touch on the question of resource allocation. (Judgments in the above cases were pending before the courts at the time of writing.)

There is an appeal against the *CEHURD & Others* judgment before the Supreme Court, and it remains to be seen what the decision will be.

Towards Optimum Utilisation of Litigation as a Tool for Promoting the Right to Health

Based on the foregoing discussion, it is clear that although there is no express provision on the right to health under the Constitution, Uganda's legal framework offers a number of avenues for health rights litigation. It will therefore take a stronger civil society and an activist judiciary to take up the challenge and be creative and courageous enough to further build on the steps taken so far. It has been noted that the failure of civil society to use the judiciary could, in addition to lack of legal skills, be attributed to the general perception of the judiciary as conservative and resistant to change, and excessively slow in delivering justice due in part to logistical and staffing impediments,[74] as well as limited knowledge about ESCRs. The limited pragmatism of the courts has also been attributed to the fact

72 Civil Suit No 111 of 2012.

73 Civil Suit No 212 of 2013.

74 C Mbazira, 'The Status of Economic, Social and Cultural Rights in Uganda: The Huge Potential' (2013) 1 *Economic and Social Rights Advocacy (ESRA) Brief*, available at www.iser-uganda.org (accessed 27 February 2015).

that litigation is sometimes undertaken by lawyers with limited experience and knowledge of human rights litigation, coupled with the failure to build strategic partnerships that would bring value to the cases.[75]

There are, however, many opportunities to exploit in advancing health rights litigation, including the flexible *locus standi*, the calibre of the incoming judges in the Constitutional and Supreme Courts,[76] and a growing interest among lawyers and civil society in strengthening their capacity to engage in strategic litigation.[77]

As stated by Gloppen,

> The success or failure of litigation depends on (a) the ability of groups whose rights are violated to articulate their claims and voice them into the legal system – or have the rights claimed on their behalf; (b) the responsiveness of the courts at various levels towards the social claims that are voiced; (c) the capability of the judges – that is, their ability to find adequate means to give legal effect to social rights; (d) whether the social rights judgments that are handed down have authority in the sense that they are accepted, complied with and implemented through legislation and policy.[78]

Accordingly, the following recommendations are made to strengthen health rights litigation in Uganda.

Capacity Building for Judges and Civil Society

The capacity of judges to come up with appropriate remedies requires professional competence and creativity, access to relevant knowledge and command of the necessary legal remedies.[79] There is therefore a need to sensitise judges through a combination of introduction to the normative framework, experience sharing with counterparts in jurisdictions with similar challenges and exposure to victims of health rights violations. Civil society also needs to build capacity in human rights knowledge, monitoring, research and documentation of violations of the right to health to be better able to identify cases for potential litigation and have adequate evidence to sustain the court cases.

75 JC Mubangizi and C Mbazira, 'Constructing the Amicus Curiae Procedure in Human Rights Litigation: What Can Uganda Learn from South Africa?' (2012) 16 *Law, Democracy and Development* 119, 209.

76 Mbazira (n 75 above).

77 For example, a network of public interest lawyers has been formed by the Public Interest Law Clinic at Makerere University.

78 S Gloppen, *Social Rights Litigation as Transformation: South African Perspectives*, CHr Michelsen Institute Working Paper 2005: 3 (CMI 2005) 4.

79 Oloka-Onyango, 'Reviewing Chapter Four of the 1995 Constitution' (n 23 above) 53-54.

The Judiciary Should Develop a Framework within which to Adjudicate the Right to Health

Pushing the boundaries of the right to health requires engaging some of the most doctrinally difficult challenges by, for example, confronting questions such as the following: What precisely are the minimum core obligations? What are the proper benchmarks for maximum available resources? What pace of progress does progressive realisation require?[80] The courts also need to find the most appropriate arguments to address the separation of powers concerns that would invariably be raised.[81]

Adopt Creative Strategies for Litigation

In the absence of a substantive right to health and the fact that a constitutional amendment to that effect is not foreseeable in the near future, the success of health rights cases will depend on innovative approaches by the litigators. As noted by Byrne, the lack of express constitutional protection for health rights provides courts, lawyers and activists with significant but not insurmountable challenges for enforcement.[82] Some of the following approaches could be included.

Exploit existing constitutional provisions to argue for justiciability

As noted earlier, there are constitutional provisions that can be used to read an enforceable right to health into the Constitution. These include articles 8A, 45 and 287. Activists should also take advantage of the wording of article 50 of the Constitution, which also allows for bringing cases where there is a threat of violation of a human right. The word 'threat' lowers the evidential burden.

Utilising the derivative approach

This would require adopting wide interpretations of existing rights, for example the right to life, or freedom from torture, inhuman and degrading treatment or punishment, which are guaranteed under the Constitution. Regarding the right to life, the Human Rights Committee has stated that:

> [T]he right to life has been too often narrowly interpreted. The expression 'inherent right to life' cannot properly be understood in a restrictive manner, and the protection of this right requires that States adopt positive measures. In this connection, the Committee considers that it would be desirable for States parties to take all possible measures to reduce infant

---

80 EA Friedman and LO Gostin, 'Pillars for Progress on the Right to Health: Harnessing the Potential of Human Rights through a Framework Convention on Global Health' (2012) 14 *Health and Human Rights* 4, 10.

81 Oloka-Onyango (n 25 above) 53-54.

82 I Byrne, 'Making the Right to Health a Reality: Legal Strategies for Effective Implementation', at http://www.interights.org/doc/health%20paper.doc (accessed 27 February 2015).

mortality and to increase life expectancy, especially in adopting measures to eliminate malnutrition and epidemics.[83]

This approach has been commonly used in the Indian courts, as seen earlier.[84]

Use of equality and non-discrimination as cross-cutting issues

Non-discrimination and equality are fundamental human rights principles and critical components of the right to health because they imply that states must recognise and provide for the differences and specific needs of groups that generally face particular health challenges such as higher mortality rates or vulnerability to specific diseases.[85] In this regard, the Committee on Economic, Social and Cultural Rights has stated that there is no justification for the lack of protection of vulnerable members of society from health-related discrimination, be it in law or in fact.[86]

This approach was also applied in the Canadian case of *Eldridge v British Columbia*,[87] where deaf individuals challenged the failure of a provincial government to provide sign-language interpreters as part of its publicly funded health care system. The Court held that this constituted discrimination on the basis that government should ensure that in providing general benefits to the population they should guarantee that disadvantaged members of society have the resources to take full advantage of these benefits and, in this context, effective communication was an indispensable component of the delivery of medical services.

Coalition building and use of amicus curiae

One of the successes of *CEHURD & Others* is that it resulted in a coalition advocating for maternal health.[88] However, this came as a consequence and not as a strategy prior to the start of the litigation process. Going forward, activists need to build coalitions before litigation and make use of *amicus curiae*, for example coming from academics, medical practitioners, international human rights experts and the Uganda Human Rights Commission, to enrich the litigation process. *Amicus curiae* have so far not featured in litigation, partly because the procedures of intervention are not adequately developed and the *amicus curiae* procedure has not been established as part of legal and judicial practice.[89]

---

83 Human Rights Committee, General Comment No 6, para 5.

84 *Paschim Banga* case (n 48 above).

85 World Health Organization and Office of the High Commissioner for Human Rights, 'The Right to Health', Fact Sheet No 31 (2000).

86 See Committee on Economic, Social and Cultural Rights, General Comment No 14, para 18.

87 [1997] 3 SCR 624.

88 M Mulumba et al, 'Holding the Ugandan Government to Account for Maternal Mortality' *Equinet Newsletter*, 1 December 2011, available at http://www.equinetafrica.org/ newsletter/index.php?issue=130 (accessed 27 February 2015).

89 Mubangizi and Mbazira (n 76 above) 209.

Conclusions

The use of litigation as a strategy for the realisation of health rights is still growing in Uganda and it will take innovation, courage and activism from both the judiciary and civil society to maximise its full potential. It must, however, be emphasised that the success of court action will depend upon cases being instituted and effective implementation of the various court orders.[90] Accordingly, litigation must necessarily be complemented by other strategies, including continuous research and monitoring, advocacy and social mobilisation.

References

Books, Chapters, Articles, etc.

Byrne, I, 'Making the Right to Health a Reality: Legal Strategies for Effective Implementation', paper presented at Commonwealth Law Conference, London, September 2005, available at http://www.interights.org/doc/health%20paper.doc (accessed 27 February 2015).

Coomans, F, 'Reviewing Implementation of Social and Economic Rights: An Assessment of the "Reasonableness" Test as Developed by the South African Constitutional Court' (2005) 65 *Heidelberg Journal of International Law* 167-196.

Friedman, EA and Gostin, LO, 'Pillars for Progress on the Right to Health: Harnessing the Potential of Human Rights through a Framework Convention on Global Health' (2012) 14 *Health and Human Rights* 4-19.

Gloppen, S, *Social Rights Litigation as Transformation: South African Perspectives*, CHr Michelsen Institute Working Paper 2005: 3 (CMI 2005).

Initiative for Social and Economic Rights, 'A Political Question? Reflecting on the Constitutional Court's Ruling in the Maternal Mortality Case (*CEHURD & Others v Attorney General of Uganda*)', ISER Position Paper (2012), available at http://www.iser-uganda.org (accessed 27 February 2015).

Kasimbazi, E and Kibandama, A, *Environmental Law in Uganda* (Kluwer Law International 2011).

Mbazira, C, 'You are the "Weakest Link" in Realizing Socio-economic Rights: Goodbye: Strategies for Effective Implementation of Court Orders in South Africa', Socio-Economic Rights Project, Community Law Centre, University of Western Cape (2008).

Mbazira, C, *Public Interest Litigation and Judicial Activism in Uganda: Improving the Enforcement of Economic, Social and Cultural Rights*, Human Rights and Peace Centre Working Paper 24 (HURIPEC 2009).

Mbazira, C, 'Uganda and the UN Treaty Bodies: Reflections on the Past and Thoughts for the Future in the Implementation of Economic, Social and Cultural Rights' in Office of the High Commissioner for Human Rights (ed), *Uganda and the United Nations Human*

90 C Mbazira, 'You are the "Weakest Link" in Realizing Socio-economic Rights: Goodbye: Strategies for Effective Implementation of Court Orders in South Africa', Socio-Economic Rights Project, Community Law Centre, University of Western Cape (2008).

Rights Mechanisms: A Compilation on the Occasion of the 60th Anniversary of the Universal Declaration of Human Rights (OHRC 2009).Mbazira, C, 'The Status of Economic, Social and Cultural Rights in Uganda: The Huge Potential' (2013) 1 *Economic and Social Rights Advocacy (ESRA) Brief*, available at www.iser-uganda.org (accessed 27 February 2015).

Mubangizi, JC and Mbazira, C, 'Constructing the Amicus Curiae Procedure in Human Rights Litigation: What Can Uganda Learn from South Africa?' (2012) 16 *Law, Democracy and Development* 119-218.

Mulumba, M, Kabanda, D and Nabayunga, H, 'Holding the Ugandan Government to Account for Maternal Mortality' *Equinet Newsletter*, 1 December 2011, available at http://www.equinetafrica.org/ newsletter/index.php?issue=130 (accessed 27 February 2015).

Namusobya, S, 'Why ISER' (2013) 1 *Economic and Social Rights Advocacy Brief*, available at www.iser-uganda.org (accessed 27 February 2015).

Oloka-Onyango, J, 'Reviewing Chapter Four of the 1995 Constitution: Towards the Progressive Reform of Human Rights and Democratic Freedoms in Uganda', study presented to the Human Rights Network-Uganda, February 2013.

Tomasevski, K, 'Strengthening Pro-poor Law: Legal Enforcement of Economic and Social Rights', in T O'Neil (ed) *Human Rights and Poverty Reduction: Realities, Controversies and Strategies* (Overseas Development Institute 2006), available at http://www.odi.org.uk/sites/odi.org.uk/files/odi-assets/publications-opinion-files/2398.pdf (accesses 27 February 2015).

World Bank, 'Quality of Uganda's Education and Health Sectors Poses Risk to Long-term Economic Progress', World Bank press release, 19 November 2013, available at http://www.worldbank.org/en/news/press-release (accessed 27 February 2015).

World Health Organization, 'Uganda Health Profile', last updated May 2013.

World Health Organization and Office of the High Commissioner for Human Rights, 'The Right to Health', Fact Sheet 31 (2000), available at http://www.ohchr.org/Documents/Publications/Factsheet31.pdf (accessed 27 February 2015).

World Health Organization and Uganda Ministry of Health, 'Health and Human Rights in Uganda: Fact Sheet' (2009).

International and Regional Instruments

African Charter on Human and Peoples' Rights 1981, OAU Doc CAB/ LEG/67/3 rev 5, 21 ILM 58, entered into force 21 October 1986.

Committee on Economic, Social and Cultural Rights, General Comment No 9, 'The domestic application of the Covenant' (Nineteenth session 1998) UN Doc E/C.12/1998/24 (1998).

Committee on Economic, Social and Cultural Rights, General Comment No 14, 'The right to the highest attainable standard of health' (Twenty-second session 2000) UN Doc E/C.12/2000/4 (2000).

Convention on the Elimination of All Forms of Discrimination Against Women, 1249 UNTS 13, adopted 18 December 1979.

Human Rights Committee, General Comment No 6, 'Article 6 (The right to life)' (Sixteenth session 1982) HRI/GEN/Rev 1 (1994).

International Covenant on Economic, Social, and Cultural Rights, 993 UNTS 3, adopted 16 December 1966.

International Convention on the Elimination of All Forms of Racial Discrimination, UN Doc A/RES/65/200, adopted 4 April 2011.

International Convention on the Rights of the Child, 1577 UNTS 3, adopted 20 November 1989.

Protocol to the African Charter on Human and Peoples' Rights on the Rights of Women in Africa (2nd ordinary session of the Assembly of the African Union) AHG/Res 240 (XXXI), adopted 11 July 2003, entered into force 25 November 2005.

Universal Declaration of Human Rights, GA Res 217A (III), UN Doc A/810 at 71 (1948).

Reports

Report of the UN Special Rapporteur on the right of everyone to the enjoyment of the highest attainable standard of physical and mental health, Paul Hunt (Mission to Uganda March 2005) UN Doc E/CN.4/2006/48/Add 2 (2006).

Save the Children, *Surviving the First Day: State of the World's Mothers 2013* (Save the Children 2013).

Uganda Bureau of Statistics, *2012 Statistical Abstract* (UBOS 2012).

Uganda Bureau of Statistics and ICF International Inc., *Uganda Demographic and Health Survey 2011* (UBOS and ICF International 2012).

Uganda Human Rights Commission, *1st Annual Report* (UHRC 1997).

Uganda Human Rights Commission, *15th Annual Report* (UHRC 2012).

Uganda Ministry of Finance, Planning and Economic Development, *Poverty Status Report. Poverty Reduction and the National Development Process: Reducing Vulnerability, Equalizing Opportunities and Transforming Lives* (MFPED 2012).

Uganda Ministry of Finance, Planning and Economic Development, National Budget Framework Paper, FY 2013/2014 (MFPED 2013).

Uganda Ministry of Health, *The Second National Health Policy: Promoting Peoples' Health to Enhance Socio-economic Development* (MoH 2010).

Uganda Ministry of Health, *Annual Health Sector Performance Report, 2011/2012.*

Uganda Ministry of Health, Health Systems 20/20 and Makerere University School of Public Health *Uganda Health System Assessment 2011* (Health Systems 20/20 project, Abt Associates 2012).

United Nations Development Programme, *Human Development Report 2013. The Rise of the South: Human Progress in a Diverse World* (UNDP 2013).

World Bank, *Uganda – Demography and Economic Growth in Uganda* (World Bank 2011), available at www-wds.worldbank.org (accessed 27 February 2015).

Cases

ACODE v Attorney General and National Environment Management Authority High Court Miscellaneous Application (No 0100 of 2004).

Attorney General v Major David Tinyefunza Supreme Court Constitutional Appeal No 1 of 1997.

BAT Ltd. v TEAN Ltd High Court (Civil Application No 27/2003).

CEHURD & Others v Attorney General Constitutional Petition No 16 of 2011.

CEHURD and Others v Executive Director of Mulago National Referral Hospital and AG Civil Suit No 212 of 2013.

CEHURD and Others v Nakaseke District Local Administration Civil Suit No 111 of 2012.

Certification of the Constitution of the Republic of South Africa Constitutional Court of South Africa, Case CCT 23/96, September 6, 1996.

Constitutional Court of Colombia, Decision (Sentencia) SU-225/98, May 20, 1998.

Eldridge v British Columbia [1997] 3 SCR 624.

Grootboom v Oostenberg Municipality and Others 2000 (3) BCLR 277 (C).

Khosa and Others v the Minister of Social Development and Others case CCT 12/03.

Marbury v Madison 5 US 137 (1803).

Minister of Health and Others v Treatment Action Campaign and Others 2002 (5) SA 721 (CC).

Paschim Banga Khet Mazdoor Samity v State of West Bengal (1996) 4 SCC 37.

Patricia Asero Ochieng and Others v Attorney General Petition No 409 of 2009.

Salvatori Abuki and Another v Attorney General Constitutional Case No 2 of 1997.

The Environmental Action Network Limited (TEAN) v British American Tobacco (BAT) Ltd Miscellaneous Application No 70 of 2002.

Thomas Okumu v BAT & Mastermind Tobacco Limited Miscellaneous Application No 0678 of 2000, arising out of Civil Suit No 465 of 2000.

Uganda Electricity Transmission Company Ltd v De Samaline Incorporation Ltd High Court Miscellaneous Cause (No 181 of 2000).

Vincent Oribi v British American Tobacco (BAT) Miscellaneous Application No 0569 of 2000, arising out of Civil Suit No 207 of 2000.

Chapter 6

Litigating Health Rights Issues: The Nigerian Experience

Josephine Odikpo and Ebenezer Durojaye

Although the right to health is not specifically referred to as a human right in the Universal Declaration of Human Rights, article 25 of the Declaration recognises the rights of every person to a standard of living adequate for the health and well-being of himself and his family, including medical care. Other international instruments have declared the enjoyment of the highest attainable standard of health as one of the fundamental rights of every human being without discrimination. The Constitution of the World Health Organization rightly contains this declaration. Article 12 of the UN International Covenant on Economic, Social and Cultural Rights (ICESCR 1966) and, indeed, the African Charter on Human and Peoples' Rights (1981) also affirm the right of an individual to enjoy the best attainable standard of physical and mental health.[1] These include the prevention, treatment and control of epidemic, endemic, occupational and other diseases. The Declaration of Alma-Ata (1978),[2] the Convention on the Rights of the Child (1989)[3] and the African Charter on the Rights and Welfare of the Child (1990)[4] also contain similar declarations on health as a fundamental human right. It can be argued that when article 3 of the Universal Declaration of Human Rights, article 6 of the International Covenant on Civil and Political Rights and section 33 of the Constitution of the Federal Republic of Nigeria 1999 on the right to life are read together with the above covenants and declarations, the effect is clearly to elevate the right to health as a fundamental human right deserving of respect and protection by any responsible government.[5] This would clearly be in consonance with the decision reached at the Vienna Programme of Action to the effect that the enjoyment of civil and political rights and economic, social and cultural rights are 'indivisible and interdependent and interrelated'.[6]

---

1 See art 16 of the African Charter on Human and Peoples' Rights (OAU Doc CAB/LEG/67/3/Rev 5), adopted 27 June 1981, entered into force 21 October 1986.

2 This was the product of the International Conference on Primary Health Care held on 12 September 1978.

3 See art 24.

4 See art 14.

5 O Oluduro and O Ayankogbe, 'Legal Issues Raised by HIV/AIDS in Nigeria' (2001) *Journal of Law and Social Sciences* 154–166.

6 See Vienna Declaration and Programme of Action A/CONF.157/23.

Also, while the Fundamental Objectives and Directive Principles of State Policy as stated in chapter II of the Nigerian Constitution are non-justiciable,[7] nonetheless they lay down the most fundamental basis upon which the 1999 Constitution is predicated as they form the fundamental principles and policies that enable legislative enactment and enforcement in Nigeria. Consequently, in *Ukpo v Imoke*[8] the Court of Appeal held that the security and welfare of the citizens shall be the primary purpose of the government. Thus, the government has an obligation to provide that the health, safety and welfare of all persons in employment shall be safeguarded and not endangered or abused and also that there are adequate medical and health facilities for all persons.[9]

Health Challenges in Nigeria

Most of Nigeria's disease burden is preventable, poverty being a major cause of the problem. With about 840 deaths per 100,000 live births, Nigeria is said to have one of the highest maternal mortality ratios in the world.[10] The likelihood of a woman dying during pregnancy or childbirth is put at 1 in 23 compared to 1 in 9,200 for Malta.[11] Other poor countries such as Lesotho and Swaziland have better maternal mortality ratios than Nigeria. Nigeria is said to have the second largest number of maternal deaths after India, with about 50,000 women dying during pregnancy and childbirth each year.[12] Sadly, while deaths arising from childbirth or pregnancy have almost been eliminated in developed countries, many developing countries, including Nigeria, are still grappling with the challenge of maternal mortality. Indeed, maternal mortality ratios provide some of the most telling evidence of inequity between rich and poor countries and urban and rural areas.

While deaths during pregnancy are generally preventable, maternal mortality has remained one of the leading causes of death and morbidity among women in Africa.[13] The reasons why women die during pregnancy are well known, and include problems such as haemorrhage (25 per cent), unsafe abortion (13 per cent), eclampsia (12 per cent), infections (16 per cent) and obstructed labour and other direct causes (16 per cent).[14] Although these are the general causes of maternal deaths, the reasons women die from pregnancy may differ from country to country.[15] There are also indirect causes such as

7 Sec 14 of the 1999 Constitution.

8 (2009) 1 NWLR PART 1121 at 106.

9 Sec 17(3) paras c-d, Constitution of the Federal Republic of Nigeria 1999.

10 World Health Organization, UNICEF, UNFPA and World Bank, *Trends in Maternal Mortality: 1990 to 2008* (WHO 2010).

11 Ibid.

12 Ibid.

13 See World Health Organization, UNICEF and UNFPA, *Maternal Mortality in 2000: Estimates* (WHO 2004).

14 World Health Organization, *The World Health Report 2005 – Make Every Mother and Child Count* (WHO 2005).

15 For instance, a report has shown that unsafe abortion constitutes about 30–40 per cent of all maternal deaths in Kenya. See Center for Reproductive Rights, *Failure to Deliver: Violations*

HIV/AIDS, malaria, anaemia and hepatitis (20 per cent). These complications can be addressed through provision of emergency obstetric care services, but such services are generally unavailable in poor regions. Beyond the medical reasons other reasons for deaths during pregnancy and childbirth include the three delays – delay in reaching treatment, delay in identifying the problem and delay in getting help. In Chapter 2, Gladys Mirugi-Mukundi examines in detail some of the sexual and reproductive health challenges facing Africa.

In Nigeria the number of deliveries attended to by skilled medical personnel is disappointingly put at 37 per cent, lower than the average in the region.[16] More disappointingly, Nigeria is one of the countries that has not made appreciable efforts towards reducing maternal deaths as envisaged under goal 5 of the UN Millennium Development Goals (MDGs). The number of deaths during pregnancy may be aggravated due to socio-cultural factors including low status of women, early marriage and a general lack of respect for women's rights. In addition, corruption, misappropriation of resources and inadequate allocation of resources to the health sector often contribute to the high maternal mortality in the country.

In addition to the challenge of high maternal mortality, Nigeria is also grappling with the devastating effects of the HIV/AIDS pandemic. It is estimated that 4.1 per cent of the population is infected with HIV, translating to about 3.1 million people living with HIV, thus making Nigeria home to the second-largest number of people living with HIV in sub-Saharan Africa (South Africa has the largest number) and the largest number in West Africa.[17] The major mode of HIV transmission in Nigeria is through unsafe heterosexual sexual intercourse. Of late, however, there seems to have been an increase in the infection rate through homosexual activities.[18] Other modes of transmission include blood transfusions, unsafe injections and mother-to-child transmission. It is estimated that AIDS has claimed 2 million lives since 1986,[19] and annually an estimated 215,000 HIV-related deaths and 281,000 new infections occur in the country.[20]

---

of Women's Human Rights in Kenyan Facilities (CRR 2007) 24. In Zimbabwe, a study has shown that lack of access to transportation is responsible for 28 per cent of maternal deaths in rural areas. See Centre for Reproductive Rights, *Briefing Paper: Surviving Pregnancy and Childbirth: An International Human Right* (CRR 2005). In Ethiopia, early marriage has been attributed as a major cause of maternal death. See S Hailu et al, 'Health Facility-based Maternal Deaths Audit in Tigray, Ethiopia' (2009) 23 *Ethiopia Journal of Health Development* 115.

16 A Bankole et al, *Barriers to Safe Motherhood in Nigeria* (AGI 2009) 4.

17 Federal Ministry of Health, *Report of the National HIV/Syphilis Sentinel Sero Prevalence Survey* (FMOH 2010).

18 VA Owuliri and OM Jolayemi, 'Reaching Vulnerable and High Risk Groups in Nigeria' in O Adeyi et al (eds) *AIDS in Nigeria: A Nation on the Threshold* (Harvard University Press 2006) 310.

19 National Agency for the Control of AIDS, *Update on HIV/AIDS Epidemic and Response in Nigeria* (NACA 2011).

20 Ibid.

Legal Framework for Realising the Right to Health in Nigeria

Health is not just a blessing one wishes for,[21] but a fundamental human right recognised constitutionally and in regional and international covenants, some of which Nigeria has ratified. Accordingly, the government of Nigeria is required not only to implement schemes that will improve the health status of its citizens but also to institutionalise systems that will ensure, promote and protect their right to good health.

Sadly, the country has not made any appreciable progress in the realisation of its citizens' right to good and affordable health care. The health care system is grossly underfunded and poorly managed. Access to safe essential drugs and facilities is severely limited, staff morale is low and ethics and professionalism hardly drive the provision of health care services. The human rights of patients are violated with impunity. Respect for privacy, confidentiality and patients' right to participate in decisions concerning their care is almost non-existent. Health care in Nigeria is influenced by local and regional factors that impact the quality or quantity present in a location. With a population of about 170 million people, Nigeria is currently the most populated country in Africa. Its population is expected to rise to 390 million by the end of 2050.[22] The Gross Domestic Product (GPD) is estimated to be US$522.180 billion and the per capital income US$3,002 by 2015.[23] It is a country that is rich in mineral resources such as oil, natural gas, bauxite, tantalite, limestone, coal, tin, iron ore, niobium, lead and zinc. Nigeria is the 12th largest producer of oil in the world. Despite this, the Nigerian government has failed woefully to deliver decent health care services for its people.

Nigeria's overall health system performance was ranked 187th among its 191 Member States by the World Health Organization in 2000[24] and it commits between 6 and 7 per cent of its annual budget to health. The average life expectancy in the country is 51.4 years[25] and about 20 per cent of children die before the age of 5.

National Health Policies in Nigeria

The National Health Policy represents the collective will of the government and people of Nigeria to provide a comprehensive health care system that is based on primary health care.[26] It describes the goals, structure, strategy and policy direction of the health care delivery system in Nigeria. It defines the roles and responsibilities of the three tiers of

---

21 See speech made by Kofi Annan, former UN Secretary General, available at http://www.unfpa.org/resources/quotes-human-rights (accessed 24 February 2015).

22 World Population Review, at http://worldpopulationreview.com/countries/nigeria-population/ (accessed 7 January 2015).

23 International Monetary Fund, at http://www.imf.org/external/pubs/ft/weo/2013/02/weodata/weorept.aspx?pr.x=50&pr.y=10&sy=2013&ey=2013&scsm=1&ssd=1&sort=country&ds=.&br=1&c=694&s=NGDPD%2CNGDPDPC%2CPPPGDP%2CPPPPC&grp=0&a (accessed 7 January 2015).

24 World Health Organization, *World Health Report* (WHO 2000) 8.

25 World Bank 'Life Expectancy at Birth, Total (Years)', at http://data.worldbank.org/indicator/SP.DYN.LE00.IN (accessed 6 February 2015).

26 Revised National Health Policy, September 2004.

government without neglecting non-governmental actors. Its long-term goal is to provide the entire population with adequate access not only to primary health care but also to secondary and tertiary services through a well-functioning referral system.

The overall objective of the National Health Policy is to strengthen the national health system such that it will be able to provide effective, efficient quality, accessible and affordable health services that will improve the health status of Nigerians through the achievement of the health-related MDGs by 2015.

By virtue of section 4 (4) and Part II of the Second Schedule of the Constitution, health care in Nigeria is usually the sole responsibility of the three tiers of government – federal, state and local. However, private providers of health care have a visible role to play in health care delivery as a result of Nigeria's economy. The federal government's role (although not limited as matters of health are within the concurrent list in the Nigerian Constitution 1999 as amended) is to coordinate the affairs of the university, teaching hospitals and federal medical centres (tertiary health care) while the state government manages the various general hospitals (secondary health care) and the local government focuses on dispensaries (primary health care).

Nigerian Constitutional Provisions on Health

Section 1(1) of the Nigerian Constitution 1999 (as amended) states that 'This Constitution is supreme and its provisions shall have binding force on the authorities and persons throughout the Federal Republic of Nigeria.' This law forms the grund norm of all legislation in Nigeria and thus section 1(3) states that 'If any other law is inconsistent with the provisions of this Constitution, this Constitution shall prevail, and that other law shall, to the extent of the inconsistency, be void.'

Under chapter IV of the Constitution a number of fundamental rights are enshrined including the rights to life, privacy, dignity, fair hearing and freedom from discrimination. Though these rights are civil and political in nature, they can be indirectly invoked to advance the right to health in the country. These provisions are greatly influenced by the provisions of the Universal Declaration of Human Rights, which clearly states in its preamble that 'recognition of the inherent dignity and of the equal and inalienable rights of all members of the human family is the foundation of freedom, justice and peace in the world'.

Fundamental objectives and principles of state policy

One of the significant innovations of the Nigerian Constitution of 1979 was the inclusion of the chapter on 'Fundamental Objectives and Directive Principles of State Policy', an idea probably borrowed from other common law countries such as India. Due to the novelty of the chapter, it was thought expedient to define what is meant by the terms 'fundamental objectives' and 'directive principles'. Fundamental objectives are the 'directive principles' laid down by the policies which are expected to be pursued in the efforts of the nation to realise the national ideals.[27] They are non-justiciable and not enforceable until and unless otherwise enacted by an Act of the National Assembly. Thus, socio-economic rights, including the right to health, fall under the Fundamental Objectives and Directive Principles of State Policy under chapter II of the Constitution. These principles and policies are embodied to include fundamental obligations of government, the government and the people, political objectives, economic objectives and social objectives.[28]

It should be noted that Section17 of the Constitution provides as follows:

> (1) The State social order is founded on ideals of Freedom, Equality and Justice,
>
> (2) In furtherance of the social order-
>
> (a) every citizen shall have equality of rights, obligations and opportunities before the law;
>
> (b) the sanctity of the human person shall be recognised and human dignity shall be maintained and enhanced;
>
> (c) governmental actions shall be humane;
>
> ...
>
> (e) the independence, impartiality and integrity of courts of law, and easy accessibility thereto shall be secured and maintained.
>
> (3) The State shall direct its policy towards ensuring that-
>
> ...
>
> (c) the health, safety and welfare of all persons in employment are safeguarded and not endangered or abused;
>
> (d) there are adequate medical and health facilities for all persons.

To aid the realisation of these objectives, the drafters of the Constitution have ensured that both the federal and state governments can enact laws in relation to the health sector of the country. Consequently, successive governments at all levels have attempted to formulate policies to affect the standard and quality of health in the country.

In addition to the Constitutional provisions, it is instructive to note that Nigeria is one of the few countries in Africa that has domesticated the African Charter on Human and

---

27 J Akande 'Fundamental Objectives and Directive Principles of State Policy within the Framework of a Liberal Economy: A Note' in IA Ayua, DA Guobadia and AO Adekunle (eds) *Nigeria – Issues in the 1999 Constitution* (NIALS 2000) 198.

28 See secs 13–17 of the Nigerian Constitution 1999 (as amended).

Peoples' Rights.[29] The African Charter avoids the previous compartmentalisation of rights by explicitly guaranteeing civil and political rights and economic, social and cultural rights in one instrument.

Article 16(1) provides that 'Every individual shall have right to enjoy the best attainable state of physical and mental health.' Under these provisions, the right to health is therefore guaranteed. Moreover, Article 16(2) further provides that states parties to the instrument 'shall take the necessary measures to protect the health of their people and to ensure that they receive medical attention when they are sick'. Chapters 1 and 9 of this volume discuss the content and meaning of the right to health guaranteed under international and regional human rights instruments, including the Africa Charter.

Challenges in Litigating Health Rights in Nigeria

Most often, violation of rights in health care institutions leads to violation of other rights such as the right to life, work, housing and education, among others. Opportunities for redress of these violations are mostly lacking. At times patients are given drugs with the label peeled off and are thus denied necessary education about the drugs, leading sometimes to adverse drug reactions and death. Youths and women seeking reproductive health care are treated with scorn and disdain depending on the disposition of the health care provider. They are rarely consulted about their diagnosis or in making decisions about their treatment. The situation is even worse for vulnerable groups such as the uneducated, the poor, women, children and patients with stigmatising diseases like HIV/AIDS.[30] Patients are reluctant to seek redress for fear of negative reprisals.

Litigation affords an individual the opportunity to challenge human rights violations and seek compensation for perceived wrongful acts. However, observation shows that health care providers in Nigeria behave as if they are immune from litigation even in the presence of gross malpractice and negligence. In a study conducted from January 2006 to March 2007 attempts were made to find out the attitudes of Nigerians towards health rights litigation.[31] The study was both quantitative and qualitative. The qualitative aspect of the study was conducted through the use of in-depth interviews with 50 randomly selected adults from different ethnic, cultural and social backgrounds. The study was carried out in Ibadan, the largest city in Nigeria. The study sought to assess the use of orthodox medical practice by Nigerians, examine Nigerian experiences of unethical practice or injustice, and identify attitudes of Nigerians to health rights litigation and factors responsible for their attitudes to litigation. The results showed that while Nigerians make use of hospitals and are aware of their rights as consumers of health care services, they exhibit poor attitudes

---

29 See the African Charter on Human and Peoples' Rights (Ratification and Enforcement) Act, Cap A9, Laws of the Federation of Nigeria (LFN) 2004.

30 S Iwuagwu et al, *Background Document on HIV and Human Rights in Nigeria* (Futures Group International 2003).

31 MO Oyetunde 'A Pilot Study Assessing Litigation in Health Care Services in Nigeria' (2011) *African Journal of Medicine and Medical Sciences* 85.

to litigation for various reasons. According to the study, these attitudes were the result of prevailing socio-cultural factors in Nigeria, which do not promote litigation. This would seem to coincide with the view of Odinkalu who has noted that litigating the right to health in Nigeria remains a great challenge due to a number of factors including an unfriendly legal regime, the high cost of litigation and delays in the justice system.[32]

Moreover, litigating health rights as a public interest legal issue involving state actors or agencies is almost impossible in the current legal atmosphere where there is no explicit constitutional guarantee for such a right.

Litigation in Nigeria is time-consuming, costly and cumbersome. Some judicial divisions are overcrowded with cases and in most cases litigants are sceptical about taking up matters because of fear of reprisal attacks or corruption and the inability to recover the 'subject or thing'; government agencies have been known to frustrate execution of court judgments.

Also, due to the fact that the right to health is not justiciable in the country, most of the litigation on health in Nigeria before 2000 dealt with issues that were contractual in nature or that related to breach of a tortuous liability. Nigerian courts have consistently held that the provisions of chapter II of the Constitution, which include the right to health, are not amenable to judicial remedies. One such instance in which this position has been affirmed is *Archbishop Okogie and Others v The Attorney General of Lagos State*.[33] In that case, the applicant challenged the policy of the Lagos state government to abolish private schools within the state claiming that it was in violation of the right to education guaranteed under section 16 (chapter II) of the 1979 constitution, which is similar to the provision of the 1999 Constitution. The Court held that by virtue of section 6 of the 1979 constitution (similar to section 6 of the 1999 Constitution) the provisions of chapter II were not enforceable and that it was not in the power of the court to make any pronouncement on them. Rather this should be done by either the executive or the legislative arm of government. If ever there had been any hope of litigating on socio-economic rights (contained in chapter II of the Nigeria Constitution) prior to *Okogie*, this hope was dealt a deadly blow by the Court in that case. By this decision, the Court has more or less closed the door to prospective socio-economic rights litigants in Nigeria.[34]

Some of the cases in the health sector have touched on the law of torts, particularly the doctrine of informed consent to protect the individual's right to bodily integrity, personal dignity, autonomy and self-determination. This confers on the individual the right to refuse any medical test or treatment, advice or counsel even if his/her doctor or family considers this as necessary for his/her health. Thus, in the Nigerian case of *Medical and Dental Practitioners Disciplinary Tribunal v Okonkwo*,[35] the Supreme Court of Nigeria upheld

32 See C Odinkalu, 'The Impact of Economic and Social Rights in Nigeria: An Assessment of the Legal Framework for Implementing Education and Health as Human Rights' in V Gauri and D Brinks (eds) *Courting Social Justice: Judicial Enforcement of Social and Economic Rights in the Developing World* (Cambridge University Press 2008) 183.

33 (1981) 2 NCLR 350.

34 See, for example, ST Eborah, 'The Future of Economic, Social and Cultural Rights Litigation in Nigeria' (2007) 1 *Review of Nigerian Law and Practice* 109, 116.

35 [2001] 7 NWLR 206.

the personal decision of a Jehovah's Witness to refuse consent to blood transfusion in exercise of this right. Also, a court held in 2002 that a doctor has no right to amputate a patient's finger without consent.[36]

In some cases, litigation on health has occurred in relation to personal injury cases or the Workmen's Compensation Act cases. A case of note in this regard is *Strabag Construction Nig. Ltd v Ogarekpe.*[37] The plaintiff was employed by the respondent as an electrician in November 1983. On 17 January 1984, the plaintiff and five others were carrying out an electrical wiring job and the plaintiff was on top of a tower crane being installed at a considerable height. As the installation was being done, the crane shifted and fell down and the plaintiff/respondent and the others on the crane were seriously injured. The plaintiff broke his hand and his armpit was severed. His doctor, an orthopaedic surgeon who operated on his hand and treated him, put his permanent disability at 25 per cent and stated that he was no longer fit to perform his normal duties as an electrical technician. The plaintiff then sued the defendant for negligence. The court held in favour of the plaintiff.

Another barrier to health rights litigation in the country has to do with lack of knowledge about human rights issues on the part of lawyers and judges. Often, lawyers and judges are not well-grounded in international human rights law, especially with regard to the right to health, including HIV/AIDS. The implication of this is that most lawyers are unable to cite relevant and appropriate international human rights instruments to advance their cases. Equally, most judges are unable to apply relevant human instruments or draw examples from other jurisdictions on similar issues to come to a logical conclusion as regards cases before them. This has hindered the development of jurisprudence on the right to health in the country. This situation is not peculiar to the right to health. By virtue of their orientation some judges have not been exposed to international human rights principles and norms and thus they are unwilling or unable to apply international human rights standards to cases before them even when the opportunity presents itself.

As mentioned earlier, Nigeria has ratified most of the international human rights instruments relating to the right to health and has even gone a step further to incorporate the African Charter into its domestic law. Despite this, the courts have been reluctant to invoke some of the principles contained in these instruments based on the provision of section 12(1) of the Constitution. This section provides that 'No treaty between the Federation and any other country shall have the force of law to the extent to which any such treaty has been enacted into law by the National Assembly.' The import of this provision would seem to be that unless a treaty has been enacted into domestic law by the legislature, it cannot be enforced in Nigeria. This would seem to coincide with the reasoning of the dualist school of thought.[38] Often, Nigerian courts have construed the

36 *Okekearu v Tanko* 2002, 15 NWLR Part 791 at 657 SC.

37 1991, 1 NWLR Part 170 at 733 CA.

38 According to the dualists, championed by Triepel and Anzilotti, the sources of international law and municipal law differ greatly from each other. While municipal law is often derived from age-old customs and conventions applicable in a particular state and legislative enactments, international law on the other hand is mainly derived from custom grown up in a community of states and treaties agreed upon by independent states. See J Dugard, *International Law: A South African Perspective* (Juta 2005) 47.

provision of this section restrictively to refuse application of international human rights treaties to cases brought before them.

In *General Sani Abacha v Chief Gani Fawehinmi*,[39] the Supreme Court of Nigeria, which is the highest court in the country, was called upon to consider the legal status of the African Charter vis-à-vis the Constitution. The Supreme Court held that the African Charter has become part of Nigerian law and therefore is enforceable in the country like any other statute in accordance with section 12 of the 1979 Constitution. The Court noted that it would be uncharitable of Nigeria to accede to an international treaty only to turn around and jettison the content of this treaty. Thus, the Court explained further:

> By Cap. 10 the African Charter is now part of the laws of Nigeria and like all other laws the courts must uphold it. The Charter gives to citizens of member states of the Organization of African Unity rights and obligations which rights and obligations are to be enforced by our courts, if they must have any meaning. No doubt Cap. 10 is a statute with international flavour. Being so, therefore, I would think that if there is a conflict between it and another statute, its provisions will prevail over those of that other statute for the reason that it is presumed that the legislature does not intend to breach an international obligation. To this extent I agree with their Lordships of the Court below that the Charter possesses 'a greater vigour and strength' than any other domestic statute ... Thus in the likely event of a conflict between Constitutional provisions and the provisions of the African Charter, the Nigerian Constitution will prevail as the superior Law. This makes it almost impossible to enforce the provisions of the African Charter on rights protection for Nigerian Citizens who are relying upon its provisions not contained in the Nigerian Constitution.[40]

It should be noted that for the purposes of litigating under chapter IV of the Nigerian Constitution or, as in recent development, a claim to exercise or protect the right to health *simplicita*, litigants in Nigerian courts must bring their action in accordance with the Fundamental Rights Procedure Rules.[41] The procedure laid down by the rules is as follows:

- An applicant must apply to court for leave to enforce his fundamental rights under the provisions of order 2 rule 2(3) made by motion ex parte.
- It must be supported by statements that set out the name and description of the applicant.
- It will clearly set out the reliefs being sought and the grounds thereof.
- This must be accompanied by a verifying affidavit deposing to the facts to be relied on by the applicant.[42]

---

39 (2001) 1 CHR 20.

40 *General SaniAbacha v Chief GaniFawehinmi*, paras F-G.

41 The fundamental rights enforcement rules made by the CJN pursuant to sec 43(3) of the 1979 Constitution and sec 42(3) of the 1999 Constitution defines 'fundamental rights as any of the fundamental rights provided in the Chapter IV of the Constitution'. See *Fajemirokun v CB NIG.LTD* (2009) 5 NWLR Part 1135 at 588 SC.

42 See *AFRIBANK Nig Plc. v Adigun* [2009] 11 NWLR Part 1152 at 334.

This is to ensure a speedy dispensation of justice and to bring all matters before the court so as to 'free' the litigant from unnecessarily suffering rights infringement a moment longer. Initially, these rules were only applicable to the fundamental provisions contained in the chapter IV provisions of the Constitution. However, the Court has held in *Ohakosim v Commissioner of Police Imo State*[43] that by virtue of the African Charter on Human and Peoples' Rights (Ratification and Enforcement) Act Cap A9, Laws of the Federation of Nigeria 2004, the African Charter on Human and Peoples' Rights constitutes part of the laws of Nigeria and must be upheld by all courts in the country. Hence, the rules must also by interpretation apply to enforcements of the African Charter and all other instruments domesticated and enacted in Nigeria.

Health Rights Litigation Post-2000

In two decisions, which will serve as the 'leading cases' for litigating health rights in Nigeria, the courts have boldly ruled to advance individuals' right to health as provided under the African Charter. The first of these cases is *Festus Odafe and Others v Attorney General of the Federation and Others*.[44] Subsequent to the grant of leave on 25 November 2002 to the applicants to enforce their fundamental rights in respect of the relief stated in the statement in support of the application, the applicants by motion on notice dated 29 November 2002 and filed on 2 December 2002 petitioned the Court for the following reliefs:

> 1. A declaration that the continuous detention and the consequent segregation and discrimination of the applicants as confirmed HIV/AIDS patients is an infraction of the applicants' constitutionally guaranteed rights to dignity of the human person and their right to freedom from discrimination provided for in sections 34(1)(a) and 42(1) of the 1999 Constitution, respectively.
>
> 2. A declaration that the applicants as confirmed HIV/AIDS patients have a right to proper medical treatment while in prison custody sequel to the Prisons Act, the Prisons Regulation Law and the United Nations Standard Minimum Rules for the Treatment of Prisoners.
>
> 3. A declaration that the failure of the officers, servants, agents and privies of the respondents to give the applicants as confirmed HIV/AIDS patients proper medical attention while in prison custody amounts to inhuman and degrading treatment and an infraction of their fundamental rights as guaranteed under section 34 and section 42 of the 1999 Constitution of the Federal Republic of Nigeria, and article 5 of the African Charter on Human and Peoples' Rights.

43 2009, 13 NWLR Part 1164 at 229.

44 Federal High Court of Nigeria, Port Harcourt judicial division, 23 February 2004, suit FHC/PH/CS/680/2003 Judge: Nwodo (2004) AHRLR 205.

The Court held, inter alia, that the denial of medical attention to the applicants amounted to a violation of the right to health as guarranteed under article 16 of the African Charter. It was further held that given the HIV status of the applicants, the refusal of the prison authorities to priovide them with medical attention amounted to inhuman and degrading treatment in violation of the Consitutional provision. However, the Court reasoned that section 42 of the Constitution does not prohibit discrimination based on health or disease status and as such the denial of medical treatment based on HIV status of the applicants did not amount to a violation of the right to non-discrimination guaranteed in section 42. It has been argued elsewhere that this interpretation of the Court is not only restrictive but also falls short of principles of international human rights law.[45] It is, therefore, imperative that an enabling environment is created where the rights of all people, including HIV positive persons, are respected and where discriminatory practices against people living with HIV/AIDS are addressed.

In *Georgina Ahamefule v Imperial Medical Centre and Another*,[46] Justice Caroline O. Olufawo of Ikeja High Court, Lagos, during the preliminary hearing of the case prevented Georgiana Ahamefule, a nurse, who was dismissed from her job at the Imperial Hospital, Ebute-Metta, Lagos, from appearing to testify in her case out of fear that she would infect those in court with HIV. The lawsuit was filed and litigated by the Social and Economic Rights Action Centre (SERAC), a non-governmental organisation based in Lagos, on Georgiana Ahamefule's behalf over a 12-year period. The hospital terminated her appointment on 23 October 1995 because of her HIV status. It also refused to carry out post-abortion evacuation after she suffered a miscarriage as a result of the trauma of the termination of her employment based on HIV status. Ahamefule had worked at the hospital for five years. The plaintiff brought an action claiming that the termination of her employment was unlawful and actuated by malice. She further claimed that her termination of employment based on HIV status was unlawful and in contravention of articles 2 and 18(3) of the African Charter. It was also contended that her denial of treatment due to her HIV status was a violation of her right to health as guaranteed in article 16 of the African Charter of Human and Peoples' Rights (Ratification and Enforcement) Act, Cap 10 Laws of the Federation of Nigeria and article 12 of the International Covenant on Economic, Social and Cultural Rights (ratified by Nigeria in 1993). She asked for damages of about N5 million.

The High Court held, inter alia, that the purported termination of the plaintiff's employment was illegal, unlawful and actuated by malice and extreme bad faith. It held further that the defendants' action in subjecting the plaintiff to HIV testing without her informed consent constituted an unlawful battery on her and that the defendants' action in not affording the plaintiff pre-test and post-test counselling services constituted an unlawful negligence of a professional duty to the plaintiff.

45 See E Durojaye, 'Discrimination Based on HIV/AIDS Status: A Comparative Analysis of the Nigerian Court's Decision in *Festus Odafe and Others v Attorney General of the Federation and Others* with other Commonwealth Jurisdictions' (2007) 11 *Law, Democracy and Development* 133.

46 Suit No ID/1627/2000, delivered on 27 September 2012, per Hon. Justice YO Idowu, Lagos High Court (unreported).

The Court further noted that the defendants' action in denying the plaintiff medical care on grounds of her HIV-positive status constituted a flagrant violation of the right to health guaranteed under article 16 of the African Charter on Human and Peoples' Rights (Ratification and Enforcement) Act CAP 10 Laws of the Federation of Nigeria and article 12 of the International Covenant on Economic, Social and Cultural Rights. The plaintiff was then awarded general damages of N5 million for the wrongful termination of employment and an additional N2 million as compensation for unlawful conduct of HIV testing without the plaintiff's informed consent and for the defendants' negligence.

This decision is significant in the sense that it is the first judicial pronouncement in Nigeria to recognise the unlawfulness of HIV testing without the individual's informed consent. Further, it is equally definitive on the point that conducting HIV tests on an individual without pre-test and post-test counselling constitutes unlawful negligence. The case also establishes the principle that denial of medical care on grounds of HIV-positive status constitutes a flagrant violation of the right to health. The monetary damages of 7 million naira awarded against the hospital and its chief medical director sends a strong signal that this kind of unjustifiable and unlawful discrimination against people living with HIV will no longer be tolerated.

No doubt this decision represents a major victory not only for Georgina Ahamefule but for all those living with HIV in Nigeria, as well as the general population. In the sense that its pronouncements have clearly extended the constitutional provisions on fundamental rights to include a right to health, it has empowered Nigerians to seek remedies under the African Charter provisions. It is also a major triumph of justice over illegality and unfairness. However, the decision needs to be celebrated with caution for a number of reasons. First, it fails to address the major issue before the Court – discrimination based on HIV status.[47] By failing to consider whether the termination of the plaintiff's employment amounted to discrimination under the Constitution, the Court would seem to have fallen into the same pit as the earlier judgment in *Odafe*.[48] In that case, the Court ruled that section 42 of the Nigerian Constitution did not prohibit discrimination on the basis of one's health or HIV status, and therefore the applicants' claim failed. This decision has been criticised for its narrow interpretation of the Constitution and for failing to consider articles 2 and 3 of the African Charter.[49]

Second, given the serious human rights violations that HIV-positive women often encounter in Nigeria, as exemplified by the plaintiff's experience in *Ahamefule*, the Court could have been more sensitive to the gender dimension raised by this case. Failure of the Court to consider the applicable constitutional provisions and the gender dimension has deprived the plaintiff of the justice she deserves.

These cases have shown that despite the fact that the right to health is not explicitly guaranteed in the Constitution, opportunities exist for health rights litigation in Nigeria.

47 For a detailed analysis of this case, see E Durojaye, 'So Sweet so Sour: A Commentary on the Nigerian High Court's Decision in *Georgina Ahamefule v Imperial Hospital & Another* Relating to the Rights of Persons Living with HIV' (2013) *African Human Rights Law Journal* 464.

48 (2004) AHRLR 205 (NgHC 2004).

49 See Durojaye (n 45 above) 137.

Civil society groups need to be more creative in litigating on this issue and there need for more training for lawyers and judges on human rights issues general and health rights litigation in particular.

Conclusions

This chapter has examined the various health challenges in Nigeria and the attempts to litigate health right cases. It has been demonstrated that due to a number of barriers, including non-recognition of the right to health as an enforceable right under the Constitution and lack of knowledge on international human rights principles on the part of judges and lawyers, jurisprudence on health rights has not been well developed in the country. Despite these challenges, recent developments in the country, as shown in the cases of *Odafe* and *Ahamefule*, would seem to show that Nigerian courts are becoming bolder in finding for the violation of the right to health based on the provisions of the African Charter. Whether or not this is sustainable given the decision of the Supreme Court in *Abacha v Gani Fawehinmi*[50] is another issue to be considered. It is yet to be seen how the Supreme Court decision in *Gani Fawehinmi* will be applied, if and when a similar case comes before the courts. It is hoped that with the courts' recent pronouncements, which have affirmed the application of the African Charter provisions in Nigeria, and with the on-going reforms in the judicial system, more litigants will be free to seek redress for infringements of their right to health before Nigerian courts.

References

Books, Chapters, Articles, etc.

Akande, J, 'Fundamental Objectives and Directive Principles of State Policy within the Framework of a Liberal Economy: A Note' in IA Ayua, DA Guobadia and AO Adekunle (eds) *Nigeria – Issues in the 1999 Constitution* (NIALS 2000) 198–234.

Bankole, A et al, *Barriers to Safe Motherhood in Nigeria* (AGI 2009).

Center for Reproductive Rights, *Briefing Paper: Surviving Pregnancy and Childbirth: An International Human Right* (CRR 2005).

Center for Reproductive Rights, *Failure to Deliver: Violations of Women's Human Rights in Kenyan Facilities* (CRR 2007).

Dugard, J, *International Law: A South African Perspective* (Juta 2005).

Durojaye, E, 'Discrimination Based on HIV/AIDS Status: A Comparative Analysis of the Nigerian Court's Decision in *Festus Odaife and Others v Attorney General of the Federation and Others* with other Commonwealth Jurisdictions' (2007) 11 *Law, Democracy and Development* 133–151.

50 SC/45/1997. This ruling refers to the supremacy of laws and regarded the provisions of the African Charter as inferior to the Nigerian Constitution.

Durojaye, E, 'So Sweet so Sour: A Commentary on the Nigerian High Court's Decision in *Georgina Ahamefule v Imperial Hospital & Another* Relating to the Rights of Persons Living with HIV' (2013) *African Human Rights Law Journal* 464–480.
Eborah, ST, 'The Future of Economic, Social and Cultural Rights Litigation in Nigeria' (2007) 1 *Review of Nigerian Law and Practice* 109–124.
Federal Ministry of Health, *Revised National Health Policy* (FMOH 2004).
Federal Ministry of Health, *Report of the National HIV/Syphilis Sentinel Sero Prevalence Survey* (FMOH 2010).
Hailu, S, Enqueselassie, F and Berhane, Y, 'Health Facility-based Maternal Deaths Audit in Tigray, Ethiopia' (2009) 23 *Ethiopia Journal of Health Development* 115–119.
Iwuagwu S, Durojaiye, E. Oyebola, B. Oluduro, B. and Ayankobe, O, *Background Document on HIV and Human Rights in Nigeria* (Futures Group International 2003).
National Agency for the Control of AIDS, *Update on HIV/AIDS Epidemic and Response in Nigeria* (NACA 2011).
Odinkalu, C, 'The Impact of Economic and Social Rights in Nigeria: An Assessment of the Legal Framework for Implementing Education and Health as Human Rights' in V Gauri and D Brinks (eds) *Courting Social Justice: Judicial Enforcement of Social and Economic Rights in the Developing World* (Cambridge University Press 2008) 183–223.
Oluduro, O and Ayankogbe, O, 'Legal Issues Raised by HIV/AIDS in Nigeria' (2001) *Journal of Law and Social Sciences* 154–166.
Owuliri, VA and Jolayemi, OM, 'Reaching Vulnerable and High Risk Groups in Nigeria' in O Adeyi, PJ Kanki, O Idutolu and JA Idoko (eds) *AIDS in Nigeria: A Nation on the Threshold* (Harvard University Press 2006) 310–322.
Oyetunde, MO, 'A Pilot Study Assessing Litigation in Health Care Services in Nigeria' (2011) *African Journal of Medicine and Medical Sciences* 85–89.
World Health Organization, *World Health Report* (WHO 2000).
World Health Organization, *The World Health Report 2005 –Make Every Mother and Child Count* (WHO 2005).
World Health Organization, UNICEF, UNFPA & World Bank, *Trends in Maternal Mortality: 1990 to 2008* (WHO 2010).
World Health Organization, UNICEF and UNFPA, *Maternal Mortality in 2000: Estimates* (WHO 2004).
World Bank 'Life Expectancy at Birth, Total (Years)', at http://data.worldbank.org/indicator/SP.DYN.LE00.IN (accessed 6 February 2015).

International and Regional Instruments

African Charter on Human and Peoples' Rights, OAU Doc CAB/LEG/67/3/Rev 5, adopted 27 June 1981, entered into force 21 October 1986.
African Charter on Human and Peoples' Rights (Ratification and Enforcement) Act, Cap A9, Laws of the Federation of Nigeria (LFN) 2004.
African Charter on the Rights and Welfare of the Child, OAU Doc CAB/LEG/24.9/49, adopted 1990, entered into force 29 November 1999.
Constitution of the Federal Republic of Nigeria 1999.

Convention on the Rights of the Child, A/RES/44/25, adopted 20 November 1989, entered into force 2 September 1990.

Declaration of Alma-Ata, adopted at the International Conference on Primary Health Care, held in Alma-Ata, USSR, September 1978, available at www.who.int/hpr/archive/docs/almaata.html.

International Covenant on Civil and Political Rights, adopted 16 December 1966, entered into force 23 March 1976.

International Covenant on Economic, Social and Cultural Rights, A/Res/21/2200, adopted 16 December 1966, entered into force 3 January 1976.

Vienna Declaration and Programme of Action, A/CONF.157/23, adopted by the World Conference on Human Rights (Vienna), 14–25 June 1993.

Cases

AFRIBANK Nig Plc. v Adigun [2009] 11 NWLR Part 1152.

Archbishop Okogie and Others v The Attorney-General of Lagos State (1981) 2 NCLR 350.

Fajemirokun v CB NIG.LTD (2009) 5 NWLR Part 1135.

Festus Odafe and Others v Attorney General of the Federation and Others (2004) AHRLR 205 (NgHC 2004).

General Sani Abacha v Chief Gani Fawehinmi (2001) 1 CHR 20.

Georgina Ahamefule v Imperial Hospital and Another, Suit No ID/1627/2000, delivered on 27 September 2012.

Medical and Dental Practitioners Disciplinary Tribunal v Okonkwo [2001] 7 NWLR 206.

Ohakosim v Commissioner of Police Imo State 2009, 13 NWLR Part 1164.

Okekearu v Tanko 2002, 15 NWLR Part 791.

Strabag Construction Nig. Ltd v Ogarekpe 1991, 1 NWLR Part 170.

Ukpo v Imoke (2009) 1 NWLR PART 1121.

Chapter 7

The Right to Health in Mauritius: Is the State Doing Enough or is the Constitutional Protection of the Right to Health Still Required?

Amar Roopanand Mahadew[1]

The World Health Organization has defined health as 'a state of complete physical, mental and social well-being and not merely the absence of disease or infirmity'.[2] Perhaps the best person to ensure that one stays in good health is oneself. However, it is important to understand the nature of the responsibility of states when it comes to the need of a citizen to feel well physically and socially without disease or infirmity. The state has a role to play because every individual is entitled to the right to health, which places some responsibilities and obligations on the state. Indeed, the right to health is not to be understood and interpreted as the right to be healthy. Rather, it consists of freedoms and entitlements, which take into cognizance the individual's biological and social conditions as well as the state's available resources, both of which may preclude a right to be healthy for reasons beyond the control of the state.[3]

In Chapter 1 of this book, Olubayo Oluduro and Ebenezer Durojaye discuss in detail the normative framework for the right to health. But before examining the legal framework on health in Mauritius, a few remarks on the international and regional standards are necessary. Article 12 of the International Covenant on Economic, Social and Cultural Rights (ICESCR) provides for the right to the highest attainable standard of health. The role of the state is therefore defined by the obligations it may have to allow its citizens to reach that standard. These obligations are of paramount importance since, as highlighted by the African Commission on Human and Peoples' Rights in the *Purohit* case, 'Enjoyment of the human right to health as it is widely known is vital to all aspects of a person's life and well-being, and is crucial to the realization of all the other fundamental human rights

1 I am extremely grateful to Dr Ebenezer Durojaye and Prof Julia Nielsen-Sloth for their constant support and encouragement.

2 See World Health Organization, 'WHO Definition of Health', available at http://www.who.int/about/definition/en/print.html (accessed 27 February 2015).

3 UN Committee on Economic, Social and Cultural Rights, General Comment No 14, 'The right to the highest attainable standard of health' (2000) UN Doc E/C./12/2000/4, para 9.

and freedoms.'[4] Mauritius acceded to the ICESCR on 12 December 1973 without entering any declarations or reservations. So far Mauritius has submitted two state reports to the Committee on Economic, Social and Cultural Rights (CESCR), in 1994 and 2008.[5]

Mauritius is a state that aspires to provide the highest attainable standard of health to its citizens. The mission statement of the Ministry of Health and Quality of Life demonstrates this objective as it aims at enhancing the health status of the population, improving the quality of health care delivery with a view to increasing patients' satisfaction, enhancing social equity through the provision of a wider range of health services to the whole population and ensuring that the health sector is consolidated and that health services remain accessible to every citizen.[6] To what extent the state has been successful in implementing those aims will be discussed in a subsequent section where the major health challenges are analysed. Suffice it to state that regarding death due to diseases such as diabetes mellitus or social problems related to health such as alcoholism, Mauritius is ranked first and tenth respectively based on death rate per 100,000 population. On the other hand, the country is doing well in the field of diseases such as influenza and pneumonia, lung diseases, tuberculosis and ulcers.[7]

The discussion on the right to health in Mauritius is a complex one since the right to health is not enshrined in the Constitution as is the case for all socio-economic rights. Yet the country has managed to do fairly well in the field of public health and medical services.[8] The adoption and practice of social policies based on the welfare state system could explain this relative success.[9] However, one may question whether the legal framework for the protection and promotion of the right to health in Mauritius is effective. To what extent have local courts been successful in upholding the right to health of citizens? What are the specific challenges affecting litigation on the right to health? And does the law need amendments for a better legal structure relating to the right to health? This chapter aims to answer the above questions by first painting a picture of the major health challenges that Mauritius is currently facing. An analysis of the existing legal framework in relation to the right to health will then be provided before proposing concrete recommendations.

4 *Purohit and Another v The Gambia* (2003) AHRLR 96 (ACHPR 2003) para 80.

5 See Office of the High Commissioner for Human Rights, 'Ratification, Reporting & Documentation for Mauritius', available at http://tbinternet.ohchr.org/_layouts/TreatyBodyExternal/Countries.aspx (accessed 27 February 2015).

6 See Ministry of Health and Quality of Life, 'Mission and Vision', available at http://health.gov.mu/English/the-ministry/Pages/Mission-and-Vision.aspx (accessed 12 October 2013).

7 World Health Rankings, 'Health Profile Mauritius', available at http://www.worldlifeexpectancy.com/country-health-profile/mauritius (accessed 27 February 2015).

8 See Commonwealth Health Online, 'Health in Mauritius', available at http://www.commonwealthhealth.org/africa/mauritius/ (accessed 27 February 2015).

9 H Kasseeah and V Tandrayen-Ragoobur, 'Assessing the Formal Social Protection System in Mauritius' (2011) 1 *Research Journal of Social Science and Management* 82.

Health Challenges in Mauritius – An Overview

The Republic of Mauritius comprises two islands, the main one known as the republic of Mauritius and the smaller one known as Rodrigues. It gained independence in 1968 and became a republic in 1992 with a Westminster system of government. It is a small country with an area of around 2,000 km^2 and a population of about 1,253,000. Since independence, Mauritius has been able to leave behind the status of under-developed country to acquire the label of an upper middle level economy with political stability.[10] Mauritius has experienced a transition from the era of communicable diseases to that of non-communicable ones. It is reported that communicable diseases as well as problems related to maternal and child health have declined and have been effectively controlled.[11] However, non-communicable and chronic diseases such as diabetes, heart attacks, circulatory problems and cancers are on the rise, and it is these which currently represent the greatest health challenges in Mauritius. Problems related to blood circulation such as strokes, cardiac arrest and heart diseases are caused by a change of lifestyle, which in turn is caused by rapid industrialisation. The health and nutritional welfare of the Mauritian community has been heavily affected by the lack of time available to attend to exercise and diet because of the general stressful working lifestyle of Mauritian society.[12]

This analysis of the health situation and its challenges in Mauritius includes an overview of some vital statistics regarding health, the health delivery system, the personnel in the medical sector and activities undertaken in private and public health institutions. The major diseases that pose a health challenge are discussed and relevant steps and policies taken by the government analysed. In addition, specific sections are dedicated to issues such as health in schools and cigarette and alcoholic problems, sexual and reproductive health, diabetes, cancer and HIV/AIDS, as it is believed that those issues merit particular attention.

Some Vital Statistics in the Health Sector

As noted earlier Mauritius is an island state with a population of 1,253,000 inhabitants with a ratio of 970 males per 1,000 females.[13] The infant mortality rate as at June 2012 was 13.4 per 1,000 live births, a decrease compared to the 2007 figure which was 15.3. The maternal mortality rate was measured at 0.65 per 1,000 live births, which is equal to nine maternal deaths in the year 2012. Life expectancy has increased from 67.4 years to 70.2 years for men and from 74.6 to 77.3 years for women in the period 2000 to 2012.[14] There has been a drastic decrease in the number of HIV/AIDS cases among Mauritians, with

10 National Investment Promotion Agency of Mauritius, 'About Mauritius', available at http://www.investmauritius.com/Mauritius.aspx (accessed 10 October 2013).

11 World Health Organization, 'WHO Country Cooperation Strategy at a Glance: Mauritius' (2014).

12 'Health and Well Being of Young People – Will Modern Lifestyle Lead to their Downfall?' *Le Defi*, 11 May 2012, 8.

13 Ministry of Health and Quality of Life, *Health Statistics Report 2012*, available at http://health.gov.mu (accessed 10 October 2013).

14 World Health Rankings (n 6 above).

figures dropping from 542 cases in 2006 to 320 cases in 2012. In 2012, 33 cases of malaria, 13 cases of dengue and 1 case of chikungunya were reported.

Scabies cases reported in Area and Community Health Centers have decreased from 29,630 in 2009 to 8,522 in 2012. Of all the deaths reported in 2012, 31.4 per cent were caused by diseases of the circulatory system, 27.1 per cent were the result of endocrine, nutritional and metabolic diseases (mainly diabetes), 12.3 per cent were due to neoplasms (cancers), 8.2 per cent were due to respiratory diseases, and injury and poisoning were responsible for 5.4 per cent.[15] A slight decrease has been noted in mortality due to the main non-communicable diseases such as heart disease, strokes, diabetes, cancer and chronic respiratory disease from 488 per 100,000 population to 482 in 2012.[16]

There has been a growth in the capacity of government hospitals as well as in the number of medical staff in the last 10 years as investment in the medical sector has been a government priority. The number of nurses and midwives working in government hospitals increased by 12 per cent from 2005 to 2012. Approximately 3,500 beds were available in hospitals to accommodate patients in 2012.[17]

The Health Delivery System

The main island of Mauritius has five regional hospitals with a total capacity of 2,538 beds and two district hospitals with a total of 108 beds.[18] There are some public health institutions that specialise in certain health areas, namely a psychiatric hospital with a bed capacity of 680, hospitals for chest diseases (61 beds), the ENT (Ear, Nose and Throat) hospital with 53 beds, a specialised eye hospital with 59 beds and a hospital for heart disease which has a capacity of 67 beds. The private health sector is equally significant as Mauritians do have recourse to private institutions for treatment.[19] The Island has up to 17 private institutions with a bed capacity of 705. Twenty Area Health Centres and 116 Community Health Centres also provide free medical care in the country. Basic health services such as treatment of common diseases and injuries, advice on family planning and child and maternal care are provided in these centres.

Private health institutions have flourished over the last decade. Depending on their medical insurance scheme and their financial background, a significant number of Mauritians make use of private medical institutions for treatment. In 2012, around 200,000 patients received medical treatment and 21,000 have undergone surgeries in private institutions, thus highlighting the importance of such institutions in the health sector. The concept of private health institutions has also given rise to medical tourism.[20]

15 Ministry of Health and Quality of Life, *Health Statistics Report 2012* (n 12 above) 7.

16 Ibid, 8.

17 Ibid, 9.

18 Mauritius Tourism Promotion Authority, 'Private Clinics, Hospitals and Healthcare', at http://www.tourism-mauritius.mu/it/Private-Clinic-Hospitals-Health-Care/ (accessed 27 February 2015).

19 Board of Investment, 'Mauritius – A Destination for Healthcare, Wellness and Leisure', Board of Investment Newsletter No 43, 10.

20 Ministry of Health and Quality of Life, *Health Statistics Report 2012* (n 12 above).

Tourists have the opportunity to combine health care, leisure and well-being in one trip.[21] For instance, tourists visiting the Island often seek cosmetic and dental surgeries using modern technology.

School Health, Cigarettes and Alcoholism

Nurses and doctors regularly visit schools and educational institutions in Mauritius to monitor the health condition of students and to find out whether there are new diseases or infections among young persons.[22] In 2001 the World Health Organization in collaboration with UNAIDS, UNESCO and UNICEF initiated a health in schools survey known as the Global School-based Student Health Survey (GSHS).[23] In 2012, 615 pre-primary schools were visited by the government nursing staff working for school health and 19,093 children were subjected to medical check-ups of which 5 per cent were diagnosed with nits and lice. Around 60,000 students were made to undergo health tests in 283 primary schools around the Island. About 1,000 of them were referred to eye specialists for defective vision. About 13,619 of the students in the first year of primary schooling were immunised against diphtheria & tetanus (DT) and poliomyelitis.[24]

Alcoholism and cigarettes are major contributors to health challenges in Mauritius.[25] The consumption of alcohol and cigarettes is significantly high in Mauritius. Alcohol consumption, for instance, has become rampant among Mauritians, particularly young men and women. Major road accidents are regularly caused by drink driving.[26] Consequently, liver disease and lung cancer have become some of the most serious causes of mortality in Mauritius.[27] According to statistics from the Mauritius Revenue Authorities, around 1 billion cigarette sticks were imported in 2012, even though this was a slight decrease from 2009 when the figure was around 1.3 billion.[28] The number of litres of imported or locally produced alcoholic drink has increased to 56 million compared to 54.8 million in 2009.

---

21 Mauritius Tourism Promotion Authority (n 17 above).

22 Ministry of Health and Quality of Life and World Health Organization, *Global School-based Student Health Survey Country Report: Mauritius* (Ministry of Health and Quality of Life 2007) 8.

23 World Health Organization, Chronic Diseases and Health Promotion, 'Global School-based Student Health Survey' (2007, 2011), available at http://www.who.int/chp/gshs/mauritius/en/ (accessed 12 October 2014).

24 Statistics relating to the expanded programme on immunisation (2007), available at http://www.google.mu/url?sa=t&rct=j&q=&esrc=s&source=web&cd=2&ved=0CDEQFjAB&url=http%3A%2F%2Fhealth.gov.mu%2FEnglish%2FDocuments%2Fstatsm07%2Fmat07m%2Fmat_p28b.pdf&ei=qppwUo24LpCQhQfdqIGgAQ&usg=AFQjCNEo0W454OzrJGvjHufE1p1NF2NTHA&bvm=bv.55617003,d.d2k (accessed 13 June 2014).

25 R Abdool, 'Alcohol Policy and Problems in Mauritius', paper prepared for the World Health Organization Alcohol Policy in Developing Societies Project (2000).

26 'Alcoholism: A Disease Which is Gaining Ground' *Le Defi*, 31 August 2012, 7.

27 World Health Rankings (n 6 above).

28 Y Buglow, 'Can Mauritius become a Smoke-free Island', Le DefiGroup Media, 31 May 2013, available at http://www.defimedia.info/news-sunday/society/item/32877-can-mauritius-become-a-smoking-free-island.html (accessed 5 December 2013).

Regular increase in prices of alcohol and cigarette through taxation by the authority has proved successful in lowering the rate of consumption among Mauritians.[29]

Major Health Complications and the Challenges Accompanying Them

This section looks at the major diseases in Mauritius, some of which are directly responsible for the high rate of morbidity while others require more attention as potential serious health threats. Measures taken by the government in terms of health-related policies to curtail these health challenges are then discussed.

It is an unfortunate fact that at least one person in every Mauritian household will be a diabetes mellitus patient. According to a 2011 World Health Organization (WHO) report, the prevalence of diabetes among Mauritians is estimated to be at 15.53 per cent.[30] According to the WHO data published in April 2011, deaths from diabetes mellitus in Mauritius had reached 2,094 or 27.06 per cent of total deaths.[31] Diabetes affects 24 per cent of Mauritians aged between 23 and 74 years while 25 per cent of Mauritians have reached the pre-diabetic stage.[32] An ageing population, a sedentary lifestyle, an unhealthy diet, stress and the fact that most Mauritians are of Asian origin (where genetically diabetes is prevalent) are the reasons for such a high number of diabetes patients.

Various steps have been taken by the government to counter the serious problem of diabetes in Mauritius. To begin with, the treatment of diabetes is completely free in government hospitals irrespective of age, social or financial background. Community health centres provide not only medicines such as insulin for diabetic patients but also nutritionist and counselling services to monitor strictly the diet and eating patterns of diabetic patients. However, over the years it has become clear that reliance on treatment without programmes of sensitisation and screening is not enough to tackle the problem. Other policies and schemes such as 'Screening and Counselling at your Doorstep' have been launched by the government.[33] A country-wide programme of prevention has been adopted by way of the National Strategy Plan of Action for Diet, Physical Activity and Health and the Framework Convention on Tobacco Control. A National Plan of Action for Nutrition has also been implemented. The government has prioritised the establishment of a National Service Framework for Diabetes for Mauritius, outlining the steps and measures for diabetes prevention and standards for diabetes care and interventions required.

Cardiovascular problems and heart disease are another group which represents a serious health challenge in Mauritius. They are among the major causes of death and they include blood circulation problems, coronary disease, heart attacks and strokes. Heart-

---

29 See DT Jamison, JG Breman, AR Measham et al (eds) *Disease Control Priorities in Developing Countries* (World Bank 2006), esp ch 46 'Tobacco Addiction' and ch 47 'Alcohol'.

30 World Health Organization, *World Health Statistics* (WHO 2011).

31 Ibid.

32 'Group Diabetes – Mauritius Ranks 3rd in the world' *Le Defi*, 22 November 2011, 11.

33 Government of Mauritius, 'Health Minister Launches "Screening and Counselling at your Doorstep" Programme', available at http://www.gov.mu/English/News/Pages/Health-Minister-Launches-%E2%80%9CScreening-and-Counselling-at-your-Doorstep%E2%80%9D-Programme.aspx (accessed 27 February 20015).

related problems have been noted among individuals of different ages, from as young as 21 to 70 and above.[34] Diabetes and changes in lifestyle such as physical inactivity have been recognised as the primary reasons for an elevated rate of cardiovascular disease in Mauritius.[35] A massive sensitisation campaign has been organised by the government and medical research has been encouraged in the area. Medical researchers are involved in the study of genetic factors underlying the susceptibility to premature coronary heart disease in the country.[36] In a report published by the WHO in April 2011, Mauritius had around 1,381 deaths caused by heart disease and this accounted for 17.84 per cent of the total number of deaths.[37]

HIV/AIDS is another health challenge that the country is currently facing. To date, a total of 692 cases of HIV/AIDS have been reported[38] and 23 cases of HIV/AIDS were registered among the Mauritian population by the Virology Laboratory Services of the Ministry of Health and Quality of Life in May 2013. The monthly average of new cases, which was 46 in the years 2006 to 2010, decreased to 33 in 2011 and 27 in 2012.[39] The HIV/AIDS epidemic in Mauritius is concentrated in the sense that the prevalence in the general population is low (about 0.2 per cent) while the prevalence in the high-risk groups of intravenous drug users, commercial sex workers (CSWs) and prison inmates is high (between 15 and 20 per cent). Out of 2,126 prison inmates, 485 are HIV positive (23 per cent).[40] The overall prevalence for the 14–49 age group is estimated at about 2 per cent.[41] The mode of transmission of HIV has shifted from heterosexual sexual activities to intravenous drug use, accounting for over 80 per cent of the mode of transmission.[42]

The discourse on sexual and reproductive health has changed over the years in Mauritius. In the 1950s and early 1960s the focus was on population growth and family planning. It was predicted that the population would grow to 2.7 million by 2000 but after successful policies of family planning, the population growth was contained to slightly over 1.2 million. The focus has now shifted to improving the sexual and reproductive health of the people with the free provision of contraceptives, antenatal care and postnatal care.[43] Sexual and reproductive health was taken on board by different components of various ministries. In 2009, the government came up with a comprehensive policy entitled 'The National Sexual

---

34 'Preventing Cardiovascular Diseases' *Le Defi*, 5 October 2012, 18.

35 C Jahangeer, 'The Effect of Risk Factors on Cardiovascular Diseases in Mauritius' (2010) 1 *American Medical Journal* 48.

36 Mauritius Research Council, 'Biomedical Research' (September 2001) 21.

37 Cited by J Tuomilehto, 'The Prevalence of Coronary Heart Disease in the Multi-ethnic and High Diabetes Prevalence Population of Mauritius' (1993) 233 *Journal of Internal Medicine* 187.

38 Statistics on HIV/AIDS (as at end of May 2013), available at health.gov.mu/English/Statistics/Documents/HIVMay13.pdf (accessed 14 June 2014).

39 Ibid.

40 Ibid.

41 See S Ramchurn, 'Epidemiology of HIV/AIDS in Mauritius' (University of Mauritius 2008–2009).

42 Statistics on HIV/AIDS (n 37 above).

43 Ministry of Health and Quality of Life, *National Sexual and Reproductive Health Strategy and Plan of Action 2009–2015* (Ministry of Health and Quality of Life 2008) 8.

and Reproductive Health Strategy and Plan of Action 2009'. The aim of the policy is to provide effective guidance and good quality delivery of sexual and reproductive health. The objectives are in line with the 1994 Cairo International Conference on Population and Development Plan of Action to which Mauritius is a signatory.[44]

As noted above, current health problems in Mauritius have to do with the increase in non-communicable diseases. Medical treatment is completely free in the country and medical insurance is not required for that purpose. How has the country been able to provide such services and what are the legal avenues for redress if, for instance, an individual feels that his or her right to health has been violated? The next section considers the legal framework relating to the right to health in Mauritius. The Constitution, Acts of parliament and policies as well as the welfare system of governance are analysed as they are all directly or indirectly connected to the right to health in Mauritius.

The Right to Health in Mauritius

To describe the legal framework relating to the right to health, it is relevant to examine the Constitution of Mauritius. The Constitution was drafted in 1968, which was the year during which Mauritius became independent following British colonial rule. The Constitution has a Bill of Rights in its chapter 2 containing exclusively civil and political rights. There are no socio-economic rights in the Mauritian Constitution, and as such, the right to health is absent from the Bill of Rights. The absence of socio-economic rights from the Constitution has been brought to the attention of the country by the United Nations Committee on Economic, Social and Cultural Rights. The Committee has asked the government whether there is any plan to include such rights in the Constitution.[45] In response to this question, the Mauritian Mission noted:

> Mauritius fully subscribes to the view that all human rights are indivisible, interdependent and interrelated. In this regard, side by side with the strengthening of the protection of civil and political rights, Mauritius has spared no efforts to advance the realization of economic, social and cultural rights for its citizens through, inter alia, measures to combat poverty and enhance social enlistment. Mauritius is a welfare state offering free education, free health services, universal old age pensions, social security aid and benefits for widows, orphans and persons with disabilities, free public transport for students and old-aged persons and other financial assistance schemes to the needy.[46]

---

44 International Conference on Population and Development (ICPD) UN A/CONF.171 (13) (18 October 1994). See http://www.unfpa.org/public/home/sitemap/icpd/International-Conference-on-Population-and-Development (accessed 27 February 2015).

45 See Committee on Economic, Social and Cultural Rights, *Examination of the Second, Third and Fourth Periodic Reports of the Implementation by Mauritius of the International Covenant on Economic, Social and Cultural Rights* (7 May 2010).

46 Ibid, introductory para.

It should be noted that there is a tendency by the government to rely on the existence of the welfare system and provide health services to the citizens by way of a welfare scheme instead of a constitutional guarantee. Consequently, the right to health is not explicitly recognized in the Constitution as it is in the South African Constitution[47] or even as a series of directive principles for policy-making as in the Indian Constitution.[48] As part of the welfare system, an array of Acts of Parliament deal with health directly or indirectly and these are analysed in the following section. Mauritius is a state party to the ICESCR and therefore is bound by article 12, which provides for the right to health. Also, this section examines how the courts have interpreted the state's obligation under international treaties and whether they make use of international provisions on human rights in local cases.

Acts of Parliament on Health in Mauritius

The most important legislative Act of Parliament relating to health is the Public Health Act of 1925. It covers a wide range of fields and activities that fall under the domain of public health. The Act can be divided into several parts, namely into substantive issues such as sanitation, infectious or communicable diseases, dangerous epidemic diseases, leprosy and protection of food. It is also an important law with regard to the administrative aspects of health in Mauritius with sections dealing with certification of death, food and water supply, cemeteries, cremation and hospitals and dispensaries. One of the important components of the right to health is the right to a healthy natural and workplace environment, as highlighted by the Committee on Economic, Social and Cultural Rights.[49] The Public Health Act has an important section devoted to a healthy environment and sanitation in the context of the tourist activities of the country. Regulations with regard to sanitation and requirements for holding lodging houses have been extended to include proper and regulated certification and licences issued by the Sanitation Authority so that there are no health dangers posed to the population in general.[50]

Mauritius has been subject to malaria since 1867 when 43,000 people were killed after a violent epidemic broke out. However, since 1954 there has not been any case of death due to malaria reported in the country.[51] The Public Health Act has played an important role in containing and gradually eradicating malaria. Inspection and control of infectious or communicable diseases has been effective due to various legal and administrative measures taken by the government. Criminalisation of conscious exposure to infectious diseases has been used as a way to reduce the transmission of infectious diseases such as malaria.[52] It is a criminal offence to expose oneself to the public if one knows that one is infected with an infectious disease. There are other provisions with regard to diseases such as

47 Sec 27 of the Constitution of the Republic of South Africa.

48 Arts 36 to 51 of the Constitution of India.

49 Committee on Economic, Social and Cultural Rights, General Comment No 14, para 15.

50 Secs 9–18 of the Public Health Act 1925.

51 Communicable Diseases Control Unit, 'The History of Malaria in Mauritius', available at http://health.gov.mu/English/Documents/Bulletins/mal-history.pdf (accessed 27 February 2015).

52 Sec 49 of the Public Health Act 1925.

cholera, yellow fever, plague and smallpox.[53] It can be said that the Public Health Act is also heavily administrative in nature as it provides for detailed information on hospitals and dispensaries as well as cemeteries.

The HIV and AIDS Act of 2007 is another important piece of legislation with regard to health in Mauritius. This Act regulates various aspects of HIV/AIDS, ranging from HIV testing facilities to disposal of syringes and confidentiality of information. Perhaps the most important section of the Act is the provision on HIV or AIDS not being a disability.[54] Discrimination based on the status of HIV/AIDS is a criminal offence by way of section 18 of the Act. HIV testing facilities are provided in all public health institutions free of charge.[55] In addition, only a certified medical practitioner can make a request for an HIV test on another person. The Pharmacy Act of 1985 is another law that regulates medicines and pharmaceutical products in Mauritius. It established a Pharmacy Board that exercises control over the manufacture, importation, distribution and sale and possession of any drugs.[56] It also regulates the pharmaceutical business in general with provisions dealing with the operation of pharmacies, prescription books and the quality of pharmaceutical products.

The Food Act of 1998 is an equally important piece of the health puzzle in Mauritius. The Food Act provides for effective and efficient protection for consumers against those who jeopardise the health of Mauritians by putting them at risk from contaminated and unhealthy food. It was deemed fit to have a law against unhealthy food not only because of the health risk but also because of the heavy costs it presents to the already overburdened health and hospital services.[57] International norms and standards as recommended by the Codex Alimentarius Commission have been applied to the drafting of the Food Act and its subsequent Food Regulations. Food is an important part of the tourism industry and the Food Act ensures that food is of excellent quality and does not pose any health threat to foreigners in Mauritius.

It is clear that there exists an array of legislation with respect to health in Mauritius. However, a closer look at the legal framework would reveal that health-related measures and policies are much more the result of the welfare state policies of the country. From the discussion above, it is clear that Mauritians do not enjoy the right to health per se, since there is no explicit recognition of this right in the Constitution. The next section analyses the constraints of having the 'right' to health only as a result of a welfare system.

A Right to Health Based on the Welfare System of Governance

A summary of the important Acts of Parliament relating to health in Mauritius clearly shows that it is the administrative aspects of health that are regulated by law in Mauritius.

53 Sec 79 of the Public Health Act 1925.

54 Sec 3 of the HIV and AIDS Act 2007.

55 Sec 5 of the HIV and AIDS Act 2007.

56 Sec 4 of the Pharmacy Act 1985.

57 The Food Act 1998, available at http://health.govmu.org/English/Documents/foodact.pdf (accessed 27 February 2015).

None of the above-mentioned Acts define the right to health or elaborate on the essential components of the right to health. They do not provide any legal basis on which litigation on health issues is possible. Returning to the Constitution, as the right to health does not form part of the Bill of Rights, the only option would be an individual case if a situation reveals some elements of discrimination, for reliance on the court to apply the implied rights theory is highly dubitable, as will be discussed below. The legal framework is therefore weak in Mauritius when it comes to the right to health, and health services provided as part of the welfare state system of governance can be both a blessing and a curse to the right to health.

The concept of the welfare state is based on key roles played by government to promote and protect socio-economic rights by ensuring equality of opportunity, equitable distribution of wealth and public responsibility. In other words, there is strong or extensive public state intervention on behalf of society or citizens in defining social security.[58] The Mauritian government has without doubt intervened, and favourably so, in the health sector based on its welfare state policies. Mauritius is one of very few countries where medical services ranging from simple check-ups to the most important surgeries are free of cost. It would therefore be incorrect to conclude that the welfare system has not helped in supporting the health of the citizens. Even the Acts of Parliament relating to health have been instrumental in the protection and promotion of the health of Mauritians. However, it is not enough, as the legal framework for health remains very weak.

First, the Constitution does not provide for any socio-economic rights in the Bill of Rights and this implies that litigation based on socio-economic rights is not possible. The Acts of Parliament discussed above are mostly administrative and not substantive on health. Second, the sparse legal provisions on health afforded by Acts of Parliaments are easily amended by a simple majority in Parliament whereas a provision of a right to health enshrined in the Constitution could only be amended or altered by a qualified majority.[59] This would suggest that health is somewhat left to the mercy of the government and it can easily change its position on health policies as health is not guaranteed as a right. Third, the absence of health as a right prohibits litigation which in turn hampers the development of judicial precedents on the right to health that could guide the executive on further policies in relation to health.[60]

In as much as the welfare state system is critical for an effective right to health with regard to its practical implementation, the lack of constitutional protection of the right to health in Mauritius leaves the picture incomplete. The country has done fairly well as the statistics given above have shown. However, the right to health is not guaranteed. So, instead, can Mauritians rely on international human rights instruments to which Mauritius is a party and under which the country has some obligations? Also, how has the Supreme Court provided guidance with regard to the interpretation of cases on the right to health

58 TK Kasongo, 'The Welfare State within the Context of Liberal Globalisation in Africa' (2006) 9 *African Journal of International Affairs* 20.

59 Sec 47 of the Constitution of Mauritius.

60 See JP Costa, 'The European Court of Human Rights and its Recent Case Law' (2003) 38 *Texas International Law Journal* 467.

and what have been the impediments on the road to litigation on the right to health in the country? The following section attempts to provide some clarity on these matters.

Judicial Constraints towards Litigating the Right to Health Based on International Human Rights Law

Human rights litigation is very much in its infancy in Mauritius. There are various reasons for this which will be analysed later. Currently, section 17 of the Constitution is the only existing provision that provides opportunities for redress in the event of a violation of civil and political rights guaranteed in the Bill of Rights. It is believed that while individual cases have their importance in the promotion and protection of human rights, public interest litigation has a deeper impact by affecting a greater number of individuals. Public interest litigation can in fact influence the overall policies and laws of the government. The publicity that human rights litigation based on class action obtains is an additional benefit in the sense that it creates greater awareness.[61] Litigation based on a specific human right can also be a good way to hold the government accountable and answerable to the public.[62] The widespread and far-reaching effect of litigation is evident in the famous South African case of *Minister of Health and Others v Treatment Action Campaign*.[63] Public interest litigation is a concept that is completely foreign to the judicial system of Mauritius. The absence of public interest litigation in Mauritius was highlighted in the case of *Quedou v State of Mauritius*[64] where, comparing Mauritius to India, the Court was of the view that:

> The situation is different in India with the development of 'Public Interest Litigation' following the decision of the Supreme Court of India in the case of Banhma Mukti Morcha v. Union of India [1984 3 SCC 161] in which it was held that a member of the public acting bona fide can move the court for relief where fundamental rights are allegedly infringed, on behalf of a person unable to do so because of poverty, disability or social position. But Mauritius, like many other Commonwealth States including the majority of the Caribbean Commonwealth States, has remained committed to the doctrine which states that an individual has no right to bring an action in Court to litigate a question which is of general public interest. He or she must have relevant personal interest in order to be given locus standi.[65]

Public interest litigation has been quite successful in India. Despite the fact that the right to health is only regarded as part of the Directive Principles of State Policy, through

61 E Durojaye, 'Litigating the Right to Health in Nigeria: Challenges and Prospects' in M Killander (ed) *International Law and Domestic Human Rights Litigation in Africa* (Pretoria University Law Press 2010) 149, 154.

62 HV Hogerzeil et al, 'Is Right to Essential Medicines as Part of the Fulfilment of the Right to Health Enforceable through the Courts?' (2006) 368 *Lancet* 305.

63 (2002) 10 BCLR 1033 (CC).

64 (2004) SCJ 40.

65 Ibid, 5.

public interest litigation, many cases have been successfully considered and adjudicated by the Supreme Court of India even though it is not mandated to decide matters regarding socio-economic rights.[66]

The Dilemma of Locus Standi *before the Supreme Court of Mauritius*

The requirement for *locus standi* before the Supreme Court of Mauritius is quite stringent and strictly applied. It can be argued that the requirement of legal standing is important to save the precious time of the court and prevent frivolous cases being entered by individuals or groups of individuals for their own publicity or benefit.[67] However, a highly restrictive interpretation of *locus standi* can be a breach of the right to be heard by a court of law and contrary to the principles of natural justice.[68] Based on section 17 of the Mauritian Constitution and the Supreme Court Constitutional Relief Rules 2000,[69] constitutional redress can only be brought by a party who has sufficient interest in the matter. Most of the time, it is the victim himself/herself and no one else. In *Noordally v Attorney General and Director of Public Prosecution*,[70] it was held that section 17 of the Constitution would appear to mean that an application can only be entertained if it is made by the complainant and no one else, while the present motion was made on behalf of two persons, by the wife of one of them. The Supreme Court of Mauritius held that where it is physically impossible for a complainant to enter action under section 17, the court may allow somebody else to do it on their behalf but in no other circumstances can section 17 be derogated from.

According to the Supreme Court in *Tengur v Ministry of Education and Scientific Research and Another*,[71] the plaintiff claimed that the tax paid by him was used by the state to provide grants to catholic colleges that practised discrimination in the recruitment of pupils. In the capacity of a tax payer, indirectly he claimed to have an interest in the matter and to satisfy the requirement of legal standing before the Court. The Supreme Court held that the plaintiff did not have sufficient interest. There is no connection between the status of the plaintiff as a taxpayer and the precise nature of the alleged constitutional infringement, namely discrimination under section 16 of the Constitution or impediment in sending to a RCEA school a child of whom the plaintiff is parent or guardian by reason only that the school is not a school established or maintained by the government.

It can be seen from the decisions above that judicial activism is not practised in Mauritius. The Supreme Court has not used the implied rights theory to interpret human rights in the Constitution. The fact that there is no public interest in the legal structure

66 See S Muralidhar, 'The Expectations and Challenges of Judicial Enforcement of Social Rights' in M Langford (ed) *Social Rights Jurisprudence* (Cambridge University Press 2008) 102.

67 See M Astley, 'Attaining Locus Standi as a Private Party in Judicial Review Proceedings in European Community Law: A Virtually Impossible Task?' (2009) 2 *Student Support.*

68 See B Hough, 'A Re-examination of the Case for a Locus Standi Rule in Public Law' (1997) 28 *Cambrian Law Review* 83–104, available at ibal.bmth.ac.uk/pdfdocs/86.pdf (accessed 27 February 2015).

69 Sec 2 of the Supreme Court (Constitutional Relief) Rules 2000.

70 (1986) MR 220/SCJ 339.

71 (2002) SCJ 48/MR 166.

of Mauritius implies that there has been insufficient education and sensitisation around subjects relating to the right to health.

Can Judicial Intervention Lead the Way towards Protection of the Right to Health?

In the absence of the right to health in the Constitution and the possibility of public interest litigation or class action, the only glimpse of hope may be judicial intervention in terms of the application of implied rights theory or purposive interpretation of existing rights such as the right to life to include the right to health. Implied right theory has been practised by judicial bodies such as the Supreme Court of India and quasi-judicial ones such as the African Commission on Human and Peoples' Rights.[72] For instance, in the *Olga Tellis* case, the Supreme Court of India interpreted the right to life to include the right to shelter and livelihood even if it finally concluded that there was no obligation on the part of the state to provide slum dwellers with shelter.[73] The question that follows therefore is whether the Supreme Court of Mauritius will adopt this 'progressive' method of interpretation of human rights law.

In the case of *Suhootoorah v Al Rahman Co Ltd*,[74] there was an attempt by the Supreme Court to interpret the right to life in a quite broad way. It was a case concerning environmental nuisance in which the Court had to interpret whether a healthy environment was part and parcel of the right to life. The Court was of the view that peace and quiet should not become a luxury item which only the affluent can enjoy in the hospitality industry. It should be a natural right protected under the right to life enshrined in section 4 of the Constitution to mean quality of life and not quantity of life. However, it has been noted that in Mauritius the doctrine of separation of powers is respected in a strict manner. The judiciary will not encroach on the field of the executive to dictate on policy matters even if such action would be warranted by the need to uphold human rights. This is shown in the case of *Parvez Carrimkhan v Tin How Lew Chin & Others*[75] whereby, despite being against the provisions of the Best Loser System in the Constitution, the Supreme Court could only interpret the provisions without ordering the government to amend them immediately even though it was allegedly violating the fundamental rights of individuals.

It can therefore be said that the only kind of cases adjudicated upon by the Supreme Court have been cases in relation to medical negligence where the right to health of patients has been affected and breached and they were given compensation by the Court. Based on civil law, there is a contractual relationship between the doctor and the patient such that if there is a breach, a contractual action for compensation is available to the

72 See *Social and Economic Rights Action Centre (SERAC) and Another v Nigeria* (2001) AHRLR 60 (ACHPR 2001).

73 *Olga Tellis v Bombay Municipal Corporation* (1985) 3 SCC 545.

74 2013 SCJ 273.

75 (2000) SCJ 260.

victim.[76] There has been one case concerning access to essential medicines but it was more geared towards the trade aspect with the parallel importation of 'strepsils' at issue.[77] It is clear that due to the non-interventionist nature of the Supreme Court, the chances of promotion and protection of the right to health via the Court, even as a component of the right to life, seem minute. The absence of public interest litigation and the requirement for *locus standi* are further stumbling blocks.

Can We Rely on International Human Rights Law Then?

Mauritius is indeed a state party to the ICESCR that enshrines the right to health in its article 12. To what extent can such provision be invoked in the Supreme Court by individuals? The situation is not very clear in Mauritius. The Constitution is silent on the issue of the application of international law by Mauritian courts. However, it is accepted that the dualist doctrine is followed in Mauritius. In other words, because of fundamental differences between international and domestic laws in a dualist legal system, enabling legislation is required to transform or incorporate international law into national law.[78] In the case of *Permal v The Illois Trust Fund*, it was held that 'it remains true that the Agreement [between UK-Mauritius on compensation to Illois] by itself does not have the force of law ... nevertheless specific provisions of an agreement, treaty or convention do have force of law in the kind of legal system that we have to the extent that they are given effect to it in an Act of Parliament or other enactment'.[79] The provisions of international human rights instruments such as the International Covenant on Civil and Political Rights, the ICESCR and the Convention on the Elimination of Discrimination against Women have been cited in several cases but merely from an inspirational point of view.[80] Therefore it is

76 See *J Chan Chiang and Another v Medical and Surgical Centre* (2011) INT 55; *Kaudeer AR & Others v PS Ministry of Health* (2008) SCJ 113; *Pirbacosse Shireen v State of Mauritius* (2008) SCJ 65; *Gopee WA v State of Mauritius* (2007) SCJ 303; *Ramdawon P Dr v The Medical Council of Mauritius* (2006) SCJ 303.

77 *Reckitt & Colman (Overseas) Limited v Mohamad Nawaz Dauhoo and the Mauritius Revenue Authority* (2012) SCJ 495.

78 F Viljoen, *International Human Rights Law in Africa* (Oxford University Press 2007) 18.

79 (1984) SCJ 173 at 7.

80 *Bajan M v The State* (2010) SCJ 348 – 'While those provisions [Article 2 of the Seventh Protocol to the European Convention on Human Rights] are not applicable to us, and we can but draw useful guidelines, we are quite happy to observe that the provisions of section 82(2) of our Constitution are in fact compatible with the provisions of the Seventh Protocol'; *Pulluck v Ramphul* (2005) SCJ 196 – 'It was submitted that those provisions were in breach of certain named articles of the International Covenant on Civil & Political Rights and of the Convention on the Elimination of All Forms of Discrimination against Women to which Mauritius is a party. As stated in *Jordan v Jordan* (2000) MR 22, whilst it is a well-recognised canon of interpretation that domestic legislation should, if possible, be construed so as to conform to international instruments to which the State is a party, it is the practice in Mauritius that any treaty or convention must as a rule be incorporated into domestic law before the courts will apply it. The provisions contained in international instruments can therefore hardly be of help to respondents when there is no evidence of their incorporation into our domestic law'; *Marguerite VEP v The Prime Minister of Mauritius* (2014)

not possible for an individual to base a case on article 12 of the ICESCR in violation of the right to health in the Supreme Court of Mauritius.

What is the Way Forward?

As it currently stands, the legal framework relating to the right to health does not provide any protection whatsoever to individuals. However, the welfare state system and all the free medical services provided so far diminish the importance of constitutional protection of the right to health as well as the possibility of litigating the right to health based on class action or public interest litigation. A lack of education on fundamental rights and obligations of the state has made it such that the utmost importance of having the right to health in the Bill of Rights is not properly understood in Mauritius.

There should be a strong lobby for socio-economic rights including the right to health in the Constitution of Mauritius. The right to health should be justiciable by the Supreme Court, thus providing the possibility to challenge the policies that are in place to combat health issues such as diabetes, cardiovascular disease and other non-communicable ailments. This will allow cases to be heard and most importantly trends and standards to be set by which policy-makers will have to abide. On the occasion of the Law Day celebrated on 4 March 2013, the Chief Justice questioned the necessity of socio-economic rights in the Constitution on the basis that '75% of Mauritians own a house so why do we need the right to shelter in the Constitution?'[81] Such statements certainly reveal the level of understanding of the importance of granting constitutional protection to socio-economic rights. Intense education and sensitisation campaigns are required targeting policy-makers, lawyers, judges, students and even the 'common people'.

The inclusion of socio-economic rights in the Constitution would serve no purpose if the possibility to litigate was not provided. This is another unfortunate area where no concrete steps have been taken. Reflecting on this situation, it would seem that the legislature has not provided for these rights simply because the judiciary or even civil society organisations have never demanded them. Civil society organisations have never been vibrant in Mauritius. This can perhaps be explained by the fact that accountability, answerability and communication between the government and citizens have been quite easy and smooth due to the very democratic nature of the system of governance. Thus civil society organisations have never been required to lobby or carry forward the agenda of the population as has been the case in other African countries. It is argued that for socio-economic rights, particularly the right to health, to be respected in a more effective way, the introduction of public interest litigation is mandatory. This was one of the recommendations of the Law Reform Commission of Mauritius that unfortunately fell on

---

SCJ 37 – 'It is to be noted that that Convention is not applicable to Mauritius and that the case for the applicant cannot be that Mr Otton is being removed from Mauritius.'

81 See Inaugural talk to celebrate Law Day in Mauritius by Chief Justice, 4 March 2013, available at http://www1.gov.mu/scourt/pub/newsDocs/INAUGURAL%20TALK%20TO%20CELEBRATE%20LAW%20DAY.pdf (accessed 27 February 2015).

deaf ears.[82] The cost of justice and judicial services is very high in Mauritius. An individual who genuinely feels that his right to health has been violated would most probably not consider going to court as it is expensive unless it was a case of compensation for medical negligence as discussed above. Having public interest litigation and NGOs to take up such cases would be an advantage to the individual in terms of easing the financial burden, but also to the public in general as the effects of such cases are far-reaching and target a wider range of persons.

Finally, the status of international human rights law is ambiguous in Mauritius. There seems to be a commitment on the part of the government to abide by international legal standards on human rights, including the right to health. However, how the court would interpret or even accept arguments based on provisions from regional or international human rights instruments remains unclear. The Constitution has to be amended to state clearly whether international laws are to be considered part of national laws or whether the process of transformation of norms is still required. The framework must be re-visited and amended in a clear and straightforward manner.

While there are non-governmental organisations working in the field of health in Mauritius, their roles are limited to sensitising the population about particular diseases. There are no civil society organisations that are set up to litigate on right to health issues. This is explained by the fact that public interest litigation is not part of the legal scene. Human rights litigation has never been a practice in Mauritius and debates on introducing it are also rare. This is perhaps due to the lack of education on human rights. It is believed that very few lawyers, magistrates and judges are well equipped to deal with cases involving highly technical aspects of socio-economic rights. This certainly calls for massive training of the judiciary on socio-economic rights issues.

Conclusions

It is difficult to demonstrate the importance of having the right to health as a constitutional right that can be adjudicated by the Supreme Court especially in a country where citizens undoubtedly enjoy a relatively high standard of health with a free health system. All the political parties that have been in power since independence have worked towards the improvement of health in Mauritius. However, currently it is only a privilege and not a right as such. A change in political regime and method of governance, for instance, could jeopardise the current health system in the sense that it consists only of benefits provided by Acts of Parliament that can be changed easily.

The absence of cases on the right to health is another indication that health-related policies have never been challenged in court. In such circumstances, the accountability of the government cannot be maximised as there is no formal forum such as a court of law where these policies can be questioned and challenged. This chapter has discussed how inadequate and incomplete the legal framework concerning the right to health is in

82 See Law Reform Commission of Mauritius, *Law Relating to NGOs: Legislative Proposals for a New Legal and Regulatory Framework* (November 2008).

Mauritius. Providing health services as part of a welfare system should be complementary to a constitutionally protected legal framework on the right to health which is properly implemented. Health as a component of a welfare system should not replace the constitutional right to health.

References

Books, Chapters, Articles, etc.

Abdool, R, 'Alcohol Policy and Problems in Mauritius', paper prepared for the World Health Organization Alcohol Policy in Developing Societies Project (2000).

'Alcoholism: A Disease Which is Gaining Ground' *Le Defi*, 31 August 2012, 7.

Astley, M, 'Attaining Locus Standi as a Private Party in Judicial Review Proceedings in European Community Law: A Virtually Impossible Task?' (2009) 2 *Student Support*.

Board of Investment, 'Mauritius – A Destination for Healthcare, Wellness and Leisure', Board of Investment Newsletter No 43, 10.

Commonwealth Health Online, 'Health in Mauritius', available at http://www.commonwealthhealth.org/africa/mauritius/ (accessed 27 February 2015).

Communicable Diseases Control Unit, 'The History of Malaria in Mauritius', available at http://health.gov.mu/English/Documents/Bulletins/mal-history.pdf (accessed 27 February 2015).

Costa, JP, 'The European Court of Human Rights and its Recent Case Law' (2003) 38 *Texas International Law Journal* 455–467.

Durojaye, E, 'Litigating the Right to Health in Nigeria: Challenges and Prospects' in M Killander (ed) *International Law and Domestic Human Rights Litigation in Africa* (Pretoria University Law Press 2010) 149–172.

Government of Mauritius, 'Health Minister Launches "Screening and Counselling at your Doorstep" Programme', available at http://www.gov.mu/English/News/Pages/Health-Minister-Launches-%E2%80%9CScreening-and-Counselling-at-your-Doorstep%E2%80%9D-Programme.aspx (accessed 27 February 20015).

'Group Diabetes – Mauritius Ranks 3rd in the world' *Le Defi*, 22 November 2011, 11.

'Health and Well Being of Young People – Will Modern Lifestyle Lead to their Downfall?' *Le Defi*, 11 May 2012, 8.

Hogerzeil, HV, Samson, M, Casanovas, JV and Rahmani-Ocora, L, 'Is Right to Essential Medicines as Part of the Fulfilment of the Right to Health Enforceable through the Courts?' (2006) 368 *Lancet* 305–311.

Hough, B, 'A Re-examination of the Case for a Locus Standi Rule in Public Law' (1997) 28 *Cambrian Law Review* 83–104, available at ibal.bmth.ac.uk/pdfdocs/86.pdf (accessed 27 February 2015).

Jahangeer, C, 'The Effect of Risk Factors on Cardiovascular Diseases in Mauritius' (2010) 1 *American Medical Journal* 46–50.

Jamison, DT, Breman, JG, Measham, AR et al (eds) *Disease Control Priorities in Developing Countries* (World Bank 2006).

Kasongo, TK, 'The Welfare State within the Context of Liberal Globalisation in Africa' (2006) 9 *African Journal of International Affairs* 1–40.

Kasseeah, H and Tandrayen-Ragoobur, V, 'Assessing the Formal Social Protection System in Mauritius' (2011) 1 *Research Journal of Social Science and Management* 82–94.

Mauritius Tourism Promotion Authority, 'Private Clinics, Hospitals and Healthcare', at http://www.tourism-mauritius.mu/it/Private-Clinic-Hospitals-Health-Care/ (accessed 27 February 2015).

Muralidhar, S, 'The Expectations and Challenges of Judicial Enforcement of Social Rights' in M Langford (ed) *Social Rights Jurisprudence* (Cambridge University Press 2008) 102–123.

National Investment Promotion Agency of Mauritius, 'About Mauritius', available at http://www.investmauritius.com/Mauritius.aspx (accessed 10 October 2013).

'Preventing Cardiovascular Diseases' *Le Defi*, 5 October 2012, 18.

Ramchurn, S, 'Epidemiology of HIV/AIDS in Mauritius' (University of Mauritius 2008–2009).

Tuomilehto, J, 'The Prevalence of Coronary Heart Disease in the Multi-ethnic and High Diabetes Prevalence Population of Mauritius' (1993) 233 *Journal of Internal Medicine* 187–194.

Viljoen, F, *International Human Rights Law in Africa* (Oxford University Press 2007).

World Health Organization, 'WHO Definition of Health', available at http://www.who.int/about/definition/en/print.html (accessed 27 February 2015).

World Health Organization, *World Health Statistics* (WHO 2011).

World Health Organization, 'WHO Country Cooperation Strategy at a Glance: Mauritius' (2014).

World Health Organization, Chronic Diseases and Health Promotion, 'Global School-based Student Health Survey', available at http://www.who.int/chp/gshs/mauritius/en/ (2007, 2011) (accessed 12 October 2014).

World Health Rankings, 'Health Profile Mauritius', available at http://www.worldlifeexpectancy.com/country-health-profile/mauritius (accessed 27 February 2015).

International and Regional Instruments

Committee on Economic, Social and Cultural Rights, General Comment No 14, 'The right to the highest attainable standard of health' (2000) UN Doc E/C./12/2000/4.

Committee on Economic, Social and Cultural Rights, *Examination of the Second, Third and Fourth Periodic Reports of the Implementation by Mauritius of the International Covenant on Economic, Social and Cultural Rights* (7 May 2010).

Convention on the Elimination of All Forms of Discrimination against Women (CEDAW), adopted 18 December 1979, entered into force 3 September 1981.

The Food Act, Act No 1 of 1998, available at http://health.govmu.org/English/Documents/foodact.pdf (accessed 27 February 2015).

International Conference on Population and Development (ICPD) UN Doc A/CONF.171/13 (18 October 1994).

International Covenant on Economic, Social and Cultural Rights, A/Res/21/2200, adopted 16 December 1966, entered into force 3 January 1976.

International Covenant on Civil and Political Rights, GA Res. 2200A (XXI), 999 UNTS 171, adopted 16 December 1966, entered into force 23 March 1976.

Reports

Law Reform Commission of Mauritius, *Law Relating to NGOs: Legislative Proposals for a New Legal and Regulatory Framework* (Law Reform Commission of Mauritius 2008).

Mauritius Research Council, 'Biomedical Research' (September 2001).

Ministry of Health and Quality of Life, *National Sexual and Reproductive Health Strategy and Plan of Action 2009–2015* (Ministry of Health and Quality of Life 2008).

Ministry of Health and Quality of Life, *Health Statistics Report 2012*, available at http://health.gov.mu (accessed 10 October 2013).

Ministry of Health and Quality of Life, 'Mission and Vision', available at http://health.gov.mu/English/the-ministry/Pages/Mission-and-Vision.aspx (accessed 12 October 2013).

Ministry of Health and Quality of Life and World Health Organization, *Global School-based Student Health Survey Country Report: Mauritius* (Ministry of Health and Quality of Life and WHO 2007).

Office of the High Commissioner for Human Rights, 'Ratification, Reporting & Documentation for Mauritius', available at http://tbinternet.ohchr.org/_layouts/TreatyBodyExternal/Countries.aspx (accessed 27 February 2015).

Cases

Bajan M v The State (2010) SCJ 348.

Gopee WA v State of Mauritius (2007) SCJ 303.

J Chan Chiang and Another v Medical and Surgical Centre (2011) INT 55.

Kaudeer AR & Others v PS Ministry of Health (2008) SCJ 113.

Marguerite VEP v The Prime Minister of Mauritius (2014) SCJ 37.

Minister of Health and Others v Treatment Action Campaign (2002) 10 BCLR 1033 (CC).

Noordally v Attorney General and Director of Public Prosecution (1986) MR 220/SCJ 339.

Olga Tellis v Bombay Municipal Corporation (1985) 3 SCC 545.

Parvez Carrimkhan v Tin How Lew Chin and Others (2000) SCJ 260.

Pirbacosse Shireen v State of Mauritius (2008) SCJ 65.

Permal v The Illois Trust Fund (1984) SCJ 173.

Pulluck v Ramphul (2005) SCJ 196.

Purohit and Another v The Gambia (2003) AHRLR 96 (ACHPR 2003).

Quedou K v State of Mauritius (2004) SCJ 40.

Ramdawon P Dr v The Medical Council of Mauritius (2006) SCJ 303.

Reckitt & Colman (Overseas) Limited v Mohamad Nawaz Dauhoo and the Mauritius Revenue Authority (2012) SCJ 495.

Social and Economic Rights Action Centre (SERAC) and Another v Nigeria (2001) AHRLR 60 (ACHPR 2001).

Suhootoorah v Al Rahman Co Ltd 2013 SCJ 273.

Tengur v the Ministry of Education and Scientific Research and Another (2002) SCJ 48/MR 166.

Chapter 8

Litigating the Right to Health in Kenya: An Analysis of Selected Cases

Jacinta Nyachae and Paul Ogendi

Previously, the defunct 1963 Constitution of Kenya codified civil and political rights but excluded social and economic rights under its Bill of Rights.[1] This scenario, undoubtedly, presented unprecedented challenges in socio-economic rights litigation in Kenya. As a consequence, socio-economic cases were rarely litigated in court. It was not until 2010 that the new Constitution[2] extended the Bill of Rights to include social and economic rights alongside the civil and political rights.[3] The incorporation of social and economic rights, including the right to health,[4] in the Bill of Rights has brought with it several benefits. First, it has made Kenya the envy of many nations for its progressiveness, as did the 1996 South African Constitution in the case of South Africa. Second, it has greatly aided socio-economic rights litigation in Kenya.

The fact that social and economic rights are guaranteed in the Constitution is indeed very encouraging. This is because constitutions and their bills of rights are a special kind of regulatory law through which all other laws are made and executed.[5] Accordingly, the purpose of the Bill of Rights is to 'elevate the individual as against the broader community, the private interest as against the general interest; it represents a restraint to the free course of utilitarianism'.[6] Put differently, enforcing the bill of rights is an essential component of constitutionalism.[7] By its very nature, a constitutional democracy is 'a far higher form of

1 See generally the following provisions of the 1963 Constitution: art 71 on the right to life; art 72 on the right to personal liberty; art 73 on the freedom from slavery and forced labour; art 74 on the freedom from inhuman treatment; art 75 on the right to property; art 76 on the freedom from arbitrary search or entry of private premises; art 77 on the right to the protection of the law; art 78 on the freedom of conscience; art 79 on the freedom of expression; art 80 on the freedom of assembly and association; art 81 on the freedom of movement; art 82 on the freedom from discrimination.

2 Promulgated on 27 August 2010.

3 See generally art 43 of the 2010 Constitution.

4 Art 43(1)(a).

5 FI Michelman, 'The Constitution, Social Rights, and Liberal Political Justification' (2001) *Institutional Journal of Constitutional Law* 13, 14.

6 JB Ojwang and JA Otieno-Odek, 'The Judiciary in Sensitive Areas of Public Law: Emerging Approaches to Human Rights Litigation in Kenya' (1988) 35 *Netherlands International Law Review* 31.

7 See generally HWO Okoth-Ogendo, 'Constitutions without Constitutionalism: Reflections on an African Paradox' in D Greenberg et al (eds) *Constitutionalism & Democracy: Transitions in the*

government than either pure democracy or undemocratic constitutional governments'.[8] Through constitutionalism, violations of human rights are redressed by the High Court acting as the constitutional court to protect and safeguard the 'private interest founded upon the guaranteed rights' of the individual.[9] In this case, the High Court also acts as the 'court of human rights'.[10] It serves to give vague constitutional rights the much needed 'specific substance' in order to be useful.[11]

However, unlike civil and political rights, the challenge with adjudicating social and economic rights is that they are nuanced. This is partly because they are claims on government for something 'new', something that does not already exist. Some of the rights require government to create programmes, usually to spend money and perhaps other scarce social resources, and often to order priorities in ways it might not otherwise do. The constitutional problems raised by these economic and social rights revolve primarily around constitutionally requiring the government to create social and economic programmes which it has not yet established, and to meet needs that its people ordinarily cannot cope with on their own.[12]

Against this background, this chapter examines some of the health challenges in Kenya and then discusses the legal framework in relation to realising the right to heath in the country. More importantly, the chapter discusses the attempt by the Kenyan court to clarify the nature of government obligations in relation to the right to health. In this regard, the chapter examines in detail two recent cases that consider the implications of anti-counterfeiting legislation for access to life-saving medications for people living with HIV and the health impact of detention of a TB patient within the prison environment in Kenya. The strength and weakness of these cases for the realisation of the right to health are discussed and suggestions are provided on how the right to health can better be guaranteed in Kenya.

Major Health Challenges in Kenya

Kenya's health sector challenges are diverse. According to the *Kenya Health Policy 2014–2030*, for instance, globalisation, political instability and the emerging regional and national macro-economic challenges triggered by the global economic downturn and climate change have all had a negative impact on the health sector.[13] In addition, there exists also 'limitations in the regulatory and resource capacity and utilisation [that] have constrained

---

Contemporary World (Oxford University Press 1993).

8 CS Nino, *The Constitutions of Deliberative Democracy* (Yale University Press 1996) 1.

9 Ojwang and Otieno-Odek (n 6 above) 32.

10 Ibid, 47.

11 H Schwartz, 'Economic and Social Rights' (1993) 8 *American University Journal of International Law and Policy* 551, 562.

12 Ibid, 553, 554.

13 Ministry of Health, *Kenya Health Policy 2014–2030: Towards Attaining the Highest Standard of Health* (2014) 6, available at http://www.health.go.ke/images/policydocs/KHP%20Final%20 booklet.pdf (accessed 11 April 2014).

the health sector's ability to harness fully the existing technology to manage most of the direct causes of ill health and death'.[14]

On the HIV and AIDS scourge, in particular, the 2007 Kenya AIDS Indicator Survey estimates that 7.4 per cent of the Kenyan population aged 15 to 65 is infected.[15] In figures, this translates to about 1.4 million Kenyans living with HIV, thereby making the HIV and AIDS epidemic one of the biggest health challenges facing Kenya at the moment.[16] The situation is exacerbated by the fact that in 2009, for example, only about 48 per cent of Kenyans living with HIV had access to antiretroviral treatment.[17] In this regard, access to essential medicines is also a major public health challenge in the country.

Legal Framework Relating to the Right to Health

Kenya has legal commitments with regard to the right to health at the international, regional, sub-regional and national levels.

International Instruments

Until recently, Kenya could not enforce international and regional laws directly in its domestic courts pursuant to a court precedent. The 1970 precedent in *Okunda v Republic*,[18] in effect, meant that Kenya was a dualist state and therefore all international and regional laws had to be implemented locally by way of a legislative enactment.[19] However, this changed with the promulgation of the new Constitution in 2010. The paradigm shift to a monist state means that Kenya can now directly apply international and regional laws. In particular, article 2(6) of the Constitution of Kenya clearly states that all treaties ratified 'form part of the law of Kenya'. As expected, the judiciary has also interpreted this constitutional provision to mean that they are 'bound by the Constitution to have regard to these treaties'.[20] It is unclear whether 'to have regard' satisfies the standard set in the Constitution. In our view, the language used above could be interpreted to mean a non-binding commitment. As such, it is not mandatory in Kenya to apply international law at all times. Moreover, it is not clear how the courts will resolve any conflicts that may arise between domestic and international or regional law.

International principles are also recognised under Kenyan laws. According to Ambani, article 2(5) of the Constitution on applicability of international principles in Kenya would arguably allow for the 'acceptance and applicability of norms that have attained customary

14 Ibid, 7.

15 Kenya AIDS Indicator Survey (2012) 12.

16 Ibid.

17 World Health Organization, *Health Situation Analysis in the African Region: Atlas of Health Statistics, 2011* (WHO 2011) 78.

18 [1970] EA 453.

19 Ojwang and Otieno-Odek (n 6 above) 29.

20 *P.A.O & 2 Others v AG* [2012] eKLR, para 55.

international law status in the municipal courts'.[21] In this regard, therefore, with or without an international or regional treaty ratified by Kenya, international crimes such as genocide, apartheid, slavery and torture are illegal in Kenya.

Accordingly, therefore, Kenya has multiple obligations under international law with regard to the right to health. These obligations begin, almost ostensibly, with article 25 of the Universal Declaration of Human Rights,[22] and transcends to more legally binding instruments ratified by Kenya including article 12 of the International Covenant on Economic, Social and Cultural Rights (ICESCR),[23] article 24 of the Convention on the Rights of the Child (CRC),[24] article 12 of the Convention on the Elimination of All Forms of Discrimination Against Women (CEDAW)[25] and article 25 of the Convention on the Rights of Persons with Disabilities.[26]

Being part of these international treaties has made it possible for Kenya to benefit from direct contributions from the relevant international bodies. Illustratively, in 1993, the Committee on Economic, Social and Cultural Rights (CESCR) noted that the introduction of treatment charges in Kenya's public health system affected adversely vulnerable groups and other members of Kenyan society.[27] Later, on the same issue, in 2008, the CESCR recommended the 'waiver of maternity fees in public hospitals and health facilities ... without compromising the quality of services'.[28] This vital contribution to the right to health would not have been possible if Kenya, like South Africa, had not ratified the ICESCR.[29] In fact, maternity charges have currently been abolished in Kenya pursuant to a presidential directive commencing on 1 June 2013.

The final point to make in this section is that the CESCR has provided an elaborate conceptual framework that has successfully been employed in Kenyan courts, particularly on the right to health. It was through the CESCR jurisprudence that the right to health in Kenya became 'closely related to and dependent' on other human rights, including

21 JO Ambani, 'Navigating Past the "Dualist Doctrine": The Case for Progressive Jurisprudence on the Application of International Human Rights Norms in Kenya' in M Killander (ed) *International Law and Domestic Human Rights Litigation in Africa* (Pretoria University Law Press 2010) 32.

22 Universal Declaration of Human Rights, adopted by the General Assembly on 10 December 1948.

23 International Covenant on Economic, Social and Cultural Rights, 16 December (1966). Kenya acceded to the Convention on 1 May 1972. It reserved article 10(2)3.

24 Convention on the Rights of the Child (1989). Kenya ratified the Convention on 30 July 1990.

25 Convention on the Elimination of All Forms of Discrimination against Women (1979). Kenya ratified the Convention on 9 March 1984.

26 Convention on the Rights of Persons with Disabilities (2006). Kenya acceded to the Convention on 19 May 2008.

27 Committee on Economic, Social and Cultural Rights, 'Concluding observations on Kenya' (1993) para 17.

28 Committee on Economic, Social and Cultural Rights, 'Concluding observations on Kenya' (2008) para 32.

29 South Africa has yet to ratify the ICESCR. This has meant that, unlike Kenya, the country is unable to benefit from CESCR jurisprudence.

the 'right to food, housing, work, education, human dignity, life, non-discrimination, equality, the prohibition against torture, privacy, access to information, and the freedoms of association, assembly and movement'.[30] Arguably, the right to health also follows the elements established by the CESCR as follows: availability, accessibility (non-discrimination, physical accessibility, economic accessibility or affordability, and information accessibility), acceptability and quality.[31] This jurisprudence has assisted litigants in giving substance to the abstract right to health provision under the Kenyan Constitution.

Regional Instruments

Regional instruments ratified by Kenya are treated in the same way as international instruments. Therefore, article 2(6) of the Constitution can be interpreted to also include regional instruments as forming part of Kenyan law. Put differently, the use of the words 'international treaties' under article 2(6) of the Constitution also encompasses 'regional treaties'. In comparison to the use of international instruments, there has been dismal usage of regional instruments in Kenya. However, this does not mean that they are not legally binding under Kenyan law.

Notwithstanding, it is still important to highlight the obligations of Kenya under the right to health at the regional level. Just as at the international level, Kenya has ratified various regional instruments that provide for the right to health. To begin with, the African Charter on Human and Peoples' Rights (African Charter) codifies the right to health under its article 16.[32] Second, the African Charter on the Rights and Welfare of the Child also provides for the right to health under its article 14(1).[33] Third, article 14 of the Protocol to the African Charter on the Rights of the Women also enshrines the right to health.[34] Fourth, the African Youth Charter also enshrines the right to health under its article 16.[35]

Lastly, in 2009, the African Commission on Human and Peoples' Rights (hereafter African Commission) adopted a set of principles and guidelines on economic, social and cultural rights to give meaning to the various obligations under the African Charter. This document provides for specific core obligations under each social and economic right, including the right to health as well as disease specific obligations, particularly, for malaria,

---

30 CESCR, General Comment No 14, 'The right to the highest attainable standard of health' (2000) para 3.

31 Ibid, para 12.

32 African Charter on Human and Peoples' Rights (African Charter), adopted on 27 June 1981, entered into force 21 October 1986. Kenya acceded to the African Charter on 23 January 1992.

33 Protocol to the African Charter on the Rights and Welfare of the Child, adopted in Addis Ababa, Ethiopia, July 1990, entered into force 29 November 1999. Kenya acceded to the Protocol on 25 July 2000.

34 Protocol to the African Charter on the Rights of the Women (2003).

35 African Youth Charter, adopted by the Seventh Ordinary Session of the African Union Head of States and Governments, held in Banjul, The Gambia on 2 July 2006.

HIV and AIDS, tuberculosis, neglected tropical diseases and other infectious diseases.[36] These principles and guidelines are very comprehensive and if properly utilised could aid in litigation especially in the area of the right to health. Sadly, just like many other regional instruments, the uptake of these guidelines and principles has been unsatisfactory.

Sub-regional Instruments

The situation at the sub-regional level with regard to human rights in general is nuanced. An analysis of the legislative framework reveals weak human rights commitments including in the area of the right to health. The East African Community (EAC) Treaty,[37] for example, only encourages cooperation in the area of health to address the main diseases, including HIV and AIDS, cholera, malaria, hepatitis and yellow fever.[38] Luckily, this cooperation is already being seen especially in the area of HIV and AIDS. A notable achievement is the enactment of the HIV and AIDS Prevention and Management Bill at the EAC Legislative Assembly in 2012 which has, in its text, a human rights language. Illustratively, article 33 provides for the right to health care services access for persons living with HIV and AIDS in the region. Once enacted into law, this legislation will be a key advocacy tool for realising health reforms in the HIV and AIDS sector in the region, including in Kenya.

Perhaps the most important step being undertaken in respect of human rights in the region is the process that was initiated to adopt an EAC Bill of Rights. According to Ebobrah, this is 'by far the most important human rights standard-setting activity' in the region.[39] Once enacted, the EAC Bill of Rights, apart from setting the minimum standards on human rights in the region, will be instrumental in spearheading far-reaching reforms.[40]

National Laws

Nationally, there are a plethora of laws on the right to health. First, and perhaps most importantly, the 2010 Constitution of Kenya under article 43(1)(a) enshrines the right to health including reproductive health care. Moreover, article 53(1)(c) also secures the right to health for children and article 46(1)(c) obligates the government to protect the health of consumers in Kenya. The HIV and AIDS Prevention and Control Act (HAPCA) secures the right to health care services including access to medicines for persons living with HIV and AIDS under section 19.[41] Section 9 of the Children's Act[42] also secures the right to health for children under the age of 18 years in Kenya.

---

36 Principles and Guidelines on the Implementation of Economic, Social and Cultural Rights in the African Charter on Human and Peoples' Rights (2009) paras 38–63.

37 East African Community (EAC) Treaty, signed on 30 November 1999, entered into force 7 July 2000.

38 See generally art 118(a) of the EAC Treaty.

39 ST Ebobrah, 'Human Rights Developments in African Sub-regional Economic Communities during 2010' (2011) 11 *African Human Rights Law Journal* 216, 220.

40 Ibid, 221.

41 Act 14 of 2006, Laws of Kenya.

42 Act 8 of 2001, Laws of Kenya.

Other Laws

As part of the constitutional implementation process, Kenya is currently developing a National Health Law Bill. Once enacted, it will be the principal legislation implementing the right to health as enshrined in article 43(1) of the Constitution. It will also serve to clarify the obligations of the government with regard to the right to health in Kenya as well as implementing some of the courts' decisions.

A Critical Analysis of Relevant Cases Relating to the Right to Health

In this section, relevant cases relating to the right to health in Kenya are discussed. The selected cases include *P.A.O & 2 Others v AG*[43] and *Daniel Nge'tich & Patrick King'etich Kirui v AG.*[44]

P.A.O & 2 Others v AG

This case was filed at the High Court in 2009 after the enactment of the Anti-Counterfeit Act.[45] Pleadings were amended in line with the new Constitution in 2010. The hearing of the case and the judgment of the High Court took place in April 2012, almost three years after the filing of the case. The delay is partly attributable to the transition from the old Constitution to the new Constitution in August 2010. It is also important to note that the enactment of the new Constitution fundamentally assisted this case.

The main issue in this case was whether the Anti-Counterfeit Act as enacted was constitutional. In order to prove that the Act was unconstitutional, the petitioners identified section 2 of the Act on the definition of counterfeiting as well as sections 32 and 34 on offences and enforcement as being unconstitutional. According to the petitioners, the above sections violated the obligations of the state to ensure conditions are in place under which its citizens can lead a healthy life. Moreover, if these provisions were to be implemented, they would deny the petitioners access to essential medicines, thus infringing their constitutional rights to life, health, and dignity under articles 26(1), 28 and 43(1) of the Constitution respectively. Lastly, the provisions would also infringe article 53 on access to basic health care for children.

The facts of this case are as follows. After the successful enactment of the Act in 2008, three petitioners describing themselves as living positively with HIV challenged the Act at the High Court seeking, among other things, a declaration that the Act as enacted would be unconstitutional in so far as it would affect or would be likely to affect access to affordable and essential drugs and medicines. The issues raised by the three petitioners had also been raised during the process of negotiations and enactment of the Act by civil society organisations (CSOs) in Kenya. As expected, therefore, the three petitioners were

43 [2012] eKLR.

44 Petition 3 of 2010.

45 Act 13 of 2008, Laws of Kenya.

later joined by the AIDS Law Project (ALP) as an interested party and by Annan Grover, the United Nations Special Rapporteur on the right to health, as amicus.

In summary, the petitioners relied on four arguments to support their case. First, they argued that their economic situation made them dependent on the cheap and free medicines that were currently being offered by the government through specialised programmes as well as other programmes initiated and being implemented by various development partners including Medicins Sans Frontieres (MSF) or 'Doctors without Borders'. Accordingly, any interference with the opportunity to access the widely used generic medicines would mean that the cost of antiretroviral drugs would be too expensive, thus denying them their right to enjoy the highest attainable standard of health. Second, the petitioners also argued that their lives were being sustained by generic antiretroviral drugs being supplied by the government as guaranteed under the HIV and AIDS Prevention and Control Act 2006. Therefore, the enforcement of the anti-counterfeit legislation would lead to the arbitrary denial of these essential medicines and thus the violation of their constitutional rights to life, health and dignity. Third, the failure by the government to expressly exempt generic drugs from the application of the anti-counterfeiting legislation as well as the failure to take into account relevant provisions guaranteeing essential medicines in the HIV and AIDS Prevention and Control Act 2006 and also the Industrial Property Act 2001 imposes an unnecessary burden on consumers of generic drugs to prove whether or not they are counterfeits. Lastly, they argued that section 2 of the Act allowed for the extra-territorial enforcement of the intellectual property right which was undesirable in Kenya since such rights are usually territorial in nature. The petitioners recommended that the definition of the term 'counterfeit' should be limited to the definition provided under article 51 of the Agreement on Trade Related Aspects of Intellectual Property Rights (TRIPs) as counterfeit trademark.

The interested party, ALP, in support of the petitioners' case, brought into the court three other perspectives. First, they observed that the Act violated the right to equality for persons living with HIV to enjoy the right to life, health and dignity like others. Second, they also observed that the Act would violate the right to family life as enshrined under article 45(1) of the Constitution since people living with HIV are usually removed from normal family life if they are debilitated and unable to care for themselves as a result of illness. Lastly, they observed that the Act posed a threat to the right of every child to basic health care as guaranteed under article 53(2) of the Constitution. It was their argument that the government had failed to consider the best interest of the child while enacting the Act.

The amicus, on his part, and arguing in favour of the petitioners, stated that the failure to expressly exempt generic medicines from the application of the Act meant that the manufacture, sale and distribution of generic equivalents of patented medicines would be adversely affected. According to the amicus, conflating generic medicines with counterfeit medicines would lead to the confiscation of legitimate generic medicines and an escalation in medicine prices in Kenya. As a result, the limited access to essential medicines would qualify as a violation of the constitutional and international right to health, which cannot be justified on the basis of international intellectual property law obligations.

On the opposing side, the respondent relied on three main arguments. First, the respondent stated that section 2 of the Act did not in any way target generic medicines and therefore there was no case of ambiguity in the definition of 'counterfeiting' as alleged by the petitioners; since the definition of 'counterfeiting' is 'clear and specific' under the Act. Second, the Act contains a proviso which sufficiently safeguards access to generics alongside other essential goods as secured under the Industrial Property Act 2001. Lastly, the Act was meant to protect consumers from harm resulting from using counterfeit products. In this respect, the Act is an enabler of human rights, including the right to life, as opposed to an infringement.

In deciding this case, while relying on national laws including the Constitution, Judge Mumbi Ngugi also relied heavily on international law. This was especially so when discerning the meaning and implications of the right to health. As stated above, international law forms part of the law of Kenya under article 2 of the 2010 Constitution. As expected, Judge Ngugi quoted with approval the international instruments as well as the jurisprudence emanating from the CESCR to interpret the Constitution. In particular, on the right to health, she relied on article 12 of the ICESCR, article 12 of the CEDAW and article 24 of the CRC. She also relied on General Comment No 14 on the right to health and General Comment No 17 on the right of everyone to benefit from the protection of the moral and material interests resulting from any scientific, literary or artistic production of which he or she is the author.[46] The former aided Judge Ngugi in reaching the conclusion that the right to health 'embraces a wide range of socio-economic factors that promote conditions in which people can lead a healthy life' while the latter aided the Judge to conclude that 'state parties have a duty to prevent unreasonably high cost for access to essential medicines'. In finding for a violation on the part of Kenya, Judge Ngugi relied on the South African case of *Minister of Health and Others v Treatment Action Campaign and Others*[47] where the esteemed South African Constitutional Court posited that the failure of the state to ensure access to Nevirapine for pregnant mothers was a violation of the constitutional right to the highest attainable standard of health. In *P.A.O & 2 Others*, Kenya was found to be in violation of its constitutional and international law obligations under the right to health by the enactment of the anti-counterfeit legislation.

Listed below are the strengths of the *P.A.O and 2 Others* case with regard to the right to health litigation in Kenya:

1. The existence of a justiciable socio-economic rights catalogue in the Constitution, and in particular, article 43(1) on the right to health, strengthened the petitioners' case and arguments before the High Court. As noted above, this case was filed in 2009 and the basis of the challenge was limited to the shaky constitutional rights to life and dignity. The amendment of the petition after the promulgation of the new Constitution in 2010

46 Committee on Economic, Social and Cultural Rights, General Comment No 17, 'The right of everyone to benefit from the protection of the moral and material interests resulting from any scientific, literary or artistic production of which he or she is the author' (2006) UN Doc E/C.12/GC/17.

47 (1) 2002 (10) BCLR 1033 (CC).

succeeded in rooting the case in a firmer right to health. Ultimately, however, the Judge observed that the three are inextricably linked.

2. This case is a good example of effective utilisation of international law and jurisprudence. Ambani observes that previously people had to forego rights and freedoms secured under international law even after ratification by Kenya.[48] This case was a departure from the past. In particular, the jurisprudence coming from the CESCR proved very useful in assisting the Judge in discerning the meaning and the implications of the right to health. Without extensive reliance on the CESCR jurisprudence it would have, perhaps, been very difficult to link the petitioners' case with the right to health narrative.

3. The place of foreign decisions was also affirmed in this case. The effective utilisation of foreign authorities, specifically the *Minister of Health and Others v Treatment Action Campaign and Others*, proved very useful in determining the right to health violation. This step should be encouraged in all cases brought before the court in order to improve the quality of judicial decisions by making use of popular precedents made outside the country.

4. The participation of the interested party, ALP, and the amicus, Grover, further assisted the petitioners' case by bringing on board other perspectives that could not or had not been articulated by the petitioners. The effect was to make the case watertight, leaving no gaps or weaknesses that could be exploited by the respondents on appeal. This explains why the case was never appealed.

Listed below are the weaknesses of the case in regard to the perspective of right to health litigation in Kenya:

1. Comparatively, there was limited, if not non-utilisation, of regional and sub-regional instruments providing for the right to health. Glaringly, there was no mention of the African Charter at all despite its prominence in the continent. In the same way, the principles and guidelines for socio-economic rights developed by the African Commission were not used despite being even more specific in terms of the obligations of the government with regard to the HIV and AIDS epidemic in Africa. This oversight should be addressed through proper dissemination of these instruments to lawyers in the continent.

2. Notwithstanding that the use of international jurisprudence and norms should be encouraged, direct importation should be discouraged. It is important to contextualise the jurisprudence and norms emanating from the international level and apply them in a manner relevant to the country. In the future, it would be desirable to develop specific norms for the Kenyan situation, as is already happening in South Africa through the development of the 'reasonableness test' in socio-economic rights litigation. Ultimately, it would be very beneficial if

---

48 Ambani (n 21 above) 31.

> the court [were to] try to convince a prospective international monitoring body that its approach is better … or that the international body should allow national divergence under doctrines such as the margin of appreciation.[49]

Daniel Nge'tich & Patrick King'etich Kirui v AG50

This case was not filed as a constitutional petition under article 43 of the Constitution on the right to health. Its importance, however, is in illustrating the broadness of the right to health question in the country. The right to health can be approached from many angles, as illustrated in this case.

Briefly, this case was filed by the AIDS Law Project (ALP) and the Kenya Legal and Ethical Issues Network on HIV & AIDS (KELIN), a local CSO, on behalf of Daniel Nge'tich and Patrick King'etich Kirui, who were detained in prison, pursuant to the relevant provisions of the Public Health Act, for defaulting tuberculosis (TB) treatment and thereby posing a risk to members of the public. The purpose of the detention was to ensure adherence to TB treatment and protect the public health. However, in their petition, the petitioners argued that the continued detention of the TB patients in prison was unconstitutional. In particular, they argued that this constituted a violation of their constitutional rights to movement and reasonable administrative action and a violation of their fundamental rights as enshrined under articles 39(1), 47(1) and 51(1) of the Constitution. The petitioners also relied on article 24(1) on the limitation of rights to prove that the limitation in this case was unconstitutional. The respondent did not oppose the petition.

The presiding Judge, Justice Philomena Mwilu, held that the decision to confine the TB patients for a period of eight months in order to guarantee adherence to treatment was unconstitutional. As a remedy, she ordered the immediate release of the two patients and instructed that their TB treatment be supervised from home by a duly appointed public health officer.

This case is very important because it addresses the issue of detention of TB patients. The determination by Judge Mwilu that detaining TB patients in prison was unconstitutional is indeed a positive outcome. It ushers in a new era in which public health interventions must be undertaken in conformity with the new Constitution. In other words, it will no longer be possible to treat persons suffering from communicable diseases, including TB, as being inferior to other human beings. Second, this case is also important because it provides a good example of how to indirectly litigate socio-economic rights using civil and political rights narrative. For instance, the petitioners in this case relied on the right to movement and the right to administrative action.

On the flipside, the ruling in this case fails to employ international and regional laws and jurisprudence. As a result, the ruling is short and precise, with the decision not

49 M Killander and H Adjoholon, 'International Law and Domestic Human Rights Litigation in Africa: An Introduction' in M Killander (ed) *International and Domestic Human Rights Legislation in Africa* (Pretoria University Law Press 2010) 15.

50 Petition 3 of 2010.

substantiated satisfactorily. This rigid application of the law is undesirable since it sets a very weak precedent with regard to the issues raised in the case. Moving forward, it would be beneficial for litigants and judges to embrace international and regional as well as foreign jurisprudence in contentious cases like this one.

Challenges and Opportunities

This section of the chapter examines the challenges and opportunities available for health rights litigation in Kenya.

Challenges

The challenges facing health rights litigation include the lack of a national health law, limited use of regional instruments and the limited capacity of judicial officers.

The fact that Kenya has yet to enact a comprehensive national health law means that article 43(1)(a) of the Constitution on the right to health remains vague or abstract. This partly explains why courts have had to rely heavily on international jurisprudence to give meaning to some of these sections, as was seen in the *P.A.O & 2 Others* case. However, moving forward, the negotiation of a comprehensive national health law in order to give meaning to the abstract right to health in the Constitution seems inevitable. It is hoped that comprehensive national health legislation, if properly harnessed, would also serve to prevent a possible floodgate of cases on the right to health in Kenya.

In the cases discussed above, it is clear that international instruments as opposed to regional instruments are preferred in Kenya. No logical explanation has been given to support this trend. In fact, one would expect regional instruments to be more popular than international instruments based on proximity and legitimacy. The reason for the dismal usage of regional instruments is partly because of poor dissemination. Other reasons are attitudinal – litigants regard regional instruments as inferior to international standards. While there is no problem relying on international instruments, in Kenya, as an African country, litigants should adopt a direct policy that promotes the use of regional laws and jurisprudence in the courts.

The limited capacity of judicial officers and lawyers was best illustrated by the *Daniel Nge'tich & Patrick King'etich Kirui* case. The ruling, although favourable, failed to take into account international and foreign jurisprudence. This may be explained by reason of lack of capacity on the part of judicial officers and lawyers. Moving forward, it is imperative to build the capacity of judicial officers and lawyers in order for them to dispense their roles effectively and competently. Already, the University of Pretoria, Centre for Human Rights, has in place an annual short course on the judicial enforcement of social and economic rights that also targets lawyers and judges. Similar training should be encouraged at the national level.

Opportunities

Opportunities available for health rights litigation in Kenya include the existence of justiciable socio-economic rights, an elaborate international and regional framework on the right to health, and devolution.

Unlike in many other countries in the world, in Kenya the Constitution explicitly recognizes justiciable socio-economic rights. This presents a unique opportunity for adjudicating these rights. Therefore, Kenyans must embrace public interest litigation as a means towards the realisation of socio-economic rights. South Africa, another country with justiciable socio-economic rights, provides a good example of a country that has succeeded in socio-economic rights adjudication judging by its rich and popular jurisprudence.

Section 2 of the Constitution is unique in that it allows for the application of international and regional laws in Kenya as well as international principles. This is indeed a major departure from the principle set in the *Okunda* case where international norms had to be transformed into national laws before they could be enforced locally. The *P.A.O & 2 Others* case is a good example of how this opportunity can be beneficial to litigants and judicial officers. However, Killander and Adjolohon have observed that monist countries (like Kenya) in most cases oppose or make little use of international law in interpreting constitutional rights.[51] According to the authors, the role of international law in interpretation 'relates to the interpretation of constitutional provisions, statutory interpretation and the development of the common law and customary law'.[52] Therefore, Kenyans must embrace international and regional laws in order to achieve maximum benefits.

Kenya has embraced devolution as a means of government. Article 6 of the 2010 Constitution declares that Kenya is divided into 47 counties as enumerated under the first schedule. Under the fourth schedule, county governments will be responsible for various social and economic rights. In respect of the health service, for example, county governments will control county health facilities and pharmacies, ambulance services, promotion of primary health care, licensing and control of undertakings that sell food to the public, veterinary services (excluding regulation of the profession), cemeteries, funeral parlours and crematoria, and refuse removal, refuse dumps and solid waste disposal. This move by Kenya is consistent with the growing international acceptance and increasing recognition of the role of local governments in human rights realisation. Indeed, some human rights obligations may be traced at the functional level of sub-national governments as opposed to national governments.[53] Consequently, therefore, national governments have no option but to rely on local/sub-national governments to implement specific human rights obligations.[54] However, some factors such as political culture, the legal system and the level of economic development influence the practice of local governments with

---

51 Killander and Adjoholon (n 49 above) 4.

52 Ibid, 15.

53 CM Bosire, 'Local Government and Human Rights: Building Institutional Links for the Effective Protection and Realisation of Human Rights in Africa' (2010) 11 *African Human Rights Law Journal* 147, 150.

54 Ibid, 151.

regard to human rights realisation.[55] Therefore, it is critical to incorporate a rights-based approach to county governments in Kenya.[56]

The Way Forward

Based on the above discussion, it can be seen that certain steps need to be taken to ensure the realisation of the right to health in Kenya. Consequently, the following suggestions are made to effect a more enabling environment for health rights litigation.

Enactment of the National Health Legislation

As stated above, Kenya is in the process of negotiating a comprehensive national health law. However, this process has been delayed, thereby compromising the implementation of the right to health as codified under article 43(1)(a) of the Constitution. Once enacted, the national health law will provide much needed details as to the content of the right to health in Kenya. According to Langford, the role of legislation in both the principled and the pragmatic perspective includes that 'it is often more precise and contextualised and has the direct authoritative and democratic imprimatur of the legislature'.[57] In its absence, the courts are left with the responsibility to define the right to health by setting 'invariable universal standards'.[58]

Ratification of the Optional Protocol to the ICESCR

While Kenya has ratified the ICESCR, it has yet to ratify its Optional Protocol. The implication of non-ratification of the Optional Protocol to the ICESCR is that individuals' communications cannot be entertained before the CESCR. This has the effect of limiting the work of the CESCR to reports submitted by government on social and economic rights and to some extent civil society parallel reports. Individuals, therefore, are denied an opportunity to benefit from the protection of this treaty body.

Promote Full Utilisation of Regional Laws alongside International Laws in Litigating Socio-economic Rights

As noted above, while there is a considerable uptake of international norms this is not true with regard to regional norms. The *P.A.O and 2 Others* case is illustrative of this point.

---

55 Ibid, 156.

56 Ibid.

57 M Langford, 'The Justiciability of Social Rights: From Practice to Theory' in M Langford (ed), *Social Rights Jurisprudence: Emerging Trends in International and Comparative Law* (Cambridge University Press 2008) 3.

58 L Stewart, 'Adjudicating Socio-economic Rights under a Transformative Constitution' (2010) 28 *Penn State International Law Review*, 487, 494.

While the litigants made excellent use of international and foreign norms they failed to make any reference to regional norms, particularly from the African Union.

Develop Capacity of Stakeholders (Lawyers, Judges and CSOs) to Litigate Social-economic Rights

In order to achieve the best results in the nuanced socio-economic rights adjudication undertaking, it is crucial to build the capacity of all stakeholders, including judges and lawyers. In fact, before deciding the *P.A.O and 2 Others* case, the presiding judge attended a socio-economic rights short course at the Centre for Human Rights, University of Pretoria. The short course is believed to have contributed to the deep knowledge of international human rights law exhibited in her judgment. The same cannot be said of the *Daniel Nge'tich and Patrick King'etich Kirui* decision.

Encourage Public Interest Litigation in Socio-economic Rights Litigation and Provid Legal Aid in Civil Cases

The often complicated nature of socio-economic rights means that litigating them requires elaborate preparation and resources. There are only two ways in which litigation in this area can be encouraged: first, through public interest litigation as seen in the cases discussed above; second, through support from legal aid activities, especially in cases involving private individuals or civil cases. Legal aid extended to civil proceedings has seen immense progress being made in the areas of 'consumer protection, social security, housing, family law, minority rights, public health and environmental protection'.[59] Durbach observes that

> [w]ith the increasing ratification of human rights treaties and conventions by states, including the International Covenant on Economic, Social and Cultural Rights, the incorporation of socio-economic rights in domestic legislation, constitutions and Charters or Bills of Rights, and a growing appreciation by the courts of the necessary interdependence of human rights (political, social and economic), the grounds for making a distinction between criminal and civil proceedings when affording legal aid, are becoming less tenable.[60]

Conclusions

This chapter has discussed the some of the health challenges currently facing Kenya. It has also discussed the legal framework for the realisation of the right to health in the country. Furthermore, we have examined some of the health rights cases in Kenyan courts and the approaches of the courts in these cases. Moving forward, Kenya and other countries will

---

59 A Durbach, 'The Right to Legal Aid in Social Rights Litigation' in M Langford (ed), *Social Rights Jurisprudence: Emerging Trends in International and Comparative Law* (Cambridge University Press 2008) 59.

60 Ibid, 63.

have to provide legal aid to supplement public interest litigation in socio-economic rights litigation. Another justification for this is that most cases involve the poorer people in the community who are unable to afford legal fees.

References

Books, Chapters, Articles, etc.

Ambani, JO, 'Navigating Past the "Dualist Doctrine": The Case for Progressive Jurisprudence on the Application of International Human Rights Norms in Kenya' in M Killander (ed) *International Law and Domestic Human Rights Litigation in Africa* (Pretoria University Law Press 2010), 25–36.

Bosire, CM, 'Local Government and Human Rights: Building Institutional Links for the Effective Protection and Realisation of Human Rights in Africa' (2010) 11 *African Human Rights Law Journal* 147–170.

Durbach, A, 'The Right to Legal Aid in Social Rights Litigation' in M Langford (ed) *Social Rights Jurisprudence: Emerging Trends in International and Comparative Law* (Cambridge University Press 2008) 59–72.

Ebobrah, ST, 'Human Rights Developments in African Sub-regional Economic Communities during 2010' (2011) 11 *African Human Rights Law Journal* 216–250.

Kenya AIDS Indicator Survey (2012), at http://www.nacc.or.ke/index.php?option=com_booklibrary&task=view&id=56&catid=124&Itemid=122 (accessed 23 October 2014).

Killander, M and Adjoholon, H, 'International Law and Domestic Human Rights Litigation in Africa: An Introduction' in M Killander (ed) *International Law and Domestic Human Rights Litigation in Africa* (Pretoria University Law Press: 2010) 3–22.

Langford, M, 'The Justiciability of Social Rights: From Practice to Theory' in M Langford (ed) *Social Rights Jurisprudence: Emerging Trends in International and Comparative Law* Cambridge University Press 2008) 3–45.

Michelman, FI, 'The Constitution, Social Rights, and Liberal Political Justification' (2001) 1 *International Journal of Constitutional Law* 13–34.

Ojwang, JB and Otieno-Odek, JA, 'The Judiciary in Sensitive Areas of Public Law: Emerging Approaches to Human Rights Litigation in Kenya' (1988) 35 *Netherlands International Law Review* 29–52.

Okoth-Ogendo, HWO, 'Constitutions without Constitutionalism: Reflections on an African Paradox' in D Greenberg, SN Katz, MB Oliviero and SC Wheatley (eds) *Constitutionalism & Democracy: Transitions in the Contemporary World* (Oxford University Press 1993) 65–82.

Ministry of Health, *Kenya Health Policy 2014–2030: Towards Attaining the Highest Standard of Health* (2014), at http://www.health.go.ke/images/policydocs/KHP%20Final%20booklet.pdf (accessed 11 April 2014).

National AIDS Control Council, *Kenya AIDS Indicator Survey* (2012) 12, at http://www.nacc.or.ke/attachments/article/403/KAIS_II_2014_Final_Report.pdf (accessed 24 July 2014).

Nino, CS, *The Constitutions of Deliberative Democracy* (Yale University Press 1996).
Schwartz, H, 'Economic and Social Rights' (1993) 8 *American University Journal of International Law and Policy* 551–565.
Stewart, L, 'Adjudicating Socio-economic Rights under a Transformative Constitution' (2010) 28 *Penn State International Law Review* 487–512.
World Health Organization, *Health Situation Analysis in the African Region: Atlas of Health Statistics 2011* (WHO 2011).

International and Regional Instruments

African Charter on Human and Peoples' Rights, adopted 17 June 1981, entered into force 21 October 1986.
African Charter on the Rights and Welfare of the Child, OAU Doc. CAB/LEG/24.9/49, adopted 11 July 1990, entered into force 29 November 1999.
African Commission on Human and Peoples' Rights, 'Principles and Guidelines on the Implementation of Economic, Social and Cultural Rights in the African Charter on Human and Peoples' Rights' (November 2010).
African Youth Charter, adopted 2 July 2006, entered into force 8 August 2009.
Committee on Economic, Social and Cultural Rights, 'Concluding observations on Kenya' (1993) UN Doc E/C.12/1993/6.
Committee on Economic, Social and Cultural Rights, 'Concluding observations on Kenya' (2008) UN Doc E/C.12/KEN/CO/1.
Committee on Economic, Social and Cultural Rights, General Comment No 14, 'The right to the highest attainable standard of health' (2000) UN Doc E/C.12/2000/4.
Committee on Economic, Social and Cultural Rights, General Comment No 17, 'The right of everyone to benefit from the protection of the moral and material interests resulting from any scientific, literary or artistic production of which he or she is the author' (2006) UN Doc E/C.12/GC/17.
Convention on the Elimination of All Forms of Discrimination against Women (CEDAW), adopted 18 December 1979, entered into force 3 September 1981.
Convention on the Rights of the Child, A/RES/44/25, adopted 20 November 1989, entered into force 2 September 1990.
Convention on the Rights of Persons with Disabilities, UN Doc A/61/611, adopted 13 December 2006, entered into force 3 May 2008.
East African Community (EAC) Treaty (1999).
International Covenant on Economic Social and Cultural Rights, adopted 16 December 1966, entered into force 3 January 1976 (UN *Treaty Series*, vol 993, 3).
Protocol to the African Charter on Human and People's Rights on the Rights of Women in Africa, CAB/LEG/66.6, adopted 11 July 2003, entered into force 25 November 2005.
Universal Declaration of Human Rights, GA Res 217A (UN Doc A/810) at 71 (1948).

Cases

Daniel Nge'tich & Patrick King'etich Kirui v AG Petition 3 of 2010.

Minister of Health and Others v Treatment Action Campaign and Others (1) 2002 (10) BCLR 1033 (CC).
Okunda v Republic [1970] EA 453.
P.A.O & 2 Others v AG [2012] eKLR.

Chapter 9

Challenges in Litigating the Right to Health in Mozambique: A Critical Analysis

Satang Nabaneh[1]

> One of the central features of human rights is accountability. Without accountability, human rights can become no more than window-dressing.[2]

The right to health is enshrined in the Constitution of Mozambique, which is the supreme law of the land.[3] At independence, Mozambique inherited from Portugal an unstable health system characterised by shortages of qualified doctors, inadequate health structures and a lack of access to medicines and other essentials which catered to only 44 per cent of the population.[4] It is estimated that there are only three doctors per 100,000 people.[5] The population of Mozambique is estimated to be between 21 and 23 million as of 2011.[6]

---

1 I would like to thank Professor Hansungule, Dr Comoane of the Mozambique Administrative Tribunal, Orquidea Massarongo of the Centre for Human Rights, Faculty of Law of the Eduardo Mondlane University of Mozambique, and Ms Farida Mamad, member of the National Human Rights Commission of Mozambique. Special thanks and appreciation also goes to the various people who provided comments and material which have deeply enriched this chapter. I would also like to thank Ebenezer Durojaye for his support. All errors and omissions in the text are of course my sole responsibility.

2 Paul Hunt as cited in H Potts, 'Accountability and the Right to the Highest Attainable Health' (2008) 1.

3 Adopted on 16 November 2004.

4 UNDP, *Mozambique National Human Development Report 2007: Challenges and Opportunities: The Response to HIV and AIDS* (UNDP 2007) 14–15, available at http://hdr.undp.org/en/reports/national/africa/mozambique/NHDR_2007_HIV_AIDS_MOZAMBIQUE.pdf (accessed 27 February 2015). See also S Chao and K. Kostermans, *Improving Health for the Poor in Mozambique: The Fight Continues* (World Bank 2001) 15.

5 PEPFAR, 'Mozambique: Operational Plan Report FY 2010', 3, available at http://www.pepfar.gov/documents/organization/145728.pdf (accessed 31 March 2013).

6 This is according to the 2007 Population Census and the World Bank's data and statistics on Mozambique as of 2011, available at http://ddpext.worldbank.org/ext/ddpreports/ViewSharedReport?&CF=&REPORT_ID=9147&REQUEST_TYPE=VIEWADVANCED (accessed 1 March 2015).

Mozambique remains one of the poorest countries in the world.[7] According to the United Nations Development Programme (UNDP) Human Development Index of 2013, Mozambique is ranked 185th out of 187 countries compared to its 184th position in 2011.[8] Nevertheless, it ranks among the top ten fastest growing economies in the world, with 7 per cent growth recorded in the two decades since the end of the civil war in 1992.[9] Notwithstanding the recent discovery of natural resources, including coal, other minerals and natural gas, which have attracted significant foreign direct investment, more than 50 per cent of the population still lives below the national poverty line, surviving on less than US$0.50 per day. Most of the poor live in the rural areas.[10]

Mozambique's poor health indicators were acknowledged by the former UN Special Rapporteur on the Right to Health, Paul Hunt, during his mission to Mozambique.[11] The Special Rapporteur noted that barriers to access to health, including the shortage of health professionals, inadequate number of health care facilities, reported corruption in the health sector and weak civil society participation in decision-making processes, hinder the enjoyment of the right to health in Mozambique.[12] This has also been recognised by the Committee on the Convention on the Rights of the Child who have noted that 'health services remain inadequate in terms of coverage and quality'.[13]

According to data from the National Statistics Institute (Instituto Nacional de Estatística, INE), about 46 per cent of children under 5 years of age suffer from chronic malnutrition in Mozambique.[14] The under 5 mortality rate is estimated at 97 per 1,000 live births.[15] The Committee on the Convention on the Elimination of All Forms of Discrimination against Women has further noted the high maternal mortality rate in the country.[16]

The country also has one of the highest rates of HIV infection in sub-Saharan Africa with women between the ages of 15 and 49 comprising 13.1 per cent of those infected,

---

7 See Economic Commission for Africa and African Union, *Economic Report on Africa 2012: Unleashing Africa's Potential as a Pole of Global Growth* (ECA and AU 2012) 38; World Bank, *Africa Development Indicators 2011* (World Bank 2011).

8 UNDP, *Human Development Report 2013. The Rise of the South: Human Progress in a Diverse World* (UNDP 2013) 143.

9 UNICEF, '2012 Annual Report: Mozambique', 4, available at http://unicef.org.mz/annualreport2012 (accessed 25 February 2013).

10 Ibid.

11 See Report of the Special Rapporteur, Paul Hunt, 'Mission to Mozambique' (2005) UN Doc E/CN.4/2005/51/Add 2, 13.

12 Ibid.

13 Committee on the Rights of the Child, 'Concluding Observations: Mozambique' (2009) CRC/C/MOZ/CO/2, para 17.

14 Instituto Nacional de Estatística, available at http://www.ine.gov.mz/Dashboards.aspx?key=536916 (accessed 1 March 2015).

15 UNICEF (n 8 above) 4.

16 Concluding Comments of the Committee on the Elimination of Discrimination against Women: Mozambique (2007) CEDAW/C/MOZ/CO/2, para 36.

compared to men who comprise 9.2 per cent.[17] It is further estimated that women aged 15–24 are three times more likely to be infected with HIV compared to men.[18]

Even though there is a constitutionally entrenched right to health, the statistics demonstrate that the chances of the state fulfilling this obligation are slim in view of the practical challenges on the ground. For the state to fulfil this right, the citizens will have to demand it and hold the state accountable through litigation.

This chapter will focus on analysing the right to health in Mozambique. First, it examines the constitutional entrenchment of the right to health in Mozambique; second, it discusses the possibilities of litigating the right to health; and third, it examines the challenges to litigating the right to health such as the requirement of *locus standi*, and the lack of knowledge of international human rights standards by both judges and lawyers. The chapter finally explores the opportunities for litigating the right to health in Mozambique.

The Protection and Recognition of the Right to Health

The right to health has been given recognition in a number of important international and regional human rights instruments. Although in Chapter 1 Olubayo Oluduro and Ebenezer Durojaye have provided an overview of the recognition of the right to health under international and regional human rights instruments, in this chapter an attempt will be made to contexualise the discussion in Chapter 1 within the legal framework of Mozambique.

Global Level

Mozambique is a state party to the International Covenant on Civil and Political Rights (ICCPR) and its second Optional Protocol relating to the abolition of the death penalty,[19] the International Convention on the Elimination of All Forms of Racial Discrimination (ICERD),[20] the Convention on the Elimination of All Forms of Discrimination against Women (CEDAW),[21] the Convention against Torture and Other Cruel, Inhuman or Degrading Treatment or Punishment (CAT)[22] and the Convention on the Rights of the Child (CRC).[23] Several of these international human rights instruments recognise the right to the highest attainable standard of health.[24]

The International Covenant on Economic, Social and Cultural Rights (ICESCR) is one of the most important treaties on the right to health. Article 12 of the ICESCR provides that state parties 'recognise the right of everyone to the enjoyment of the highest

17 UNICEF (n 8 above) 5.
18 Ibid.
19 Ratification Resolution No 5/91, of 12 December 1991.
20 Ratification Resolution No 4/83.
21 Ratification Resolution No 4/93 of 2 June 1993.
22 Ratification Resolution No 8/91 of 20 December 1991.
23 Ratification Resolution No 19/90 of 10 October 1990.
24 See arts 12 and 16 of the CEDAW, and art 24 of the CRC.

attainable standard of physical and mental health'. It further encompasses determinants to the right to health.

The Covenant obliges state parties to take appropriate measures that include, inter alia:

> (c) the prevention, treatment and control of epidemic, endemic, occupational and other diseases;
>
> (d) and the creation of conditions which would assure to all medical service and medical attention in the event of sickness.[25]

The Committee on Economic, Social and Cultural Rights (CESCR) which is responsible for overseeing the implementation of the Covenant, has stated that:

> health is a fundamental human right indispensable for the exercise of other human rights. Every human being is entitled to the enjoyment of the highest attainable standard of health conducive to living a life in dignity.[26]

Despite the fact that socio-economic rights are entrenched in the Constitution of Mozambique, the country has not ratified the ICESCR or its optional protocol, which has now come into force.

Relevant Laws at the Regional and Sub-regional Levels

African regional level

At the regional level, Mozambique is a party to the African Charter on Human and Peoples' Rights (hereafter African Charter),[27] the African Charter on the Rights and Welfare of the Child (hereafter African Children's Charter)[28] and the Protocol to the African Charter on the Rights of Women in Africa (hereafter African Women's Protocol).

Under the African Charter, article 16 provides that 'everyone has the right to enjoy the best attainable state of physical and mental health'. As the African Commission on Human and Peoples' Rights (hereafter African Commission) explained in *Purohit v The Gambia*:

> Enjoyment of the right to health as is widely known is vital to all aspects of a person's life and well being, and is crucial to the realisation of all the other fundamental human rights and freedoms.[29]

---

25 Arts 12(20)(c)(d).

26 Committee on Economic, Social and Cultural Rights, General Comment No 14, 'The right to the highest attainable standard of health' (2000) UN Doc E/C.12/2000/4, para 1.

27 Ratification Resolution No 9/88 of 25 August 1988.

28 Ratification Resolution No 20/98.

29 *Purohit and Another v The Gambia* (2003) AHRLR 96 (ACHPR 2003) para 80.

Similarly, the African Women's Protocol provides for the right to health. Article 14 requires states to 'ensure that the right to health of women, including sexual and reproductive health, is respected and promoted'. The Protocol is the first human rights treaty that recognises women's reproductive rights as human rights and provides for women's protection from HIV/AIDS as well as a the right to medical abortion. The African Children's Charter also recognises the right to health for children.[30]

Given that Mozambique has guaranteed the right to health care in its constitution and ratified the African Charter and its Protocol on Women's Rights in Africa, it is incumbent upon the country to ratify the ICESCR and its protocol.[31]

Southern African Development Community (SADC) region

In addition to the above enumerated international and regional human rights instruments relevant to the right to health, there exist normative instruments at the Southern African level that further guarantee the right to health.

The SADC treaty does not encompass individual rights but obliges member states to act in accordance with the principles of human rights, democracy and the rule of law.[32] Article 5 on the objectives of SADC implies the obligation to promote, respect and fulfil socio-economic rights including the right to health. The objectives include promotion of 'sustainable and equitable economic growth and socioeconomic development'[33] and to 'combat HIV/AIDS or other deadly and communicable diseases'.[34] While these objectives may not be directly enforceable, they guide the actions and conduct of all member states. Article 6(1) of the treaty obliges states in pursuance of the objectives to

> undertake to adopt adequate measures to promote the achievement of the objectives of SADC, and shall refrain from taking any measure likely to jeopardise the sustenance of its principles, the achievement of its objectives and the implementation of the provisions of the treaty.

This clearly shows that member states have both the positive obligation of promoting and fulfilling the objectives of SADC, as well as the negative obligation to refrain from impeding the realisation of the objectives and principles.

Other instruments that have been adopted include the SADC Charter on Fundamental Social Rights (hereafter Social Charter), the SADC Protocol on Gender and Development and the Protocol on Health.

Article 3(1) of the SADC Social Charter encompasses the embodiment of:

---

30 Art 14(1) of the African Children's Charter.

31 The former UN Special Rapporteur on the Right to Health Paul Hunt during his mission to Mozambique made the same recommendation, see Report of the Special Rapporteur (n 10 above) 6.

32 Art 4(c) of the SADC Treaty (1992/1993).

33 Art 5(1)(a).

34 Art 5(1)(i).

> the recognition by governments, employers and workers in the Region of the universality and individuality of basic human rights proclaimed in instruments such as the United Nations Universal Declaration of Human Rights, the African Charter on Human and Peoples' Rights, the Constitution of the ILO, the Philadelphia Declaration and other relevant international instruments.

This means that all human rights in these instruments are applicable in the sub-region. The phrase 'other relevant international instruments' implies the inclusion of important instruments such as the ICESCR. The Social Charter focuses on governing labour relations and it is limited in scope as it is aimed at workers alone. In this regard, it provides for the right to health for every worker in the region.[35]

In addition, the SADC Protocol on Gender and Development provides for access to health care for children.[36] It further obliges state parties to 'undertake to adopt and implement, by 2015, legislative frameworks, polices, programmes and services to enhance gender sensitive, appropriate and affordable health care'.[37] Other provisions include the obligation of state parties to 'enact legislation that addresses the prevention and treatment of HIV/AIDS and the care and support of those living with or affected by HIV/AIDS'.[38]

The SADC Protocol on Health was adopted in 1999 and came into force in 2004. In its preamble, the Protocol acknowledges that 'a healthy population is a prerequisite for sustainable human development'. It further recognises that 'a close cooperation in the area of health is essential for the effective control of diseases and for remedying general health concerns in the region'.[39] The Protocol does not explicitly recognise the individual's right to access health care and essential medicines. Instead, states are urged to cooperate with each other in terms of raising funds to acquire medicines, technology and other resources needed by citizens.[40] These instruments serve as benchmarks for Mozambique's obligations and duties relating to the right to health.

Mozambique's Legal Framework for the Protection of the Right to Health

Following the brief analysis of the right to health provided for under international and regional human rights instruments, this section will examine the extent to which Mozambique's laws comply with the above standards.

35 See art 12 of the SADC Social Charter on protection of health, safety and environment.
36 Art 11 of the Protocol. Mozambique has ratified the Protocol.
37 Art 26 of the Protocol.
38 Art 27 of the Protocol.
39 Preamble of the SADC Protocol on Health.
40 See art 19 of the SADC Protocol on Health.

Constitutional Entrenchment of the Right to Health in Mozambique

As a former colony of Portugal, Mozambique's legal system inherited certain colonial laws with regard to controlling the economy and political power. Since independence, Mozambique has promulgated three constitutions, in 1975, 1990 and 2004 respectively, which also shows the progression in terms of the entrenchment of socio-economic rights in the Constitution, including the right to health. For instance, the 1975 Mozambican Constitution included only the right to education and work.[41] The 1990 Constitution provided for the right to education,[42] and to medical and health care.[43] The 2004 Constitution also recognises the right to health as a justiciable right.

The Constitution of the Republic of Mozambique is the supreme law of the land. The Preamble recognises that:

> the Constitution reaffirms, develops and deepens the fundamental principles of the Mozambican state, enshrines the sovereign character of the democratic state, based on pluralism of opinion, party organization and respects and guarantees the fundamental rights of the citizens.

The Constitution contains a comprehensive catalogue of rights and freedoms under Title III which are in line with various international and regional human rights treaties to which Mozambique is a party. The Constitution proclaims that the fundamental aim of Mozambique is 'the defence and promotion of human rights and the equality of citizens before the law'.[44]

Although Mozambique is not a state party to the ICESCR, its constitutional provisions on socio-economic rights are influenced by the treaty.[45] The Constitution contains a Bill of Rights that explicitly provides for fundamental rights. Article 89 of the Constitution states that 'all citizens shall have the right to medical and health care, *within the terms of the law*, and shall have the duty to promote and protect public health'.[46] The enjoyment of the right to health care remains difficult due to the non-existence of an enabling law to give effect to it. Thus, for the right to health to become enforceable in Mozambique, an enabling law must be enacted. Nonetheless, a purposive interpretation to this provision can still result in the right being directly applicable or enforceable in court.

Thus, it is arguable that the right to health is a legal imperative and directly enforceable through the courts. Regardless of whether an enabling law is enacted, when the right to health is constitutionally entrenched in the Bill of Rights, it becomes enforceable as the Constitution gives recourse to the courts in terms of violations of any of the rights enshrined in the Constitution. It has been argued that the failure to enact an enabling law

41 See arts 29, 31 and 32 of the 1975 Constitution.

42 Arts 88–91 of the 1990 Constitution.

43 See article 43 of the Constitution.

44 Art 6(d).

45 See F Viljoen, *International Human Rights Law in Africa* (Oxford University Press 2007) 573.

46 Emphasis added.

becomes a violation in itself.[47] However, to date, the failure to enact such a law on the part of the state has not been challenged in court.

Nevertheless, the entrenchment of the right to health care in the Constitution obliges the state to ensure access to the best health care through a timely and effective quality health service.[48]

A Presidential Decree entrusts this responsibility to the Ministry of Health.[49] Article 116 of the Constitution further states that:

> 1. Medical and health care for citizens shall be organised through a national health system, which shall benefit all Mozambican people.
>
> 2. To achieve the goals of the national health system, the law shall establish the ways in which medical and health care is delivered.
>
> 3. The State shall encourage citizens and institutions to participate in raising the standard of health in the community.
>
> 4. The State shall promote the expansion of medical and health care and the equal access of all citizens to the enjoyment of this right.
>
> 5. The State shall be responsible for promoting, supervising and controlling the production, the sale and the use of chemical, biological and pharmaceutical products and other forms of treatment and diagnosis.
>
> 6. The medical and health care activities run by collective and private entities shall be carried out in accordance with the law and be subject to the supervision of the State.

Thus, article 116 of the Constitution provides that in order to ensure medical and health care for all citizens, a national health system should be organised to make it beneficial to all people in Mozambique. Access to health care is therefore available for all with assistance via the national health system.[50] Article 2 of Law 2/77 regarding the Law of National Health System provides that 'every citizen has the right to free medicines and medical care when in-patient'. Article 6 further provides that free in-patient treatment is established for drugs considered basic.

An amendment to this law through Law 4/87 of 19 January 1987 brought changes to the National Health System Act. Under the law, health care and medication, surgery,

---

47 A Mandlate, 'The Protection and Enforcement of Socio-economic Rights in Lusophone Countries in Africa: Challenges in Angola, Cape Verde and Mozambique' (2010) 11(3) *ESR Review* 22, 23.

48 Human Rights Council, National Report submitted in accordance with paragraph 159(a) of the annex of the Human Rights Council resolution 5/1: Mozambique (2011) A/HRC/WG.6/10/MOZ/1, para 86.

49 See Decree No 11/95.

50 Art 1 of Lei 2/77 of 19 January for the Law of the National Health Systems.

laboratory tests and all necessary treatment carried out during hospitalisation is only free after payment of a minimum rate of hospitalisation – that is, the gratuity only exists for processes carried out during admission in hospital and is subject to payment of the fee. This simply means that medical treatment in public hospitals is free when the patient is hospitalised. When he continues with the treatment as an out-patient, the gratuity is limited to the basic drugs necessary to treat the patient. However, for out-patient treatment (*tratamento ambulatório*), the patient has to pay for a minimum rate of consultation which is not applicable for cases of malaria and tuberculosis.[51]

Notably, an HIV-related legislation was adopted in 2002 to protect people living with HIV from discrimination in the workplace and to combat stigma related to HIV/AIDS.[52] Some of its provisions include protection of privacy and confidentiality, voluntary testing and counselling, and access to treatment and care for people living with HIV/AIDS.

Despite the constitutional rhetoric, it is not uncommon to find major challenges to access to health care especially in the rural areas of the country. The statistics emerging from the United Nations bodies are demonstrative of the challenges experienced in access to health care. Despite these challenges, as this chapter will show, there has hardly been any litigation related to the right to health, thus creating the need to interrogate the force of international law and human rights norms in Mozambique.

The Place of International Law and Human Rights Norms in Mozambique

Mozambique has a monist system. Upon ratification, a treaty (*tratados*) or an agreement (*acordos*) becomes law when ratification or accession is followed by its publication in the National Gazette (*Boletim da República*).[53] Upon publication, the international law theoretically becomes enforceable in the courts. However, international law has never been directly enforced in the country. For instance, there is no evidence of enforcement of the African Charter in the courts.

The Constitution contains an explicit provision which integrates international law into national law once the treaties have been ratified. According to the Constitution, international law has the same legal effect in theory as laws under the Constitution and legislation promulgated by the Assembly of the Republic and the government.

Article 18(2) of the Constitution on international law establishes that:

> Norms of international law shall *have the same force in the Mozambican legal order, as have infra-constitutional legislative acts of the Assembly of the Republic and Government*, according to the respective manner in which they are received.[54]

51 See arts 1 & 2 of Law 4/87 of 19 January which amended the Law of National Health System, in particular art 1.

52 HIV Law 5 of 2002.

53 See arts 144, 199, 204 and 205 of the Constitution, which give explicit procedures for ratification of treaties and international agreements respectively.

54 Emphasis added.

Article 17.2 of the Constitution further provides that the state 'shall accept, observe and apply the principles of the Charter of the United Nations and the Charter of the Organisation of African Unity'. This is further reinforced by article 43 of the Constitution, which provides that the Bill of Rights shall be interpreted 'in harmony with the Universal Declaration of Human Rights and the African Charter on Human and Peoples' Rights'.

These constitutional provisions mean that all ratified international human rights instruments to which Mozambique is a party shall apply at all levels after the publication in the country's official Gazette. They also imply that international standards in the field of human rights can be invoked and are directly applicable in the courts of the country. However, in Mozambique, most of the instruments are not published in the official Gazette.

An assertion can be made that although Mozambique is monist, in practice, however, ratified international human rights instruments are rarely applied in courts. In essence, the country is just as much a dualist state. The country is de jure monist and de factor dualist like any other.

Judicial Enforcement of the Right to Health

Judicial enforcement of the right to health ensures the realisation of the right. In ensuring access to justice, litigation can serve as an avenue for realising the health needs of individuals while holding governments accountable for violations of the right.[55] For example, South Africa has one of the most progressive health rights jurisprudences which holds the government accountable.[56] Litigation therefore becomes a key strategy especially when the right to health is justiciable as is the case in Mozambique. The Constitution of Mozambique not only provides for the right to health care but also for adjudication when such a right is violated. Article 70 of the Constitution states that 'Every citizen shall have the right of recourse to the courts against acts that violate their rights and interests recognised by the Constitution and the laws.' Article 89 further states that 'All citizens shall have the right to present petitions, complaints and claims to the competent authority in order to demand the restitution of their rights violated or in defence of the public interest.' The Constitution further provides in article 81(2) as follows:

> The right of popular action shall consist of: a) The right to claim for the injured party or parties such compensation as they are entitled to; b) The right to advocate the prevention, termination or judicial prosecution of offences against the public health, consumer rights, environmental conservation and cultural heritage.

This provision recognises the right of 'popular action' (*direito de acção popular*) which gives individuals and groups the right to bring cases to court in relation to issues such as public

55 BM Meier and AE Yamin, 'Right to Health Litigation and HIV/AIDS Policy' *Journal of Law, Medicine & Ethics* (2011) 81, 82.

56 See S Liebenberg, 'South Africa' in M Langford (ed) *Social Rights Jurisprudence: Emerging Trends in International and Comparative Law* (Cambridge University Press 2008) 75–101.

health. The Constitution further stipulates that the Courts are 'to guarantee and strengthen the rule of law as an instrument of legal stability, and they must guarantee respect for the laws and safeguard the rights and freedoms of citizens'.[57]

However, the rules that govern the jurisdiction of the domestic courts are not clear about which of the courts have jurisdiction over human rights matter. For instance, the Constitution provides under article 241(1) that 'the Constitutional Council is a sovereign public office with special jurisdiction to administer justice in *matters of a legal constitutional nature*'.[58] The Constitutional Council (*Conselho Constitucional*) is mandated to administer justice in constitutional matters and issues related to elections though it is not a judicial body.[59] Article 244(2) of the Constitution further provides that judgments of the Council become 'binding on all citizens, institutions and other legal persons, they shall not be subject to appeal and they shall prevail over other decisions'.

Noticeably, however, the Constitutional Court is not defined as a court in the Constitution. According to the Constitution, Mozambique has three categories of courts: Supreme Court (*Tribunal Supremo*), Administrative Courts (*Tribunais Administrativos*) and Courts of Justice (*Tribunais Judicias*).[60] The Supreme Court is the highest court in the country,[61] although the Courts of Justice have the ordinary jurisdiction in civil and criminal matters and exercise their jurisdiction over all areas not assigned to other jurisdictional orders.[62] Nhampossa has argued that since judicial actions on socio-economic rights are against the state, the state cannot appear before the Courts of Justice.[63] It remains unclear whether the Courts of Justice will have the jurisdiction to adjudicate matters where the state is a party in the matter.[64]

The Administrative Courts have jurisdiction over matters concerning disputes relating to the legality of administrative acts.[65] In the recent case of *Ruth Silvestre Muianga*, the applicant, with the support of the Mozambican League of Human Rights (Liga dos Direitos Humanos – LDH), brought an action for enforcement of extra-contractual liability against the Mozambican state.[66] This case concerned the death of the late Ruth Elias Muianga, an 11-year-old boy who was killed by the Police of the Republic of Mozambique (PRM) during the food riot of 1–2 September 2010. It was alleged that the PRM and Ministry of Interior violated the rule of law and fundamental rights of citizens.[67]

---

57 Art 212(1)(2) of the 2004 Constitution.

58 Emphasis added.

59 Art 244(1) of the 2004 Constitution.

60 Art 223(1) of the 2004 Constitution.

61 Art 225(1) of the 2004 Constitution.

62 Art 223(4) of the 2004 Constitution.

63 JV Nhampossa, 'Challenges to the Implementation and Enforcement of Socio-economic Rights in Mozambique' (unpublished thesis 2009) 21.

64 Ibid.

65 Art 230(2) of the 2004 Constitution.

66 Tribunal Administrativo, Primeira secção, Processo no. 2 214/2010–1.a: Acordao no 89/2012 (Judgment of the Administrative Court). A copy of the judgment is on file with the author.

67 Ibid, paras 5–8.

The applicant further asserted that the indiscriminate use of real bullets violated various human rights instruments that Mozambique is a party to.[68] The state failed in its main responsibility of ensuring effective protection and realisation of human rights and fundamental freedoms as determined by the Constitution under article 58(2) which states that 'the State shall be responsible for damages caused by the unlawful acts of its agents, in the performance of their functions, without prejudice to rights of recourse available under the law'.

The application was heard by the Administrative Court which held that the applicant bore the right to indemnification for damages and has standing as the mother of the minor who was shot by a member of the PRM. The PRM is tasked to 'ensure public order and safety' pursuant to article 102 of Law No 9/2001 of 7 July.[69] The Court further held that the state was liable for the actions of the PRM and asked the state to pay damages amounting to 500,000 Metacais.[70]

Initially, the case illustrates that the Court is more comfortable hearing cases dealing with civil and political rights. The utilisation of instruments that Mozambique has ratified is evident in the applicant's argument to strengthen the rights enshrined in the Constitution, and invoke the ICCPR and the African Charter.[71]

The decision of the Administrative Court represents a significant development in the Court's jurisprudence. It illustrates, despite its strict formalities, how the rights enshrined in the Constitution can be used to support such a finding. However, the Court did not explicitly refer to article 58(1) of the Constitution which states that 'everyone shall have the right to claim compensation in accordance with the law, for damages caused by a violation of their fundamental rights'. The shortcoming of the decision is that it appears the Court did not utilise the opportunity to expound and clarify on its jurisdiction to hear cases dealing with human rights matters, rather it simply enquired whether the actions of the PRM are attributable to the state. A critical area that remains to be tested is whether the Court will exercise jurisdiction in socio-economic violations including the right to health in terms of state actions.

It is, therefore, posited that there is a need for an explicit provision with regard to which court has jurisdiction over human rights matters. This is particularly important as it is related to the general principle set out in article 56(1) of the Constitution that 'individual rights and freedom shall be guaranteed by the State and shall be exercised within the framework of the Constitution and the Law'.

Factors Hampering Right to Health Litigation in Mozambique

It is a tragic irony that despite the innovative provisions on the right to health which can facilitate litigation in Mozambique, my research has not uncovered any litigated cases on

68 Ibid, para 9.
69 Ibid, para 14.
70 Ibid, para 15.
71 Ibid, para 28.

the right to health. Judicial enforcement on the right to health is non-existent. Reflecting on this reveals the imperative for an analysis of the barriers for litigating the right to health. Such barriers include the lack of usage of international law, the rules and procedures that govern who can constitute cases before the courts and how just procedure should be taken.

Jurisprudential Challenges

The Constitutional Council has been reviewing constitutional cases dealing with electoral disputes between political parties.[72] The Supreme Court, in the case of *President of the Republic of Mozambique v Bernardo Sacarolha Ngomacha*, held that customary law must be in line with constitutional principles and international agreed instruments for the protection of human rights.[73]

Domestic courts in Mozambique rarely rely on standards found in international instruments.[74] Domestic norms are usually preferred to international norms in litigating human rights issues. In most cases, Portuguese jurisprudence is quoted in submissions before the court.[75] Thus, it is hard to find judgments that cite international law instruments.

Although ratified treaties are part and parcel of the domestic legal order, the approach of the courts in their limited usage of international law points to the fact that it is not adhered to.[76] The potential of international and regional instruments, including the African Charter, as interpretative tools has not been utilised.[77] As a civil law system, precedents are not usually followed and litigation on human rights and constitutional matters are not common. This further limits legal practitioners from depending on precedents set by international and regional human rights systems or other domestic courts.

Legal Standing

The Constitution gives citizens by virtue of articles 70 and 89 of the Constitution the right of recourse when there is a violation of their rights. Article 81(2) of the Constitution is innovative in recognising the right of 'popular action' on behalf of individuals or groups on issues of public health. The difficulty, however, is with regard to the modalities on how such cases can be instituted.

Litigation on violations of the right to health faces the obstacle of the *locus standi* at the Constitutional Court. This requirement is based on the premise that the Courts of Justice

---

72 Afrimap, OSISA and OSMP, *Mozambique*, Public Broadcasting in Africa series (Open Society Foundations 2010) 5.

73 Supreme Court (*Tribunal Supremo*), criminal section I, Proc 5/2004-A. As cited in Afrimap/OSISA, *Mozambique: Justice Sector and the Rule of Law* (OSISA 2006) 132.

74 See Mandlate (n 46 above) 23.

75 Afrimap/OSISA (n 72 above) 62.

76 See the judgment in *Ruth Silvestre Muianga* (n 65 above).

77 See A Mandlate and F Mamad, 'Mozambique' in Centre for Human Rights, *The Impact of the African Charter and Women's Protocol in Selected African States* (University of Pretoria Law Press 2012).

and the Administrative Courts[78] may not exercise jurisdiction over right to health cases, but rather the Constitutional Court will have jurisdiction as it deals with constitutional matters. According to article 245(2) of the Constitution, legal standing before the Council is extended to the President of the Republic, the President of the Assembly of the Republic, at least one-third of the deputies of the Assembly of the Republic, the Prime Minister, the Attorney General of the Republic, the Ombudsman and 2,000 citizens.

In terms of direct access for citizens, the right of popular action will be applicable. The standing law regime in Mozambique requires 2,000 citizens to institute a case at the Constitutional Council. The requirement for 2,000 citizens limits judicial enforcement as such a requirement is complex and it would be difficult to institute such cases. The effect of this provision is that the Court shall not receive petitions from individuals or their representatives, who allege that their right to health has been violated if they are less than 2,000 people. The only option for such individuals is to go to the Assembly and convince two-thirds of the deputies to take the case or go through the Ombudsman (*Provedor de Justiça*), although, despite approval from Parliament,[79] an individual has not yet been appointed to the position.[80]

The strict requirement for legal standing before the Constitutional Council might perhaps serve as one of the major impediments for judicial enforcement of socio-economic rights including the right to health. The rule of *locus standi* can impede access to justice for those who have experienced violations of their fundamental rights. As stated by Chaskalson P in *Ferreira v Levin No*, a broader approach to standing ensures 'constitutional rights enjoy full measure of protection to which they are entitled to'.[81]

In addition, the Technical Unit for Law Reform (*Unidade Técnica de Revisão Legal* – UTREL) established under the Ministry of Justice should, under its mandate, prepare legislation to give effect to this constitutional provision as the proper framework is absent.

Lack of Knowledge of International Law

Another barrier facing litigation of the right to health in Mozambique is the lack of knowledge of international human rights law on the part of both judges and lawyers.[82] As the Special Rapporteur on the independence of judges and lawyers, Gabriela Knaul, on her missions to Mozambique in 2009 and 2010, respectively, explains:

> Making justice accessible to all starts with an adequate knowledge of human rights and fundamental freedoms, and the functions and services provided by the system of administration of justice.[83]

---

78 The Administrative Court has shown willingness to exercise jurisdiction over civil and political rights cases.

79 According to art 256 of the Constitution.

80 Human Rights Council, National Report (n 47 above) para 37.

81 1996 (1) SA 984 (CC).

82 Mandlate (n 46 above) 23.

83 Report of the Special Rapporteur on the independence of judges and lawyers, Gabriela Knaul, on her missions to Mozambique (2011) UN Doc A/HRC/17/30/Add 2, para 45.

Magistrates do not have the adequate understanding of human rights law.[84] This means that most lawyers are unable to cite international human rights law while judges are unable to draw conclusions through application of relevant international human rights law. Yet, Mozambique is well known for hosting the adoption of the Protocol on the Rights of Women in Africa and had a commissioner, Madam Melo, who served in the African Commission.

Very few non-governmental organisations (NGOs) are concerned with issues relating to violations of the right to health. They are mostly concerned with civil and political rights.[85] In addition, they lack adequate knowledge of international human rights law with the exception of few.[86] Key among them is the Human Rights League (Liga dos Direitos Humanos – LDH) which has observer status before the African Commission. It does a fair amount of human rights work, including instituting cases in the domestic courts and submitting shadow reports to the Commission. In addition to LDH, there are a few other national organisations that engage in this type of work.[87]

Human and Financial Constraints[88]

There is a dearth of qualified lawyers willing to take up socio-economic rights cases in Mozambique. It is estimated that in 2010, 610 lawyers were registered with the Mozambican Bar Association (OAM)[89] in an estimated population of 22.5 million.[90] This 'corresponds to a ratio of one lawyer to 36,885 people'.[91] The Special Rapporteur on the independence of judges and lawyers has also raised concerns in relation to the shortage of qualified lawyers outside the capital, where some provinces such as Gaza or Niassa do not have a resident advocate.[92]

In addition, the state has established the Institute for Legal Assistance and Representation (Instituto do Patrocínio e Assistência Jurídica – IPAJ), a free legal aid body to provide legal services including representation in court for clients who have obtained a declaration of

84 The same is said to be applicable in Cape Verde and Angola which have the same legal system as Mozambique.

85 This view is shared by Mandlate and Mamad (n 76 above) 109.

86 Ibid.

87 Other organisations include Women in Law and Southern Africa, Mozambique (Mulher e Lei na África Austral), the Women's Forum (Fórum Mulher), the Mozambican Association of Women in Legal Careers (Associação Moçambicana de Mulheres de Carreira Jurídica) and the Mozambican Association of Judges (Associação Moçambicana dos Juízes).

88 See Report of the Special Rapporteur, Gabriela Knaul (n 82 above) paras 40–44.

89 Law 28/2009 governs the operation of the OAM.

90 TL Timbane, 'Novos remos do processo civil em Mocambique'. Ceremonia de lancamento do Codigo de Processo Civil UTREL (2010) as cited by Mandlate (n 46 above) 23.

91 Mandlate (n 46 above) 23,

92 Report of the Special Rapporteur, Gabriela Knaul (n 82 above) para 90.

poverty (*atestado de pobreza*), issued by the City Council.[93] However, IPAJ staff lack the skills to handle socio-economic rights cases, including the right to health.[94]

Although Mozambique is one of the fastest growing economies, this is not reflective of the socio-economic circumstances of its citizens. It should be noted that the majority of Mozambicans live in abject poverty and are unaware of their rights.[95] Citizens face financial challenges in accessing courts due to distance from courts and poor transport networks. Court fees are also exorbitant.[96] The cost of litigating is still relatively high even when the case is pro bono and the fees are waived because of the expenses incurred with regard to transport to court and accommodation away from home.[97]

Prospects for Litigating the Right to Health in Mozambique

The Constitution of Mozambique provides for the right to health as a fundamental right. In addition, other rights such as the right to life, dignity and liberty provide an important entry point for the enforcement of the right to health. It must be borne in mind that the right to health is dependent on the enjoyment of other rights – food, housing, work, education, access to information and freedom of association and movement.[98] Health litigation can greatly contribute to holding the government accountable to laws and policies as well as ensuring implementation.[99] There is much potential for litigating health-related cases.

Litigation is vital in empowering individuals and NGOs to raise claims of human rights violations in court. It seeks to hold governments accountable to their right to health obligations.[100] This is in light of their obligation to respect, protect and fulfil the right to health. These obligations have been described as 'a positive expectation on the part of the state to move its machinery towards the realisation of the rights'.[101] This will only be possible in Mozambique when civil society organisations and human rights lawyers file test cases on the right to health.

---

93 The main legal instruments governing the provision of legal aid and services in Mozambique are Law 6/94 and Decree No 54/95.

94 Mandlate (n 46 above), 23.

95 See Report of the Special Rapporteur, Gabriela Knaul (n 82 above) para 46.

96 Court fees in Mozambique are regulated by the Code of Court Costs Decree No 48/89, updated by Decree No 14/96.

97 Afrimap/OSISA (n 72 above) 15.

98 UN Committee on Economic, Social and Cultural Rights, General Comment No 14, 'The right to the highest attainable standard of health', UN Doc E/C.12/2000/4, para 8.

99 See S Gloppen, 'Litigation as a Strategy to Hold Governments Accountable for Implementing the Right to Health' (2008) 10 *Health and Human Rights* 21.

100 See HV Hogerzeil et al, 'Is Access to Essential Medicines as Part of the Fulfillment of the Right to Health Enforceable through the Courts?' (2006) 368 *Lancet* 305.

101 *Social and Economic Rights Action Centre (SERAC) and Another v Nigeria* (2001) AHRLR 60 (ACHPR 2001) para 47.

Important steps to encourage litigating the right to health are the creation of a conducive environment, the development of clear rules and procedures governing litigation, the establishment of the National Human Rights Commission and intensive human rights education.

Jurisdiction and Standing

The rules governing which court has jurisdiction over human rights matters must be made clear. In addition, the rules of standing before the Constitutional Council, which require 2,000 citizens before a case can be instituted, are problematic. These serve as barriers to accessing justice in relation to violations of fundamental human rights.

Recognising the inextricable link between the rule of standing and its potential to impede or facilitate access to justice, it is suggested that the procedural rules should be amended to make it flexible so that potential applicants can approach the relevant judicial body. Inspiration can be drawn from section 38(d) of the South African Constitution which grants standing to 'anyone acting in the public interest'.[102] The provision for 'anyone' and not necessarily a group of 2,000 citizens will provide an opportunity for human rights litigation including health-related litigation. Such a broad and wide scope of standing will allow individuals and non-citizens to access the courts. It should be noted, however, that the mere relaxing of the rules governing standing may not lead to the building of a human rights litigation culture.

Strengthening of Human Rights Education

Human rights education is vital for both lawyers and judges. This must be on an ongoing basis on issues relating to international law and human rights.[103] There is evidence to show that fulfilment of human rights is achievable through litigation by citation of international law.[104]

Human rights education should be included in the curriculum for law students. This is evident in the Faculty of Law at the Eduardo Mondlane University (Universidade Eduardo Mondlane) which has established the Centre for Human Rights (Centro dos direitos humanos) focusing on providing legal education. The Faculty currently runs an LLM in Human Rights.[105] In addition, the Politeque University (Universidade A Politecnica) and the Catholic University of Mozambique (Universidade Catolic de Mocambique) have introduced human rights education at the undergraduate level.[106]

---

102 Constitution of South Africa, 1996.

103 See the Bangalore Principles of Judicial Conduct adopted by the Judicial Group on Strengthening Judicial Integrity, as revised at the Round Table Meeting of Chief Justices held at the Peace Palace, The Hague (25–26 November 2002) paras 6.3–6.6.

104 J Singh et al, 'Do Human Rights Matter to Health?' (2007) 370 *Lancet* 521, 526.

105 I experienced this as a student of the LLM in Human Rights and Democratisation in Africa at the Centre for Human Rights, Eduardo Mondlane University during my second semester in 2012.

106 Mandlate and Mamad (n 76 above) 110.

National Human Rights Commission (NHRC)

The National Human Rights Commission (NHRC) was established in 2009 to uphold human rights in Mozambique.[107] Its mandate is to receive complaints of violation of human rights and refer them to the relevant body for protection. It also proposes law reform and ratification of international instruments. Members of the NHRC have already been sworn in although it has yet to begin operations.[108] Concerns have been raised about political influence in the appointment of the commissioners.[109]

The Commission's mandate should be expanded so as to develop a practice of public inquiry into systematic violations of human rights, especially socio-economic rights, including the right to health. It should also conduct human rights impact assessments into budget allocations and monitoring of public funds allocated to health.

The NHRC should also collect information on measures that have been taken by organs of the state for realising socio-economic rights, including the right to health. These reports could subsequently be tabled before Parliament to influence changes in policy and inquiry areas.

Thus, the Commission has the potential to provide a greater degree of independent oversight on human rights matters. However, it is left to be seen whether it will utilise its potential to the maximum while drawing inspiration from similar bodies such as the South African Human Rights Commission.

Conclusions

This chapter has discussed the reasons for the lack of health-related litigation in Mozambique. These include jurisprudential challenges and ambiguity concerning jurisdiction of courts on human rights matters, the lack of knowledge of international human rights law on the part of judges and lawyers, and human and financial constraints. The chapter has also identified opportunities for litigating the right to health in Mozambique, such as increased activism and strategic litigation by civil society organisations and human rights lawyers, as well as continuous training for lawyers and judges and the inclusion of human rights education in the law school curriculum and law faculties in the country.

When considering the right to health in Mozambique, one is struck by the relative absence of cases, despite the possibilities available in the Constitution. Judicial cases do not mention international or regional human rights treaties. The recent decision in the *Ruth Silvestre Muianga* case in which the State of Mozambique was held liable for the indiscriminate use of real bullets during the 2010 food riot demonstrates that there is still

107 Ibid.

108 Email correspondence with Farida Mamad, member of the National Human Rights Commission, 4 April 2013. See also UN Mozambique, 'Human Rights Commission in Mozambique Presented Publicly', available at http://www.mz.one.un.org/por/Noticias/Noticias2/Human-Rights-Commission-in-Mozambique-Presented-Publicly (accessed 31 March 2013).

109 See Mandlate and Mamad (n 76 above) 112 n.

some capacity for citizens to have faith in the judicial function and demand that justice be done, especially in cases where the state violates human rights and fundamental freedoms of citizens.[110]

This chapter suggests that it will be partly incumbent on the judiciary to inquire into alleged breaches of the state's obligations relating to the right to health by addressing the issue of judicial efficiency. The degree to which the Mozambican judiciary is called upon to settle cases involving socio-economic rights also reveals the non-litigating culture of the civil society. It is therefore vital that Mozambican civil society, through its numerous NGOs, submits cases on the right to health which can serve to maximise the enforcement of the right to health.[111] Indeed, judicial enforcement of the right to health holds promise for the realisation of state duties in guaranteeing the right to health in Mozambique.

References

Books, Chapters, Articles, etc.

Gloppen S, 'Litigation as a Strategy to Hold Governments Accountable for Implementing the Right to Health' (2008) 10 *Health and Human Rights* 21–36.

Hogerzeil HV, Samson, M, Casanovas, JV and Rahmani-Ocora, L, 'Is Access to Essential Medicines as Part of the Fulfilment of the Right to Health Enforceable through the Courts?' (2006) 368 *Lancet* 305–311.

Liebenberg, S, 'South Africa' in M Langford (ed) *Social Rights Jurisprudence: Emerging Trends in International and Comparative Law* (Cambridge University Press 2008) 75–101.

Mandlate, A, 'The Protection and Enforcement of Socio-economic Rights in Lusophone Countries in Africa: Challenges in Angola, Cape Verde and Mozambique' (2010) 11(3) *ESR Review* 22–24.

Mandlate, A and Mamad, F, 'Mozambique' in Centre for Human Rights, *The Impact of the African Charter and Women's Protocol in Selected African States* (University of Pretoria Law Press 2012) 105–113.

Meier, BM and Yamin, AE, 'Right to Health Litigation and HIV/AIDS Policy' (2011) *Journal of Law, Medicine & Ethics* 81–84.

Nhampossa, JV, 'Challenges to the Implementation and Enforcement of Socio-economic Rights in Mozambique' (unpublished thesis 2009).

Potts, H, 'Accountability and the Right to the Highest Attainable Health' (2008), available at http://repository.essex.ac.uk/9717/1/accountability-right-highest-attainable-standard-health.pdf (accessed 27 February 2015).

110 League of Human Rights (Liga dos Direitos Humanos de Moçambique), press release shared by Joao Nhampossa, one of the lawyers in the case, via email on 28 March 2013.

111 The former Special Rapporteur on Health, Paul Hunt, has suggested that civil society utilise the 'explicit language of human rights, including the right to health, in their activities and campaigns' (n 10 above) 21.

Singh J, Govender, M and Mills, EJ, 'Do Human Rights Matter to Health?' (2007) 370 *Lancet* 521–527.

UN Mozambique, 'Human Rights Commission in Mozambique Presented Publicly', available at http://www.mz.one.un.org/por/Noticias/Noticias2/Human-Rights-Commission-in-Mozambique-Presented-Publicly (accessed 31 March 2015).

Viljoen, F, *International Human Rights Law in Africa* (Oxford University Press 2012).

International and Regional Instruments

African Charter on Human and Peoples' Rights, GA Dec. 115 (XVI), adopted 17 June 1981, entered into force 21 October 1986.

African Charter on the Rights and Welfare of the Child, OAU Doc. CAB/LEG/24.9/49, adopted 11 July 1990, entered into force 29 November 1999.

Bangalore Principles of Judicial Conduct adopted by the Judicial Group on Strengthening Judicial Integrity, as revised at the Round Table Meeting of Chief Justices held at the Peace Palace, The Hague (25–26 November 2002).

Committee on Economic, Social and Cultural Rights, General Comment No 14, 'The right to the highest attainable standard of health' (2000) UN Doc E/C.12/2000/4.

Committee on the Rights of the Child, 'Concluding Observations: Mozambique' (2009) CRC/C/MOZ/CO/2.

Concluding comments of the Committee on the Elimination of Discrimination against Women: Mozambique (2007) CEDAW/C/MOZ/CO/2.

Convention on the Elimination of All Forms of Discrimination against Women (CEDAW), adopted 18 December 1979, entered into force 3 September 1981.

Convention on the Rights of the Child, A/RES/44/25, adopted 20 November 1989, entered into force 2 September 1990.

Convention against Torture and Other Cruel, Inhuman or Degrading Treatment or Punishment, GA Res. 39/49, adopted 10 December 1984, entered into force 26 June 1987.

International Covenant on Civil and Political Rights, GA Res. 2200A (XXI), 999 UNTS 171, adopted 16 December 1966, entered into force 23 March 1976.

International Covenant on Economic, Social and Cultural Rights, A/Res/21/2200, adopted 16 December 1966, entered into force 3 January 1976.

International Convention on the Elimination of All Forms of Racial Discrimination, adopted 21 December 1965, entered into force 4 January 1969 (UN *Treaty Series* vol 660, 195).

Protocol to the African Charter on Human and People's Rights on the Rights of Women in Africa, CAB/LEG/66.6, adopted 11 July 2003, entered into force 25 November 2005.

SADAC Charter of Fundamental Social Rights (2003).

SADC Protocol on Gender and Development (2008).

SADC Protocol on Health (1999).

Reports

AfriMAP, OSISA and OSMP, *Mozambique*, Public Broadcasting in Africa series (Open Society Foundations 2010).

AfriMAP/OSISA, *Mozambique: Justice Sector and the Rule of Law* (OSISA 2006).

Chao, S and Kostermans, K, *Improving Health for the Poor in Mozambique: The Fight Continues*, HNP Discussion Paper (World Bank 2001).

Economic Conference for Africa and African Union, *Economic Report on Africa 2012: Unleashing Africa's Potential as a Pole of Global Growth* (ECA and AU 2012).

Human Rights Council, National Report submitted in accordance with paragraph 159(a) of the annex of the Human Rights Council resolution 5/1: Mozambique (2011) A/HRC/WG.6/10/MOZ/1.

PEPFAR, 'Mozambique: Operational Plan Report FY 2010', available at http://www.pepfar.gov/documents/organization/145728.pdf (accessed 31 March 2013).

Report of the Special Rapporteur on the independence of judges and lawyers, Gabriela Knaul, on her missions to Mozambique (2011) UN Doc A/HRC/17/30/Add 2.

Report of the Special Rapporteur on the right of everyone to the enjoyment of the highest attainable standard of physical and mental health, Paul Hunt, mission to Mozambique (2005) Un Doc E/CN.4/2005/51/Add 2.

UNDP, *Mozambique National Human Development Report 2007: Challenges and Opportunities: The Response to HIV and AIDS* (UNDP 2007), available at http://hdr.undp.org/en/reports/national/africa/mozambique/NHDR_2007_HIV_AIDS_MOZAMBIQUE.pdf (accessed 27 February 2013).

UNDP, *Human Development Report 2013. The Rise of the South: Human Progress in a Diverse World* (UNDP 2013).

UNICEF, '2012 Annual Report: Mozambique', available at http://unicef.org.mz/annualreport2012 (accessed 25 February 2013).

World Bank, *Africa Development Indicators 2011* (World Bank 2011).

Cases

Ferreira v Levin No and Others 1996 (1) SA 984 (CC).

Ruth Silvestre Muianga case, Tribunal Administrativo, Primeira secção, Processo no. 2 214/2010–1.a.

President of the Republic of Mozambique v Bernardo Sacarolha Ngomacha, Supreme Court (*Tribunal Supremo*), criminal section I, Proc 5/2004-A.

Purohit and Another v The Gambia (2003) AHRLR 96 (ACHPR 2003).

Social and Economic Rights Action Centre (SERAC) and Another v Nigeria (2001) AHRLR 60 (ACHPR 2001).

PART III
Comparative Regional Study

Chapter 10

Keeping Promises: Litigation as a Strategy to Concretise the Right to Health in Africa

Judy A. Oder[1]

Over the last decade, some countries in Africa have successfully controlled smallpox, polio, guinea-worm disease and river blindness.[2] Despite these positive developments, the enjoyment of the right to health remains elusive to the majority of the African continent's population.

The fulfilment of the right to health is vital to all aspects of a person's life and well-being, and is crucial to the realisation of all other fundamental human rights and freedoms.[3] The right to health is closely related to and dependent upon the rights to food, housing, work, education, privacy, human dignity, life, access to information, non-discrimination and equality, the prohibition against torture and the freedoms of association, assembly and movement. These as well as other rights and freedoms address integral components of the right to health.[4]

This chapter looks at some of the key right to health challenges in the region and how litigation could be used to respond to them. The chapter will build on discussion in Chapter 1 by Olubayo Oluduro and Ebenezer Durojaye on the normative framework for realising the right to health and Chapter 3 by Gladys Mirugi-Mukundi on a rights-based approach to realising access to sexual and reproductive health care services in Africa. The first part of the chapter discusses the major health challenges facing the region. The second section looks at the legal and human rights framework for the realisation of the right to health. The chapter then analyses the strengths and weaknesses of cases from regional mechanisms on the right to health or indirectly touching on the underlying determinants of the right to health. It includes a comparative analysis with jurisprudence of other regional bodies focusing on lessons that can be learnt by litigants in Africa. The

1 I am grateful to Andrea Coomber for her comments.

2 World Health Organization, *The Health of the People: The African Regional Health Report* (WHO 2006) 57, available at http://whqlibdoc.who.int/afro/2006/9290231033_rev_eng.pdf. (accessed 1 February 2015).

3 The African Commission on Human and Peoples' Rights in *Purohit and Moore v The Gambia* 241/2001, para 80.

4 Committee on Economic, Social and Cultural Rights, General Comment No 14 'The right to the highest attainable standard of health' (2000) para 3.

last section features challenges and opportunities for future litigation of right to health issues in Africa and concludes with concrete recommendations.

An Overview of Key Right to Health Challenges in Africa

The first part of this section looks at the some of the main health challenges across the region. These include maternal mortality, HIV/AIDS, tuberculosis and neglected diseases.

Maternal, Newborn and Child Health

Millions of mothers, newborn babies and children die every year from preventable, treatable causes. According to a World Health Organization (WHO) report, 'since the early 1990s, little or no progress has been made in maternal, newborn and child health in many parts of the region largely due to the HIV/AIDS epidemic and armed conflicts. In some parts of the region, progress in maternal, newborn and child health has been reversed.'[5]

The report adds that the main causes of maternal death are severe bleeding (haemorrhage), infection (sepsis), eclampsia, obstructed labour and unsafe abortion, but increasing numbers of mothers in this region die from indirect causes, such as HIV/AIDS, tuberculosis, malaria and anaemia.[6] According to the WHO , the major complications that account for 80 per cent of all maternal deaths are severe bleeding (mostly bleeding after childbirth), infections (usually after childbirth), high blood pressure during pregnancy (pre-eclampsia and eclampsia) and unsafe abortion.[7]

A study in West Africa showed that 'for each maternal death, a further 30 women may suffer long-lasting disabilities due to a range of conditions such as chronic anaemia, infertility and obstetric fistula. Harmful traditional practices such as female genital mutilation and nutritional taboos also contribute to poor maternal health. Female genital mutilation, which is the partial or total removal of external genitalia, is practised in 27 African states.'[8]

HIV/AIDS

The WHO reports that

> Africa is the region of the world most affected by the HIV/AIDS pandemic. It has about 11% of the world's population but is home to more than 60% of all people in the world living with HIV. In 2005, an estimated 25.8 million people were living with HIV/AIDS, 3.2

5 World Health Organization, *Health of the People* (n 1 above) xv.

6 Ibid, 18.

7 World Health Organization, 'Maternal Mortality', Fact sheet No 348 (May 2012), available at http://www.who.int/mediacentre/factsheets/fs348/en/. This web page is periodically updated.

8 World Health Organization, *Health of the People* (n 1 above) 19.

million people became infected with the virus and 2.4 million people died of AIDS in the region. In 16 countries in Africa, at least 10% of the population is infected.[9]

The WHO and the Joint United Nations Programme on HIV and AIDS (UNAIDS) declared the lack of access to antiretroviral (ARV) medicines to treat HIV/AIDS in developing countries a public health emergency in 2003.[10] A 2013 UNAIDS report found that Africa continues to be more affected by HIV than any other region of the world, accounting for 69 per cent of people living with HIV globally. Despite positive trends, in 2011 there were still 1.8 million new HIV infections across the continent, and 1.2 million people died of AIDS-related illnesses.[11]

The UNAIDS report states that the number of people in Africa receiving antiretroviral treatment increased from less than 1 million in 2005 to 7.1 million in 2012, with nearly 1 million added in the last year alone. AIDS-related deaths are also continuing to fall – reducing by 32 per cent from 2005 to 2011 – as are the numbers of new HIV infections, which have fallen by 33 per cent from 2001 to 2011. The report attributes this success to strong leadership and shared responsibility in Africa and among the global community. It also urges sustained commitment to ensure Africa achieves zero new HIV infections, zero discrimination and zero AIDS-related deaths.[12]

Those living with HIV/AIDS are prone to stigmatisation and left to the care of relatives and non-governmental institutions. For example, while considering Kenya's periodic report in 2008, the Committee on Economic, Social and Cultural Rights expressed concern that 'children and orphans affected by HIV/AIDS are not adequately supported by the state party and that the care for these children and the task of monitoring their school attendance is frequently delegated to their extended families and to community and faith-based organisations, without adequate support and supervision from the state party'.[13]

Tuberculosis

The WHO has concluded that every year there are an estimated 2.4 million new tuberculosis cases and half a million tuberculosis-related deaths in Africa. The African region accounted for 24 per cent of notified cases in 2003, despite having only 11 per cent of the world's population. Of the 22 high-burden countries that are responsible for 80 per cent of all new tuberculosis cases, nine are in this region: the Democratic Republic of the Congo (DRC),

---

9 Ibid, 44.

10 Joint United Nations Programme on HIV/AIDS, *Keeping the Promise: Summary of the Declaration of Commitment on HIV/AIDS* (UNAIDS 2002) 5.

11 UNAIDS Press Release, 'UNAIDS reports more than 7 million people now on HIV treatment across Africa – with nearly 1 million added in the last year – while new HIV infections and deaths from AIDS continue to fall', available at http://www.unaids.org/en/resources/presscentre/pressreleaseandstatementarchive/2013/may/20130521prupdateafrica/; http://www.unaids.org/en/media/unaids/contentassets/documents/unaidspublication/2013/20130521_Update_Africa.pdf.

12 Ibid.

13 Committee on Economic, Social and Cultural Rights, Concluding observations on Kenya (2008) para 26.

Ethiopia, Kenya, Mozambique, Nigeria, South Africa, Uganda, the United Republic of Tanzania and Zimbabwe. Eleven of the 15 countries with the highest incidence are also in the region: Botswana, Kenya, Lesotho, Malawi, Namibia, Sierra Leone, South Africa, Swaziland, Uganda, Zambia and Zimbabwe.[14] In 2011, the WHO noted that Sub-Saharan Africa carried the greatest proportion of new cases per population with over 260 cases per 100,000 population in 2011.[15]

The WHO study further elaborates that 'on average, about one-third of tuberculosis patients notified in countries in Africa are co-infected with HIV, and in most countries in southern Africa – such as Lesotho, Malawi, South Africa, Swaziland, Zambia and Zimbabwe – over two thirds of children and adults with tuberculosis are co-infected with HIV'.[16] The TB Alliance describes tuberculosis and HIV/AIDS as 'fatally synergistic':

> In high-burden countries, people with HIV/AIDS are 20 times more likely to contract TB than those not suffering from HIV/AIDS, and reciprocally, TB bacteria can hasten the progression of an HIV infection, causing patients to become sicker more rapidly.[17]

Neglected Diseases

According to the WHO, diseases such as sleeping sickness, visceral leishmaniasis and Buruli ulcer 'continue to take their toll in the region, but they no longer figure on the disease-control agenda of the developed world'.[18] Drug research and development to treat these diseases has stalled, but they still have a considerable impact on human development in the region. While the focus has been on other diseases these neglected diseases have become worse. As the WHO study notes, 'Raising the profile of neglected diseases is the first step towards curing them'.[19]

Determinants Affecting the Enjoyment of the Right to Health

The UNICEF/WHO Joint Monitoring Programme for Water and Sanitation found that in 2002 only 58 per cent of the population of sub-Saharan Africa had access to a safe water supply. According to the findings of the UNICEF/WHO Programme, 'Hundreds of thousands of Africans, particularly children, die every year from diseases caused by micro-organisms, certain chemicals in the water supply, or diseases caused by poor sanitation.'[20] Another source of damage to health in the African region is chemical pollution, which can cause effects ranging from acute intoxication to birth defects and cancer.[21]

---

14 World Health Organization, *Health of the People* (n 1 above) 48.

15 World Health Organization, 'Tuberculosis', Fact sheet No 104 (2013), available at http://www.who.int/mediacentre/factsheets/fs104/en/ (accessed 5 February 2015).

16 World Health Organization, *Health of the People* (n 1 above) 49.

17 TB Alliance, 'TB and HIV', available at http://www.tballiance.org/why/tb-hiv.php.

18 World Health Organization, *Health of the People* (n 1 above) 56.

19 Ibid.

20 Ibid, 86.

21 Ibid, 87.

Emergency Situations

In January 2006, the WHO's Health Action in Crisis unit listed 46 countries worldwide as experiencing a crisis – of these, 25 were in the African region. According to the WHO study, 'In health terms, the direct effects of war, civil conflict, floods, droughts, famine and infectious disease are formidable. These factors reduce the resilience of people and of health systems, and they are quickly compounded when shelter, water, nutrition, security, sanitation and disease control are inadequate.'[22] The study also found that 'crises are often characterised by a high level of sexual violence against women and young children'.[23]

Apart from states' failure to deal with the above challenges, other issues continue to compromise the enjoyment of the right to health in the region.

Violations in Health Care Settings

Several human rights violations take place in health care settings across Africa. Examples of these include locking up patients who cannot pay their medical bills, denial of emergency medical care, denial of medication and counselling for people living with HIV/AIDS and the degrading treatment afforded individuals in mental hospitals.[24]

Health Systems and Corruption

The right to health requires an effective, responsive, integrated and good quality health system that is accessible to all.[25] The WHO has identified six essential building blocks that make up health systems: health services (medical and public health); health workforce; health information system; medical products, vaccines and technologies; health financing; and leadership, governance and stewardship.[26] Although debatable, these building blocks provide a useful way of looking at health systems and can be thought of as building blocks for the realisation of the right to health.[27]

Health systems of several countries in the region are frail and not fully operative.[28] Corruption is a threat to the enjoyment of the right to health in the region. In 2011 the UN-backed Global Fund Against Aids, Tuberculosis and Malaria announced it was

---

22 Ibid, 92.

23 Ibid, 93.

24 For a detailed discussion of violations in health care settings, see J Oder, 'Pay Up or You'll be Detained! Improved Health Systems and Accountability as a Response to Violations Arising in Healthcare Settings' (2011) Human Rights Abuse and Health Care, 16.4 *INTERIGHTS Bulletin* 166–171.

25 P Hunt and G Backman, 'Health Systems and the Right to the Highest Attainable Standard of Health' (2008) 10 *Health and Human Rights* 81–92.

26 World Health Organization, *Everybody's Business: Strengthening Health Systems to Improve Health Outcomes: WHO's Framework for Action* (WHO 2007).

27 G. Backman et al., 'Health Systems and the Right to Health: An Assessment of 194 Countries' (2008) 372 *Lancet* 2050.

28 World Health Organization, *Health of the People* (n 1 above) 102.

strengthening financial safeguards following corruption claims in Mali, Mauritania, Djibouti and Zambia.[29] It has been reported that 'Uganda lost US$12m from the same fund over poor accountability'[30] and that in January 2011 Germany, the third biggest donor to the fund after the US and France, had suspended the €200m it pledged for 2011, asking for an investigation into the fraud and misuse of money in four countries – Mauritania, Mali, Zambia and Djibouti. During the same period Ireland delayed a decision to continue its donations to the fund.[31]

The above health challenges clearly indicate that states are falling short of their human rights obligations, set out in regional and international treaties, to protect the right to health.

The Legal and Human Rights Framework of the Right to Health in Africa

The African Charter on Human and Peoples' Rights (African Charter) is the key regional human rights instrument. Considered below are other regional human rights instruments that protect the right to health. Litigants can file cases alleging violations of these treaty provisions before the African Court on Human and Peoples' Rights (African Court), the African Commission on Human and Peoples' Rights (African Commission) and the African Committee on the Rights and Welfare of the Child (Children's Committee). Cases from some countries can also be filed before UN treaty bodies.

Principles in these regional human rights instruments contain immediate obligations of states in respect of the right to health, for example the obligation to take steps, the prohibition of retrogressive steps, minimum core obligations and the obligation to prevent discrimination in the enjoyment of economic, social and cultural rights.[32] In this context, an understanding of the key substantive and structural challenges outlined above and juxtaposition of these with states' regional and international obligations is critical to developing and litigating right to health cases.

The African Charter specifically provides that these treaty bodies can draw from principles of international human rights law in considering the conformity of states' action or inaction with regional treaties.[33]

---

29 'Global Fund Against Aids Cracks Down on Fraud' *BBC News*, 5 February 2011, available at http://www.bbc.co.uk/news/world-europe-12371723 (accessed 5 February 2015).

30 C Wendo and C Businge, 'Uganda loses US$12m Global Fund' *New Vision*, 28 October 2008, available at http://www.newvision.co.ug/D/8/12/656872 (accessed 5 February 2015).

31 S Boseley, 'Can the Global Fund Weather the Corruption Storm?' Infectious Diseases: Sarah Boseley's global health blog, 28 January 2011, available at http://www.guardian.co.uk/society/sarah-boseley-global-health/2011/jan/28/aids-infectiousdiseases (accessed 5 February 2015).

32 African Commission on Human and Peoples' Rights, 'Principles and Guidelines on the Implementation of Economic, Social and Cultural Rights in the African Charter on Human and Peoples' Rights', sec H, para 16.

33 African Charter on Human and Peoples' Rights, art 60; Protocol to the African Charter on the Establishment of the African Court on Human and Peoples' Rights (1997) art 7; African Committee on the Rights and Welfare of the Child.

Article 16 of the African Charter provides that every individual shall have the right to enjoy the best attainable state of physical and mental health and obliges state parties to take the necessary measures to protect the health of their people and to ensure that they get medical attention when they are sick. Article 24 provides that peoples shall have the right to a general satisfactory environment favourable to their development.

The above articles require the state to respect, protect and fulfil the right to health. The obligation to respect requires states to respect the right to health by refraining from denying or limiting equal access to the right to health for all persons.[34] The obligation to protect requires states to protect individuals and communities from violations and requires the investigation and prosecution of perpetrators of such violations and the provision of legal and other remedies to victims.[35] The obligation of the right to fulfil requires states to adopt appropriate legislative, administrative, budgetary, judicial, promotional and other measures to fully realise the right to health.[36]

Children's Rights

Health provisions in the African Charter on the Rights and Welfare of the Child (Children's Charter)[37] provide specific protection for children's health rights.[38] It provides that every child shall have the right to enjoy the best attainable state of physical, mental and spiritual health and obliges states to take measures to pursue the full implementation of this right.[39] It requires states, inter alia, to reduce infant and child mortality rates and to ensure the provision of necessary medical assistance and health care to all children, with emphasis on the development of primary health care.[40]

The different challenges that children face include being vulnerable to malnutrition and infectious diseases during their early years and to sexual, reproductive and mental health problems during puberty. All children should be treated equally and the needs of children from minorities or vulnerable groups such as children from minority or indigenous communities, intersex children and, generally, young girls and adolescent girls, should be addressed.[41]

---

34 *SERAC v Nigeria*, Communication 155/96, para 50.

35 Ibid, para 46.

36 World Health Organization and Office of the High Commissioner for Human Rights, 'The Right to Health', Fact sheet No 31 (2000) 27.

37 OAU Doc CAB/LEG/24.9/49, entered into force 29 November 1999.

38 See Children's Charter, art 14; Protocol to the African Charter on Human and Peoples' Rights on the Rights of Women in Africa, art 14.

39 Children's Charter, art 14(1).

40 Children's Charter, art 14(2)(a)(b).

41 World Health Organization and Office of the High Commissioner for Human Rights (n 35 above) 14.

Women's Rights

The Protocol to the African Charter on Human and Peoples' Rights on the Rights of Women in Africa (Women's Protocol)[42] urges states to respect the right to health including sexual and reproductive health and details the appropriate measures states should take in this regard.[43] It urges states to take appropriate measures to ensure that women have the right to live in a healthy and sustainable environment.[44]

Women experience some peculiar health challenges; governmental interventions responding to these issues should be specifically tailored as appropriate responses. Societal realities that affect women's health and how they live include the prevalence of poverty and economic dependence, their experience of violence, gender bias in the health system and society at large, discrimination on the grounds of race or other factors, the limited power many women have over their sexual and reproductive lives and their lack of influence in decision-making. Some groups of women have particular health problems and face double or multiple layers of discrimination not only because they are women but because they belong to vulnerable groups. For example, women living in poor areas, those living with HIV/AIDS, indigenous and rural women will face other forms of bias and difficulty accessing health services.[45]

Sex workers, women belonging to sexual minorities, older women or female prisoners are groups of women that face specific health issues because of their particular situations. Some women face particular health issues and particular forms of discrimination, with some groups, including refugee or internally displaced women, women in slums and suburban settings, indigenous and rural women, women with disabilities or women living with HIV/AIDS, facing multiple forms of discrimination, barriers and marginalisation in addition to gender discrimination.[46]

Internally Displaced Persons

The African Union Convention for the Protection and Assistance of Internally Displaced Persons in Africa (Kampala Convention) provides that all persons have a right to be protected against arbitrary displacement.[47] The Convention also proscribes members of armed groups from denying internally displaced persons the right to live in satisfactory conditions of dignity, security, sanitation, food, water, health and shelter; and from

42 CAB/LEG/66.6 (13 September 2000).

43 Women's Protocol, art 14.

44 Women's Protocol, art 17.

45 World Health Organization and Office of the High Commissioner for Human Rights (n 35 above) 12.

46 Ibid. See also United Nations Declaration of Commitment on HIV/AIDS, paras 13 and 14, available at http://www.un.org/ga/aids/coverage/FinalDeclarationHIVAIDS.html (accessed 5 February 2015).

47 Kampala Convention, art 4.

separating members of the same family.[48] It details states' obligations relating to protection and assistance during internal displacement.[49]

Persons Living with HIV/AIDS

The African Commission has undertaken initiatives to elaborate standards with interpretive value. Its resolution on HIV/AIDS declares the pandemic a human rights issue and calls on states to allocate national resources that reflect a determination to fight the spread of HIV/AIDS.[50] In 2010, the African Commission established a Committee on the Protection of the Rights of People Living with HIV (PLHIV) and Those at Risk, Vulnerable to and Affected by HIV. The Committee was set up to, among other things, 'seek, request, receive, analyse and respond to reliable information from credible sources including individuals, community-based organisations, non-governmental organisations, specialised agencies, inter-governmental organisations and state parties on the situation and rights of PLHIV and those at risk'. It will also engage 'state parties on their responsibilities to respect, protect and fulfil the rights of people living with HIV and those at risk', and 'recommend concrete and effective strategies' to better protect them.[51]

Having access to drugs is critical in the context of states' obligation in respect of persons living with HIV/AIDS.

The Office of the United Nations High Commissioner for Human Rights has indicated that 'states are obliged to develop national health legislation and policies and to strengthen their national health systems … key issues related to access to medicines must be taken into account such as sustainable financing, availability and affordability of essential medicines; price and quality control; dosage and efficacy of medicines; procurement practices and procedures, supply chains and so on'.[52]

States are obliged to protect persons living with HIV/AIDS from prejudice. They should prohibit discrimination on the grounds of health status, including definite or alleged HIV/AIDS status. National strategies, plans and programmes should incorporate positive measures to respond to aspects that hinder the equal access of these vulnerable populations to prevention, treatment and care.[53]

48 Kampala Convention, art 7(2)(d).

49 Kampala Convention, art 9.

50 ACHPR/Res.53 (XXIX) 01.

51 Mandate of the Committee on the Protection of the Rights of People Living with HIV (PLHIV) and Those at Risk, Vulnerable to and Affected by HIV (2010), available at http://www.achpr.org/mechanisms/hiv-aids/ (accessed 4 February 2015).

52 United Nations Office of the High Commissioner for Human Rights, 'Access to Medicines – a Fundamental Element of the Right to Health', available at http://www.ohchr.org/EN/Issues/Development/Pages/AccessToMedicines.aspx (accessed 8 February 2015).

53 World Health Organization and Office of the High Commissioner for Human Rights, 'The Right to Health', Fact sheet No 31 (2000) 12–20.

The African Commission's Principles and Guidelines on Economic, Social and Cultural Rights

In 2011 the African Commission adopted principles and guidelines on economic and social rights to elaborate the African Charter's provisions and to provide guidance to states and stakeholders on the implementation of the African Charter's economic, social and cultural rights provisions. They provide that the right to health care requires an effective and integrated health system which is responsive to national and local priorities, and accessible to all.

The principles and guidelines call on states to adopt and implement a comprehensive national public health strategy and plan of action. This plan should include special attention to basic and primary health care, and specific measures to ensure coverage of all age groups, in particular in marginalised urban and rural areas.[54] It also details disease specific obligations in relation to malaria, HIV/AIDS, tuberculosis, neglected tropical diseases and other infectious diseases.[55] The guidelines are a useful resource for groups and lawyers undertaking right to health litigation.

The Abuja Framework

The Abuja Framework for Action for the Fight against HIV/AIDS, TB and Other Related Infectious Diseases[56] and the Solemn Declaration on Gender Equality in Africa[57] are decisions by the Assembly of Heads of States and Governments of the African Union that have a bearing on the protection of the right to health.

The extensive normative framework at the regional level and the various challenges provide opportunities for litigation of the right to health in Africa. The next section focuses on right to health litigation before the African Commission juxtaposed with right to health jurisprudence from other regional and international human rights mechanisms, with a focus on lessons for litigants from the region.

Litigation of Right to Health Issues

The African Commission has looked at some of the challenges facing the right to health in Africa against states' regional obligations. However, it is worth noting here that there has not generally been much litigation of economic and social rights at either regional or national levels.

---

54 African Commission on Human and Peoples' Rights (n 29 above) C, para 54 i.

55 Ibid, C, para 54 xix.

56 AHG/228(XXXVII) Annex III.

57 Adopted at the Assembly of Heads of State and Government, 6–8 July 2004.

Limited Litigation of the Right to Health

At the national level there are various barriers to the litigation of the right to health and in some states it is not provided as a right in national constitutions and legislation. A lack of awareness that the right to health can be claimed and the focus of human rights lawyers on civil and political rights cases, which are more straightforward, can also be impediments to litigating the right to health. There are limited resources to develop right to health cases from scratch and conservative benches sometimes see their consideration of right to health issues as interference with the executive's role in setting and implementing health policies. If there is limited or no engagement of health issues within the national judicial system, it is highly unlikely that cases will proceed to regional or international human rights mechanisms.[58]

Strategic Litigation of Right to Health Cases

In both national and regional litigation, there is need for clarity regarding the trajectory of the process. While the region has both civil and common law judicial systems, the context in each country varies and national legislation and policies will also differ.

To have the most impact, right to health cases should be litigated strategically. Strategic litigation entails going to court to seek a remedy beyond an individual case. It involves a number of steps that need to be taken into account.

The first stage will include the identification of issues, key actors and the problem. It also helps to be clear about what resources the litigants command, for example the litigants' capabilities as individuals or groups – financial resources, legal skills, relevant information and organisational capacity.[59]

The second stage of the litigation process comprises the engagement with the court, including the admissibility of the matter and the actual litigation process. Also key to the process is establishing whether the court accepts right to health cases and the claims made before it. Related to this aspect is the legal basis of the judgment or how the judges conceptualise the right to health.[60]

Strategic cases can be devised by litigants in response to a specific problem or they can emerge from ordinary cases. They can be litigated in a tactical way and argued and pursued in a strategic manner. Cases developed from scratch require detailed preparation – often lengthy and costly research, finding appropriate applicants and formulating arguments to reach an identified litigation objective. In cases that have developed organically, the applicants' lawyers will often appreciate the potential of the case to have a wider impact beyond the interests of their clients. Meticulous reasoning, supporting evidence and amicus curiae interventions make these cases strategic. Cases that evolve organically are

58 The author works with lawyers litigating the right to health across Africa.

59 S Gloppen, 'Litigating Health Rights: Framing the Analysis' in AE Yamin and S Gloppen (eds) *Litigating Health Rights: Can Courts Bring More Justice to Health?* (Harvard University Press 2011) 31.

60 Ibid, 34.

less expensive but issues could arise regarding the facts or in relation to national level proceedings that may have predated the engagement of strategic lawyers.[61]

The impact of a strong judgment depends on whether the decision is complied with and how it is implemented. It is vital to identify the authorities responsible for the remedies specified in the judgment and to assess to what extent the authorities comply with the judgment and the role of enforcements mechanisms,[62] where they exist.

The right to health cases below have been litigated before the African Commission and at regional and international levels. As will be seen, the small volume of litigation at the regional level does not reflect the issues raised by the health challenges in the region.

African Commission

The right to health in the context of environmental degradation

In *Social and Economic Rights Action Centre (SEAC) & Another v Nigeria*, the state was alleged to have violated the right to health by failing to fulfil the minimum duties required by this right through directly participating in the contamination of air, water and soil and thereby harming the health of the Ogoni population.[63] It was also alleged to have failed to protect the population from the harm caused and to provide or permit studies of potential or actual environmental and health risks caused by oil operations in the area.[64] The Commission found the Nigerian government in violation of the right to health and the right to a clean environment by participating in the contamination of air, water and soil and thereby harming the health of the Ogoni population, and by failing to protect the Ogoni population from the harm caused by private actors.[65] In this decision the Commission extended the scope of protection afforded by the African Charter to violations perpetrated by non-state actors.

The finding of a violation based on environmental degradation and its threat to, and destruction of, Ogoni sources of livelihood was a positive step forward by the African Commission in the purposive interpretation of the right to life.[66] It marked a departure from earlier decisions in which violations of the right to life were based on executions, assassinations, arrests and detentions without trial, torture and other acts that either threatened or actually harmed the individuals concerned.[67] In linking respect for the right to life to the right to health and a healthy environment the Commission's decision reinforces the indivisibility and interdependence of human rights.

---

61 A Coomber, 'Strategically Litigating Equality: Reflections on a Changing Jurisprudence' (2012) 15 *European Anti-Discrimination Law Review* 11.

62 Gloppen (n 58 above) 36.

63 Comm No 155/96.

64 Ibid, para 50.

65 Ibid, paras 50, 52.

66 JC Nwobike 'The African Commission on Human and Peoples' Rights and the Demystification of Second and Third Generation Rights under the African Charter: *SERAC & Anor v Nigeria*' (2005) 1 *African Journal of Legal Studies* 129, 135.

67 Ibid.

The Commission observed that the respondent state was obliged to respect the right to health[68] and a satisfactory environment.[69] It noted that this entailed largely non-interventionist conduct from the state, for example not to carry out, sponsor or tolerate any practice, policy or legal measures violating the integrity of the individual.[70] While indicating that states are required to undertake certain measures to protect the right to health, the Commission pointed out that this right can also be respected when states refrain from carrying out or condoning acts which undermine the right to health.

For litigants, this case is an example of how good preparation – particularly clarity and precision in setting out the claims and the remedies sought – can lead to a positive decision. The Commission does not have restrictions in regard to submission of evidence; the applicants submitted video evidence to buttress their contention.

An obsolete mental health framework

In *Purohit and Moore v The Gambia* the African Commission considered the substantive content of the right to health when it looked at the archaic mental health legislation of the Gambia.[71] The applicants alleged that the legislative regime in the Gambia for mental health patients violated the right to enjoy the best attainable state of physical and mental health (article 16) and the right of the disabled to special measures of protection in keeping with their physical and moral needs (article 18(4)).[72]

Holding that the Gambia fell short of satisfying the requirements of articles 16 and 18(4) of the African Charter, the Commission stated that the enjoyment of the right to health is crucial to the realisation of other fundamental rights and includes the right of all to health facilities, as well as access to goods and services, without discrimination of any kind.[73]

In holding that mental health patients should be accorded special treatment to enable them to attain and sustain their optimum level of independence and performance, the Commission referred to article 18(4) and drew from the standards outlined in the Principles for the Protection of Persons with Mental Illness and the Improvement of Mental Health Care.[74] It used the Principles to flesh out what mental health care constituted and stated that the scheme of the Lunatics Detention Act was lacking in therapeutic objectives, as well as in the provision of matching resources and programmes of treatment of articles 16 and 18(4) of the African Charter.[75]

In this case, the Commission recognised the poverty that renders African states incapable of providing necessary amenities, infrastructure and resources to facilitate the enjoyment of the right. It read the obligation of state parties into article 16 when it stated that states should 'take concrete and targeted steps, while taking full advantage of their

68 African Charter, art 16.
69 African Charter, art 24.
70 *SEAC & Another v Nigeria*, Comm No 155/96, para 52.
71 *Purohit & Moore v The Gambia*, Comm No 241/2001.
72 Ibid, paras 3–9.
73 Ibid, para 80.
74 A/RES/46/119 adopted 17 December 1991.
75 *Purohit & Moore v The Gambia*, Comm No 241/2001, para 81

available resources, to ensure that the right to health is fully realised in all its aspects without discrimination of any kind'.[76] Critics have suggested that this is a 'watering down' of the obligation imposed on states by article 16.[77]

In the Commission's view, persons who have been institutionalised are not included within the protective scope of article 6, which deals with 'liberty and security' and prohibits arbitrary arrest and detention.[78] This interpretation is disappointing, in particular because the vulnerability of those institutionalised is increased by that fact that general medical practitioners – who are not necessarily psychiatrists – may make those important diagnoses.[79] The decision demonstrates that sometimes a court or mechanism may not agree with arguments before them. It's important, post-decision, to figure out how such loopholes can be addressed.

In earlier cases, the Commission had briefly considered the right to health in cases that were mainly focused on civil and political rights violations. In *Media Rights Agenda v Nigeria* it looked at access to doctors for detainees.[80] Similarly, in *Malawi African Association and Others v Mauritania* it considered the poor prison conditions and found that the responsibility of the state in relation to the right to health is heightened in cases in which the individual is incarcerated.[81] In *Free Legal Assistance Group and Others v Zaire* the Commission found that mismanagement of public finances, the government's failure to provide basic services to the populace and the shortage of medicines in hospital amounted to a violation of article 16.[82]

Lessons from Other Jurisdictions

The selected cases below litigated before international and regional human rights institutions give insight into key right to health cases from other regions. While the contexts in the respondent countries vary, there are lessons that litigants from the region can draw from.

Human Rights Committee

In *KL v Peru*, KL, a 17-year-old, was pregnant with an anencephalic foetus. Although Peruvian abortion law permits abortion when the life or health of the mother is in danger,

76 Ibid, para 84.

77 M Langford and A Nolan, *Litigating Economic, Social and Cultural Rights: Legal Practitioners Dossier* (Centre on Housing Rights and Evictions 2006) 101.

78 *SEAC & Another v Nigeria*, Comm No 155/96, para 52, paras 64–68. The Commission stated, 'Article 6 of the African Charter was not intended to cater for situations where persons in need of medical assistance or help are institutionalized' (para 68).

79 F Viljoen and C Odinkalu, *The Prohibition of Torture and Ill-treatment in the African Human Rights System: A Handbook for Victims and their Advocates*, OMCT Handbook Series 3 (OMCT 2006), 45.

80 *Media Rights Agency and Others v Nigeria*, Comm Nos 105/93, 128/94, 130/94 and 152/96 (1998).

81 *Malawi African Association and Others v Mauritania*, Comm Nos 54/91, 61/91, 98/93, 164/97 to 196/97 and 210/98 (2000), para 116.

82 *Legal Assistance Group and Others v Zaire*, Comm Nos 25/89, 47/90, 56/91, 100/93, para 4.

KL was denied an abortion and had to deliver the baby and breastfeed her for the four days she survived. On 17 November 2005, the UN Human Rights Committee rendered its decision establishing that denying access to a legal abortion in the case of *KL v Peru* constitutes a violation of the International Covenant on Civil and Political Rights (ICCPR). The ruling specifically establishes violations of the right to be free from cruel, inhumane, and degrading treatment (article 7), privacy (article 17) and special protection of the rights of a minor (article 24), among other things. The Human Rights Committee did not find a right to life violation even though the applicant's life was placed in grave danger.[83] On a procedural level, because there were no effective domestic remedies at the domestic level, the Human Rights Committee considered the merits of the case.

This matter illustrates that litigants should not shy away from instituting right to health cases in national courts as regional human rights bodies may provide redress that is unavailable domestically. Where there are no remedies at the national level litigants should make reference to any petitions filed before national judicial bodies in their applications to regional and international mechanisms to avoid admissibility challenges. This case once again shows the importance of clearly highlighting the various vulnerabilities of those whom the case is about. In this case, as KL, a minor , lost her daughter, the resulting judgment offers greater protection for both girls' and women's reproductive health.

CEDAW Committee

In the case of *Ms A.S. v Hungary*, Ms AS, a member of the Roma community, needed an emergency Caesarean section upon going into labour. Immediately before the surgery, a doctor asked Ms AS to sign consent forms on which the doctor had handwritten a statement that Ms AS consented to a sterilisation procedure. Ms AS did not understand the statement or that she had been sterilised until after the operation had taken place. In her communication to the CEDAW Committee, it was found that Ms AS had exhausted her domestic remedies because under Hungarian law she was unable to appeal this decision to the Constitutional Court given the nature and facts of her case. Hungary was found to have violated AS's rights to (1) fully informed consent to medical procedures; (2) right to information on family planning; (3) right to appropriate services in connection with pregnancy and the post-natal period; and (4) right to determine the number and spacing of her children, under articles 10(h), 12 and 16(1)(e) of the Convention on the Elimination of Discrimination Against Women.[84]

The Committee also found that the communication was admissible, even though the operation occurred before the Optional Protocol entered into force for Hungary, because sterilisation was a continuous injury, and because sterilisation is permanent and irreversible as success of reversal is low.[85]

As a result of the decision Hungary amended its Public Health Act in 2008. Finally, in February 2009 the Ministry of Social Affairs and Labour announced that it would

83 *KL v Peru*, at http://reproductiverights.org/sites/crr.civicactions.net/files/documents/KL%20HRC%20final%20decision.pdf (accessed 15 February 2015).

84 *Ms A.S. v Hungary* (2004), Comm No 4/2004, CEDAW/C/36/D/4/2004, para 11.5.

85 Ibid, para 10.4.

compensate Ms AS according to the Committee's recommendations. This is a landmark decision in which for the first time an international body held a state responsible for failing to provide a woman with necessary information and failing to obtain full consent prior to a sterilisation procedure.[86]

The case indicates the importance of setting out clear remedies that impact not just the applicant but also policy and legislation. While changes resulting from a decision may not happen soon after a decision has been rendered, it is important to have an implementation strategy, especially in respect of cases taken before quasi-judicial human rights mechanisms which may not have specific implementation procedures.

This matter also indicates that violations that first occur before the coming into force of a treaty can be considered by a treaty body if they are continuing. Applications regarding violations that occurred before states' ratification or accession to the African Court Protocol, the Children's Charter or any of the UN Optional Protocols establishing individual complaints mechanisms can be filed before these mechanisms if the impact of those violations are still being felt.

The case of *Maria de Lourdes da Silva Pimentel v Brazil* concerns Alyne da Silva Pimentel Teixeira, a Brazilian woman, who died in 2002 when she was six months pregnant. She was examined in a health centre, and after her situation worsened she was informed that her foetus had died. She delivered a still birth in a private health facility through a curettage surgery and became disoriented.[87] The private clinic had no transport available, so she had to wait eight hours to be transferred to a public health hospital, where no beds were available. She had been left unattended in the hallway of the public hospital for 21 hours when she died.[88]

The Centre for Reproductive Rights and Advocacia Cidada Pelos Direitos Humanos filed against the State of Brazil in 2007 to the CEDAW Committee which held that the Brazilian state was negligent in not exercising due diligence to ensure appropriate pregnancy services. It had neglected its duty to regulate and monitor private health care institutions, failed to address discrimination against a woman who was poor and of African descent, and failed to ensure effective judicial protection for the family. The CEDAW Committee made several recommendations to Brazil to comply with its international human rights obligations, including appropriate compensation to the family, and more generally ensuring women's rights to safe motherhood and affordable access to emergency obstetric care.[89]

This case lays down states' positive obligations in respect of maternal mortality issues. It implicates states' obligations with regard to the oversight and supervision of private health facilities. This case, like some of the others discussed here, exemplifies the need to

---

86 Centre for Reproductive Rights, '*AS v Hungary*', available at http://reproductiverights.org/en/case/as-v-hungary-united-nations-committee-on-the-discrimination-against-women (accessed 10 February 2015).

87 *Maria de Lourdes da Silva Pimentel v Brazil* (2008), Comm No 17/2008, CEDAW/C/49/D/17/2008, para 2.6.

88 Ibid, para 2.12.

89 Ibid, para 8.

request remedies that address not only specific violations in respect of the victim but also wider structural challenges in the health system.

Inter-American Commission on Human Rights

In the case of *Jorge Odir Miranda Cortéz v El Salvador*, a petition was filed on 24 January 2000 against the state of El Salvador before the Inter-American Commission on Human Rights (IACHR), alleging violation of the rights to life, health and full development of personality of a group of persons living with HIV. The case was grounded on the state's failure to provide them with the triple therapy medication needed to prevent them from dying and to improve their quality of life. The petitioners also claimed that the situation of the said persons constituted an instance of cruel, inhumane and degrading treatment. The IACHR requested the state to adopt urgent precautionary measures in respect of the alleged victims, in this case so that they could receive relevant medical services and antiretroviral medication.[90]

On 20 March 2009, the IACHR published its report on the merits of the case (Report 27/09) stating that it did not find a violation in the present case, as the state has, according to the Inter-American organ, effectively pursued the progressive realisation of the rights enshrined in article 26 of the American Convention. The IACHR found that the measures of the state were sufficiently expeditious to accomplish that aim effectively. It stated that it was not possible to speak of any direct violation of the right to health of Jorge Odir Miranda Cortez or the other 26 persons identified, as would have been the case if, for instance, it were shown that the state refused to provide care to any of them. According to it, during the processing of the case the Salvadoran health services progressively broadened free coverage to other persons infected with HIV/AIDS, subject to medical screening. It also reported that the petitioners had not alleged any backtracking in the sense of suspension of benefits that any of them were already receiving.[91]

One key lesson to draw from this case is the use of provisional measures to seek redress in respect of right to health violations. Where immediate interventions are required to put an end to on-going violations, this procedure may provide much needed remedies. The case also shows that in litigating right to health issues, litigants should expect to encounter issues around progressive realisation and availability of resources in the treaty mechanism's analysis or in the state's arguments. Litigants should therefore be prepared to illustrate with relevant statistics and information the state's policies and plans, if any, in respect of the issues at hand.

Opportunities

The contextual and normative framework together with the challenges sets the stage for the litigation of the right to health.

---

90 *Jorge Odir Miranda Cortéz et al. v El Salvador*, Case 12.249, Report No 29/01. OEA/Ser.L/V/II.111 Doc 20 rev (2001).

91 Inter-American Commission on Human Rights, Report No 27/09, Merits, Jorge Odir Miranda Cortes et al. El Salvador, 20 March 2009.

For increased right to health litigation at the regional level, there has to be litigation or at least attempts to seek redress from national judicial systems. Litigation has taken place in countries with no specific right to health constitutional provisions with the use of, for example, right to life, freedom from degrading treatment and dignity provisions. The increasing right to health litigation in the region on issues around discrimination of persons living with HIV/AIDS, forced sterilisation and maternal mortality are positive developments which can be built upon.

For the last two decades, the African Commission has been the main human rights monitoring mechanism. There are now two other regional mechanisms that can consider right to health cases. The Children's Committee and the African Court have competence to consider right to health cases and develop standards. The Court's decisions will be binding on states. In choosing in which forum to file a case, litigants should take into account the following issues: the expertise of the bench or members of the mechanism, the procedure of the institution, the duration of the process and the role of the treaty body in the implementation process.

The African Commission through its special mechanisms works on other thematic issues, namely persons living with HIV/AIDS, women's rights, conditions of detention and the rights of older persons, which points to its engagement and expertise on these issues. Cases related to these issues could be entry points for health rights litigation before the Commission as these are clearly areas the Commission is interested in and where it has placed resources.

The Optional Protocol to the International Covenant on Economic, Social and Cultural Rights (ICESCR) enables the Committee on Economic, Social and Cultural Rights to consider complaints from the region when the Optional Protocol comes into force and states from the region ratify it. Recently the African Commission passed a resolution urging African states to ratify the ICESCR, and the Optional Protocol to the ICESCR and to take immediate steps, individually and through international assistance and cooperation, to protect the rights and respect and fulfil their obligations under these instruments subject to their available resources.[92]

In the last few years, there has been a wave of demand for political freedoms across the region as Africans have become more aware of their rights and have demanded accountability from their leaders. With time, this coming of age in terms of demand for rights will hopefully filter through to mobilisation and demand for the enjoyment of right to health and other economic, social and cultural rights.

Existing networks at national, sub-regional, regional and international levels provide excellent opportunities to collaborate and develop strategies related to litigation of the right to health. Linked to these are also specific right to health movements and civil society organisations that are already focusing on right to health litigation. Right to health litigants from the region should tap into these to share experiences, build their capacities and learn from each other.

---

92 African Commission, Resolution 223 on the Optional Protocol to the International Covenant on Economic, Social and Cultural Rights, available at http://www.achpr.org/sessions/51st/resolutions/223 (accessed 11 February 2015).

The last decade has seen increased state engagement with regional human rights treaty bodies. The procedures of the African Commission, the African Court and the Children's Committee are ways through which litigants and regional groups with a focus on right to health can engage with these institutions and states on specific right to health issues. The African Commission's and the Children's Committee's state reporting procedures, special mechanisms and ordinary sessions are all ways through which states can be reminded of their obligations in respect of the right to health.

Challenges

One of the key challenges related to the right to health concerns the lack of awareness of health as a right. There is also limited knowledge by relevant stakeholders of the treaty bodies and how they work. This situation is arguably one of the main reasons why there is limited litigation of right to health issues. Litigants and community groups could collaborate to educate the public on the right to health.

There is scanty data and statistics in relation to health issues in the region. Not only is there limited data on communicable diseases[93] but the lack of or insufficient disaggregated data makes litigation difficult, as numbers are needed not only for evidentiary purposes but also in assisting the state to respond appropriately to the remedies ordered by human rights mechanisms.

The lack of specific constitutional or statutory legislation delineating the right to health and strict standing rules that limit who can file cases have been cited by lawyers and groups in the region as barriers to litigation. Lack of funds and resources to develop strategic cases is a key problem often referred to by human rights lawyers and organisations in the region. Sometimes right to health violations involve sensitive and personal issues that individuals may not want to have publicised through litigation processes. Litigation is a lengthy and expensive process which leads to some applicants withdrawing or giving up before the conclusion of a case.[94]

Litigation in the region has been in response to specific or particular situations. While such litigation may be conducted strategically, it means that data collection and key events relevant to the litigation of the case are only undertaken after the violations have taken place. Developing right to health cases from scratch would be a way of dealing with some of the inherent and deep right to health challenges in the region. This would allow litigators to chart the course of the litigation and not react to circumstances.

For the judiciaries in the region to provide substantive analyses of the right to health issues in cases before them it is important that they are familiarised with economic and social rights cases. One of the judiciary's key roles of developing standards is curtailed if their expertise in respect of economic, social and cultural rights issues is limited.

In a recent case in Uganda, in which the state argued the political question doctrine in the context of separation of powers, the Court agreed with the state and ruled that it does

93 World Health Organization, *Health of the People* (n 1 above) 77.

94 Interights has organised consultative meetings and litigation surgeries at which these issues repeatedly come up.

not have power to determine or enforce its jurisdiction on matters that require analysis of the health sector or make a review of their implementation.[95] The case is an instance of the argument for increased familiarisation of domestic judges with economic, social and cultural rights principles.

The challenges related to the right to the health in the region are numerous and encompass substantive, procedural and structural issues. The situation as it is seems overwhelming and may put off potential litigants; this is where careful thought and planning are needed to litigate specific issues that could have a wider impact.

Access to the African Court by non-governmental organisations and individuals is limited and is only possible after states have made a declaration allowing individual petition.[96] At the time of writing this chapter, only litigants from Burkina Faso, Ghana, Malawi, Mali, Rwanda and Tanzania can file right to health cases before the African Court, and only after exhausting or making attempts to exhaust local remedies.

Conclusions

Targeted strategic litigation at both the national and regional levels on some of the challenges outlined in this chapter would certainly be a way of concretising the right to health detailed in the various regional instruments. Some challenges would be easier to litigate than others. However, strategic litigation alone is a limited tool. Where judgments are successful, their implementation presents an additional set of challenges in terms of affecting change. The most successful cases are those that are brought in the context of a broader social and/or political movement,[97] where there are parallel advocacy and lobbying efforts and engagements with the media.[98] Litigation of an issue in isolation can have an impact on case law, but is unlikely to resonate on the ground or beyond those most directly affected.[99] In litigating the right to health, greater thought and preparation are needed as litigants may be confronted with judicial conservatism and resource and procedural challenges.

The courts' interpretations of economic, social and cultural rights provisions in treaties would also assist the various duty-bearers to tailor health interventions and policies and bring them in line with states' international human rights obligations. The challenges discussed here illustrate that various duty-bearers, beyond ministries of health, are implicated in the protection of the right to health. Information, statistics and reports prepared by various governmental departments focusing on issues related to women, children, persons living with disabilities, sexual minorities, environment, finance, water

95 *Centre for Health Rights and Development & Others v Attorney General*, Petition 16/2011 UGCC 4 [5 June 2012].

96 African Court Protocol, art 34(6).

97 See INTERIGHTS, *Strategic Litigation of Race Discrimination in Europe: From Principles to Practice* (ERRC/INTERIGHTS/MPG 2004), 25.

98 Gloppen (n 58 above).

99 Coomber (n 55 above) 2.

and sanitation in the context of health are critical and can be used to support right to health litigation.

Commitment from states in the region to realising the right to health is central. Formulating and implementing national plans and availing sufficient resources to the health sector indicate a state's willingness to respect its obligations. The political will and financial support that helped stamp out small pox, polio, guinea-worm disease and river blindness is needed to deal with the continent's health crisis.

References

Books, Chapters, Articles, etc.

Backman, G et al., 'Health Systems and the Right to Health: An Assessment of 194 Countries' (2008) 372 *Lancet* 2047–2085.

BBC, 'Global Fund Against Aids Cracks Down on Fraud' *BBC News*, 5 February 2011, available at http://www.bbc.co.uk/news/world-europe-12371723 (accessed 5 February 2015).

Boseley, S, 'Can the Global Fund Weather the Corruption Storm?' *Infectious Diseases: Sarah Boseley's global health blog*, 28 January 2011, available at http://www.guardian.co.uk/society/sarah-boseley-global-health/2011/jan/28/aids-infectiousdiseases (accessed 5 February 2015).

Coomber, A, 'Strategically Litigating Equality: Reflections on a Changing Jurisprudence' (2012) 15 *European Anti-Discrimination Law Review* 11–23.

INTERIGHTS, *Strategic Litigation of Race Discrimination in Europe: From Principles to Practice* (ERRC/INTERIGHTS/MPG 2004).

Gloppen, S, 'Litigating Health Rights: Framing the Analysis', in AE Yamin and S. Gloppen (eds) *Litigating Health Rights: Can Courts Bring More Justice to Health?* (Harvard University Press 2011).

Hunt, P and Backman, G, 'Health Systems and the Right to the Highest Attainable Standard of Health' (2008) 10 *Health and Human Rights* 81–92.

Joint United Nations Programme on HIV/AIDS, *Keeping the Promise: Summary of the Declaration of Commitment on HIV/AIDS* (UNAIDS 2002).

Langford, M and Nolan, A, *Litigating Economic, Social and Cultural Rights: Legal Practitioners Dossier* (Centre on Housing Rights and Evictions 2006).

Nwobike, J, 'The African Commission on Human and Peoples' Rights and the Demystification of Second and Third Generation Rights under the African Charter: *SERAC & Anor v Nigeria*' (2005) 1 *African Journal of Legal Studies* 129–146.

Oder, J, 'Pay Up or You'll be Detained! Improved Health Systems and Accountability as a Response to Violations Arising in Healthcare Settings' (2011) Human Rights Abuse and Health Care 16.4 *INTERIGHTS Bulletin* 166–171.

TB Alliance, 'TB and HIV', available at http://www.tballiance.org/why/tb-hiv.php (accessed 5 February 2015).

UNAIDS Press Release, 'UNAIDS Reports More Than 7 Million People Now on HIV Treatment across Africa – with Nearly 1 Million Added in the Last Year – while New HIV Infections and Deaths from AIDS Continue to Fall', available at http://www.unaids.org/en/resources/presscentre/pressreleaseandstatementarchive/2013/may/20130521prupdateafrica/;http://www.unaids.org/en/media/unaids/contentassets/documents/unaidspublication/2013/20130521_Update_Africa.pdf.

United Nations Office of the High Commissioner for Human Rights, 'Access to Medicines – a Fundamental Element of the Right to Health' (n.d.).

Viljoen, F and Odinkalu, C, *The Prohibition of Torture and Ill-treatment in the African Human Rights System: A Handbook for Victims and their Advocates*, OMCT Handbook Series 3 (OMCT 2006).

Wendo, C and Businge, C, 'Uganda Loses US$12m Global Fund' *New Vision*, 28 October 2008.

World Health Organization, *Everybody's Business: Strengthening Health Systems to Improve Health Outcomes: WHO's Framework for Action* (WHO 2007).

World Health Organization, *The Health of the People: The African Regional Health Report* (WHO 2006), available at http://whqlibdoc.who.int/afro/2006/9290231033_rev_eng.pdf (accessed 1 February 2015).

World Health Organization, 'Maternal Mortality', Fact sheet No 348 (May 2012).

World Health Organization, 'Tuberculosis', Fact sheet No 104 (October 2013).

World Health Organization and Office of the UN High Commissioner for Human Rights, 'The Right to Health', Fact Sheet No 31 (2000).

International Instruments and Documents

Abuja Framework for Action for the Fight against HIV/AIDS, TB and Other Related Infectious Diseases, AHG/228 (XXXVII) Annex III (2001).

African Charter on Human and Peoples' Rights, OAU Doc CAB/LEG/67/3 rev 5, entered into force 21 October 1986.

African Charter on the Rights and Welfare of the Child, OAU Doc CAB/LEG/24.9/49, entered into force 29 November 1999.

African Commission on Human and Peoples' Rights, 'Principles and Guidelines on the Implementation of Economic, Social and Cultural Rights in the African Charter on Human and Peoples' Rights' (November 2010).

African Commission on Human and Peoples' Rights, 'Resolution on HIV/AIDS Pandemic – Threat Against Human Rights and Humanity' adopted at 29th Ordinary Session of the African Commission held in Tripoli, Libya, ACHPR Res 53/(XXIX)01.

African Commission on Human and Peoples' Rights, 'Resolution 223 on the Optional Protocol to the International Covenant on Civil and Political Rights', adopted at the 51st Ordinary Session held in Banjul, The Gambia (2 May 2012).

African Union, African Summit on HIV/AIDS, Tuberculosis and Other Related Infectious Diseases, Abuja, Nigeria, 24–27 April 2001, OAU/SPS/ ABUJA/3.

African Union, Convention for the Protection and Assistance of Internally Displaced Persons in Africa (Kampala Convention), 22 October 2009, entered into force 6 December 2012.

African Union, Draft Kampala Declaration on Refugees, Returnees and Internally Displaced Persons in Africa, Ext/Assembly/AU/PA/Draft/Decl. (I) Rev 1 (October 2009).

Committee on Economic, Social and Cultural Rights, Consideration of reports submitted by States parties under articles 16 and 17 of the Covenant [on Economic, Social and Cultural Rights] concluding observations of the Committee on Economic, Social and Cultural Rights: Kenya, E/C.12/KEN/CO/1 (2008).

Committee on Economic, Social and Cultural Rights, General Comment No 14, 'The right to the highest attainable standard of health' (art 12 of the Covenant), 11 August 2000, UN Doc E/C.12/2000/4 (2000).

International Covenant on Civil and Political Rights, GA Res. 2200A (XXI), 999 UNTS 171, adopted 16 December 1966, entered into force 23 March 1976.

Mandate of the Committee on the Protection of the Rights of People Living with HIV (PLHIV) and Those at Risk, Vulnerable to and Affected by HIV, adopted at Resolution the 47th Ordinary Session held in Banjul, The Gambia, ACHPR Res 63.

Protocol to the African Charter on the Establishment of the African Court on Human and Peoples' Rights, OAU Doc OAU/LEG/AFCHPR/PROT (III) (1997), entered into force 25 January 2004.

Protocol to the African Charter on Human and Peoples' Rights on the Rights of Women in Africa CAB/LEG/66.6/Rev 1 (2003), entered into force 25 November 2005.

Solemn Declaration on Gender Equality in Africa, African Union, Addis Ababa, Ethiopia, 6–8 July 2004.

UN Declaration of Commitment on HIV/AIDS, UNGA Res S-62/2, 27 June 2001.

UN Principles for the Protection of Persons with Mental Illness and the Improvement of Mental Health Care, A/AES/46/119, adopted 17 December 1991.

Cases

Centre for Health Rights and Development & Others v Attorney General, Petition 16/2011 UGCC 4 [5 June 2012].

Free Legal Assistance Group and Others v Zaire, African Commission on Human and Peoples' Rights, Comm Nos 25/89, 47/90, 56/91 and 100/93 (4 April 1996).

Jorge Odir Miranda Cortez et al. v. El Salvador, Case 12.249, Report No 29/01, OEA/Ser.L/V/II.111 Doc 20 rev. (7 March 2001).

Karen Noelia Llantoy Huamán v. Peru (2005) Communication No 1153/2003, UN Doc CCPR/C/85/D/1153/200.

Malawi African Association and Others v. Mauritania, African Commission on Human and Peoples' Rights, Comm Nos 54/91, 61/91, 98/93, 164/97 to 196/97 and 210/98 (11 May 2000).

Maria de Lourdes da Silva Pimentel v. Brazil (2008) Communication No. 17/2008, CEDAW/C/49/D/17/2008.

Media Rights Agenda and Others v Nigeria, African Commission on Human and Peoples' Rights, Comm Nos 105/93, 128/94, 130/94 and 152/96 (31 October 2008).
Ms A.S. v Hungary (2004) Communication No. 4/2004, CEDAW/C/36/D/4/2004.
Purohit and Moore v. The Gambia, African Commission on Human and Peoples' Rights, Comm No 241/2001 (2003).
Social and Economic Rights Action Centre (SERAC) & Another v Nigeria (2001) AHRLR 60 (ACHPR 2001).

Chapter 11

The Protection of the Right to Health through Individual Petitions before the Inter-American System of Human Rights

Oscar Parra-Vera[1]

The Inter-American System of Human Rights is composed of the Inter-American Commission on Human Rights (IACHR or 'Commission') and the Inter-American Court (IACtHR or 'Court'). The Commission makes country and thematic reports, and examines petitions alleging violations of human rights. Also, the Commission is empowered to adopt precautionary measures taking into account the gravity and urgency of the situation. When the recommendations adopted by the Commission in a specific case are not subject to compliance, the Commission has the power to submit a case before the Inter-American Court.[2] This chapter examines some examples regarding the advances of the Commission and the Court in the development of standards regarding the right to health in the context of individual petitions. It is important to take into account that some scholars have argued against the justiciability of economic, social and cultural rights in the Inter-American System. This is based on the difficulty of accessing the system and/or the possibility of inequity of impact. Also, there is a strong argument for a direct protection of the right to health under article 26 of the American Convention on Human Rights (hereinafter the 'American Convention') or indirect protection through civil and political rights.[3]

---

1 The opinions expressed are those of the author alone and are not to be attributed to the Inter-American Court or its Registry. I would like to thank Jorge Parra Norato and Laura Lyons Cerón for research assistance and Fernanda Parra for her support in the English version of this chapter.

2 Inter-American Commission on Human Rights, Rules of Procedure (approved by the Commission at its 137th regular period of sessions, held from 28 October to 13 November 2009, and modified on 2 September 2011 and during the 147th Regular Period of Sessions, held from 8 to 22 March 2013, for entry into force on 1 August 2013), art 45.

3 See, for example, the discussion between James Cavallaro and Tara Melish: J Cavallaro and E Schaffer, 'Less as More: Rethinking Supranational Litigation of Economic and Social Rights in the Americas' (2004) 56 *Hastings Law Journal* 217; T Melish, 'Rethinking the "Less as More" Thesis: Supranational Litigation of Economic, Social and Cultural Rights in the Americas' (2006) 39 *New York University Journal of International Law and Politics* 385; J Cavallaro and E Schaffer, 'Rejoinder: Finding Common Ground to Promote Social Justice and Economic, Social and Cultural Rights in the Americas' (2006) 39 *New York University Journal of International Law and Politics* 345; T Melish, 'Counter-rejoinder: Normative Neutrality and Technical Precision, the Role of the lawyer in

This chapter will consider some of these arguments and provide an overview of eight subthemes about the direct and indirect protection of right to health: justiciability under the American Declaration, under article 26 of the American Convention, the protection of right to health through the right to 'life with dignity' and the duty to guarantee inspection, surveillance and control in the rendering of health care services. The chapter then considers specific issues regarding vulnerable groups. In particular, the chapter analyses the right to health and its connection with the right to personal integrity, with emphasis on health care for persons with disabilities and persons deprived of liberty. Finally, the chapter examines other important issues such as confidentiality and sexual and reproductive rights.

Justiciability of the Right to Health under the American Declaration

The Inter-American Commission has the powers to investigate and resolve individual petitions alleging violations of the American Declaration of Human Rights by states that are not parties to it. For example, in *Ache People v Paraguay*, the Commission found the lack of medical assistance and provision of medicines during some epidemics to be a breach of the right to the preservation of health and to well-being established in article XI of the American Declaration.[4]

Another relevant example is the case of *Yanomami v Brazil*. In this case, the Inter-American Commission found that a state may incur responsibility for the violation of the right of preservation of health and to well-being of the indigenous community 'for having failed to take timely and effective measures' in order to avoid a considerable number of deaths caused by epidemics of influenza, tuberculosis, measles, venereal diseases and so on suffered by community members as a consequence of the invasion, carried out without prior and adequate protection for the safety and health of the Indians, of construction workers, geologists, mining prospectors and farm workers who came to their lands after the discovery of tin and other metal ores in the region, and also because of the construction of a highway.[5]

In some cases against Cuba, it is possible to see breach of the same right due to problems with access to health or quality of food within the prison system.[6]

Supranational Social Rights Litigation' (2006) 39 *New York University Journal of International Law and Politics* 385; J Cavallaro ans S Brewer, 'La Función del Litigio Interamericano en la Promoción de la Justicia Social' (2008) 8 *Sur. Revista Internacional de Derechos Humanos* 85. See also OR Ruiz-Chiriboga, 'The American Convention and the Protocol of San Salvador: Two Intertwined Treaties. Non-enforceability of Economic, Social and Cultural Rights in the Inter-American System' (2013) 31 *Netherlands Quarterly of Human Rights* 156, the concurring opinion of Judge Eduardo Ferrer Mac-Gregor Poisot to the Judgment of the Inter-American Court of Human Rights in the case of *Suárez Peralta v Ecuador* of 21 May 2013.

4 *Ache People v Paraguay* IACHR OEA/Ser.L/V/II.50 Doc 13 Rev 1 (2 October 1980) 34–35.

5 *Yanomami v Brazil* Case No 7615, IACHR Resolution No 12/85 of 5 May 1985, 10 & operative para 1.

6 IACHR, Resolution No 3/82, Case 6091, Cuba, 8 March 1982; Resolution No 45/81, Case 4402, Cuba, 25 June 1981; Resolution No 46/81, Case 4429, Cuba, 25 June 1981; Resolution

Justiciability of the Right to Health under Article 26 of the American Convention

The American Convention on Human Rights (ACHR), adopted in 1969, consists of a Preamble and three other parts. The First Part is entitled 'State Obligations and Rights Protected' and has five chapters. The First Chapter establishes the general obligations for State Parties and the second refers to civil and political rights. The title of the Third Chapter is 'Economic, Social and Cultural Rights' and it contains only one article – article 26, 'Progressive Development'.

Regarding the economic, social and cultural (ESC) rights, the Pact of San José 'derives' those rights from the Charter of the Organization of American States (OAS), adopted in 1948 and modified in 1967. Article 26 provides that:

> The States Parties undertake to adopt measures, both internally and through international cooperation, especially those of an economic and technical nature, with a view to achieving progressively, by legislation or other appropriate means, the full realization of the rights implicit in the economic, social, educational, scientific, and cultural standards set forth in the Charter of the Organization of American States as amended by the Protocol of Buenos Aires.

Determining the scope of article 26 has generated many doctrinal debates within the jurisprudence of the Court. The most important of these is whether the American Convention allows direct justiciability of social rights. This is supported by an interpretation that considers that 'the rights' enshrined in the OAS Charter are not 'strictly speaking, rights'. Positions that consider that article 26 does not include social rights highlight the project presented by the Inter-American Commission before the Specialised Inter-American Conference of 1969, which did not include these rights,[7] and with the understanding of the progress clause as 'a standard of non-justiciability'.[8] Other positions highlight the fact that the Additional Protocol to the American Convention on ESC rights (Protocol of San Salvador, adopted in 1988) only establishes the justiciability of the right to education and unionisation and does not include most social rights, including the right to health, as justiciable rights. Based on these positions, it is argued that social rights cannot be subject to litigation through article 26 of the Convention.[9]

For the purposes of this chapter, it is not necessary to delve into this debate.[10] Here we are only interested in highlighting some important doctrinal positions and developments in the jurisprudence of the Inter-American System. In this regard, Abramovich and Rossi

---

No 47/81, Case 4677, Cuba, 25 June 1981; Resolution No 2/82, Case 2300, Cuba, 8 March 1982; Resolution No 3/82, Case 6093, Cuba, 8 March 1982.

7 M Craven, 'The Protection of Economic, Social and Cultural Rights under the Inter-American System of Human Rights' in D Harris and S Livingstone, *The Inter-American System of Human Rights* (Oxford University Press 1998) 297–306.

8 Cavallaro and Schaffer (n 2 above), 225–227 and 267–269.

9 Ruiz-Chiriboga (n 2 above).

10 For more detail, see O Parra-Vera, *Justiciabilidad de los Derechos Económicos, Sociales y Culturales ante el Sistema Interamericano* (Comisión Nacional de los Derechos Humanos 2011), 67.

have noted that article 26 clearly refers to the 'adoption of measures' to give 'full effect' to 'rights'. In this sense, its literal interpretation leads to the conclusion that it does not formulate mere programmatic objectives.[11] These rights, according to the wording of the norm, must be inferred from the economic, social and cultural rights of the OAS Charter. It should also be noted that Sergio Garcia Ramirez has argued that article 26 encompasses rights and that '[a]ll rights ... contained in the Pact of San José and accepted by the States ... are subject to a general regime of supervision and decisions, or put in another way, "means of protection"'.[12]

If these starting points are accepted (that the American Convention establishes social rights), the subsequent task lies in the interpretation of article 26 to determine i) what are the rights that can be inferred in light of the reference to the OAS Charter, ii) what is the scope of the progressive development clause, and iii) how do states' obligations operate in relation to these rights.[13]

In resolving these legal issues, if any doubts or conflicting positions exist, the Inter-American Court has stated that in interpreting the Convention, the most favourable alternative for the protection of the rights guaranteed under the treaty must always be preferred in accordance with the principle of norm most favourable to a human person.[14] Moreover, it is essential to recognise the consistent jurisprudence of the Inter-American Court, following the European Court of Human Rights on this matter, in considering human rights conventions as 'living instruments' that must be interpreted in light of current conditions and that the interpretation of rights must be made 'in the context of the evolution of the fundamental rights of the human person in contemporary international law'.[15] The interpreter's task is then to update the normative scope of the Convention. Furthermore, as highlighted by Hector Faundez, article 29(d) of the American Convention

---

11 V Abramovich and J Rossi, 'La tutela de los derechos económicos, sociales y culturales en el artículo 26 de la Convención Americana sobre Derechos Humanos' in C Martin, D Rodríguez-Pinzón and J Guevara (eds) *Derecho Internacional de los Derechos Humanos* (Fontamara 2004).

12 S García Ramírez, 'Protección jurisdiccional internacional de los derechos económicos, sociales y culturales' (2003) 9 *Cuestiones Constitucionales* 127, 139 and 141.

13 See T Melish, *La Protección de los Derechos Económicos, Sociales y Culturales en el Sistema Interamericano de Derechos Humanos* (CDES Yale Law School 2003), 379–392; Abramovich and Rossi (n 10 above) 457–478; H Faúndez Ledesma, 'Los derechos económicos, sociales y culturales en el sistema interamericano' in VV.AA., *El Sistema Interamericano de Protección de los Derechos Humanos: su jurisprudencia sobre debido proceso, DESC, libertad personal y libertad de expresión* (IIDH 2004) 98–102 and 113–120; C Courtis, 'La protección de los derechos económicos, sociales y culturales a través del artículo 26 de la Convención Americana sobre Derechos Humanos' in C Courtis, D Hauser and G Rodríguez Huerta (eds) *Protección internacional de los derechos humanos. Nuevos desafíos* (Porrúa-ITAM 2005) 1.

14 See, inter alia, *Mapiripán Massacre v Colombia*, Merits, Reparations and Costs, Judgment of 15 September 2005, I/A Court HR Series C No 134, para 106.

15 The Right to Information on consular assistance in the framework of the guarantees of the due process of law, Advisory Opinion OC-16/99 of 1 October 1999, I/A Court HR Series A No 16, para 114; Juridical Condition and Rights of the Undocumented Migrants (Advisory Opinion OC-18/03 of 17 September 2003) I/A Court HR Series A No 18, para 120.

states that none of its provisions can be interpreted in the sense of excluding or limiting the effect of the American Declaration of Rights and Duties of Man and other acts of the same nature.[16] It is important to note that this Declaration explicitly guarantees various social rights, including the right to health.

Most of the postions that have been canvassed in interpreting article 26 have been based on the OAS Charter, while consideration has not been given to the American Declaration or the pro person principle for its determination. According to this view, the principle of the most favourable interpretation should only be used to set the scope of the norm in question, which establishes limitations to derive competence.[17]

However, the Court has noted that the interpretation of the Convention must be comprehensive, in such a way that it harmonises the literal, teleological, systematic and historical methods.[18] The role of the systematic approach could support the position that applying the principle of most favourable interpretation helps in harmonising the rights guaranteed in the OAS Charter, the American Declaration[19] and the Protocol of San Salvador,[20] as well as other international instruments relevant to the subject (such as the International Covenant on Economic, Social and Cultural Rights (ICESCR) and International Labour Office (ILO) Conventions).[21]

Other interpretive elements can be useful in addressing these problems. With regard to the proper interpretation of the rights enshrined in article 26, it is important to note that this chapter considers several other provisions of the OAS Charter. In the case of the right to health, considerations are given to articles 34(i)[22] and 34(l)[23] of the OAS Charter, article XI of the Declaration and article 10 of the Protocol of San Salvador.

The Court has had two important rulings on the scope of article 26. While these cases do not address the right to health directly, they illustrate the potential and limits of this article in regard to the enforceability of such a right. In the case of the *Five Pensioners*, the Inter-American Commission argued that the unjustified decline in the degree of development

---

16 Faúndez Ledesma (n 13 above) 100.

17 Abramovich and Rossi (n 10 above).

18 *González et al ('Cotton Field') v Mexico*, Preliminary Objection, Merits, Reparations and Costs, Judgment of 16 November 2009, I/A Court HR Series C No 205.

19 CEJIL, *La protección de los derechos económicos, sociales y culturales y el Sistema Interamericano* (CEJIL 2005) 75.

20 T Melish, 'Enfoque según el artículo 26: Invocando los DESC que se derivan de la Carta de la OEA' in T Melish, *La Protección de los Derechos Económicos, Sociales y Culturales en el Sistema Interamericano de Derechos Humanos* (CDES Yale Law School 2003) 383–388.

21 Courtis (n 13 above) 8–29; CEJIL (n 19 above) 76–78; V Krsticevic, 'La protección de los derechos económicos, sociales y culturales en el Sistema Interamericano' in CEJIL, *Construyendo una agenda para la justiciabilidad de los derechos sociales* (CEJIL 2004) 167–173.

22 Art 34(i) Protection of man's potential through the extension and application of modern medical science.

23 Art 34(l) Urban conditions that offer the opportunity for a healthful, productive, and full life.

of the right to social security constitutes a violation of article 26.[24] The Court found that there has been a breach of the right to property (article 21 of the Convention) but rejected the violation of right to social security. It further noted that 'the progressive development' of ESC rights, should be measured

> in function of the growing coverage of economic, social and cultural rights in general, and of the right to social security and to a pension in particular, bearing in mind the imperatives of social equity of the entire population but not in function of the circumstances of a very limited group of pensioners, who do not necessarily represent the prevailing situation.[25]

Taking into account this consideration, the Court rejected 'the request to rule on the progressive development of economic, social and cultural rights in Peru, in the context of this case'.[26]

This judgment was criticised, among other reasons, for not implementing the obligations to respect and guarantee in regard to social rights, and for the confusion generated between the collective dimension of social rights and their national scope, as well as a number of concerns regarding the public policy analysis.[27] Six years later, in the case of *Acevedo Buendía v Peru*, the Inter-American Court modified some components of its jurisprudence in the *Five Pensioners*.[28] The Court stated that article 26 enshrines economic, social and cultural rights, and imposes on states the obligations to respect and guarantee (prevent, protect and enforce) these rights. This is a first step to overcoming many of the concerns of the past. The emphasis on the obligations that derive from social rights will be essential to an analysis of the specific international responsibility regarding such rights.

With respect to the obligations of progressivie realisation and non-retrogression, the Court referred to the doctrine of the Committee on Economic, Social and Cultural Rights (CESCR) of the United Nations. The Court noted that the obligation to adopt measures to boost progressive measureas could be subject to accountability and referred to the following standards:

> The UN Committee on Economic, Social and Cultural Rights has indicated that: 'in considering a communication concerning an alleged failure of a State party to take steps to the maximum of available resources … will examine the measures that the State party has effectively taken, legislative or otherwise. In assessing whether they are "adequate" or "reasonable", the Committee may take into account, *inter alia*, the following considerations: a) [t]he extent to which the measures taken were deliberate, concrete and targeted towards the fulfillment of economic, social and cultural rights; b) [w]hether the State party exercised

24 *'Five Pensioners' v Peru*, Merits, Reparations and Costs, Judgment of 28 February 2003, I/A Court HR Series C No 98.

25 Ibid, para 147.

26 Ibid, para 148.

27 For a major analysis of these critics, see Parra-Vera (n 9 above).

28 *Acevedo Buendía et al ('Discharged and Retired Employees of the Office of the Comptroller') v Peru*, Preliminary Objection, Merits, Reparations and Costs, Judgment of 1 July 2009, I/A Court HR Series C No 198.

its discretion in a non-discriminatory and nonarbitrary manner; c) [w]hether the State party's decision (not) to allocate available resources was in accordance with international human rights standards; d) [w]here several policy options are available, whether the State party adopted the option that least restricted Covenant rights; e) [t]the time frame in which the steps were taken[; and] f) [w]hether the steps had taken into account the precarious situation of disadvantaged and marginalized individuals or groups and, whether they were nondiscriminatory, and whether they prioritized grave situations or situations or risk.'[29]

As a corollary to the above-mentioned, the Court defined criteria for analysing the regressive measures, relying on the view of the CESCR. It noted that 'those measures that are deliberately retrogressive in this regard would require the most careful consideration and must be fully justified by reference to the totality of [social] rights' 'in the context of the full use of the maximum available resources'. It also noted that:

> In accordance with the Committee on Economic, Social and Cultural Rights, '[s]hould a State party use "resource constraints" as an explanation for any retrogressive steps taken, ... would consider such information on a country-by-country basis in the light of objective criteria such as: a) [t]he country's level of development; b) [t]he severity of the alleged breach, in particular whether the situation concerned the enjoyment of the minimum core content of the Covenant; c) [t]he country's current economic situation, in particular whether the country was undergoing a period of economic recession; d) [t]he existence of other serious claims on the State party's limited resources; for example, resulting from a recent natural disaster or from recent internal or international armed conflict; e) [w]hether the State party had sought to identify low-costs options; and f) [w]hether the State party had sought cooperation and assistance or rejected offers of resources from the international community for the purposes of implementing the provisions of the Covenant without sufficient reason.'[30]

Also, the Inter-American Court recognised that in 2009 the Inter-American Commission had reasoned that in order to assess whether a regressive measure is compatible with the American Convention, it must be 'determined whether strong enough reasons justify it'. This momentous ruling of the Inter-American Commission, in the case of the *National Association of Ex-Employees of the Peruvian Social Security Institute et al v Peru*,[31] analysed the change, through a constitutional and legal reform in how the alleged victims had been exercising their right to a retirement pension. Although no human rights violation was declared, a methodology for the analysis of these cases was established. Specifically, the Commission stated that the prohibition of retrogression requires an analysis of the

29 Committee on Economic, Social and Cultural Rights, 'An evaluation of the obligation to take steps to the "maximum of available resources" under an Optional Protocol to the Covenant' (Thirty-eighth session) E/C.12/2007/1, 21 September 2007, para 8.

30 Ibid, para 10.

31 *National Association of Ex-Employees of the Peruvian Social Institute et al v Peru*, Admissibility and Merits Case of 27 March 2009, IACHR Case 12.670 Report No 38/09, paras 140–147.

individual damage of a right in relation to the collective implications of the measure, taking into account strong enough reasons. This means assuming that the prohibition of retrogression is a principle (that is, an optimisation mandate that can be considered with other principles) and not a rule (that is, a norm that applies under the rules all/nothing), and thus not all regression is prohibited.[32]

As noted, the jurisprudence of the Commission and the Court has focused more on the scope that the application of article 26 can have in specific contentious cases. These trends emerged in 2009 and have not yet been applied in specific cases on the right to health. Prior to that year, several reports were issued that are silent on the right to health under article 26 of the American Convention.

For example, in the case of *Odir Miranda et al v El Salvador*, the Commission admitted the petition for the right to health, in the framework of article 26, but in the respective report on the merits, it considered that there was no violation of this right. The case involved 27 HIV positive persons who were denied access to medication that integrated the triple therapy necessary to prevent death and improve their quality of life. The Inter-American Commission ordered the government of El Salvador to adopt urgent precautionary measures for the victims in the case in order for them to obtain the relevant medical care and antiretroviral medications. The Supreme Court of Justice of El Salvador rendered a decision ordering the distribution of medicines to the petitioners as of December 2000. In 2003, the Commission issued its report on the merits, which was published in 2009. In that report, the Commission found no violation of the right to health considering that measures had been adopted to provide the appropriate medical care.[33]

As analysed in subsequent segments of this chapter, the Inter-American Court has not applied article 26 in its jurisprudence directly to the right to health, but has included some references about this right in the context of cases regarding rights such as life and personal integrity. This practice was criticised by the concurring opinion of Judge Margarette

32 On the role of the distinction between principles and rules for a better approach regarding the judicial application of the prohibition of regresssion, see R Uprimny and D Guarnizo '¿Es posible una dogmática adecuada sobre la prohibición de regresividad? Un enfoque desde la jurisprudencia constitucional colombiana' in E Ferrer Mac-Gregor and A Zaldívar (eds) *Homenaje a Héctor Fix Zamudio* (UNAM 2008).

33 *Jorge Odir Miranda Cortez et al v El Salvador*, Merits Report of 20 March 2009, IACHR Case 12.249 Report No 27/09: In the merits report No 27/09, the Commission considered that 'the State demonstrated … that it took what steps it reasonably could to provide medical treatment to the persons included in the record. The IACHR finds that, in the circumstances, the measures of the State were sufficiently expeditious to accomplish that aim effectively. It is not possible, therefore, to speak of any direct violation of the right to health of Jorge Odir Miranda Cortez or the other 26 persons identified in Case 12.249, as would have been the case if, for instance, it were shown that the State refused to provide care to any of them. Moreover, during the processing of the instant case the Salvadoran health services progressively broadened free coverage to other persons infected with HIV/AIDS, subject to medical screening. Furthermore, the petitioners have not alleged any backtracking in the sense of suspension of benefits that any of them were already receiving.'

Macaulay in *Furlan and Next of Kin v Argentina*,[34] decided in 2012. This case deals with the problems of access to rehabilitation services for a child with mental disability. The case is analysed in more detail in later parts of this chapter. The Court only considered the breach of articles 8 and 25 of the Convention (judicial guarantees, judicial protection and access to justice). In addition, the Court considered the negative impact of lack of access to rehabilitation in the context of the right to personal integrity.

Justice Macaulay noted that, even though she voted in favour of the Court's judgment, it was also possible to resolve the case from another perspective regarding the direct justiciability of economic, social and cultural rights under the scope of article 26 of the American Convention, particularly under the duty to respect and guarantee the right to health and the right to social security. Judge Macaulay pointed out that it is necessary to define the social rights set out in the Charter of the Organization of American States as regards the American Declaration. Likewise, Macaulay highlighted that in the *Furlan* case there were regulations that clearly established some grounds for access to various benefits established in relation to the right to health and the right to social security. Taking into consideration the allegation of obstacles to access to those benefits, it is noted that the issue was not a discussion about the progressive realisation or retrogression of these rights. Indeed, it was a controversy about the duty to guarantee the right to health and the right to social security, matters that required the use of sources related to the ICESCR and the authorised interpretation of the CESCR.

On the other hand, Judge Macaulay noted that the Protocol of San Salvador could be used for the interpretation of the scope of the American Convention in the specific case. Although the Protocol enshrines only the justiciability of the right to education and some labour union rights (article 19), it does not establish any provision aimed at limiting the scope of the American Convention. Consequently, when interpreting the Convention the interpreter must carry out a systematic interpretation of both treaties, taking into account their object and purpose. Moreover, the Vienna Convention demands an interpretation in good faith of the terms of article 26, recognising that the American Convention did not establish distinctions when pointing out that its jurisdiction covers all the rights guaranteed in articles 3 to 26 of that Convention. Furthermore, article 4 of the Protocol of San Salvador establishes that none of the rights recognised or in force in a state can be restricted or infringed by virtue of international conventions, with the excuse that the Protocol mentioned before does not recognise them or recognises them to a lesser degree. Finally, the Vienna Convention states that an interpretation should not lead to a manifestly absurd or unreasonable result. In this regard, the conclusion is that the Protocol of San Salvador limits the scope of the Convention; this would lead to the absurd consideration that the American Convention can have some effects among the Participating States of the San Salvador Protocol while having another effect for the states that are not parties to the said Protocol.

---

34 *Case of Furlan and Next of Kin v Argentina*, Preliminary Objections, Merits, Reparations and Costs, Judgment of 31 August 2012, I/A Court HR Series C No 246.

In this sense, Judge Macaulay stressed that the Court, as the authorised interpreter of the Convention, has to update the normative sense and therefore the normative value of article 26. She pointed out:

> what matters is not the subjective intention of the State's delegates at the time of the San José's Conference or during the discussion of the Protocol of San Salvador, but the objective intention in the text of the American Convention, taking into account that the duty of the interpreter is to update the normative meaning of the international instrument. In addition, it is not acceptable to use a historical interpretation, based on the hypothetical intention about the Convention of the delegates who adopted the Protocol of San Salvador, to discredit the explicit content of the American Convention.

In 2013 another important development in this debate was made by Judge Eduardo Ferrer Mac-Gregor Poisot in a concurring opinion in the case *Suárez Peralta v. Ecuador*.[35] Judge Ferrer Mac-Gregor expressed that article 26 'needs to be interpreted in light of our times and in accordance with the relevant advances in international human rights law and in constitutional law'. In particular, he highlighted that:

> The necessary evolutive interpretation of Article 26 of the American Convention must also be derived from the full recognition in many Constitutions of the protection of the right to health as a social right, which represents a regional trend. And this trend can also be appreciated in the evolution of the case law of the highest national jurisdictions granting effectiveness to this social right; at times even directly and not only in connection with civil and political rights.

Moreover, Judge Ferrer Mac-Gregor defended an interpretation that attempts to grant primacy to the normative value of article 26 of the American Convention interpreted in light of the Protocol of San Salvador. In this understanding, the Additional Protocol is not able to reduce the normative value of the American Convention if this objective is not expressly stated in that instrument in relation to the obligations *erga omnes* established in articles 1 and 2 of the American Convention, general obligations that apply to all rights, even economic, social and cultural rights, as the Inter-American Court has explicitly recognised in the *Acevedo Buendía* judgment. In summary, Judge Ferrer Mac-Gregor calls for an interpretation that establishes the greatest practical effects possible for the Inter-American norms as a whole, as the Inter-American Court has been doing with regard to civil and political rights:

> This vision of direct justiciability means that the methodology to attribute international responsibility is circumscribed to the obligations regarding the right to health. This signifies the need for more specific arguments on the reasonableness and proportionality of a certain type of public policy measures. In view of the sensitive nature of an assessment in this

35 Concurring Opinion of Judge Eduardo Ferrer Mac-Gregor Poisot to the Judgment of the Inter-American Court of Human Rights in the case of *Suárez Peralta v Ecuador*, 21 May 2013.

> sense, the Inter-American Court's decisions acquire greater transparency and strength if the analysis is made *directly* in this way with regard to the obligations surrounding the right to health, instead of with regard to the sphere more closely related to the consequences of certain effects on personal integrity; that is, indirectly or by connectivity with the civil rights. Similarly, the reparations that the Court traditionally grants, and that in many cases have an impact on services related to the right to health, such as measures of rehabilitation and satisfaction, may acquire a real causal nexus between the right violated and the measure decided with all its implications. Furthermore, when we speak of direct justiciability, this implies changing the methodology based on which compliance with the obligations of respect and guarantee (Article 1(1) of the Pact of San José) is assessed, which is evidently different with regard to the right to life and the right to personal integrity, than it is with regard to the right to health and other social, economic and cultural rights … The effective guarantee of economic, social and cultural rights is an alternative that would open up new possibilities in order to achieve transparency and the full realization of rights, without artifices and directly, and thus acknowledge what the Inter-American Court has been doing indirectly or in connection with the civil and political rights.[36]

This long statement regarding Judge Macaulay's and Judge Ferrer Mac-Gregor's opinions is important to highlight the current status of the discussion as regards the direct protection of the right to health under article 26. However, there is potential to explore the realisation of the right to health through indirect application of other rights. This position is explored further in the next section of this chapter.

Justiciability of the Right to Health under a Concept of Right to a Life with Dignity

An alternative, distinct to that of direct justiciability based on article 26, can be found in Inter-American decisions issued in regard to access to the right to health through some civil and political rights. One example of this possibility is the utilisation of the right to a 'life with dignity' for the protection of the right to health.

In this regard, in the case of the *'Street Children' (Villagrán-Morales et al) v. Guatemala*, about the extrajudicial execution of 'street children' living in a state of poverty in which they were deprived of minimum conditions for a life with dignity, the Court developed a broad interpretation of the right to life to include decent living conditions. It was noted that

> in essence, the fundamental right to life includes not only the right of every human being not to be deprived of life arbitrarily, but also the right to not be prevented from having access to conditions that guarantee a dignified existence. States have the obligation to guarantee the

36 Ibid.

> creation of the conditions required to avoid violations of this basic right and, in particular, the duty to prevent its officials from violating it.[37]

This view was reiterated in *'Juvenile Reeducation Institute' v Paraguay*, where the Court analysed the situation of children deprived of liberty. While in a detention centre, some of these children had died under various circumstances. The Inter-American Court considered that 'to protect a child's life, the State must be particularly attentive to that child's living conditions while deprived of his or her liberty'[38] and consequently, 'regarding children deprived of their liberty and thus in the custody of the State, the latter's obligations include that of providing them with health care and education'.[39] It should be noted that in this case, the victims' representatives alleged the violation of article 26 as a result of the lack of guarantee of the minimum levels of satisfaction of social rights, and indeed this was acknowledged and accepted by the state. However, to establish the scope of the right to life, the Court took into account social rights enshrined in the Convention on the Rights of the Child and the Protocol of San Salvador, for which reason it was considered unnecessary to issue a holding on article 26 with regard to this case.

Other cases in which health has been discussed in relation to a life with dignity involve violations of the rights of indigenous communities. In one case, an indigenous community called on the State of Paraguay to return its ancestral lands.[40] The community members indicated that they were living outside of these lands and in conditions of extreme poverty, enduring factors such as unemployment, malnutrition, poor housing conditions and difficulties in accessing safe drinking water and health services.

In the case in question, the Inter-American Court established that the right to life also implied access to conditions allowing for a dignified existence. With this consideration as the basis, it was understood as the precedent to assess whether the state had met its positive obligations regarding the right to life

> in view of the provisions set forth in Article 4 of the [ACHR], in relation to the general duty to respect rights, embodied in Article 1(1) and with the duty of progressive development set forth in Article 26 of that same Convention, and with articles 10 (Right to Health); 11 (Right to a Healthy Environment); 12 (Right to Food); 13 (Right to Education) and 14 (Right to the Benefits of Culture) of the Protocol of San Salvador and the relevant provisions of the ILO Convention No. 169.[41]

Analysing the facts of the case, the Court held that the conditions of abject poverty in which the community existed and the impact that this had on the health and nutrition of

---

37 *'Street Children' (Villagrán Morales et al) v Guatemala*, Merits, Judgment of 19 November 1999, I/A Court HR Series C No 63, para 144.

38 *'Juvenile Reeducation Institute' v Paraguay*, Preliminary Objections, Merits, Reparations and Costs, Judgment of 2 September 2004, I/A Court HR Series C No 112, para 160.

39 Ibid, para 161.

40 *Yakye Axa Indigenous Community v Paraguay*, Merits, Reparations and Costs, Judgment of 17 June 2005, I/A Court HR Series C No 125.

41 Ibid, para 163.

its members had in turn affected the existence of dignified life. The Court considered that, given the circumstances of the case, this was attributable to the state. The Court reached this conclusion for several reasons, among them that the state had failed to implement positive measures necessary to ensure that these people maintained living conditions compatible with their dignity, despite having knowledge of their situation.[42] With basis in this logic of interdependence, the Court has established that the right to health ('health care'), together with the right to education, constitutes a pillar which is 'fundamental … to guarantee the enjoyment of a life with dignity'.[43] On the other hand, the Court used article 26 in its analysis of the violation of the right to life. The Court identified that the duty to 'generate minimal living conditions compatible with the dignity of the human person, and to not create conditions that hinder or impede said dignity', is a duty whose verification in the present case should be considered, inter alia, alongside the duty of progressive development contained in article 26 of the Convention, and of some social rights established in the Protocol of San Salvador.[44]

In recent jurisprudence, the Court has further developed an anaylsis concerning the right to a dignified life in relation to the obligation of prevention and the theory of risk as a reference in the attribution of international responsibility to a state. In the Case of the *Xákmok Kásek Indigenous Community v Paraguay*, the Court held that the community had not been able to recuperate its lands and its members were increasingly restricted in terms of the development of their way of life, their traditional subsistence activities and their mobility within their ancestral territories.[45]

The Court established that state assistance provided in terms of access to quality water, food, health and education services was not enough to overcome the conditions of particular vulnerability that the Xákmok Kásek community experienced. It was considered that this situation was closely linked to the lack of access to their land. Indeed, the absence of opportunity for self-sufficiency and sustainability, in accordance with ancestral traditions, led community members to rely almost exclusively on state actions. As such, this forced them to live in a way that not only marked a difference from their cultural patterns but also caused abject poverty. In this case, the Court found that both reports prepared by state institutions and a presidential decree allowed for it to be understood that the state was aware of the serious risk faced by the community.

Accordingly, the Court held that the state had not ensured basic services necessary to protect the right to a dignified life in these conditions of real, immediate and particular risk to a defined group of people. This constitutes a violation of the right to a life with dignity for the members of the community who found themselves in conditions of extreme poverty.

---

42 Ibid, paras 162–171 and 176.

43 See *Juridical Condition and Human Rights of the Child*, Advisory Opinion OC-17/02 of 28 August 2002, I/A Court HR Series A No 17, para 86.

44 *Yakye Axa Indigenous Community v Paraguay*, paras 162–163.

45 *Xákmok Kásek Indigenous Community v Paraguay*, Merits, Reparations and Costs, Judgment of 24 August 2010, I/A Court HR Series C No 214.

It is important to note that the Court adopted the standards formulated by the CESCR of the United Nations when assessing the problems faced by victims in regard to the aforementioned social rights. Moreover, this is an approach that differs in partial measure to that previously mentioned with regard to the failure to ensure a dignified life. Indeed, the attribution of responsibility in the case of *Xákmok Kásek* on matters relating to health, food and other subsistence issues arises from the risk known by the state, and its corresponding duty to prevent such a risk. It is, however, important to note that it is not possible to attribute all serious threats to survival to the state but only those that are known and can be foreseen.

Similarly, in regard to certain deaths that occurred in the community, the Court noted that several community members had died from diseases which could have been easily preventable if they had received regular and consistent medical attention or adequate control of their health. It further stressed that the predominant victims were children in the early stages of their lives, whom the state had a greater duty to protect. The Court therefore ruled that in regard to such deaths the state had violated the right to life, in that it failed to take necessary and expected measures falling within the scope of its powers to prevent or avoid the risk posed to the right to life.

The Right to Health and the Duty to Guarantee Inspection, Surveillance and Control in the Rendering of Health Care Services

In the context of some cases regarding the breach of the right to life or right to access to justice, the Inter-American Court has developed standards relating to problems in the inspection, surveillance and control of health care services.

In the case of *Ximenes Lopes v Brazil*, which deals with the death of a person with mental illness while in the care of a rest home, the Inter-American Court analysed the state's international responsibility regarding the outsourcing of health care services to a private institution.[46] In this regard, the Court stated:

> The assumptions of the State's liability for the violation of rights enshrined in the Convention may include both the acts or the failure to act attributable to State bodies or officials, as well as the failure of the State to prevent third parties from impairing the juridical rights protected by human rights. Notwithstanding, between these two extremes of liability is the conduct described in the Resolution of the International Law Commission,[47] of a person or entity which, though not a state body, is authorized by the State legislation to exercise

46 *Ximenes Lopes v Brazil*, Merits, Reparations and Costs, Judgment of 4 July 2006, I/A Court HR Series C No 149. For a more detailed analysis, see C Courtis, 'La muerte en una institución psiquiátrica en la jurisprudencia de la Corte Interamericana de Derechos humanos. El caso Damiao Ximenes Lopes c. Brasil' in C Courtis, *El mundo prometido. Escritos sobre derechos sociales y derechos humanos* (Fontamara 2009).

47 See International Law Commission, Liability of the State for internationally unlawful acts (International Law Commission 53rd session, 2001), UN Doc A/56/10, text introduced in the appendix to UN General Assembly Resolution 56/83 of 28 January 2002.

> powers entailing the authority of the State. Such conduct, either by a natural or legal person, must be deemed to be an act by the State, inasmuch as such person acted in such capacity.[48]

Regarding the obligation to secure inspection, surveillance and control in the rendering of health care services, the Inter-American Court noted 'the duty of the States to regulate and supervise the institutions which provide health care services, as a necessary measure aimed at the due protection of the life and integrity of the individuals under their jurisdiction', duty that 'includes both public and private institutions which provide public health care services, as well as those institutions which provide only private health care'.[49] The Court said that though the state may delegate the rendering of public services through so-called outsourcing, it continues to be responsible for providing such public services and for protecting the public interest concerned, in this case, health care. Above all, the Court said:

> the States are responsible for regulating and supervising at all times the rendering of services and the implementation of the national programs regarding the performance of public quality health care services so that they may deter any threat to the right to life and the physical integrity of the individuals undergoing medical treatment. They must, *inter alia*, create the proper mechanisms to carry out inspections at psychiatric institutions, submit, investigate, and solve complaints and take the appropriate disciplinary or judicial actions regarding cases of professional misconduct or the violation of the patients' rights.[50]

These statements were reiterated in the case of *Albán Cornejo et al v Ecuador*, which relates to a medical malpractice case.[51] In this judgment the Court pointed out that 'when related to the essential jurisdiction of the supervision and regulation of rendering the services of public interest, such as health, by private or public entities (as is the case of a private hospital)' the allocation of responsibility may arise 'by the omission of the duty to supervise the rendering of the public service to protect the mentioned right'.[52] Futhermore, the Court pointed out that 'Physicians are concerned with the preservation of fundamental values of individuals and of humankind as a whole'[53] and that the legislation applicable to medical malpractice should satisfy the due realisation of justice in this case.

In the case of *Suárez Peralta v Ecuador* the topic of medical bad practice was analysed again by the Court.[54] Melba Suárez Peralta had surgery for appendicitis at the Minchala private clinic, which caused her severe and permanent after-effects.The Inter-American Court declared the international responsibility of the state because of the errors, delays and omissions in the criminal investigation, which led to the application of the statute

48 *Ximenes Lopes v Brazil*, para 86.

49 Ibid, para 141.

50 Ibid, para 99.

51 *Albán Cornejo et al v Ecuador*, Merits, Reparations and Costs, Judgment of 22 November 2007, I/A Court HR Series C No 171.

52 Ibid, para 119.

53 Ibid, para 133.

54 *Suárez Peralta v Ecuador*, Preliminary Objections Merits, Reparations and Costs, Judgment of 21 May 2013.

of limitations in the proceedings, and because of the failure to guarantee and prevent a violation of the right to personal integrity, taking into account the absence of state supervision and control of the clinics (public and private) where the victim was treated.

The Court made specific reference to the concepts of interdependence and indivisibility in order to define the scope of the right to health when examining the violation of the obligation to guarantee the right to personal integrity and considered

> that although the relevant Ecuadorian regulations established mechanisms of control and supervision of medical care, this supervision and control was not carried out in the instant case, as regards control of both the services provided in the State facility, the Polyclinic of the Guayas Traffic Commission, and those provided in the private institution, the Minchala Clinic. The Court finds that this resulted in a situation of risk, which the State was aware of, that materialised in adverse effects on the health of Melba Suárez Peralta.[55]

In addition, the Court affirmed that 'the State's supervision and inspection should be designed to ensure the principles of availability, accessibility, acceptability, and quality of the medical services' and, to this end, it emphasised that 'regarding the quality of the service … health facilities must have satisfactory conditions of hygiene and trained medical personnel'.[56] In this analysis, the Inter-American Court referred expressly to different international instruments, resolutions and sources that regulate or have direct implications for the protection of the right to health.

When the judgment dealt with the violation of the right to judicial guarantees and to judicial protection, the Court determined that there had been errors, delays and omissions in the criminal investigation proceedings, and that therefore 'the State authorities did not act with due diligence or in keeping with the obligations to investigate and to ensure effective judicial protection within a reasonable time, in order to guarantee to Melba Suárez Peralta a reparation enabling her to have access to the medical treatment required by her health problems'.[57]

The Right to Health and the Right to Personal Integrity in the Context of Health Care for Persons with Disabilites

An important development of the protection of the right to health through the right to personal integrity can be observed in the above-mentioned cases of *Furlan and Next of Kin v Argentina*, regarding access to justice for children and persons with disabilities, and *Ximenes Lopes v Brazil*.

In the *Furlan* case, various irregularities in a civil trial deprived a person with disabilities from due access to health services. While the Court did not rule explicitly with regard to

55 Ibid, para 154.
56 Ibid, para 152.
57 Ibid, para 122.

the right to health, various approaches have had an impact on the indirect justiciability of this right.

The *Furlan* case relates to the lack of timely response on the part of the Argentine judicial authorities, who incurred an excessive delay in the resolution of a civil action brought against the state for harm and detriment. The medical treatment of the child and subsequently disabled adult, Sebastián Furlan, depended on the response to this action. The civil process was initiated by the father of Sebastián, following an accident that occurred as the child played in a park and a cross bar fell on his head. The crossbar was part of the debris that the army had abandoned in the park, and as such the request for compensation was directed at the Army.

In the jurisprudence of the Inter-American Court, controversies in regard to alleged unreasonableness of the time period are analysed through four components: i) the complexity of the matter, ii) the actions of the parties, iii) the actions of judicial officers, and iv) the harm to the legal status of the persons involved. In the *Furlan* case, access to adequate rehabilitation was taken into account in the analysis of the fourth element of reasonable time. The Court recalled that if the passage of time has a relevant impact on the legal status of the individual, it is necessary that the process move forward more quickly to ensure that the case is resolved in a short time.

Considering the above, the Court ruled that in cases where the controversy deals with groups in situations of vulnerability, such as disabled people, it is imperative that appropriate measures be taken. These measures may include the prioritisation of the case and its resolution by responsible authorities, in order to avoid delays in their processing and to ensure the timely resolution and execution of said proceedings. As such, the Court considerd the following as proven: i) the severe impairment to physical and mental health of Sebastián Furlan caused as a result of the accident, and his subsequent medical and psychological needs; ii) the two attempted suicides carried out by Sebastián Furlan, information which was made known to the judge, evidencing both issues with the early rehabilitation that Sebastián Furlan received, and the need for specialised medical attention given his delicate situation; and iii) an incident in which for no explanation whatsoever, Sebastián attacked his grandmother, an event which triggered a preventative detention order against him and reflected the serious psychological situation affecting him.

Accordingly, the Court found that the vulnerable state of Sebastián Furlan required greater diligence on the part of judicial authorities, as the primary objective of the case depended on the brevity of the process itself. The primary objective can be seen to be the obtainment of compensation designed to cover the debts incurred by the family over a number of years, in payment for the rehabilitation and therapies necessary to diminish the negative effects which over time had led to the current condition of Sebastián Furlan. Therefore, the Court indicated as proven that the prolongation of the processing of the case had impacted the legal status of the victim in a relevant and certain way, and has had and continues to have an irreversible impact. This is due to the delays in the awarding of compensation, which led to the victim being unable to receive treatments that could have provided him with a better quality of life. In conclusion, the Court defined the obligation of ensuring speedy trial in civil cases in which a greater chance of rehabilitation depends on the brevity of the proceeding.

In this particular case, given the effects on Sebastián Furlan of the civil proceedings and the impact that the denial of access to justice had on the possibility of accessing adequate medical care and rehabilitation, the Court considered that the right to humane treatment had also been violated.

In providing remedies in this case, the Court mentioned developments regarding the right to rehabilitation in the terms of international law, particularly taking into account article 25 of the UN Convention for Persons with Disabilites. This article establishes the right to the enjoyment of the highest attainable standard of health without discrimination on the basis of disability and the obligation to take all appropriate measures to ensure access for persons with disabilities to health services, including health-related rehabilitation. Moreover, the Court cited article 23 of the Convention on the Rights of the Child, regarding health care for mentally or physically disabled children. The Court ordered a specific rehabilitation in relation to the 'life-plan'[58] of Sebastian Furlan through an interdisciplinary team and taking into account the 'social model for disability'.

Also, taking into account the accessibility problems regarding social security and health legislation and policies, the Court ordered the adoption of measures to ensure that as soon as a person is diagnosed with serious problems or consequences relating to a disability, a charter of rights must be given to the individual or to his family group summarising in a clear and accessible manner the benefits established in the law, the standards for the protection of persons with mental disabilities established in the judgment, and the relevant public policies, as well as the institutions that can provide assistance in this matter.

In the *Ximenes Lopes* case, the Court considered that states have the duty to guarantee the provision of effective health care services to all persons with mental illness. This duty entails the obligation of the state to ensure the access to basic health care to all persons, the promotion of mental health, the provision of such services in the least restrictive possible way, and the prevention of mental illness.[59]

Moreover, taking into account the agression suffered by the victim, the Court said that due to their psychological and emotional condition, persons with mental illness are particularly vulnerable to any health treatment, and such vulnerability is greater when they are admitted to mental health institutions. The Court said that this 'increased vulnerability' is due to 'the imbalance of power between patients and the medical staff responsible for their treatment, as well as to the high degree of intimacy which is typical of the treatment of psychiatric illnesses'. In this context, the Court set out some standards regarding personal autonomy and the right to health:

---

58 'This notion is different from the notions of special damages (*daño emergente*) and loss of earnings (*lucro cesante*) ... [T]he so-called [proyecto de vida] deals with the full self-actualisation of the person concerned and takes account of her calling in life, her skills, her particular circumstances, her potentialities, and her ambitions, thus permitting her to set for herself, in a reasonable manner, specific goals, and to attain those goals ... [D]amage to the "life-plan" ... implies the loss or severe diminution, in a manner that is irreparable or reparable only with great difficulty, of [a person's] prospects of self-development.' See *Loayza Tamayo v Peru*, Reparations and Costs, Judgment of 27 November 1998, I/A Court HR Series C No 42.

59 *Ximenes Lopes v Brazil*, para 128.

> The Court considers that any health treatment administered to persons with mental illness should aim at achieving the patient's welfare and the respect for his or her dignity as a human person, which is translated into the duty to adopt the respect for the intimacy and autonomy of persons as guiding principles for administering psychiatric treatment. The Court concedes that the foregoing principle is not absolute, since the patients' needs themselves may sometimes require the adoption of measures without their consent. Notwithstanding, mental illnesses should not be understood as a disability for determination and the assumption that persons with mental illness are capable of expressing their will, which should be respected by both the medical staff and the authorities, should prevail. When the patients' inability to give their consent has been proven, their next of kin, legal representatives or pertinent authorities will give the consent required as regards to the treatment to be administered thereto.[60]

Also, Mr Ximenes Lopes was subject to restraint. The Court noted that the use of restraint poses a high risk of doing harm to the patient or causing his or her death and that falls and lesions during such procedures are quite common. The Court considered that restraint 'is one of the most aggressive measures to which a patient under psychiatric treatment can be subjected' and 'it should be used as a last resort and with the only purpose of protecting the patient, or else the medical staff or third persons, when the behavior of the patient involved is such as to pose a threat to their safety'. Furthermore, and bearing in mind that any treatment should be chosen on the basis of the patient's best interest and the respect for his or her autonomy, the Court established that health care staff should apply the least restrictive possible restraint techniques and only for such period of time as it is absolutely necessary and under conditions which respect the patient's dignity and minimise the risks of impairing his or her health.

The Right to Health of Persons Deprived of Liberty under the Right to Personal Integrity

In a number of cases related to violations of the rights of persons deprived of liberty, the Court has identified that the state has an obligation to provide detained persons with regular medical provision and care, and with adequate treatments when needed.[61] Similarly, the Court has also noted that the lack of adequate medical care could in itself be considered a violation of articles 5(1) and 5(2) of the American Convention, depending on various factors including the specific circumstances of the person in question, the nature of the condition that they suffer from, the time that passes without medical attention and

60 Ibid, para 130.

61 See *Tibi v Ecuador*, Preliminary Objections, Merits, Reparation and Costs, Judgment of 7 September 2004, I/A Court HR Series C No 114, para 156; *Montero Aranguren et al (Detention Center of Catia) v Venezuela*, Merits, Reparations and Costs, Judgment of 5 July 2006, I/A Court HR Series C No 150, para 102; *García Asto and Ramírez Rojas v Peru*, Preliminary Objection, Merits, Reparations and Costs, Judgment of 25 November 2005, I/A Court HR Series C No 137, para 227.

the cumulative effects that this has,[62] and, in some cases, the sex and age of the individual.[63] In this matter the Court has taken into account the United Nations Standard Minimum Rules for the Treatment of Prisoners and the Principles for the Protection of All Persons under Any Form of Detention or Imprisonment.

In this regard, the Court in *Vélez Loor v Panama* examined the legality of the detention of an Ecuadorian citizen in Panama as a result of his failure to carry the documentation necessary to remain within the country.[64] The victim was taken to prison. In regard to the conditions of his detention, the Court considered that the deficiencies in the supply of drinking water in the detention centre had been constant. Furthermore, the Court found evidence that an apparent skull fracture that Mr Vélez Loor had suffered was not treated with specialised medical attention or adequate medication, and indeed was not properly treated. In particular, it was noted that despite his recurring problems with headaches and dizziness, and the identification by the physicians who treated him that there was need for a CAT scan of his brain, this scan was not carried out and Mr Vélez Loor did not receive adequate or timely medical attention for this injury. This may have had a negative impact on his health, and was contrary to the decent treatment to which he was entitled.

In the case of *Vera Vera et al v Ecuador*, the Court analysed the detention of a 20-year-old young man who had been chased by a group of persons who apparently accused him of committing assault and armed robbery. During the confusion, Mr Vera Vera was shot, but the origin of the shot was unknown. Upon arrest, the police noted that he had received a gunshot wound to his left breast and took him to the police station. From there, he was transferred to a hospital where the existence of a gunshot wound was confirmed. It was noted in the record that on two occasions Mr Vera Vera had vomited. Even so, he was discharged by three doctors on duty given that, according to their opinion, 'his wound did not merit hospitalization' and he was prescribed 'general care'. Upon entering prison, a report was rendered and established that, among other things, he must have a radiograph to rule out any permanent injury, the projectile should be removed and permanent medical monitoring put in place a to prevent complications. Despite a request to transfer him to a health care centre to extract the bullet from the firearm, the authorities stated that 'the transfer of the detainee to the [h]ospital was not justified'.

Four days later the first signs of complications appeared and Mr Vera Vera was again interned in the hospital for five days, where he could not undergo surgery because there was no doctor on duty; his condition had deteriorated significantly, so he was transferred to another hospital. The costs of this ambulance transfer were covered by Mr Vera Vera's mother. That night the victim died after an emergency intervention, because of

62 *García Asto and Ramírez Rojas*, para 226; *Miguel Castro Castro Prison v Peru*, Merits, Reparations and Costs, Judgment of 25 November 2006, I/A Court HR Series C No 160, para 302; *Montero Aranguren et al*, paras 102 and 103.

63 *'Street Children'* case, para 74; Case of *Vera Vera et al v Ecuador*, Preliminary Objections, Merits, Reparations and Costs, Judgment of 19 May 2011, I/A Court HR Series C No 224, para 44.

64 *Vélez Loor v Panama*, Preliminary Objections, Merits, Reparations and Costs, Judgment of 23 November 2010, I/A Court HR Series C No 218.

complications related to the penetration of a projectile from a firearm. It was not until the autopsy was performed that the bullet was removed.

From the expert evidence included in the case file, the Court concluded that during the first hospitalisation of Mr Vera Vera the doctors who had cared for him committed various omissions that amounted to 'gross medical negligence'. Among other irregularities was the lack of medical information that justified his discharge from the first hospital such as examinations and relevant diagnoses relating to his wounds. The Court pointed out that while Mr Vera Vera was at the Provisional Detention Center with a gunshot wound, he was not subjected to any adequate physical assessment, and in addition the police unit did not have the necessary medical equipment to perform a specialised assessment which could have helped the doctor on duty to object to his discharge from the hospital and request his immediate hospitalisation.

Therefore, the Court found that the medical care received by Mr Vera Vera in the police station was negligent in that the state had not immediately transfered Mr Vera Vera to hospitals with facilities that met his health care needs. The Tribunal stated that if Mr Vera Vera had immediately undergone appropriate surgical treatment, his chances of surviving would have been good despite his gunshot wound. The number of omissions of the state through its agents during the time that the victim was in their custody amounts to medical negligence which resulted in a painful deterioration, and finally in death, a consequence that could have been avoided with appropriate and timely medical treatment.

In the Court's view, the circusmtances leading to Mr Vera Vera's death constitute inhumane and degrading treatment to the detriment of the victim, particularly because the medical negligence 'caused the painful deterioration of his physical condition during the course of ten days, culminating in his death'. The Tribunal referred to the jurisprudence of the European Court of Human Rights noting that

> the European Court took into account factors such as the lack of pertinent emergency and specialized medical care, excessive deterioration of the physical and mental health of the person deprived of liberty and exposure to severe or prolonged pain as a result of the lack of timely and diligent medical care, excessive security conditions which the person undergoes despite his or her obvious serious health condition and with no grounds or evidence that would have required it, as well as public awareness or media communication of these situations, among other things, to assess whether there has been inhumane or degrading treatment of persons deprived of liberty.[65]

The overall conclusion was that the lack of adequate and timely attention while Mr Vera Vera was in the state's custody amounted to violations of his rights to personal integrity and life.

Similarly, with regard to cases dealing with provisional and precautionary measures relating to some of the prisons on the continent, the jurisprudence of the Inter-American Court and Inter-American Commission has further established interdependence between

---

65 *Sarban v Moldova* CEDH (No 3456/05); *Paladi v Moldova* (No 39806/05), GC, Judgment of 10 March 2009.

sanitation conditions and the guarantee of basic social goods, in detention centres, with the immediate protection of the right to a dignified life and the right to humane treatment.

Confidentiality and the Medical Act

In the case of *De la Cruz Flores v Peru*, relating to the detention of a health worker who offered sanitary assistance to members of an illegal armed group, the Court highlighted the state's duty to respect the 'right and obligation [of the physicians] to protect the confidentiality of the information to which, as physicians, they have access',[66] particularly as regards the physician's obligation to report on possible criminal acts and the duty of not to punish for any medical activity, which means that sanitary assistance should not be subject to prosecution. In that respect, the Court said that the 'medical act' is 'not only an essential lawful act, but also the physician's obligation to provide'.

Sexual and Reproductive Rights

It is possible to see the most systematic approach in this matter in *Artavia Murillo et al (in vitro fertilization) v Costa Rica*.[67] This case relates to the general ban on the practice of in vitro fertilisation in Costa Rica as of 2000, following a decision of the Constitutional Chamber of the Supreme Court of Justice. The Inter-American Court determined that the state was internationally responsible for violating the right to private and family life, and the right to personal integrity in relation to personal autonomy, sexual health, the right to enjoy the benefits of scientific and technological progress, and the principle of non-discrimination, to the detriment of the 18 victims in that case.

The Inter-American Court indicated that the right to privacy is related to (i) reproductive autonomy, and (ii) access to reproductive health services, which includes the right to have access to the necessary medical technologies to exercise that right. Therefore, the rights to private life and to personal integrity are directly and immediately related to health care. The Court considered that the absence of legal safeguards that take into consideration reproductive health may result in a serious violation of the right to autonomy and reproductive freedom. Regarding reproductive rights, it indicated that these rights are based on the recognition of the basic rights of all couples and individuals to decide freely and responsibily on the number of children, the timing of births and the interval between them, and to have information and the means to acquire this, and the right to the highest possible degree of sexual and reproductive health.

Lastly, the Court said that the right to private life and reproductive freedom is related to the right to have access to the necessary medical technology to exercise this right. The

66 *De La Cruz Flores v Peru*, Merits, Reparations and Costs, Judgment of 18 November 2004, I/A Court HR Series C No 115, para 101.

67 Case of *Artavia Murillo et al (in vitro fertilization) v Costa Rica*, Preliminary Objections, Merits, Reparations and Costs, Judgment of 28 November 2012, I/A Court HR Series C No 257.

right of access to the most advanced and effective scientific progress for the exercise of reproductive autonomy and the possibility of forming a family entails the right to accede to the best health services in assisted reproduction techniques and, consequently, the prohibition of disproportionate and unnecessary restrictions *de iure* or *de facto* to the exercise of reproductive decisions.

The Court considered that 'conception' should be understood as the moment in which the fertilised egg is implanted in the uterus, a moment that cannot be understood as a process separate from a woman's body. The Court concluded that, before conception, it was not appropriate to apply article 4 of the American Convention. In addition, the Court indicated that the embryo cannot be understood as a person for the effects of article 4(1) of the American Convention and indicated that the right to life is not absolute and that a gradual and incremental protection exists for prenatal life in keeping with its development.

Having established the foregoing, the Court indicated that the Constitutional Chamber's judgment amounted to a severe limitation of the above-mentioned rights, because the victims had to take new decisions with regard to the methods or practices they wished to attempt in order to procreate a biological child. The Court emphasised that IVF is a technique that, in most cases, is practised as a last resort when other infertility treatments have been attempted or when it is a person's only option in order to have biological children. In addition, some people had to leave the country to carry out the procedure, and this entailed, directly or indirectly, the need to make some aspects of their private life public, as well as introducing difficulties that do not arise when IVF is available in one's own country.

In addition to the above, the Constitutional Chamber's decision had a discriminatory impact with regard to disability, gender and the economic situation of some victims. The Court considered infertility as a functional limitation recognised as a disease and that people in Costa Rica who suffer from infertility, and who faced barriers arising from the Constitutional Chamber's decision, should consider themselves protected by the rights of persons with disabilities, which include the right of access to the necessary techniques to resolve reproductive health problems. The Court also found gender stereotypes that affected the women and the men, bearing in mind the prejudice, shame and difficulties they experienced owing to the role assigned to them regarding maternity and reproductive capacity. The Court also underlined that assisted reproduction technologies are especially associated with a woman's body and it was in their bodies that IVF procedures had been initiated that were subsequently interrupted. In addition, the Court noted that some of the victims did not have the financial resources to carry out IVF abroad.

Furthermore, the Court took note that embryonic loss occurs in both natural pregnancies and in techniques such as artificial insemination; consequently, the protection of the embryo that was sought by banning IVF had a very limited and modest scope. The Court therefore concluded that the Constitutional Chamber had based its decision on the absolute protection of the embryo and because it did not weigh or take into account the other conflicting rights this entailed an arbitrary and excessive intervention in the rights of the victims which made the interference disproportionate and had a discriminatory impact.

The Inter-American System has also considered some cases regarding sexual violence and rape. In the context of the present chapter, a short overview of the main cases before the Court is offered, with particular reference to access to health. There is also a short discussion on some friendly settlements before the Commission regarding obstacles to legal abortion and other cases about forced sterilisation.

In *Rosendo Cantú et al v México* the Court considered the rape of Valentina Rosendo, of the Me'paa indigenous community.[68] Once Ms Rosendo Cantú denounced the rape, a preliminary investigation was initiated before an ordinary criminal court, but the case was transferred to the military courts when it was established that military personnel could have been involved. Ms Rosendo Cantú attempted to challenge this transfer, but was unsuccessful. The Court emphasised that violence against women is an offence against human dignity and a manifestation of the historically unequal power relations between women and men that pervade every sector of society, regardless of class, race or ethnic group, income, culture, level of education, age or religion, and strike at its very foundation. Likewise, the Court considered that rape may constitute torture even when it is based on a single act or takes place outside state facilities. This is so because the objective and subjective elements that classify an act as torture do not refer either to the accumulation of facts or to the place where the act is committed, but to the intention of the act, the severity of the suffering and the purpose of the act. Moreover, the Court established that rape is an offence that generally takes place in the absence of persons other than the victim and the aggressor. Thus, one cannot expect graphic or documentary evidence, and the victim's testimony becomes fundamental. It is not unusual that the retelling of traumatic acts of this nature contain some aspects that could be considered, a priori, to show a lack of precision in the narration.

In another similar case of rape, *Fernández Ortega et al v Mexico*, the Court said that the 'lack of elemental medical resources, and also the failure of the medical officials and the officials of the Public Prosecutor's Office who initially attended Mrs Fernández Ortega to use an action protocol were especially serious and had negative consequences in regard to the attention merited to the victim and on the legal investigation of the rape'.[69]

Another case of rape and abortion was analysed by the Inter-American Commission in a friendly settlement adopted in 2007 in the case of *Paulina del Carmen Ramírez Jacinto v Mexico*.[70] Paulina Ramírez was raped when she was 14 years old. In a case of this nature, the criminal legislation authorised the performance of an abortion. However, the hospital's personnel gave a number of excuses to the complainant and her family in order not to perform the procedure. Finally, a physician convinced Paulina's mother that the abortion should not be performed because of the supposed risks of the procedure for her health. The Commission highlighted that women cannot fully enjoy their human rights without having timely access to comprehensive health care services, and to information and education in this sphere. The Commission also noted that 'the health of sexual violence

68 *Rosendo Cantú et al v Mexico*, Preliminary Objection, Merits, Reparations and Costs, Judgment of 31 August 2010, I/A Court HR Series C No 216.

69 *Fernández Ortega et al v Mexico*, Preliminary Objection, Merits, Reparations and Costs, Judgment of 30 August 2010, I/A Court HR Series C No 215, para 197.

70 *Paulina del Carmen Ramírez Jacinto v Mexico*, Friendly Settlement of 9 March 2007, IACHR Report 21/07, Petition 161–02.

victims should be treated as a priority in legislative initiatives and in the health policies and programs of Member States'. The parties reached a friendly settlement whereby Mexico's Federal Health Secretariat agreed, among other measures, to (a) conduct a national survey on medical assistance to victims of domestic violence, and (b) draft a circular addressed to state health services aimed at 'strengthening their commitment toward ending violations of the right of women to the legal termination of pregnancy'.

In the case of *X and Y (Argentina)*, the Inter-American Commission analysed the routine practice to demand that relatives who want to visit an intern in prison be subjected to vaginal inspection.[71] The petition pointed out that an intern's wife and her 13-year-old daughter were subjected to these inspections, and there were no special circumstances to justify these extraordinary measures. The Commission sought a balance between the interests of the persons who are subjected to these inspections and the interest of the state to maintain security in jails. It categorised the 'vaginal search [as] more than a restrictive measure as it involves the invasion of a woman's body'. Therefore, the Commission considered that it was necessary to meet four conditions in order to establish the legitimacy of a vaginal search or inspection: '1) it must be absolutely necessary to achieve the security objective in the particular case; 2) there must not exist an alternative option; 3) it should be determined by judicial order; and 4) it must be carried out by an appropriate health professional.' Concerning Ms Y, who was 13 years old at the time, the Commission decided that it was evident that the vaginal inspection constituted an 'absolutely inadequate and unreasonable method'. Although it is true that this decision has been criticised as it does not issue any statement about possible discrimination, given that it is deduced from the report that only women were subjected to this type of search and not men,[72] this case opened the door to several judicial pronouncements in some countries. For instance, in Colombia, the Constitutional Court has almost totally prohibited this practice.[73]

---

71 *X and Y (Argentina)*, IA Comm. HR, Case 10.506, 15 October 1996.

72 In this sense, see C Medina Quiroga 'The Inter-American Commission on Human Rights and Women, with Particular Reference to Violence' in M Castermans-Holleman, F van Hoof and J Smith (eds) *The Role of the Nation-state in the 21st Century: Human Rights, International Organisations and Foreign Policy* (Kluwer 1998) 117.

73 See, for example, judgment T-848 of 2005 and judgment T-1069 of 2005. In these sentences, the Constitutional Court of Colombia took into consideration, inter alia, that it is not reasonable to carry out a search that transgresses the right to the person's human dignity (intern or visitor) by manipulating their genitals, when it is not necessary because there are other mechanisms to guarantee security. The Court pointed out that it is not constitutionally reasonable, as the intrusive searches practised by a jail officer, such as undressing the intern or visitor, forcing her to bend or flex her legs to show her genitals to the guard, especially if these are practised in non-sanitary conditions, imply a violation of the fundamental right to not be submitted to cruel, inhuman or degrading treatments. On the other hand, it was pointed out that the intervention, registers, interferences, verifications or extractions on the bodies, such as 'intrusive searches', could be given for founded reasons 'provided that there is informed consent by the person affected and that the search is practiced in such a way that personal modesty and decorum are not offended, as well the violated physical and juridical integrity, which are conditions that demand (i) a legal mandate, (ii) judicial supervision, (iii) the

Mamérita Mestanza v Peru is a representative case of a significant number of women affected by a massive, compulsive and systematic governmental policy that emphasised sterilisation as a method to quickly modify the population's reproductive behaviour, especially that of poor, indigenous and rural zone women. Ms Mestanza, a peasant woman, about 33 years old and the mother of seven children, was harassed by the public health system to be sterilised. Based on threats because she had more than five children, her consent was obtained for a tubal ligation procedure, which took place without prior medical examination. The victim was discharged even when there were serious anomalies, and she died a few days later. The Health Center Chief was never prosecuted nor arraigned for disciplinary measures. In the respective friendly agreement, the state recognised its international responsibility for violating the Convention and the Convention on Violence against Women. It committed to carry out a thorough investigation of the facts and to punish those responsible, even at the penal administrative level, including actions among the respective professional colleges. Moreover, among other measures, it committed to the adoption of public policies on reproductive health and family planning, as well as legislative modifications in order to eliminate any discriminatory approach on reproductive health and family planning, respecting women's autonomy.[74]

In ordering remedy for diverse violations committed against the Sawhoyamaxa indigenous community in Paraguay, the Court pointed out that 'States must devote special attention and care to protect this group and must adopt special measures to secure women, especially during pregnancy, delivery and lactation, access to adequate medical care services'.[75]

In the *Miguel Castro Castro Prison* case, the Court directly took a gender approach by analysing the extrajudicial executions and attempts against personal integrity that took place during the military intervention directed against the interns of a Peruvian jail. In this case, the Tribunal established the following:

> With regard to the treatment that must be offered to women who are detained or arrested ... female detainees must be supervised and checked by female officers and pregnant and nursing women must be offered special conditions during their detention.[76]

> Within gross imprisonment conditions we can mention ... lack of attention to women's physiological needs when they were denied materials of personal hygiene, such as soap, toilet paper, feminine pads, and underwear in order to be able to change; lack of attention to pre and post natal health needs ... The damages and suffering experimented by women

---

intervention of expert personnel, and (iv) the use of adequate instruments and sanitary conditions, as the cruel, inhuman and degrading treatments are banned, and their prohibition is absolute'.

74 *María Mamérita Mestanza Chávez* v *Peru*, Friendly Agreement of 10 October 2003, IACHR Report No 71/03, Petition 12.191.

75 *Sawhoyamaxa Indigenous Community v Paraguay*, Merits, Reparations and Costs, Judgment of 29 March 2006, I/A Court HR Series C No 146.

76 *Miguel Castro Castro Prison v Peru*, para 303.

> in general and especially the pregnant women and by the inmates that were mothers were especially gross.[77]

Moreover, in this case the Court established certain parameters on medical attention in regard to the health needs of intern women:

> Another aspect that affected women was the lack of attention to their physiological needs ... The International Committee of the Red Cross has established that the State must ensure that 'sanitary conditions [in the detention centres] are adequate to maintain the hygiene and the health [of the prisoners], allowing them regular access to toilets and allowing them to bathe and to wash their clothes regularly.' Likewise, said Committee also determined that special arrangements must be made for female detainees with their period, when they are pregnant, or accompanied by their children. The omission of those excesses caused special and additional suffering to imprisoned women.[78]
>
> It was proven that in the case of the inmates Eva Challco and Sabina Quispe Rojas the State did not attend to their basic prenatal health needs, and that regarding the latter it did not offer her postnatal medical attention as well (*supra* par. 197(57)), which implied an additional violation to their right to humane treatment.[79]

In the case of the *Xákmok Kásek*, relating to the situation of a victim who died as result of maternal mortality causes, the Court noted the relation between maternal mortality, human rights, discrimination and poverty as follows:

> The death of Remigia Ruíz, who died in 2005 at 38 years of age, and who was pregnant and did not receive medical attention, reveals many of the inherent characteristics of maternal mortality, such as: death during labor without adequate medical care, a situation of exclusion or extreme poverty, lack of access to adequate health services, and a lack of documentation on cause of death, among others. In this regard, the Court underscores that extreme poverty and the lack of adequate medical care for pregnant women or women who have recently given birth result in high maternal mortality and morbidity.[80] Because of this, States must design appropriate health-care policies that permit assistance to be provided by personnel who are adequately trained to attend to births, policies to prevent maternal mortality with adequate pre-natal and post-partum care, and legal and administrative instruments for

---

77 Ibid, para 319.

78 Ibid, para 331.

79 Ibid, para 332.

80 The Court, citing the World Health Organization definition, stated that 'A maternal death is the death of a woman while pregnant or within 42 days of termination of pregnancy, irrespective of the duration and the site of the pregnancy, from any cause related to or aggravated by the pregnancy or its management, but not from accidental or incidental causes.' World Health Organization, *International Statistical Classification of Diseases and Related Health Problems, Tenth Revision*, vol. 2: *Instruction Manual* (2nd edn, Geneva 2005), 141.

health-care policies that permit cases of maternal mortality to be documented adequately. All this is because pregnant women require special measures of protection.[81]

Conclusions

There has been a lot of debate about the foundations for a direct protection of the right to health in the Inter-American System. However, the Inter-American Commission and Court have protected this right using different kinds of arguments taking into account different articles of the American Convention. This chapter has identified eight examples of this kind of progressive interpretation. Notwithstanding, it is important to expect some future litigation pursuing the direct protection of the right to health under article 26 of the American Convention in order to provide a better scrutiny of the duties of guarantee and respect of this right. In the meantime, some litigation has obtained very positive results using the connection between the right to health and civil and political rights and has had a decisive role in the protection of groups in situations of vulnerability.

Epilogue

In 2013 the Court highlighted the strong connection between the right to health and the vulnerability of internally displaced persons (IDPs). In fact, in *Operation Genesis*, the Court stated that the measures of basic assistance provided by the state during the period of displacement were insufficient, because the physical and mental conditions that those displaced had to face for almost four years were not in keeping with the minimum standards required in such cases. The overcrowding, the food, the supply and management of water, as well as the failure to adopt measures with regard to health care, reveal non-compliance with the state's obligation to provide protection following the displacement, with the direct result being the violation of the right to personal integrity of those who suffered the forced displacement.[82]

Finally, it is important to say that in 2015 there are two very important cases regarding the right to health pending before the Court. *Gonzales Lluy and Family v Ecuador* is the first case regarding HIV to come before the Inter-American Court. The other case, *Chinchilla Sandoval and Others v Guatemala*, relates to a woman with diabetes who died in prison in the context of alleged problems concerning access to adequate treatment. No doubt these two cases will add important standards in the evolution of the Inter-American jurisprudence related to health issues.

---

81 *Xákmok Kásek Indigenous Community v Paraguay*, para ?.

82 *Afro-descendant Communities Displaced from the Cacarica River Basin (Operation Genesis) v Colombia*, Preliminary Objections, Merits, Reparations and Costs, Judgment of 20 November 2013, I/A Court HR Series C No 270.

References

Books, Chapters, Articles, etc.

Abramovich, V and Rossi, J, 'La tutela de los derechos económicos, sociales y culturales en el artículo 26 de la Convención Americana sobre Derechos Humanos' in C Martin, D Rodríguez-Pinzón and J Guevara (eds) *Derecho Internacional de los Derechos Humanos* (Fontamara 2004).

Cavallaro, J and Brewer, S, 'La Función del Litigio Interamericano en la Promoción de la Justicia Social' (2008) 8 *Sur. Revista Internacional de Derechos Humanos* 85–99.

Cavallaro, J and Schaffer, E, 'Less as More: Rethinking Supranational Litigation of Economic and Social Rights in the Americas' (2004) 56 *Hastings Law Journal* 217–281.

Cavallaro, J and Schaffer, E, 'Rejoinder: Finding Common Ground to Promote Social Justice and Economic, Social and Cultural Rights in the Americas' (2006) 39 *New York University Journal of International Law and Politics* 345–383.

CEJIL, *La protección de los derechos económicos, sociales y culturales y el Sistema Interamericano* (CEJIL 2005).

Courtis, C, 'La protección de los derechos económicos, sociales y culturales a través del artículo 26 de la Convención Americana sobre Derechos Humanos' in C Courtis, D Hauser and G Rodríguez Huerta (eds) *Protección internacional de los derechos humanos. Nuevos desafíos* (Porrúa-ITAM 2005) 1–66.

Courtis, C, 'La muerte en una institución psiquiátrica en la jurisprudencia de la Corte Interamericana de Derechos humanos. El caso Damiao Ximenes Lopes c. Brasil' in C Coutis, *El mundo prometido. Escritos sobre derechos sociales y derechos humanos* (Fontamara 2009).

Craven, M, 'The Protection of Economic, Social and Cultural Rights under the Inter-American System of Human Rights' in D Harris and S Livingstone (eds) *The Inter-American System of Human Rights* (Oxford University Press 1998) 289–321.

Faúndez, Ledesma H, 'Los derechos económicos, sociales y culturales en el sistema interamericano' in VV.AA., *El Sistema Interamericano de Protección de los Derechos Humanos: su jurisprudencia sobre debido proceso, DESC, libertad personal y libertad de expresión* (IIDH 2004) 98–102 and 113–120.

García Ramírez, S, 'Protección jurisdiccional internacional de los derechos económicos, sociales y culturales' (2003) 9 *Cuestiones Constitucionales* 127–157.

Krsticevic, V, 'La protección de los derechos económicos, sociales y culturales en el Sistema Interamericano' in CEJIL, *Construyendo una agenda para la justiciabilidad de los derechos sociales* (CEJIL 2004) 167–173.

Medina Quiroga, C, 'The Inter-American Commission on Human Rights and Women, with Particular Reference to Violence' in M Castermans-Holleman, F van Hoof and J Smith (eds) *The Role of the Nation-state in the 21st Century: Human Rights, International Organisations and Foreign Policy* (Kluwer 1998) 117–134.

Melish, T, *La Protección de los Derechos Económicos, Sociales y Culturales en el Sistema Interamericano de Derechos Humanos* (CDES Yale Law School 2003).

Melish, T, 'Counter-rejoinder: Normative Neutrality and Technical Precision, the Role of the Lawyer in Supranational Social Rights Litigation' (2006) 39 *New York University Journal of International Law and Politics* 385–415.

Melish, T, 'Rethinking the "Less as More" Thesis: Supranational Litigation of Economic, Social and Cultural Rights in the Americas' (2006) 39 *New York University Journal of International Law and Politics* 171–343.

Parra-Vera, O, *Justiciabilidad de los Derechos Económicos, Sociales y Culturales ante el Sistema Interamericano* (Comisión Nacional de los Derechos Humanos 2011).

Ruiz-Chiriboga, OR, 'The American Convention and the Protocol of San Salvador: Two Intertwined Treaties. Non-enforceability of Economic, Social and Cultural Rights in the Inter-American System' (2013) 31 *Netherlands Quarterly of Human Rights* 156–183.

Uprimny, R and Guarnizo, D, '¿Es posible una dogmática adecuada sobre la prohibición de regresividad? Un enfoque desde la jurisprudencia constitucional colombiana' in E Ferrer Mac-Gregor and A Zaldívar (eds) *Homenaje a Héctor Fix Zamudio* (UNAM 2008).

World Health Organization, *International Statistical Classification of Diseases and Related Health Problems, Tenth Revision*, vol. 2: *Instruction Manual* (2nd edn, Geneva 2005).

International and Regional Instruments

Additional Protocol to the American Convention on Human Rights in the Area of Economic, Social, and Cultural Rights (Protocol of San Salvador), adopted 17 November 1988, entered into force 16 November 1999.

American Convention on Human Rights (Pact of San José), adopted 22 November 1969, entered into force 18 July 1978.

American Declaration of the Rights and Duties of Man, 1948.

Charter of the Organization of American States, adopted 30 April 1948, entered into force 13 December 1951.

Committee on Economic, Social and Cultural Rights, 'Declaration on the evaluation of the obligation to take steps to the "maximum of available resources" under an Optional Protocol to the Covenant' (Thirty-eighth session) UN Doc E/C.12/2007/1, 21 September 2007.

Convention on the Rights of the Child, A/RES/44/25, adopted 20 November 1989, entered into force 2 September 1990.

Convention on the Rights of Persons with Disabilities, A/RES/61/106, adopted 13 December 2006, entered into force 3 May 2008.

Inter-American Commission on Human Rights, 1959.

Inter-American Commission on Human Rights, Rules of Procedure (Approved by the Commission at its 137th regular period of sessions, held from October 28 to November 13, 2009, and modified on September 2nd, 2011 and during the 147th Regular Period of Sessions, held from 8 to 22 March 2013, for entry into force on August 1st, 2013).

International Covenant on Economic, Social and Cultural Rights, A/Res/21/2200, adopted 16 December 1966, entered into force 3 January 1976.

International Law Commission, Liability of the state for internationally unlawful acts (International Law Commission 53rd session, 2001), UN Doc A/56/10, text introduced in the appendix to UN General Assembly Resolution 56/83 of 28 January 2002.

Cases

Ache People v Paraguay IACHR OEA/Ser.L/V/II.50 Doc 13 Rev 1 (2 October 1980).

Acevedo Buendía et al ('Discharged and Retired Employees of the Office of the Comptroller') v Peru, Preliminary Objection, Merits, Reparations and Costs, Judgment of 1 July 2009, I/A Court HR Series C No 198.

Afro-descendant Communities Displaced from the Cacarica River Basin (Operation Genesis) v Colombia, Preliminary Objections, Merits, Reparations and Costs, Judgment of 20 November 2013, I/A Court HR Series C No 270.

Albán Cornejo et al v Ecuador, Merits, Reparations and Costs, Judgment of 22 November 2007, I/A Court HR Series C No 171.

Artavia Murillo et al (in vitro fertilization) v Costa Rica, Preliminary Objections, Merits, Reparations and Costs, Judgment of 28 November 2012, I/A Court HR Series C No 257.

De La Cruz Flores v Peru, Merits, Reparations and Costs, Judgment of 18 November 2004, I/A Court HR Series C No 115.

Fernández Ortega et al v Mexico, Preliminary Objection, Merits, Reparations and Costs, Judgment of 30 August 2010, I/A Court HR Series C No 215.

'Five Pensioners' v Peru, Merits, Reparations and Costs, Judgment of 28 February 2003, I/A Court HR Series C No 98.

Furlan and Next of Kin v Argentina, Preliminary Objections, Merits, Reparations and Costs, Judgment of 31 August 2012, I/A Court HR Series C No 246.

García Asto and Ramírez Rojas v Peru, Preliminary Objection, Merits, Reparations and Costs, Judgment of 25 November 2005, I/A Court HR Series C No 137.

González et al ('Cotton Field') v Mexico, Preliminary Objection, Merits, Reparations and Costs, Judgment of 16 November 2009, I/A Court HR Series C No 205.

Jorge Odir Miranda Cortez et al v El Salvador, Merits Report of 20 March 2009, IACHR Case 12.249 Report No 27/09.

Juridical Condition and Human Rights of the Child, Advisory Opinion OC-17/02 of 28 August 2002, I/A Court HR Series A No 17.

Juridical Condition and Rights of the Undocumented Migrants, Advisory Opinion OC-18/03 of 17 September 2003, I/A Court HR Series A No 18.

'Juvenile Reeducation Institute' v Paraguay, Preliminary Objections, Merits, Reparations and Costs, Judgment of 2 September 2004, I/A Court HR Series C No 112.

Loayza Tamayo v Peru, Reparations and Costs, Judgment of 27 November 1998, I/A Court HR Series C No 42.

'Mapiripán Massacre' v Colombia, Merits, Reparations and Costs, Judgment of 15 September 2005, I/A Court HR Series C No 134.

María Mamérita Mestanza Chávez v *Peru*, Friendly Agreement of 10 October 2003, IACHR Report No 71/03, Petition 12.191.

Miguel Castro Castro Prison v Peru, Merits, Reparations and Costs, Judgment of 25 November 2006, I/A Court HR Series C No 160.

Montero Aranguren et al (Detention Center of Catia) v Venezuela, Merits, Reparations and Costs, Judgment of 5 July 2006, I/A Court HR Series C No 150.

National Association of Ex-Employees of the Peruvian Social Institute et al v Peru, Admissibility & Merits Case of 27 March 2009, IACHR Case 12.670 Report No 38/09.

Paulina del Carmen Ramírez Jacinto v Mexico, Friendly Settlement of 9 March 2007, IACHR Report 21/07, Petition 161–02.

The Right to Information on consular assistance in the framework of the guarantees of the due process of law, Advisory Opinion OC-16/99 of 1 October 1999, I/A Court HR Series A No 16.

Rosendo Cantú et al v Mexico, Preliminary Objection, Merits, Reparations and Costs, Judgment of 31 August 2010, I/A Court HR Series C No 216.

Sarban v Moldova CEDH (No 3456/05); *Paladi v Moldova* (No 39806/05), GC, Judgment of 10 March 2009.

Sawhoyamaxa Indigenous Community v Paraguay, Merits, Reparations and Costs, Judgment of 29 March 2006, I/A Court HR Series C No 146.

'Street Children' (Villagrán Morales et al) v Guatemala, Merits, Judgment of 19 November 1999, I/A Court HR Series C No 63.

Suarez Peralta v Ecuador, Preliminary Objections Merits, Reparations and Costs, Judgment of 21 May 2013.

Tibi v Ecuador, Preliminary Objections, Merits, Reparation and Costs, Judgment of 7 September 2004, I/A Court HR Series C No 114.

Vélez Loor v Panama, Preliminary Objections, Merits, Reparations and Costs, Judgment of 23 November 2010, I/A Court HR Series C No 218.

Vera Vera et al v Ecuador, Preliminary Objections, Merits, Reparations and Costs, Judgment of May 19, 2011, I/A Court HR Series C No 224.

Xákmok Kásek Indigenous Community v Paraguay, Merits, Reparations and Costs, Judgment of 24 August 2010, I/A Court HR Series C No 214.

X and Y (Argentina), IA Comm. HR, Case 10.506, 15 October 1996.

Ximenes Lopes v Brazil, Merits, Reparations and Costs, Judgment of 4 July 2006, I/A Court HR Series C No 149.

Yakye Axa Indigenous Community v Paraguay, Merits, Reparations and Costs, Judgment of 17 June 2005, I/A Court HR Series C No 125.

Yanomami v Brazil, Case No 7615.

Index

For Product Safety Concerns and Information please contact our EU representative GPSR@taylorandfrancis.com Taylor & Francis Verlag GmbH, Kaufingerstraße 24, 80331 München, Germany

Batch number: 10726294

Printed by Printforce, the Netherlands